"Articulate and fearless, David Horowitz tracks the anti-American attitudes and professorial abuses of students that have metastasized throughout academia. *The Professors* is a must-read, not only for educators and governmental policy makers—but for every parent with high school or college-age children."

—State senator Bill Morrow
Sponsor of a California Academic Bill of Rights

"David Horowitz has single-handedly done more than anyone I know to throw light on the political abuse of our college and university classrooms by activist professors who have been enabled to do so because of the incestuous self-selection process for faculty recruitment and tenure. *The Professors* throws a harrowing light on the decline of professional standards in our schools and the efforts by faculty with political agendas to use their classrooms for indoctrination rather than education."

—State representative Dennis K. Baxley
chair of the Education Council of the Florida legislature
and chief sponsor of Florida's Academic Bill of Rights

"Horowitz's book *The Professors* is a must read for all parents planning on a quality education for their children."

—State senator Larry A. Mumper
Sponsor of academic freedom legislation in Ohio

"With documentation that will be hard to refute, David Horowitz describes the betrayal of our young people by professors who are defiantly unethical and contemptuous of academic standards. It is a form of educational malpractice. We learn that Ward Churchill, the shame of Colorado's university system, has his counterparts on campuses across the nation."

—John Andrews, former president of the Colorado Senate
and sponsor of Colorado legislation to implement an Academic Bill of Rights

"Academics on the Left like to pat themselves on the back for daring to 'speak truth to power.' David Horowitz's *The Professors* speaks some uncomfortable truths to them—to those who run American higher education today. They will hate this scathing critique, but will be hard-pressed to answer his charges."

—Professors Stephan and Abigail Thernstrom
Harvard University

THE
PROFESSORS

*The 101 Most Dangerous
Academics in America*

David Horowitz

Since 1947
**REGNERY
PUBLISHING, INC.**
An Eagle Publishing Company • Washington, DC

Cataloging-in-Publication data on file with the Library of Congress

ISBN 0-89526-003-4

Published in the United States by
Regnery Publishing, Inc.
One Massachusetts Avenue, NW
Washington, DC 20001
www.regnery.com

Distributed to the trade by
National Book Network
Lanham, MD 20706

Manufactured in the United States of America

10 9 8 7 6 5 4 3 2 1

Books are available in quantity for promotional or premium use. Write to Director of Special Sales, Regnery Publishing, Inc., One Massachusetts Avenue NW, Washington, DC 20001, for information on discounts and terms or call (202) 216-0600.

CONTENTS

INTRODUCTION

Trials of the Intellect in the Post-Modern Academy

In January 2005, Professor Ward Churchill became a figure of national revulsion when his impending visit to Hamilton College was linked to an article claiming that the victims of 9/11 were "little Eichmanns" who deserved their fate. Churchill's article produced an outcry of such force that it led to the removal of the faculty head of the host committee at Hamilton and the resignation of the president of the University of Colorado, where Churchill was professor of ethnic studies. As a result of the uproar, Churchill was removed as department chair, and university authorities began an investigation into how he had acquired his faculty position in the first place.

Far from being a marginal crank, Ward Churchill was (and still is) prominent at the University of Colorado and in the academic world at large. A leading figure in his field and widely published, his appearance at Hamilton in January 2005 would have been the fortieth campus to which he had been invited to speak in the three years after 9/11.[1] The opinions expressed in his infamous article[2] were themselves far from obscure to his academic colleagues. First published on the Internet in October 2001, they reflected views that were part of the intellectual core of his academic work, familiar both to university authorities in Colorado and to his faculty hosts at Hamilton. These facts made the scandal an event whose significances extended far beyond the fate of one individual to implicate the academic culture itself.

The Churchill spectacle was not an isolated incident at Hamilton. In the fall of 2004, a convicted terrorist named Susan Rosenberg was invited to join the faculty as a "visiting professor," to teach a course on "Resistance Memoirs." As the course title suggested, far from repudiating her political past, Susan Rosenberg embraced it. She was an active member of a network of veteran radicals, many still in jail, who remained loyal to the causes they had violently served. Rosenberg herself had been apprehended in 1984 as she was moving more than six hundred pounds of explosives into a Cherry Hill, New Jersey, warehouse. She had been sentenced to fifty-eight years in prison for her crime, but was released as one of President Clinton's last-minute pardons after serving only fourteen years of her term.

Rosenberg had been hired by Nancy Rabinowitz, a professor of comparative literature and head of the Kirkland Project on Gender, Society and Culture at Hamilton. The Kirkland Project, a self-described "social justice organization," was run by faculty and funded by a university endowment. Although the nation at large was engaged in a "War on Terror" in Iraq and only three years earlier had been the target of a massive terrorist attack, Professor Rabinowitz was oblivious to the public reaction her decision might provoke. Even when the outcries caused Rosenberg to withdraw, Rabinowitz remained adamant. Apparently unconscious of the damage she was about to inflict on herself, two schools, and the university culture, Rabinowitz followed her first misstep with a second when she decided to honor an invitation to Churchill to speak at Hamilton a month after the Rosenberg affair.

The behavior of Rabinowitz and her Kirkland colleagues reflected the insularity of a predominately left-wing academic environment that had become an echo chamber for ever more radical ideas. It was this environment that prevented the directors of the Kirkland Project from perceiving any impropriety in conferring academic legitimacy on an individual who had been sentenced to prison for terrorist acts.

Hamilton College is a small liberal arts college in rural upstate New York. Named after a conservative American Founder, its colonial architecture and sylvan views provide a setting well-suited to the contemplative life. Along with sister schools like Williams and Colgate, Hamilton aspires to be a "second-tier Ivy" and generations of graduates have sent their children there to carry on a family legacy and reap the intellectual benefits of the school they remember. It is this loyalty to tradition that maintains the flow of donations, which sustains Hamilton and attracts students who pay a yearly tuition of $30,000 to attend.

Along with other American universities, in the last several decades Hamilton has undergone a sea change. Significant departments of the school have ceased to be part of the ivory tower that its alumni recall. Many faculty members are no longer devoted to pursuits that are purely "academic," and the curriculum has been expanded to include agendas about "social change" that are overtly political and make an invitation to a convicted terrorist seem appropriate rather than merely appalling.

This transformation has been the work of an academic generation that came of age as anti-war radicals in the Vietnam era. Many of these activists stayed in school to avoid the military draft and earned PhDs, taking their political activism with them when they became tenured-track professors in the 1970s. As tenured radicals,[3] they were determined to do away with the concept of the ivory tower and scorned the contemplative life that liberal arts colleges like Hamilton created.[4] They rejected the concept of the university as a temple of the intellect, in which the term "academic" described a curriculum insulated from the political passions of the times. Instead, these radicals were intent on making the university "relevant" to current events, and to their own partisan agendas. Accordingly, they set about re-shaping the university curriculum to support their political interests, which appeared in their own minds as grandiose crusades for "social justice."

They created new institutional frameworks and fields of study, casting old standards and disciplines aside. New departments began to appear with objectives that were frankly political and maintained no pretense of including intellectually diverse viewpoints or in pursuing academic inquiries unconnected to the conclusions they might reach. Names like "Black Studies" and "Women's Studies" had political subtexts and were really devoted to Black Nationalism, feminism, and similar ideological programs. Many had been created through political protests—some violent. One of the first Black Studies programs was established at Cornell University as a concession to black radicals who occupied the administration building with loaded shotguns and refused to leave until their demands were met. Among the demands the university administration agreed to was the "right" of the radicals to appoint their own professors.

At first the new departments were presented as part of a broader social movement to "serve" minority groups previously neglected. But as the cohort of activists on academic faculties grew, the new disciplines proved insufficient to encompass the social and intellectual agendas the radicals favored. Cultural studies, peace studies, whiteness studies, post-colonial studies, and global studies—even social justice studies—came into being as interdisciplinary fields shaped by narrow, one-sided political agendas. Some of these programs attacked American foreign policy and the American military, others America's self-image and national identity. Collectively, they marked a dramatic departure from the academic interests of the past, providing institutional settings for political indoctrination: the exposition and development of radical theory, the education and training of radical cadre, and the recruitment of students to radical causes.

Because the new activist departments were "interdisciplinary," they were able to spread their influence through the traditional fields until virtually every English Department, History Department, and law school now draws on Women's Studies and African American Studies Departments for courses and faculty. The intellectual movement created has been so powerful in shaping the university curriculum that it has affected the educational philosophy of the institutions themselves. Modern research universities once defined their purposes in official templates as institutions "dedicated to the disinterested pursuit of knowledge." Under the new dispensation, they embrace the mission brought to them by radical academics and now often refer to themselves as institutions dedicated to "social change."[5]

Nancy Rabinowitz was one of the tenured radicals who had come to Hamilton to promote the new dispensation. Though formally a professor of comparative literature, she was unable to leave her activist passions at the campus gates and became the guiding influence and head of the Kirkland Project for Gender, Society and Culture, where she implemented her extra-academic agendas by inviting radicals like Susan Rosenberg to teach.

Professor Rabinowitz's connection to Rosenberg was also something more than academic. Rabinowitz had married into a famous radical family, which was linked to Rosenberg through her infamous crime. Rabinowitz's father-in-law was the celebrated Communist lawyer Victor Rabinowitz, whose clients

included Fidel Castro and other violent radicals, including the
political terrorists of the Puerto Rican FALN. Victor Rabinowitz's lifelong friend and law partner was Leonard Boudin,
also a Communist, and the father of Kathy Boudin, one of the
leaders of the Weather Underground, a terrorist cult that had
declared a formal "war" on "Amerikkka' in the 1970s, and carried
out bombings of the Pentagon, the U.S. Capitol, and other official buildings. The principal leaders of the Weather Underground later became professors (and are profiled in this book).[6]
When the terrorist cult dissolved in 1976, Kathy Boudin joined
the "May 19 Communist Movement," a Weather Underground
network splinter group, which in 1981 robbed a Brinks armored
car in Nyack, New York, murdering two guards and a policeman,
and leaving nine children fatherless. Susan Rosenberg was part
of the Weather Underground network and was indicted for the
Nyack crime.

Kathy Boudin was convicted for her role in the Nyack
robbery-murders, but Susan Rosenberg, though indicted, was
never tried. Prosecutors in the Nyack case saw no reason to pursue her after she received her fifty-eight-year sentence for other
crimes. This was the sentence from which President Clinton—
petitioned by New York Democratic congressman Jerrold
Nadler—finally released her.

Susan Rosenberg was only one of several Weather Underground terrorists who had recently surfaced and begun touring
college campuses. Still committed radicals, they had formed a
"political prisoners" network[7] and were looking to rehabilitate
themselves and their political agendas. Uncontrite about the revolutionary politics that had led to their crimes, they made
appearances at colleges across the country, where they were
invited to lecture and give seminars by radical professors who
presented them to students as advocates for "human rights."
When convicted bomber and Weather Underground member

Laura Whitehorn was invited as an official guest of the African American Studies Department at Duke University, she was presented as a human rights activist by Duke faculty. It was left to Duke students to research her history on the Internet and reveal her terrorist past and criminal conviction, and to protest the faculty deception.[8]

The professors running the Kirkland Project had presented Susan Rosenberg in equally misleading terms as "an award-winning writer, an activist, and a teacher who offers a unique perspective as a writer." She was further described as a victim of government persecution, imprisoned because of her "political activities" with the Black Liberation Army. No mention was made of her crimes or theirs, which included several murders.

Schools like Hamilton had become so exclusively politicized towards the Left that decisions like the one Nancy Rabinowitz made had come to seem normal by university standards. While some Hamilton faculty voiced moral outrage at the Rabinowitz invitation, the concerns of those involved were mainly focused on the possibility of negative public reaction. Not that the faculty sympathized with the public. Most regarded any negative response to the Rosenberg invitation as a reflection of public ignorance and attitudes that were "reactionary." In their minds, the problem raised by the hiring of a convicted terrorist was whether the free speech rights of the terrorist could be protected, not the implications of such an appointment for academic values.

While members of the Hamilton community worried about the public reaction, a sophomore named Ian Mandel stepped forward to spark the outrage that would eventually thwart Professor Rabinowitz's political agendas. As Jacob Laksin reported for *FrontPagemag.com*, "Ian Mandel had personal reasons to oppose Rosenberg's appointment. A Nyack native, he grew up with the names Waverly Brown and Edward O'Grady etched into his mind. They were the two Nyack police officers killed in the 1981 robbery [for which Rosenberg was indicted]. 'Every day of my life until I left for Hamilton, I drove by the memorial to officers Brown and O'Grady located about one mile from my house,' he recalled. Mandel explained that Nyack's tight-knit community was profoundly shaped by the murders of the two officers. 'To this day it is a tough subject for many to speak about,' he wrote. It was a measure of the anger and disgust he felt about Rosenberg's hiring that Mandel, a member of the Hamilton College Democrats, agreed to speak about it. Like many Nyack residents, Mandel had thoroughly studied the robbery. He concluded that Rosenberg was indeed involved. 'To me, and I'd assume to most members of the Nyack community and of the larger law-enforcement community, that makes Susan Rosenberg a cop-killer,' he said. Haunted by Rosenberg's grim legacy at Nyack, Mandel was determined not to let it follow him to Hamilton. 'I think that bringing Susan Rosenberg to teach a class at Hamilton is a disgrace and a black-eye to the college,' he said."[9]

Mandel was invited to appear on TV and radio talk shows. Simultaneously, police officers staged a demonstration to protest the Rosenberg outrage at a New York fundraiser for Hamilton. This, in turn, led to an alumni revolt. As the media events unfolded, donors began to withdraw their pledges from the college while irate phone calls from alumni and citizens flooded the president's office. This public pressure eventually overwhelmed the institution's resistance and led to a resolution of the crisis with Rosenberg's withdrawal from the program. The faculty radicals led by Professor Rabinowitz remained defiant, however, referring to the public's reaction as a witch-hunt.

This defiance led directly to the second incident, whose ramifications were to prove even greater than the first. Well before the Rosenberg fiasco, the Kirkland Project had scheduled Ward

Churchill to speak. Despite the damage they had already inflicted on their college, the Kirkland directors made no move to reconsider or postpone the Churchill appearance.

Like Rosenberg, Churchill's link to Rabinowitz was political rather than academic. One of the items he listed in his *curriculum vitae* was that during the 1970s he had trained members of the Weather Underground in the use of weapons and explosives. Churchill was already well-known in academic circles for his views that America was a genocidal nation, led by international criminals—views shared by the Weather Underground and many radical professors. This was why Rabinowitz and the faculty advisors to the Kirkland Project invited him in the first place, and why they did not want to cancel the invitation. Going ahead with his scheduled appearance would be an "in-your-face" gesture to a public that in their eyes had persecuted Susan Rosenberg for her political views, and to a Hamilton administration that had failed to defend her. Professor Rabinowitz and her radical faculty allies were determined to demonstrate to the unenlightened just what free speech meant.

During the crisis, several moderate faculty voices challenged this view. "If the administration cannot see the contradiction between this hire and the clearly stated mission of the college to foster scholarship and academic excellence, then God help us all," commented Robert Paquette, one of Hamilton's handful of conservative professors.[10] Economics professor James Bradfield was similarly disturbed that the Hamilton administration had adopted the radicals' view of the issue as Rosenberg's free speech. "I disagree with the administration's presenting this as a matter of free speech, which it is not," he said. "It is a matter of standards...Even if Susan Rosenberg possessed the intellect or had achieved the scholarly or artistic preeminence of people such as Albert Einstein, Milton Friedman, Lionel Trilling, or Leonard Bernstein, I would argue that her character, as manifestly demonstrated by the choices that she made as an adult over a sustained period of years, would preclude her appointment to the faculty of Hamilton College."[11]

Though in recent years Hamilton had invited a greater percentage of conservative speakers to campus than was the practice at most colleges (the numbers were still pitifully small), and though several faculty were visibly troubled by the Rosenberg invitation, opposition to the faculty radicals remained confined to a minority bold enough to express an opinion publicly. The hand of this minority was greatly strengthened by the damage the Rosenberg debacle had inflicted on the college. The revenue loss from withdrawn donations had already prompted a rumor that there might be no faculty salary increases in the coming year.[12] Consequently, Rabinowitz's determination to use the college as a platform for her political agendas became a practical matter as well.

When the spring schedule of events for the Kirkland Project was published, a government professor named Theodore Eismeier noticed Ward Churchill's name among the invited speakers. Eismeier immediately logged on to the Internet and came up with an article Churchill had written three years before, which in his eyes was a smoking gun. Written just after the attacks of 9/11, Churchill's article was called, "Some People Push Back: On the Justice of Roosting Chickens."

Churchill's imperfect sense of English syntax made his title seem more obscure than its inflammatory message warranted. What he meant was that the heinous terrorist attacks of 9/11 were a case of the *chickens coming home to roost*; that the horrors of 9/11 were Americans' just desserts. "Let's get a grip here, shall we?" Churchill wrote. "True enough, [the victims of 9/11] were civilians of a sort. But innocent? Give me a break. If there was a better, more effective, or in fact any other way of visiting some penalty befitting their participation upon the little Eichmanns inhabiting the sterile sanctuary of the twin towers, I'd really be interested in hearing about it."

In this mangled prose Churchill was merely articulating the theme of his entire academic career: America was like Hitler Germany, a nation dedicated to the extermination of minorities; its capitalist economic machine starving poor people all over the world all the time. Therefore, the "civilians" who comprised what Churchill referred to as its "technical core"—the inhabitants of the World Trade Center—were little Eichmanns, cogs in a machine that churned out mass murder. (Adolf Eichmann was the Nazi bureaucrat who organized the shipment of Jews to the gas chambers). In Churchill's view, there was no "better way of visiting some penalty befitting their participation" in the workings of America's global economy (and thus global genocide) than incinerating Americans in their place of work.

That such views could earn an individual like Churchill a full professorship at a major state university and the responsibility and power of a department chair spoke volumes about academic corruption not only in Colorado but in the ethnic studies field. That Churchill was a sought-after speaker by universities across the country was a chilling indictment of an entire system.

Theodore Eismeier was convinced that the invitation to Churchill spelled disaster for Hamilton. He sent the essay along with "other troubling writings" of Churchill's to school administrators.[13] The result was a series of meetings with Rabinowitz and the executive committee of the Kirkland Project. According to Rabinowitz's account of these meetings, there was dissension among the Kirkland board of advisors. The administration thought the event "was going to be as bad as Susan Rosenberg" and wanted the Kirkland board to defuse it by converting Churchill's speech into a panel, which would include anti-

Churchill faculty like government professor (now dean of students) Phil Klinkner. Rabinowitz protested. "Let's take a strong stand for freedom of speech," she said.[14]

Churchill's speech was hardly "free." The Kirkland Project was paying him $3,500 plus expenses to come to Hamilton, which was probably twice the cost of bringing a nationally renowned scholar in the humanities or social sciences to campus. Rabinowitz and the directors of the Kirkland Project hadn't offered Churchill this kind of money to provide students with an example of free speech. They had invited him because, like Rabinowitz, they shared his extreme views or found him academically interesting. Promoting views like Churchill's was the purpose of the Kirkland Project. This was *their* standard, and this standard—not free speech—was the issue.

As the date of Churchill's visit approached, the Syracuse *Post-Standard* published a report on the event that included interviews with the growing campus opposition. Professor Eismeier was quoted as saying that the proposed panel was "akin to inviting a representative of the KKK to speak and then asking a member of the NAACP to respond." Other media began to report the controversy. Through Internet postings, talk radio chatter, and further press coverage, the controversy picked up momentum until a Hamilton student appeared on FOX News Channel's *The O'Reilly Factor* and blew the affair wide open.

Like Ian Mandel before him, Matthew Coppo was a sophomore at Hamilton, but his relationship to the political events that provided a subtext for the occasion was more intimate. Matthew's father had been killed in the World Trade Center on 9/11 and was thus one of the innocent victims Ward Churchill had described as "little Eichmanns" who deserved to die. Matthew Coppo appeared on two consecutive segments of *The O'Reilly Factor*, the first with his mother. In the show's opening editorial segment, O'Reilly declared that Hamilton was morally wrong to have provided Churchill with an academic template and said that his hateful comments "should not be rewarded by any sane person," which was a perfectly reasonable view. As a result of the broadcast, an avalanche of angry emails (more than 8,000 according to college officials) descended on Hamilton president Joan Hinde Stewart, leading her to cancel the event.

Explaining the cancellation, Stewart presented herself and Hamilton not as the embarrassed authors of bad decisions and abysmal standards but as failed defenders of free speech. She thus accepted, for a second time, the self-serving view of Hamilton's faculty radicals that the real problem was not the behavior of the faculty Left but the public's reaction. To this claim she added an administrative concern for campus security: "We have done our best to protect what we hold most dear—the right to speak, think, and study freely—but there is a higher responsibility that this institution carries, and that is the safety of our students." Stewart alleged that threats of violence had been made, and that these had prompted her decision to cancel the event. Such threats probably were made (though it is also possible that Churchill and others exaggerated them). Threats of violence occur quite regularly, however, in regard to campus speeches and they are normally dealt with by ample campus security, including armed guards and an occasional German shepherd.[15]

Stewart made no mention of academic standards as they pertained to extending an official university invitation to someone with Churchill's views. But behind the scenes Stewart understood that the crisis was about the standards. Nancy Rabinowitz was forced to resign as chair of the Kirkland Project and a faculty committee was appointed to conduct an inquiry and offer recommendations for reform. When the inquiry was completed, Stewart announced that the Kirkland budget would be significantly cut and its missions and programs reviewed. In future all campus speakers would be paid for in part through a central fund reported to the administration, giving Stewart control over the decisions that her professors had abused.

Immediately, one member of the faculty committee stepped forward to make it known that Stewart's solution was not one the committee had recommended. Margaret Thickstun, a professor of English and the chair of Hamilton's faculty, told reporters that the president's decision was "more restrictive" than what the committee had recommended. The Hamilton faculty, in Professor Thickstun's view, didn't think there was anything wrong with the invitations to Rosenberg and Churchill or with Kirkland Project standards. "I think that the faculty as a whole felt that the Kirkland Project wasn't the issue," she said; "the media coverage was the issue."[16]

At the University of Colorado an even larger drama was unfolding. Churchill's extreme views had been known to university authorities for a long time, but they had done nothing about them. Since Churchill was a full professor and chair of an academic department, there was nothing they really could do. He was protected by tenure rules and academic freedom considerations that left university officials few options.

The University of Colorado did have a tenure review process, which was supposed to be administered annually. But the policy had not been observed in years.[17] Nor was it conceivable, even if the procedures were observed, that Churchill's tenure would be put in jeopardy simply because he had abhorrent views. A celebrated attempt by the City University of New York to fire Leonard Jeffries, a racist professor of black studies,[18] for making a flagrantly anti-Semitic speech had failed in the courts, some years earlier, because it was based on his public speech, not his classroom performance. Even his racism in the classroom, which was indisputable, was not considered by the university as possible grounds for his dismissal. The tenure protections of professors were that strong.[19]

The national publicity generated by the Hamilton crisis dramatically altered this situation by bringing Churchill's views to the attention of the public at large, who regarded them as the incomprehensible ravings of a fringe radical. The fact that the nation was at war with a ruthless enemy with whom Churchill clearly identified caused an uproar in the Colorado media, and led the governor and other officials to demand that he be fired.

In the weeks that followed, several facts about Churchill's academic career were brought to light and provided other grounds for questioning his university position. Although Churchill was a department head who received an annual salary of $120,000, he had no doctorate, which was a standard requirement for tenured positions, not to mention chairs. Moreover, his academic training had been in communications as a graphic artist rather than an academic field related to ethnic studies. The master's degree he held was from a third-rate experimental college, which did not even award grades when he attended in the 1970s. He had lied to qualify for his affirmative action hire, when he claimed on his application that he was a member of the Keetoowah Band of the Cherokee tribe. In fact, his ancestors were Anglo-Saxon and the Keetoowah Band had publicly rejected him. An investigative series by the *Rocky Mountain News* also maintained that he had plagiarized other professors' academic work and had made demonstrably false claims about American history in his own writing, literally making up American atrocities that never happened.[20]

Despite these revelations, hundreds of professors and thousands of students across the country sprang to Churchill's defense, signing petitions and protesting the "witch-hunt" of academic "liberals."[21] At the Indiana University Law School, Professor Florence Roisman took around a petition in Churchill's behalf. When law professor William Bradford, a Chiricahua Apache with a stellar academic resume, refused to sign the petition, Professor

Roisman retorted, "What kind of a native American are you?" and launched a campaign to have Bradford fired.[22] The American Association of University Professors ignored the Bradford case, but issued an official declaration of support for Churchill, invoking "the right to free speech and the nationally recognized standard of academic freedom in support of quality instruction and scholarship."[23] Churchill made a public appearance in his own defense to a cheering University of Colorado audience of fifteen hundred and went on to tour other campuses where he received a similar hero's welcome, also from large crowds.[24] These events further revealed to a troubled public the extent to which radicalism at the very edges of the American political spectrum had established a central place in the curriculum of American universities.

How could the university have hired and then raised to these heights an individual of such questionable character and preposterous views as Ward Churchill? How many professors with similar resumes had managed to acquire tenured positions at the University of Colorado and other institutions of higher learning? How pervasive was the conflation of political interests and academic pursuits on university campuses or in college classrooms? Why were the administrations seemingly unable to assert and enforce standards of academic excellence? Such were the issues the Churchill scandal raised.

The Changed University

The present volume examines 101 college professors and attempts to provide a factual basis for answering these questions. The method used is similar to the scholarly historical discipline known as "prosopography," which was defined by one of its creators and best-known practitioners, Lawrence Stone, as "the study of biographical details of individuals in the aggregate."[25] The purpose of this exercise, as Stone explains is "to establish a universe to be studied," in this case a universe of representative academics who use their positions to promote political agendas. A further purpose of prosopography is to establish patterns of conduct and patterns in careers through a study of the assembled profiles.

When viewed as a whole, the 101 portraits[26] in this volume reveal several disturbing patterns of university life, which are reflected in careers like Ward Churchill's. These include (1) promotion far beyond academic achievement (Professors Anderson, Aptheker, Berry, Churchill, Davis, Kirstein, Navarro, West, Williams, and others in this volume); (2) teaching subjects outside one's professional qualifications and expertise for the purpose of political propaganda (Professors Barash, Becker, Churchill, Ensalaco, Furr, Holstun, Wolfe, and many others); (3) making racist and ethnically disparaging remarks in public without eliciting reaction by university administrations, as long as those remarks are directed at unprotected groups, e.g., Armenians, whites, Christians, and Jews (Professors Algar, Armitage, Baraka, Dabashi, hooks, Massad, and others);[27] (4) the overt introduction of political agendas into the classroom and the abandonment of any pretense of academic discipline or scholarly inquiry (Professors Aptheker, Dunkley, Eckstein, Gilbert, Higgins, Marable, Richards, Williams, and many others).

Not all of the professors depicted in this volume hold views as extreme as Ward Churchill's, but a disturbing number do. All of them appear to believe that an institution of higher learning is an extension of the political arena, and that scholarly standards can be sacrificed for political ends; others are frank apologists for terrorist agendas, and still others are classroom bigots. The dangers such individuals pose to the academic enterprise extend far beyond their own classrooms. The damage a faculty minority can inflict on an entire academic institution, even in the absence of a scandalous figure like Ward Churchill, was recently demonstrated at Harvard, when President Lawrence Summers was censured—the first such censure in the history of the modern research university in America—because Summers had the temerity to suggest in a faculty setting an idea that was politically incorrect.[28]

The influence of radical attitudes is not confined to radicals on a given faculty, but has a tendency to spread throughout an institution. Robert Reich, a former cabinet secretary in the Clinton administration and now a professor of economics and social policy at Brandeis University, is not a political radical. But in the present academic environment Reich is a member of the faculty committee of the "Social Justice and Policy Program" in the undergraduate school. The Social and Justice Policy Program, as the name implies, is little more than a training course for students to become advocates for expanding the welfare state. It is a program of indoctrination in the strictest lexigraphical sense— "to imbue with a partisan or ideological point of view"—and thus inappropriate for an academic curriculum. The proper setting for such a course would be a training institute maintained by the Democratic Party.

One of the professors profiled in this volume, Columbia University's Todd Gitlin, explained in a 2004 essay that after the 1960s, "all that was left to the Left was to unearth righteous traditions and cultivate them in universities. The much-mocked 'political correctness' of the next academic generations was a consolation prize. We lost—we squandered the politics—but won the textbooks."[29] Professor Richard Rorty, a renowned professor of philosophy and ardent left-winger, described this development with equally refreshing candor: "The power base of the left in America is now in the universities, since the trade unions have largely been killed off. The universities have done a lot of good work by setting up, for example, African-American studies programs, Women's Studies programs, Gay and Lesbian Studies programs. They have created power bases for these movements."[30] That a distinguished philosopher like Rorty would find the political debasement of the university a development to praise speaks volumes about the changes that have taken place in the academic culture since the war in Vietnam.

Because activists ensconced in programmatic fields like black studies and women's studies also teach in traditional departments like history and English, the statements by Rorty and Gitlin actually understate the ways in which the radical Left has colonized a significant part of the university system and transformed it to serve its political ends. In September 2005, the American Political Science Association's annual meeting featured a panel devoted to the question, "Is It Time to Call It Fascism?" meaning the Bush administration. Given the vibrant reality of American democracy in the year 2005, this was obviously a political rather than a scholarly agenda.[31]

To identify 101 radical professors for this volume, it was not necessary to scour university faculties. This sample is but the tip of an academic iceberg, and it would have been no problem to provide a thousand such profiles or even ten times the number.[32] The faculty members of the entire Ethnic Studies Department, which Churchill chaired, share views similar to Churchill's and have declared their solidarity with him. Yet only the new chair of Churchill's department, Elizabeth Perez, has been selected for inclusion in these profiles.[33] None of the nine professors participating on the Political Science Association panel—or many others like it—are included. Out of the more than 250 "Peace Studies" programs whose agendas are overtly political rather than scholarly, this collection includes only half a dozen professors. The same is true for other ideological fields like women's studies, African American studies, gay and lesbian studies, postcolonial studies, queer studies, whiteness studies, and cultural studies.[34]

This book is not intended as a text about left-wing bias in the university and does not propose that this bias is necessarily a problem. Every individual, whether conservative or liberal, has a perspective and therefore a bias. Professors have every right to interpret the subjects they teach according to their individual points of view. This is the essence of academic freedom. But they also have professional obligations as teachers, whose purpose is the instruction and education of students, not to impose their biases on students as though they were scientific facts. The professorial task is to teach students how to think, not to tell them what to think. In short, it is the responsibility of professors to be professional—and therefore "academic"—in their classrooms, and therefore not to require students to agree with them on matters which are controversial.

The privileges of tenure and academic freedom are specifically granted in exchange for this professionalism. Society does not provide tenure to politicians—and for good reason. To merit their privileges—and specifically their tenure privileges—professors are expected to adhere to professional standards and avoid political attitudinizing. As professionals, their interpretations should be tempered by the understanding that all human knowledge is uncertain and only imperfectly grasped, that such knowledge must be based on the collection of evidence and evaluated according to professionally agreed on methodologies and standards. As teachers they are expected to make their students aware of the controversies surrounding the evidence, including the significant challenges to their own interpretations. Hired as experts in scholarly disciplines and fields of knowledge, professors are granted tenure in order to protect the integrity of their academic inquiry, not their right to leak into the classroom their uninformed prejudices on subjects which are outside their fields of expertise.

Professors also have a responsibility in their classrooms to respect not only the professional standards of research and inquiry but the unformed intellects of their students, who are their charges. Their teaching must not seek the arbitrary imposition of personal opinions and prejudices on students, enforced through the power of the grading process and the authority of the institutions they represent.

Although beyond the scope of this inquiry, it is a reasonable assumption that a majority of faculty members are professionals and devoted to traditional academic methods and pursuits. But these scholars are often a silent majority, intimidated from expressing their views on subjects like the Susan Rosenberg and Ward Churchill affairs because of their concern not to be labeled "racist" or "sexist" or "reactionary" by their more aggressive radical peers. Still, they are not always so intimidated, and can sometimes be seen standing up to defend academic standards under assault.

At the University of Colorado, Paul Campos, a liberal member of the law faculty and a columnist for the *Denver Rocky Mountain News*, issued one of the strongest statements on Churchill's tenured position: "To compare the victims of the 9/11 massacre to one of the chief architects of the Holocaust is both intellectually bankrupt and morally depraved. To do so in a published essay, and to repeat this opinion to the media, after being asked whether he wishes to consider it, calls into question the author's fitness to continue as a member of this university's faculty. Members of our faculty should keep in mind that a grant of tenure is not a guarantee of perpetual employment. Tenure protects against dismissal without cause; but professional incompetence and moral depravity are both sufficient grounds for firing tenured faculty."[35]

Two years earlier, a prominent member of the academic Left and a distinguished Milton scholar, Stanley Fish, wrote an article in the *Chronicle of Higher Education* in which he stressed the importance of drawing the line between political attitudinizing and scholarly discourse. His article was titled "Save the World on Your Own Time,"[36] and in it, he cautioned academics about getting involved *as academics* in moral and political issues such as the war on terror. In a paradoxical summary he warned: "It is immoral for academics or academic institutions to proclaim moral views." The reason, according to Fish, was provided long ago in a faculty report to the president of the University of Chicago. "The report declares that the university exists 'only for the limited...purposes of teaching and research,'" Fish wrote. "Since the university is a community only for those limited and distinctive purposes, it is a community which cannot take collective action on the issues of the day without endangering the conditions for its existence and effectiveness."

The conclusion Professor Fish drew was straightforward: "Teachers should teach their subjects. They should not teach peace or war or freedom or diversity or uniformity or nationalism or anti-nationalism or any other agenda that might properly be taught by a political leader or a talk-show host. Of course they should teach *about* such subjects, *something very different from urging them as commitments*—when they are part of the history or philosophy or literature or sociology that is being studied. The only advocacy that should go on in the classroom is the advocacy of what James Murphy has identified as the intellectual virtues, 'thoroughness, perseverance, intellectual honesty,' all components of the cardinal academic virtue of being 'conscientious in the pursuit of truth.'" (emphasis added)

Once the prevailing view among academic professionals, this perspective is now under significant challenge by radicals firmly entrenched in liberal arts departments. Organizations like "Historians Against the War" or the "Radical Philosophical Association"[37] directly challenge the idea of academic neutrality on controversial political issues. In 2002, Columbia University hosted a conference of academic radicals called "Taking Back the

Academy: History of Activism, History as Activism." The published text of the conference papers[38] was provided with a foreword by Professor Eric Foner,[39] who is a past president of both the Organization of American Historians and the American Historical Association, and a leading academic figure. Far from sharing Professor Fish's view that a sharp distinction should be drawn between political advocacy and the scholarly disciplines, Professor Foner embraced the idea that political activism is *essential* to the academic mission: "The chapters in this excellent volume," wrote Foner, "derive from a path-breaking conference held at Columbia University in 2002 to explore the links between historical scholarship and political activism.... As the chapters that follow demonstrate, scholarship and activism are not mutually exclusive pursuits, but are, at their best, symbiotically related."[40]

The implications of this symbiosis were drawn by the conference panels, which are listed in the table of contents as follows: "Student Movements" "Student Unions" "Historians for Social Justice" and "Bridging the Gap between Academia and Activism." This symbiosis of activism and scholarship reflected a self-conception in which radical professors would function as the mentors and protectors of student activists, deploying their intellectual skills in behalf of "progressive" political causes. History professor Jesse Lemisch, a founding member of "Historians Against the War," began his presentation with these words: "As historians, teachers and scholars, we oppose the expansion of American empire..." Speaking on the final conference panel, Professor Lemisch spelled out the connection that academic radicals like himself made between their roles as scholars and their political goals: "Being an activist is a necessary prerequisite for historians who want to see through the reigning lies, and I take it as a given that we *must* be activists. Writing history is about challenging received authority. Activist experience gives the historian experiential understanding of the power of the state, repression, social change...the depth of commitment of those with power to maintaining the standing order through their journalists, historians, police and law firms.... You can't *begin* to understand how history happens unless you have this basic training as a historian/activist. A good dose of tear gas makes us think more clearly as historians."[41]

Far from being marginal, Lemisch's endorsement of activist scholarship is shared by leaders of the academic profession. Jacquelyn Hall is a professor of history at the University of North Carolina and, like Eric Foner, a former president of the Organization of American Historians; and like Foner and Lemisch, she is also a member of "Historians Against the War." She had this to say about *Taking Back the Academy*: "In considering the broad social and political responsibilities of intellectuals in society, this book calls for a revitalized definition of what it means to be a scholar-citizen in the twenty-first century. For scholars in the humanities, that call could not be more timely. Alternatively maligned as politically irrelevant or dangerously subversive, historians and other stewards of society's subjective truths increasingly must be prepared to articulate—and defend—their function in today's marketplace of ideas and corporatized universities."[42] These are the words of an activist rather than a scholar. But at the Columbia University conference the distinction was no longer recognized.

The Law of Group Polarization

The professors profiled in this volume are drawn from public and private universities, from small institutions and large ones, and from schools that are both secular and religious. Among them are individuals prominent in their institutions and at the forefront of their professions. They are the authors of books widely used as texts in their fields. They have been funded by prestigious foundations and awarded the highest professional honors in their fields. They are department chairs and directors of academic institutes and programs and heads of large professional associations. Among them are presidents and former presidents of the American Historical Association, the American Anthropological Association, the National Ethnic Studies Association, the American Philosophical Association, the Modern Language Association, the American Sociological Association, and the Middle East Studies Association. As tenured faculty they have a prominent role in the hiring and promotion of future generations of university professors. They are representative figures, widely influential in the academic world.

At the same time and notwithstanding their impressive credentials, these professors (as their profiles demonstrate) are capable of making disturbingly shallow intellectual judgments and expressing alarmingly crude political opinions. Like Ward Churchill, their excesses implicate not only themselves but the academic culture itself.

Critics of the university have long complained that the system of tenure, which provides lifetime job security, also serves to protect mediocrity and encourage incompetence. The efforts to politicize the curriculum over the last three decades have predictably created new opportunities for both tendencies to flourish.

One factor contributing to the debasement of intellectual standards in the university is the politicized environment of the university itself. It is relatively easy for politically like-minded individuals to mistake adherence to partisan formulas for substantive thought and even intellectual achievement. Some years ago, the power of this phenomenon was demonstrated to devastating effect by a physicist named Alan Sokal.[43] Sokal was a political leftist, concerned about the debasement of intellectual standards by his political allies in the university. In a famous thought experiment, Sokal submitted a paper to *Social Text*—a "peer-reviewed" academic journal, whose articles were viewed by many as on the "cutting edge of radical theory." By design, the substance of the paper Sokal wrote and submitted was pure nonsense, but its content—also by design—was "politically correct." Sokal wanted to see if the distinguished academic editors at *Social Text* would accept a worthless article for publication if they shared its political conclusions.

"To test prevailing intellectual standards," Sokal explained, "I decided to try a modest (though admittedly uncontrolled) experiment: Would a leading North American journal of cultural studies—whose editorial collective includes such luminaries as [Duke professor] Frederic Jameson[44] and [Princeton professor] Andrew Ross—publish an article liberally salted with nonsense if (a) it sounded good and (b) it flattered the editors' ideological preconceptions."[45] The article Sokal submitted to *Social Text* was called "Transgressing the Boundaries: Towards a Transformative Hermeneutics of Quantum Gravity." Its thesis was that gravity was merely a social construct, an instrument of phallocentric hegemony. "In the second paragraph I declare, without the slightest evidence or argument, that 'physical "reality" [note the scare quotes] . . . is at bottom a social and linguistic construct.' Not our *theories* of physical reality, mind you, but the reality itself. Fair enough: anyone who believes that the laws of physics are mere social conventions is invited to try transgressing those conventions from the windows of my apartment. (I live on the 23rd floor.)"

Social Text published the article, exposing the editors to national embarrassment when Sokal revealed the hoax. "The editors of *Social Text* liked my article," he explained afterwards, "because they liked its *conclusion*: that 'the content and methodology of post-modern science provide powerful intellectual support for the progressive political project.'" One could not hope for a clearer example of why initiating inquiries with politically correct conclusions already in mind is essentially anti-intellectual. Yet conformity to the parameters of the "progressive political project" has become a widespread standard of academic judgment in universities not only for the selection and design of its curricula, but for the hiring and promotion of faculty.

While mediocrity and incompetence have always had a place in the academic world, it is also the case that never before in the history of the modern research university have entire departments and fields been devoted to purely ideological pursuits. Nor has overt propagandizing had such a respected and prominent place in university classrooms. Even more disturbingly, the last few decades mark the first time in their history that America's institutions of higher learning have become a haven for extremists.

A primary cause of this development is the overwhelming prevalence of leftists (and "liberals") on academic faculties along with the corresponding absence of other, critical, perspectives. A well-known principle of group dynamics is the "law of group polarization," which holds that if a room is filled with like-minded people, the center of the room will move towards the extreme. The room becomes an echo-chamber of approbation, while the natural clamor for attention among individuals provides an incentive to push the envelope of approved opinions to their natural limit.[46]

In many fields the academic community has become such an echo-chamber. Numerous surveys of political attitudes among university professors have established that the ratio of faculty members holding views to the left of the political spectrum over those holding conservative views ranges from 5–1 to 9–1 and is steadily increasing.[47] At Ward Churchill's university in Boulder, the figure is 30–1.[48] This reflects the academic future at schools as disparate as Stanford and Berkeley, where a 30–1 ratio already exists among junior faculty (assistant and associate professors).[49] The atmosphere created by such a one-sided dialogue is what makes possible university support for an intellectual rogue like Ward Churchill by academic organizations like the Kirkland Project, the American Association of University Professors, and thousands of professors nationwide. The law of group polarization that produces extremists like Churchill would operate even if the room of like-minded faculty were not the product of systematic exclusion. But the evidence strongly suggests that it is.

Some academics, like Paul Krugman, have challenged this claim and argue that the vast disparity in the representation of different intellectual perspectives is a matter of self-selection: "It's a fact, documented by two recent studies, that registered Republicans and self-proclaimed conservatives make up only a small minority of professors at elite universities. But what should we conclude from that? One answer is self-selection— the same sort of self-selection that leads Republicans to outnumber Democrats four to one in the military. The sort of person who prefers an academic career to the private sector is likely to be somewhat more liberal than average, even in engineering."[50]

Professor Krugman's argument about self-selection could easily have been used to explain the absence of women or African Americans on university faculties forty years ago, when they were as rare as Republicans are today. Would Professor Krugman's attitude be the same if he were called on to explain *those* disparities? It is not obvious that the military and the academy can be compared in the way that Professor Krugman proposes, since there is no intellectual apprenticeship required for inclusion in the military, and its recruitment process hardly entails the kind of pervasive inquiry into a candidate's opinions and judgments as does an academic hire. There are many Republican lawyers, to pick only one obvious profession that has an aca-

demic analogue, but the percentage of Republican law professors at academic institutions is no greater than the percentage of
Republicans on other faculties.[51]

As a political columnist, Krugman must also be aware that
not all Republicans—not even most Republicans—are businessmen, or employed in business professions. The Republican Party
is competitive with Democrats in virtually all social sectors,
while the most reliable indicator of a Democratic vote is not
class but proximity to and length of membership in academic
communities where there is a restricted marketplace of ideas. As
a professor at Princeton, which is governed by the trustees of the
"Princeton Corporation," Krugman must be aware that a significant segment of the university community is actually part of the
private sector, and a lucrative part at that for academic entrepreneurs like himself. If Republicans are motivated by a desire
to succeed in the private sector, why would they deny themelves
the opportunities provided by private corporations like Princeton and Harvard?

Krugman's self-selection hypothesis cannot explain the
results of the study by Professor Daniel Klein and Andrew Western[52] showing that the ratio of Republicans to Democrats among
junior faculty at Berkeley and Stanford is a third of what it is
among senior faculty. Nor can it explain why the percentage of
faculty conservatives should have dramatically declined in the
last twenty years, as a recent study by Rothman, Nevitte, and
Lichter shows.[53] In a survey of 1,643 faculty members drawn
from 183 colleges and universities, the authors concluded that
"over the course of fifteen years, self-described liberals grew
from a slight plurality to a five to one majority on college faculties, while the ratio of liberals to conservatives in the general
population remained relatively constant.[54] These statistics are
perfectly compatible with the view that the exclusion of conservatives began roughly thirty years ago when a generation of

political activists started to acquire power over faculty hiring and promotion committees.

Are these disparities the result of political discrimination? There is considerable reason to believe that they are. Certainly the rationale for such an agenda has long been a staple of radical thought. The political activists who flooded university faculties in the early 1970s were encouraged by their own theories to regard the university as an instrument for social change whose levers of power it was important for "progressives" to manipulate and control.

Academic radicals self-consciously drew their social strategies from the writings of the Italian Communist Antonio Gramsci, around whom an academic cult formed in the 1970s, just as they were ascending the tenure ladder. Gramsci was an innovator in Marxist theory, whose ideas focused on the importance of acquiring cultural "hegemony" as the fulcrum of revolutionary change. Gramsci explicitly urged radicals to gain control of the "means of cultural production" to further their ends. Foremost among these means were the universities and the media. The considerations that led Gramsci to these conclusions would certainly have also encouraged faculty activists to seek institutional power within the university by acquiring control of its hiring and tenure committees.[55]

Herbert Marcuse, a professor at Brandeis and a veteran of the famed "Frankfurt School" of European Marxism, was another figure whose writings flourished with the new radical presence on university faculties. His famous essay on "Repressive Tolerance," written in 1965, is a justification for the suppression of conservative speech and access to cultural platforms on the grounds that the views of right-wing intellectuals reflect the rule of an oppressive and already dominant social class. Marcuse identified "revolutionary tolerance" as "tolerance that enlarged the range and content of freedom." Revolutionary tolerance could not be neutral towards rival viewpoints. It had to be "partisan" on behalf of a radical cause and "intolerant towards the protagonists of the repressive *status quo*." This was a transparent prescription for not hiring academic candidates with conservative views. In this view, a blacklist was a potential tool of "liberation."

According to Marcuse, normal tolerance "granted to the Right as well as the Left, to movements of aggression as well as to movements of peace, to the party of hate as well as to that of humanity... actually protects the machinery of discrimination." By this logic, repression of conservative viewpoints was a progressive duty. Evaluating conservative academic candidates on their merits, without regard to their political and social opinions, was to support discrimination and oppression in the society at large. Marcuse's "dialectical argument" exerted a seminal influence in academic circles in the 1970s and provided a powerful justification for blacklisting conservatives in the name of equality and freedom.[56] The same argument would also justify the exclusion of conservative texts from academic reading lists, which is an all too common practice on liberal arts campuses.

Today senior conservative professors (and most conservative professors are now senior) find themselves regularly excluded from search and hiring committees, and a dwindling presence on university faculties. A typical case was reported to a visitor to the University of Delaware in November 2001, who asked a senior member of the history department, and its lone conservative, how a system worked that had made him such a solitary figure. The professor answered, "Well, they haven't allowed me to sit on a search committee since 1985. In that year I was its chair and we hired a Marxist. This year [2001] we had an opening for a scholar of Asian history. We had several candidates among whom the best qualified was from Stanford. Yet he didn't get the job. So I went to the chair of the search committee and asked him what had happened. 'Oh,' he said, 'you're absolutely right. He was far and away the most qualified candidate and we had a terrific interview about his area of expertise. But then we went to lunch and he let out that he was for school vouchers. And that killed it."[57] Apparently, a politically incorrect view on K-12 school voucher proposals implied incorrect views about the Ming Dynasty or the Meiji Restoration, disqualifying the bearer for academic employment. Or perhaps the radical faculty in the history department did not want to hire a loose cannon who might eventually jeopardize their control.

The bitterly intolerant attitude of the current academic culture towards conservatives is inevitably a factor in the exclusion process. In the spring of 2005, the *Skidmore College News* published an article called "Politics in the Classroom," which quoted anthropology professor Gerry Erchak to this effect: "In the hiring process you'd probably be wise not to mention your political views. If you say, 'Oh, hey, I really think Reagan was great,' or, 'I'm a Bush guy,' I can't say a person wouldn't be hired, but it's like your pants falling down. It's just horrible. It's like you cut a big fart. I just don't think you'll be called back."[58]

Faculty prejudices reflected in Erchak's comment are a pervasive fact of academic life. In the same spring, Professor Timothy Shortell[59] was elected by his peers to the chair of the sociology department at Brooklyn College. His election became a news item when it was discovered that he had written an article referring to religious people as "moral retards" and was on record describing senior members of the Bush administration as "Nazis." The recent eruption of the Churchill controversy had made Shortell's extreme attitudes newsworthy, but apparently had not impressed his department peers as the least bit unusual when they elected him.

As in the case of Ward Churchill, the public airing of Shortell's prejudices generated a reaction strong enough to persuade the president of Brooklyn College to block his appointment to the departmental chair and avoid further embarrassment to the college. But left to itself, the university process would have placed Shortell in a position to determine the composition of faculty for a generation to come. Departmental chairs at Brooklyn College exercise veto powers over faculty hiring decisions. Is it reasonable to think that someone with views like Shortell's would approve the hiring of a sociology candidate with religious views or Republican leanings? According to the survey of seventeen hundred academics by Professor Daniel Klein and Andrew Western, the ratio of Democrats to Republicans in sociology departments nationwide is 28–1.[60]

Criminology professor Michael Adams of the University of North Carolina, Wilmington, has reported an incident reflecting similar prejudice. A colleague on a search committee for the Criminology Department remarked to him that a candidate they were reviewing should not be hired because he was "too religious."[61] Too religious to study crime? Among his search committee colleagues, only Adams thought this peculiar.

The prejudice against conservatives is so ingrained and commonplace that academics do not see it as a problem at all. To them it is just the order of things. When an anthropology professor at Rollins University, an elite private school in Florida, was asked whether he was concerned that there were no conservatives in his department, he explained: "Anthropology is the study of other cultures and requires individuals who are compassionate and tolerant." Even when it was brought to his attention, the professor was completely oblivious to the intolerance of his own statement.[62] David French, the president of the Foundation for Individual Rights in Education and a graduate of Harvard Law School, spent two years as a lecturer at Cornell Law School: "During my second interview with the director of the program I was applying to join, she asked the following question: 'I note

from your *curriculum vita* that you seem to be involved in religious right issues. Do you think you can teach gay students?'
How many gay applicants at Cornell have been asked: 'Do you
think you can teach Christian students?'"[63] When a conservative
student publication at Duke University published an article
showing that conservatives were a rarity on the Duke faculty,
the chairman of the Duke philosophy department, Professor
Robert Brandon, said: "We try to hire the best, smartest people
available...If, as John Stuart Mill said, stupid people are generally conservative, then there are lots of conservatives we will
never hire."[64]

During a recent conflict over diversity at the Harvard Law
School, a candid acknowledgment of the hiring bias against conservative candidates was made by Professor Alan Dershowitz, a
faculty liberal. When the conflict came to a head the administration created a "Committee on Healthy Diversity" to assuage
left-wing students who wanted more women and racial minorities hired. While there were already a considerable number of
women and minority professors at Harvard Law, there were only
a handful of identifiable Republicans out of a faculty of 200.[65]
Seizing the opportunity the Left had seemingly provided, conservative students appealed to the Committee on Healthy
Diversity to hire more conservatives, but their pleas went unan-
swered.

Professor Dershowitz explained why their request fell on
deaf ears: "The true test for diversity for me is would people on
the left vote for a really bright evangelical Christian, who was a
brilliant and articulate spokesperson for the right to life, the
right to own guns...anti-gay approaches to life, anti-feminist
views? Would there be a push to get such a person on the faculty? Now, such a person would really diversify this place. Of
course not. I think blacks want more blacks, women want more
women, and leftists want more leftists. Everybody thinks diver-

sification comes by getting more of themselves. And that's not true diversity."[66] Of course, thanks to the relative scarcity of faculty conservatives there is no significant constituency for hiring more of them.

Academic Freedom

The activist agendas of today's academics are not only a departure from academic tradition; they are violations of established principles of academic freedom dating back to 1915. These principles, which were developed by the American Association of University Professors, have been universally embraced by American colleges and universities and are elaborated in official faculty guidelines, while remaining unenforced. Rule APM 0-10 of the University of California's *Academic Personnel Manual*, written in 1934 by its president, Robert Gordon Sproul, states:

> The function of the university is to seek and to transmit knowledge and to train students in the processes whereby truth is to be made known. To convert, or to make converts, is alien and hostile to this dispassionate duty. Where it becomes necessary, in performing this function of a university, to consider political, social, or sectarian movements, they are dissected and examined, not taught, and the conclusion left, with no tipping of the scales, to the logic of the facts.... Essentially the freedom of a university is the freedom of competent persons in the classroom. In order to protect this freedom, the University assumed the right to prevent exploitation of its prestige by unqualified persons or by those who would use it as a platform for propaganda.

On July 30, 2003—sixty-nine years after this statement was written—the passage was removed from the Berkeley personnel manual by a 43–3 vote of the Faculty Senate.[67] This was an eloquent and disturbing expression of the new academic culture, which had accommodated itself to the intrusion of partisan agendas into the curriculum. The Sproul clause was replaced by one that omitted any distinction between indoctrination and education and which made faculty the arbiter of the standard: "Academic freedom requires that teaching and scholarship be assessed only by reference to the professional standards that sustain the University's pursuit and achievement of knowledge," the new passage stated. "The substance and nature of these standards properly lie within the expertise and authority of the faculty as a body. . . . Academic freedom requires that the Academic Senate be given primary responsibility for applying academic standards. . . ." In other words, academic freedom is whatever the faculty says it is. Gone is the injunction against making converts to political, social, or sectarian agendas; gone, too, the admonition not to exploit the prestige of the university as a platform for political propaganda.

With this rewriting of university guidelines, the principle of academic freedom, which had been created to protect scholarship, had now become a license for professors to do what they liked. This was an ominous event in the life of American universities and passed virtually unnoticed; an indication of how completely this core principle of university governance had fallen into disregard, and how profoundly the university culture had changed.

The removal of the Sproul clause was the Faculty Senate's response to a dilemma created the previous year when a radical lecturer named Snehal Shingavi announced that his section of a freshman writing course would be titled "The Politics and Poetics of Palestinian Resistance." In describing the course, which was required of all freshman whose writing skills did not meet the university's standard, Shingavi wrote: "The brutal Israeli military occupation of Palestine, [ongoing] since 1948, has systematically

displaced, killed, and maimed millions of Palestinian people...
This class will examine the history of the [resistance] and the
way that it is narrated by Palestinians in order to produce an
understanding of the *Intifada*." The course description Shingavi
had placed in the official university catalogue ended with a
warning: "Conservative thinkers are encouraged to seek other
sections."[68] When FOX News Channel hosts jumped on this
attempt to exclude conservative students, the public reaction
prompted university officials to remove the warning from the
catalogue. But they allowed the course—a blatant exercise in
political propaganda—to continue as announced.

The only academic rationale for the freshman English course
was to teach incoming students the elements of style—the grammatical construction of topic sentences and paragraphs and the
like. This was why the course was offered by the English Department and not the Departments of Political Science or Middle
Eastern Studies. But instead of confronting an egregious abuse of
the classroom for political purposes, the Berkeley Faculty Senate
chose instead to conceal its hypocrisy by eliminating the section
of its academic freedom code specifically designed to draw the
distinction between education and indoctrination.

The misuse of freshman writing courses is common at many
universities, where sections are regularly built around themes
like feminism, radical environmentalism, and radical perspectives on race.[69] At the same time, there are academic freedom
guidelines still nominally in force at these schools which were
written to prevent such practices.

The faculty handbook of Ohio State University (to take a
fairly typical example) instructs professors as follows: "Academic
freedom carries with it correlative academic responsibilities. The
principal elements include the responsibility of teachers to...
differentiate carefully between official activities as teachers and
personal activities as citizens, and to act accordingly." Policy HR

64 in the Penn State policy manual is even more explicit: "No faculty member may claim as a right the privilege of discussing in the classroom controversial topics outside his/her own field of study. The faculty member is normally bound not to take advantage of his/her position by introducing into the classroom provocative discussions of irrelevant subjects not within the field of his/her study." The Penn State policy manual explains the rationale behind its restriction of professorial speech in these words:

> The faculty member is entitled to freedom in the classroom in discussing his/her subject. The faculty member is, however, responsible for the maintenance of appropriate standards of scholarship and teaching ability. It is not the function of a faculty member in a democracy to indoctrinate his/her students with ready-made conclusions on controversial subjects. The faculty member is expected to train students to think for themselves, and to provide them access to those materials, which they need if they are to think intelligently. Hence, in giving instruction upon controversial matters the faculty member is expected to be of a fair and judicial mind, and to set forth justly, without super-cession or innuendo, the divergent opinions of other investigators.

Behind these guidelines lies a liberal philosophy of education, where the professional responsibility of educators is to elevate students' ability to think, not hand them the correct opinions. This is what distinguishes democratic systems of education from their totalitarian counterparts. Under academic freedom guidelines, teachers are expected to instruct students how to assemble data from the evidential record, evaluate it, and construct an argument. They are expected to refrain from using the authority of the classroom to impose on students their personal conclusions about questions to which the answers are not verifiable or are beyond their professional expertise. It is the difference, as Stanley Fish wrote, between teaching *about* controversial issues and "urging them as commitments."

There are no "correct" answers to controversial issues, which is why they are controversial: scholars cannot agree. Answers to such questions are inherently subjective and opinion-based and teachers should not use the authority of the classroom to force students to adopt their positions. To do so is not education but indoctrination.

These principles are still enshrined in the academic freedom guidelines of the American Association of University Professors and of many large university systems, like the ones in Pennsylvania and Ohio, and until recently California.[70] But as the profiles in this book reveal, they are widely disregarded by activist professors in liberal arts programs.

Many professors featured in this volume are icons of the contemporary academy—Michael Eric Dyson, John Esposito, Eric Foner, Frederic Jameson, bell hooks, Mari Matsuda, among others. Others are more obscure and known only locally. But even the more obscure faculty in this book will be important enough figures to those students who come under their tutelage. The lack of professionalism displayed by these professors will have an impact on their education, and it would be naïve to suppose it will be a good one.

How many radical professors are there on American faculties of higher education? According to the federal government, the total number of college and university professors in the United States is 617,000. If we were to take the Harvard case reviewed at the end of this volume[71] as a yardstick, and assume a figure of 10 percent per university faculty, and then cut that figure in half to control for the possibility that Harvard may be a relatively radical institution, the total number of such professors at American universities with views similar to the spectrum represented in this volume would still be in the neighborhood of 25,000–30,000.[72] The number of students annually passing through their classrooms would be of the order of a hundred times that, or three million. This is a figure that ought to trouble every educator who is concerned about the quality of higher education and every American who cares about the country's future.

The professorial profiles that follow have been printed in alphabetical order and can be read advantageously in that sequence. The very randomness of the selection is an instruction in itself. Many hands went into making this text possible. More than thirty researchers were involved in drafting the profiles. John Perazzo managed the research, wrote some of the texts, and reviewed them all. John is the managing editor of www.DiscoverTheNetworks.org, a database on the political Left, which provided the idea for this book. Jacob Laksin and Thomas Ryan are researchers and writers for the same website and for www.FrontPagemag.com. Mike Bauer, another DiscoverTheNetworks staffer, went over the text and footnotes with a fine-toothed comb. Elizabeth Ruiz tracked down sources and generally assisted in the technical aspects of putting the text in order. I could not have completed this book without them.

I have revised and edited all of the profiles contained in this text and rewritten many, so that I no longer know where my edits begin and the original drafts end. These profiles should be treated as a collective effort, but I am ultimately responsible for their judgments and accuracy.

This book was inspired by my own educational experience at Columbia University in the 1950s. I was a Marxist at the time and wrote my classroom papers, as a seventeen-year-old, from that perspective. Even though this was the height of the Cold War and my professors were anti-Communist liberals, they never singled me out for comment the way many conservative students I have encountered are singled out today. No professor of mine ever said in the course of a classroom lecture, "Horowitz, why do Communists kill so many people?" Yet, last year, a Christian student at the University of Rhode Island named Nathaniel Nelson was singled out by his political science professor, who interrupted a class discussion in a course on "Political Philosophy from Plato to Machiavelli" to ask, "Nathaniel, why do Christians hate fags?" I do not know how my education would have been affected if my professors had become my adversaries in the classroom, but I am sure the effect would not have been positive. If my professors had made me an object of their partisan passions, the trust between teacher and student would have been irreparably ruptured and with it the ability of my teachers to provide me with the full benefits of their experience and expertise.

I am grateful to my Columbia professors for not becoming my adversaries in the classroom in the way that has become common in the classrooms of activist professors today. I am grateful to them for treating me as a seventeen-year-old, who was their student and to whom they had the same professional obligation they had to students who might agree with them on contemporary issues. I am grateful for their professionalism and for the respect they showed to their academic calling; and I am grateful for their concern for my vulnerability as a young man. In twenty years of schooling up through the graduate level, I never heard one teacher or professor, on one occasion in one classroom ever express a political opinion. Not one. It is my hope that the integrity exhibited by my teachers in that politically troubled era will be restored one day to American institutions of learning so that future generations of students can receive as full a benefit from their educational experience as I did.

My most difficult task in writing this book was living daily with the knowledge it provides of the enormous damage that several generations of tenured radicals have inflicted on our educational system; and of being cognizant of the unrelenting malice that so many of them hold in their hearts for a country that has given them the great privileges and freedoms they enjoy as a birthright.

December 2005

One Hundred and One Professors

Professor M. Shahid Alam
Northeastern University

— Professor of economics, Northeastern University, Boston

— Likens the 9/11 terrorists to America's Founding Fathers, as men who were willing to die "so that their people might live, free and in dignity"

— Claims that the al Qaeda's *jihad* is a defensive *jihad* against Western aggressors

M. Shahid Alam is one of the thousands of tenured academics at American universities whose intellectual guide is Marxism and who thinks that America's terrorist enemies are really "freedom fighters" and America a Great Satan. In an essay appearing in the December 2004 issue of *Dissident Voice* ("A Radical Newsletter in the Struggle for Peace and Justice"), Alam likened Moham-med Atta and the al-Qaeda terrorists who attacked the World Trade Center on 9/11 to the American patriots who defended themselves against the British at Lexington and Concord[1] and launched an historic movement for liberty and freedom. Wrote

Professor Alam: "On September 11, 2001, nineteen Arab hijackers too demonstrated their willingness to die—and to kill—for their dream."

Professor Alam's inflammatory and fanatic prose was published widely on the Internet. When challenged by email, he rebutted his critics with an anti-Semitic sneer: "Why is it that the only hateful mail I have received is signed by Levitt, Hoch, or Freedman?" If Professor Alam had made similar slurs about African Americans or gays, he would have been reprimanded and probably dismissed by the school administration. As his targets were only Jews, the university administration showed no interest.

In January 2005, Alam published a follow-up article[2] in Counterpunch.org, a well-known website that supports Iraq's terrorists as "resistance fighters" against American "imperialism." Alam's article was titled "The Waves of Hate: Testing Free Speech in America," and in it, he portrayed himself as a heroically misunderstood and persecuted figure who was testing the limits of free speech while "hate websites"—he named the anti-al-Qaeda blog www.jihadwatch.org, and www.littlegreenfootballs.com—hounded him for speaking the truth. In his Counterpunch article, Professor Alam defended his claims. "In their war of independence, the Americans may not have targeted civilians, but they did commit atrocities, and they did inflict collateral damage on civilians." Alam seemed surprised that people would take exception to his analogy: "I have since been wondering why my suggestion that al-Qaeda—like the American colonists before them—was leading an Islamic insurgency has provoked such a storm of vicious attacks."

See also: Professors Anderson, al-Arian, Bagby,
Massad, Mazrui

Research: Robert Spencer[3]

Professor Hamid Algar
University of California, Berkeley

— Professor of Persian and Islamic studies, University of
  California, Berkeley
— Supporter of the Ayatollah Khomeni
— The war on terror is America's aggression against the Muslim
  world.

Born in 1940, Hamid Algar has been a member of the UC
Berkeley faculty since 1965. He is the biographer of Iran's
Islamic dictator, the Ayatollah Khomeni, and ranks among the
world's leading historians of Islam. He teaches courses on Persian literature, the history of Islam, and Shi'ism, Sufism; he has
written books and articles on each of these subjects, including
more than one hundred articles in the *Encyclopaedia Iranica*. He
is also a ferocious critic of the United States and Israel.

Professor Algar personally met with Khomeini during the latter's exile in Paris, and again several times after the Iranian revolution of 1979. He translated many of Khomeini's writings and
speeches and wrote a book about those works, titled *The Roots
of the Islamic Revolution in Iran*. Professor Algar considers the
Iranian revolution "the most significant, hopeful, and profound
event in the entirety of contemporary Islamic history."[4]

In an address honoring Khomeini in 1994, Algar advocated
global jihad: "Let us remember the comprehensive jihad that
starts with our own persons and should also embrace our communal and political lives and if necessary go to the point of taking weapons in our hands to defeat the enemies of Islam."[5] Algar
immediately defined those enemies: "Let us remember the clear
analysis of the West that Imam (Khomeini) gave us . . . as a collection of international bandits . . . which has consolidated itself

since Imam's death. Let us also remember his insistence that the abominable genocide state of Israel completely disappear from the face of the globe."[6]

In Professor Algar's view, there is no "clash of civilizations" between Middle Eastern Islam and the West. "That's one of those meaningless slogans which people hold seminars and write books about," he says, "which presumes an inherent and irreducible antagonism. But what may be underway is the launching of World War IV [with "WW III" having been the Cold War], as it's been called, most recently by James Woolsey [former director of the CIA]."[7] Professor Algar is skeptical about the U.S. government's assurance that the current war on terror "isn't a war against Islam." According to Professor Algar, "'World War IV' clearly focuses on Middle Eastern Muslim states."[8]

Professor Algar sees America's war on terror largely as a product of America's imperialistic and aggressive impulses, which he says are aimed at fulfilling the goals of an agenda that long predated 9/11. The *modus operandi*, in his view, is the calculated replacement of one perceived threat—Communism—with a new perceived threat—Islam. "There always has to be a focus for hostility," he says, "to keep the juices pumped and the military machine well supplied. Now, somewhat improbably, Islam—or Muslims and Muslim countries—are fulfilling that role of a global long-term threat."[9]

In Professor Algar's view, Americans identify their adversary as "militant" Islam because "it's not politically correct to say you're against a religion as such. Therefore, an adjective has to be supplied: militant Islam, extremist Islam, Islamic terrorism, Islamic fundamentalism, political Islam. I would say that the Muslim world, or specifically the Muslim Middle East, has been chosen not because it is strong, a menace, or a threat; but, on the contrary, because it is an extremely weak and impotent adversary."[10] He gives no credence to suggestions that militant Islam chose the West as its enemy through the attacks of 9/11 and many previous acts of anti-Western terrorism. According to Professor Algar, the aggression that led to the War on Terror was instigated by the West.

In 1998, Professor Algar verbally harassed and spat on members of UC Berkeley's Armenian Student Association, who were commemorating the genocide of Armenians by the Turks. "It was not a genocide, but I wish it were, you lying pigs," Shake Hovsepian quoted Algar for *Usanogh: Periodical of Armenian Students*.[11] "You are distorting the truth about history. You stupid Armenians; you deserve to be massacred!"

The university administration at Berkeley, whose antennae are usually exquisitely sensitive to any sign of "insensitivity" among its faculty or students, had no reaction to these remarks from its most prominent professor of Islamic studies.

> *See also:* Professors Brand, Dabashi, Massad, Mazrui
>
> *Research:* Joseph D'Hippolito[12]

Professor Lisa Anderson
Columbia University

— Professor of political science, Columbia University
— Dean of Columbia's school of International and Public Affairs
— Regards America's wars of liberation in Afghanistan and Iraq as "an assault on the entire region."

A faculty member at Columbia University since 1986, political science Professor Lisa Anderson is the former president of the Middle East Studies Association. Described in her university biography as "one of this country's most eminent scholars of the Middle East and North Africa," Professor Anderson is the author of just one book, *The State and Social Transformation in Tunisia and Libya, 1830-1980.* She currently serves as the dean of Columbia's School of International and Public Affairs and co-chair of Human Rights/Middle East. She is also a member of the Council on Foreign Relations, the Carnegie Council on Ethics, and the Social Science Research Council.

Professor Anderson's most recent achievement was raising $4 million, almost entirely from Arab sources, for an "Edward Said Chair in Middle Eastern Studies."[13] Though Said was not a scholar of Islam or the Middle East, but a literary scholar and celebrated anti-Israel polemicist, Anderson found nothing peculiar in naming the chair after him. She kept the sources of the chair's funding secret for as long as possible, despite public criticism and even though New York State Law requires that such information be reported when it involves foreign funds. To occupy the chair, she selected Professor Rashid Khalidi, a long-time supporter of Yasser Arafat and one-time activist with the Palestine Liberation Organization, who depicts Israel as a "racist" nation that imposes "apartheid" on Palestinians. Professor Anderson reserved the chair for Khalidi until he could extricate himself from his position at the University of Chicago. She could not "honestly think of a better person," she said, "to recruit to Columbia."[14]

Professor Anderson was also instrumental in helping Joseph Massad, whom she had served as a PhD advisor, to secure a teaching post at Columbia. Massad believes that the "Jewish state is a racist state that does not have the right to exist," that Palestinian suicide bombers are noble "anti-colonial resistors," and that there are "stark" similarities between the plight of World War II-era Jews in Nazi concentration camps and contemporary Palestinian terrorists in Israeli prisons.

During Professor Anderson's tenure as dean, the School of International and Political Affairs has held numerous events condemning the state of Israel. In September 2002, for instance, the School of International and Public Affairs co-sponsored an African Studies Institute seminar called "South African Conversation on Israel and Palestine,"[15] which was designed to liken Israel's current social structure to the system of racial apartheid, even though the Arab citizens of Israel (more than a million strong) enjoy more rights than the citizens of any Arab state.

Professor Anderson is a fierce critic not only of Israel, but also of the United States. She views the 9/11 attacks as the Muslim world's response to "the fact of American political power in the world, and the fact of inequitable distribution of power within the United States." When writing about the "war on terror," Professor Anderson places those words in sneer quotes to convey her belief that the term is nothing more than a pretext for American empire-building by means of serial invasions. Casting the U.S. as an unprovoked aggressor in this war, she characterizes the American military operations in Afghanistan and Iraq as an "assault on the entire region" and an attempt "to rewrite the map of the entire area."[16]

> *See also:* Professors Anidjar, Brand, J. Cole,
>   De Genova, Massad
>
> *Research:* Hugh Fitzgerald[17]

Professor Gil Anidjar
Columbia University

— Assistant professor of comparative literature, Columbia

— Anti-Israel activist and apologist for Islamic radicalism

— Identifies "good teaching" with pro-Palestinian activism and "dissent"

Professor Gil Anidjar is an assistant professor of comparative literature in Columbia University's department of Middle East and Asian Languages and Cultures. Professor Anidjar's class, "Semites: Race, Religion, Literature," parses, among other issues, the use of the term "Semite" and how it has "affected various aspects of academia and individual academics."[18] There is little doubt about how it has affected academics like Professor Anidjar: for the professor, the term is merely a rhetorical cudgel with which to batter the legitimacy of the state of Israel. For instance, he has claimed in interviews[19] that "the last Semites and the only Semites" are Arabs—an argument that, though demonstrably false, is intended to undermine the legitimacy of Israel's character as a Jewish state. Stretching this argument further, Professor Anidjar has contended that "the Arabs have become the race that is still attached to its religion, whereas the Jews have in fact become Western Christians, and therefore are no longer marked, neither by race nor by religion."[20] The Columbia University administration had no reaction to these crudely racist public remarks from one of its professors.

Implicit in Professor Anidjar's remarks is that Israel has no right to exist as a Jewish state, a point reinforced by his frequent tirades against Zionism, which he assails for what he calls its "apocalyptic dimensions."[21] When speaking about Zionism, as he does in his classes, Professor Anidjar also stresses: "The argument I want to make is that it is absolutely essential to continue to insist on the colonial dimension of Zionism, and colonial in the strict sense, absolutely."[22] "Israel is absolutely a colonial enterprise, a colonial settler state."[23] Far more charitable is Professor Anidjar's appraisal of Islam. When faced with criticism of Islam he has said: "There is, in fact, a level at which I simply lack all understanding," he has said. "Can anyone seriously claim that the problem with Islamic countries is Islam?"[24]

Professor Anidjar's animus against Israel finds its most zealous expression in his role as an anti-Israel activist-academic on the Columbia campus. On November 13, 2002—billed as Columbia's "National Day of Action against Israeli Apartheid"— Professor Anidjar led a campus conference to divest Columbia from any dealings with Israeli companies.[25]

Professor Anidjar draws no distinction between his roles as an academic and activist. An academic, according to Professor Anidjar, is not one who imparts knowledge or guides students in a dispassionate quest for truth, but one who recruits them to his personal political causes. Of one such cause—"Palestinian rights"—Professor Anidjar said on the occasion of a 2005 anti-Israel gathering, "is—or it should be—the struggle of all students and all teachers, of all adjuncts and lecturers, of untenured as well as—believe me—tenured faculty."[26] Addressing himself to politically like-minded colleagues at Columbia, Professor Anidjar urged them to "Continue to support [radical anti-Israel professor] Joseph Massad and remember Palestinian rights too... Continue to voice your dissent. For that is good teaching." Professor Anidjar regards his conflation of activism and pedagogy as evidence of his "support for Academic Freedom," although he did fret, in the course of his high-pitched oration, "I fear I am beginning to sound like a raving lunatic."[27]

See also: Professors Cloud, Dabashi, Haddad, LeVine

Research: Jacob Laksin, Hugh Fitzgerald[28]

Professor Anatole Anton
San Francisco State University

— Professor of philosophy at San Francisco State University

— Former chair of the Philosophy Department

— Co-coordinator of the Radical Philosophy Association

Professor Anatole Anton is professor of philosophy at San Francisco State University and the former chair of the department. He "writes and researches on political philosophy, the philosophy of social science, and Hegel and Marx." He is also the general editor of the San Francisco State University *Series in Philosophy*.

Professor Anton is co-coordinator of the Radical Philosophy Association, an anti-capitalist group of Marxist professors who "believe that fundamental change requires broad social upheavals but also opposition to intellectual support for exploitative and dehumanizing social structures, [including] capitalism, racism, sexism, homophobia, disability discrimination, environmental ruin, and all other forms of domination." The Radical Philosophy Association supports Cuba's Communist dictatorship and opposes U.S. economic and military aid to Israel, on grounds that such aid is "perceived" as supporting "the enem[y] of Muslim nations." The Association has taken a strong stand against the war on terror in Afghanistan and Iraq. The Radical Philosophy Association attributes the terrorist threat to America's ill-advised support for "corrupt and repressive regimes" in the Third World.

In a September 27, 2004 email circulated to his colleagues, Anton wrote: "Companeros [sic], I thought a number of you might find these words by E.L. Doctorow [on the "Unfeeling President"] moving and useful and therefore might want to circulate them widely." President Bush, according to Doctorow, "does not suffer the death of our twenty-one-year-olds who wanted to be what they could be.... [He] does not know what death is. He hasn't the mind for it.... How then can he mourn? To mourn is to express regret and he regrets nothing.... He does not drop to his knees, he is not contrite, he does not sit in the church with the grieving parents and wives and children.... He does not feel for the families of the dead,... He cannot mourn but is a figure of such moral vacancy as to make us mourn for ourselves."

See also: Professor Jaggar
Research: Lisa Makson

Professor Bettina Aptheker
University of California, Santa Cruz

— Professor of Women's Studies, University of California, Santa Cruz
— Describes her teaching philosophy as "revolutionary praxis."
— Marxist-Feminist

Professor Bettina Aptheker is the daughter of a famous American Communist, the late Herbert Aptheker who, after the fall of the Soviet system (which both he and his daughter deeply regretted), was honored by the Columbia University history department and hired as a visiting law professor by the University of California (Berkeley) and as a history professor at several prestigious academic institutions.

Professor Bettina Aptheker is by her own proud admission both a Communist and a self-described "lesbian activist." Her introductory course at UC Santa Cruz (UCSC) on feminism, which she has taught since 1980, turns Marx's "historical materialism"—the idea that society progresses through successive stages from feudalism to capitalism to socialism into a theory of sexuality, and turns sexuality into a species of political consciousness-raising. Aptheker's course syllabus describes lesbianism as the "highest stage of feminism" (an obvious homage to Lenin's *Imperialism: The Highest Stage of Capitalism*). In other words, change in sexual orientation is an inevitable final stage in the development of the socially conscious individual. This is intended as serious analysis. Aptheker teaches the course to 400 students a year, and the lectures have actually been filmed at university expense as an important contribution to what the university describes as lesbian "herstory."

Aptheker describes her teaching philosophy as a "revolution-ary praxis." The crux of this approach, she has said, is to subvert the traditional mission of the university by breaking down the distinction between subjective and objective truth, what Aptheker dubs "breaking down dualisms."[29] This approach is especially relevant to women's studies, Aptheker notes, because it allows her to inject a "women-centered perspective" into the curriculum to correct what she claims was the "male-centered" bias of traditional university study.[30] Aptheker has even based an entire course around her notion of a feminist pedagogy, called "Feminist Methods of Teaching." Aptheker's contribution to women's studies also includes her marriage of radical politics to feminist sensibilities—all under the guise of an academic cur-riculum. A typical brainchild is Aptheker's graduate-level course "Feminist/Radical Pedagogies."[31]

Although a fulltime professor of feminist studies and history at the UCSC, Aptheker does not have a single work of reputable scholarship to her name. Most of her books, including *Intimate Politics: Autobiography As Witness* and *The Morning Breaks: The Trial of Angela Davis*, and *If They Come in the Morning: Voices of Resistance*" (co-authored with Angela Davis) are frankly political.

As for Aptheker's ostensibly scholarly effort, *Woman's Legacy: Essays on Race, Sex, and Class in American History* (1982), this amounts to little more than a review of Aptheker's politics. Radical feminist poet Adrienne Rich has hailed the book as "feminist to its core."[32]

On the website RateMyProfessors.com, one of Aptheker's less than happy students complains that she focuses "way too much on personal history—relied on pseudo-celebrity status to entertain the class." According to the student, Aptheker wants everyone to know that she "met my life partner, Kate Miller, at a Holly Near Concert...in October 1979."

The Santa Cruz campus is a fertile ground for Communist politics. An old Berkeley comrade of Professor Aptheker's—also the scion of a famous Communist family—Conn Hallinan, is the university's Provost. Hallinan's father, Vincent, was a wealthy lawyer who ran as the presidential candidate for the Communist-created and controlled Progressive Party in 1952. (Hallinan had to conduct his presidential campaign from his prison cell at McNeil Island federal penitentiary in Washington State, where he was serving time for tax evasion.)

The Santa Cruz faculty also includes Professor Angela Davis,[33] winner of a Lenin Peace Prize from the East German police state during the Cold War. Aptheker, Hallinan, and Davis were expelled from the Communist Party in 1991 after the failed coup against Gorbachev. Communist Party head Gus Hall supported the coup, while they did not (making them the more "liberal" faction of the Party). They formed the "Committees of Correspondence," an organization for themselves and other Gorbachev supporters.

A member of the anti-war movement during the sixties, Aptheker has not shed her reflexive opposition to U.S. military intervention. Appearing at an April 2003 UCSC faculty teach-in against the Iraq War, Aptheker proclaimed, "This war in Iraq is an obscenity." Aptheker also claimed to see similarities between the political strategies of the United States under George W. Bush and those of Nazi-era Germany. "We should make no mistake between the kinds of diplomacy Hitler's regime engaged in during the 1930s and the kinds of diplomacy the Bush administration has engaged in. There are direct parallels, and it's very frightening," said Aptheker.[34] "Our agenda should be to overthrow Bush," she informed UCSC students. Writing several months later, in the Summer 2003 issue of *The Wave*, the newsletter of the UCSC Women's Department, Aptheker let

loose with a yet more high-pitched attack on the Bush administration, accusing it of "[i]mplementing a proto-fascist program
of racist abuse directed especially toward peoples of Arab heritage, while giving license to the worst forms of persecution of
all peoples of color," and declared her assurance that "the Washington clique promises to lead us further towards an abyss of
unending imperial wars and economic catastrophe."[35]

Aptheker is similarly outspoken against Israel, and has
labored to make the UCSC campus into a focal point of anti-
Israel activism. Aptheker has signed an open letter to the U.S.
government demanding the ending of all American aid to Israel.
In 2002, she authored an article in *The Wave* pledging support
for Palestinian terrorists, whom she euphemistically described as
"anti-occupation activists."[36]

See also: Professors Davis, Furr, Jaggar,
                    Marable, Targ
Research: John Perazzo

Professor Sami al-Arian
University of South Florida

— Professor of engineering at the University of South Florida

— North American head of Palestine Islamic Jihad, a terrorist group responsible for the suicide bombing murders of more than 100 civilians in the Middle East

— "Civil liberties activist"

Before being arrested for his terrorist activities, Osama (Sami) al-Arian, a Palestinian, was a professor of engineering who operated out of the University of South Florida. Professor Al-Arian created two non-profit organizations, a think tank associated with the University called the World Islamic Studies Enterprise and the Islamic Committee for Palestine, which raised funds and recruited soldiers for Palestinian Islamic Jihad. Professor Sami al-Arian was, in fact, the North American head of Palestinian Islamic Jihad, which was one of the principal terrorist organizations in the Middle East, and responsible for suicide bombings that have taken the lives of more than a hundred people including two Americans, aged 16 and 20. An FBI surveillance video of Professor al-Arian's fundraising tour of American mosques shows him being introduced as "the president of the Islamic Committee for Palestine. . . . the active arm of the Islamic *Jihad* Movement."

Along with others in the video who praise the killing of Jews and Christians, Professor al-Arian declaims, "God cursed those who are the sons of Israel, through David and Jesus, the son of Mary. . . . Those people, God made monkeys and pigs. . . ." And further: "Let us damn America, let us damn Israel, let us damn them and their allies until death." In another speech Professor al-Arian said, "We assemble today to pay respects to the march of the martyrs and to the river of blood that gushes forth and does not extinguish, from butchery to butchery, and from martyrdom to martyrdom, from *jihad* to *jihad.*" [37] As one of the tapes reveals, at one of Professor al-Arian's fundraisers to "sponsor" Palestinian martyrs, a spokesman "begged for $500 to kill a Jew."[38]

One board member of Professor al-Arian's academic think tank was also a Palestinian professor at the university named Khalil Shiqaqi. His brother, Fathi Shiqaqi, was the well-known founder of Palestinian Islamic Jihad and its military leader in Syria. When Fathi Shiqaqi was assassinated, his replacement as head of the terrorist organization was Professor Ramadan Abdallah Shallah another director of Professor al-Arian's think tank and also a member of the faculty of the University of South Florida.

In 1997, Professor al-Arian founded the National Coalition to Protect Political Freedom. Its specific purpose was to oppose the "Anti-Terrorism and Effective Death Penalty Act"—the predecessor to the Patriot Act—which had been passed in 1996 following the bombing of the Federal Building in Oklahoma City that killed 175 innocent people. Pursuant to the Act, Palestinian Islamic Jihad was declared a terrorist organization. The Act also made "material support" for terrorist organizations illegal and authorized the use of secret evidence in terrorist cases. Professor al-Arian's brother-in-law Mazen al-Najjar—also a member of the think tank—was arrested under the terms of the Act, held for three and a half years and eventually deported after 9/11.

Professor al-Arian was the spearhead of the civil liberties coalition that formed to oppose the Patriot Act, which was, in effect, an extension of the Clinton anti-terrorism law. Professor Al-Arian's coalition partners included the National Lawyers Guild, the American Civil Liberties Union, and the Center for Constitutional Rights, whose lead spokesman in the coalition was David Cole, professor of law at Georgetown University and the lawyer for Professor al-Arian's terrorist brother-in-law, Professor Mazen al-Najjar.[39]

Professor Al-Arian had been under investigation by the FBI since 1996 and had long been publicly identified as a terrorist by close observers of the Islamic *jihad* movement, including reporters for the *Miami Herald* and Investigative Project director Steven Emerson. When Emerson began warning the public about Professor al-Arian's terrorist efforts he was ferociously attacked for "Muslim-bashing" and "McCarthyism" by prominent figures in the political Left, among whom al-Arian was by now a familiar colleague. On September 26, 2001, Professor al-Arian made the mistake of appearing on FOX News Channel's *O'Reilly Factor*. The host confronted Professor al-Arian with his videotaped calls for terrorist *jihad* and declared, "If I was the CIA, I'd follow you wherever you went." The ensuing public uproar produced enough embarrassment to University of South Florida officials that they finally suspended al-Arian from his professorship, with pay.

Professor Al-Arian responded to the suspension by adopting the posture of the victim: "I'm a minority," he said. "I'm an Arab. I'm a Palestinian. I'm a Muslim. That's not a popular thing to be these days. Do I have rights, or don't I have rights?"[40] The American left sprang to Professor al-Arian's defense. Their efforts included articles in *The Nation* and *Salon.com*, whose reporter Eric Boehlert called it, "The Prime Time Smearing of Sami al-Arian" and explained, "By pandering to anti-Arab hysteria, NBC, Fox News, Media General and Clear Channel radio disgraced themselves—and ruined an innocent professor's life."[41] The leftist head of Georgetown's Middle East studies program, Professor John Esposito, expressed concern that al-Arian not be a "victim of... anti-Arab and anti-Muslim bigotry," and Professor Ellen Schrecker, the foremost academic expert on the McCarthy era (who regards American Communists as well-meaning social reformers and innocent victims of government persecution) called al-Arian's suspension "political repression."[42]

Others who joined the al-Arian defense chorus for Professor al-Arian included the ACLU, the Center for Constitutional Rights, the University of South Florida faculty union, and the American Association of University Professors, which threatened to challenge the university's accreditation because it had "violated" Professor al-Arian's "academic freedom."[43] Meanwhile, faculty at Duke University invited Professor al-Arian to be the featured speaker at an academic symposium on "National Security and Civil Liberties." Professor al-Arian was the featured (and university-sponsored) speaker as an expert on civil liberties.

Professor Sami al-Arian was arrested for his terrorist activities in February 2003. In December 2005 he was acquitted of eight of the seventeen charges and a mistrial was declared on nine others when the jury failed to agree. In his summation, al-Arian's attorney conceded that al-Arian was an operative for Palestine Islamic Jihad. A reporter covering the trial summarized: "The trial exposed the professor as having been deeply enmeshed in the internal workings of Palestinian Islamic Jihad a terrorist group that has killed well over a hundred people in Israel, Gaza and the West Bank, mostly through its favored technique of suicide bombings."[44]

See also: Professors Cole, Shallalah

Research: David Horowitz[45]

Professor Leighton Armitage
Foothill College

— Adjunct Lecturer in political science, Foothill College, California

— Believes that Jews control the U.S. government

— Believes Israelis are Nazis

Dr. Leighton Armitage is an adjunct lecturer in political science in the Business and Social Sciences Department of Foothill College in Northern California. Foothill prepares more of its students to attend nearby Stanford and other major universities than any other two-year community college in California.

Dr. Armitage's academic expertise is in Europe and Japan, but his classroom focus is on Israel, a nation he loathes. He teaches his classes that Jewish "Nazis" control the U.S. government. He declares that Israel's security fence is illegal, immoral, and oppressive, and similar to the Ghetto Wall the Nazis erected in 1940 Warsaw to lock up the city's Jews pending their extermination in Treblinka and Auschwitz. "Few people realize how much influence they [Jews] wield,"[46] Dr. Armitage tells his students. America, he adds, is hated all around the world because of its close relationship with Israel.

With an even hand, Dr. Armitage denounces both the U.S. military's destruction of the safe houses of Iraqi terrorists, and the Israeli army's demolition of the safe houses of Palestinian terrorists. "Have you heard what we're doing now to houses of suspected terrorists in Iraq?" the professor asks. "We're blowing them up. If you're suspected of being a terrorist, your house will be blown up. Now, the Israelis do it with a bulldozer and we do it with a Howitzer and Apache gun ships, so it's different. I guess we have more fun."[47]

According to Dr. Armitage, America's ills can be attributed to the fact that Jews control the U.S. electoral system. "They're good business people, you've got to respect them for that, if for nothing else," he says. "Of course they're buying our elections, which really pisses me off. And this stuff you learn over time, it's not overt, no one tells you this and no one wants you to know it." He says that when he was an intern in Congress many years ago, a congressional assistant warned him about the evils of the "Jewish lobby."[48]

The Nazi analogy is ever present in Dr. Armitage's mind: "What are [the Israelis] doing with the Palestinians, every day? They're killing them. They're not taking their glasses and gold fillings, and everything else, as far as I know, but they are still slaughtering these people. It's exactly what Hitler did to the Jews."[49]

Dr. Armitage's remarks have been so public and so outrageous that Foothill College President Bernadine Fong apologized for them in a meeting with the Anti-Defamation League in March 2004. But even after he had revealed himself as an anti-Semite and had thoroughly embarrassed his college—and even though he is an adjunct instructor with no tenure and can be removed from the classroom if the administration simply chooses not to renew his contract—Dr. Armitage continues to be on the faculty of Foothill.

See also: Professors Christiansen, Finkelstein, Massad

Research: Lee Kaplan[50]

Professor Stanley Aronowitz

City University of New York

— Professor of sociology at City University of New York

— "We know that the charges against us—that university teaching is a scam, that much research is not 'useful,' that scholarship is hopelessly privileged—emanate from a Right that wants us to put our noses to the grindstone just like everybody else."

One of the leading figures of the academic Left, Stanley Aronowitz is a professor of sociology at City University of New York, where he has also been the director of the Center for Cultural Studies since 1988. Before his academic career, Professor Aronowitz was a union organizer for the Clothing and Oil and Chemical Workers unions.

In February 1997, Aronowitz wrote an article in the academic journal *Social Text*, titled "The Last Good Job in America," which also became the title of a book he published in 2001. Couched as a personal memoir, this article is a self-portrait of the liberal arts professor as slacker-in-residence.

In his memoir, Professor Aronowitz acknowledges that City University originally hired him "because they believed I was a labor sociologist." In fact, as he admits, this was just a scam: "First and foremost I'm a political intellectual . . . [I] don't follow the . . . methodological rules of the discipline." After being hired as a sociologist, Professor Aronowitz signed up for the then-hottest new academic fad, "cultural studies," and created the Center for Cultural Studies to escape the rigors of his original professional discipline. "Cultural Studies" provided him with a broad umbrella under which to pursue his Marxist politics and pass them on to his students.

As a member of the editorial board of *Social Text* and head of the Center for Cultural Studies, Professor Aronowitz is more than just a professor. He is an academic star with a six-figure salary and a publishing resume to match. In today's politicized university, it is thoroughly in keeping with Aronowitz's elevated academic status that his *chef d'oeuvre* is a book called *Science As Power*, whose core thesis is the view—which was last popular in the era of Joseph Stalin—that science is just an instrument of the ruling class. Of Professor Aronowitz's book, a reviewer for the *Times Literary Supplement* said: "If the author knows much about the content or enterprise of science, he keeps the knowledge well hidden."

Non-leftist readers of Professor Aronowitz's work could hardly have been surprised in 1996 when he and his fellow editors at *Social Text* fell victim to a famous academic hoax perpetrated by physicist Alan Sokal. Sokal submitted a phony paper on quantum mechanics and "post-modernism," another intellectual fashion of the academic Left. It was Sokal's intention to demonstrate that the magazine *Social Text* would publish nonsense about science, if the nonsense was politically correct.[51] Although the Sokal article created an international scandal, Professor Aronowitz's university career was unaffected. Aronowitz was promoted to distinguished professor of sociology in 1998.

The "last good job in America" turns out to be the lucrative job that Professor Aronowitz has created for himself at the expense of New York taxpayers and the economically disadvantaged minorities who make up the CUNY student body. "What I enjoy most," says Professor Aronowitz, "is the ability to procrastinate and control my own work-time, especially its pace: taking a walk in the middle of the day, reading between the writing, listening to a CD or tape anytime I want, calling up a friend for a chat." Professor Aronowitz teaches only one two-hour course a week. This is a seminar in Marxism. On Mondays and

Wednesdays, Professor Aronowitz does not bother to leave his house. These are the days devoted to writing a piece for *The Nation* on "the future of the left," and of course the article for *Social Text* on what a good job he has.

For decades, Professor Aronowitz and other academic leftists have been escaping the reality of their failed revolution in America's streets during the 1960s by colonizing the American university and politicizing its curriculum. In the course of this self-absorbed intellectual destruction, they have abused the educational aspirations of unsuspecting students, poor and well-fed alike. And even while this equal-opportunity exploitation goes on, they never lose the ability to see themselves as the victims of vast conspiracies of the political Right. "We know," writes Professor Aronowitz, "that the charges against us—that university teaching is a scam, that much research is not 'useful,' that scholarship is hopelessly privileged—emanate from a Right that wants us to put our noses to the grindstone just like everybody else."

The conclusion to Professor Aronowitz's memoir is naturally a call to arms, but phrased in the form of a reproof to his comrades for not advancing their struggle militantly enough: "We have not celebrated the idea of *thinking* as a full-time activity and the importance of producing what the system terms 'useless' knowledge. Most of all, we have not conducted a struggle for universalizing the self-managed time some of us still enjoy." Loafers of the world, unite!

Research: David Horowitz[52]

Professor Regina Austin
University of Pennsylvania

— William A. Schnader Professor of Law, University of
  Pennsylvania
— Believes black community should accommodate criminal
  behavior and find a "good middle ground between straightness
  and more extreme forms of lawbreaking."
— "Law is useful as a supplement to activism."

Regina Austin is the William Schnader Professor of Law at the
University of Pennsylvania, a feminist and "a leading authority
on economic discrimination and minority legal feminism,"[53]
according to her university website. Professor Austin is a proponent of Critical Race Theory, a school of law that combines
Marxist and racial perspectives. Pioneered by racial ideologue
Derrick Bell,[54] Critical Race Theory regards white racism as a
permanent structural dimension of American society. Critical
race theorists advocate compensatory, race-based preferences for
African Americans in employment, education, and—in Professor
Austin's case—criminal justice.

Long an outspoken advocate of racial separatism, Professor
Austin has made race/class/gender conflict the centerpiece of
her courses, which view legal issues through the narrow prism of
identity politics. Characteristic of Professor Austin's approach is
her popular seminar, "Advanced Torts: Intentional Torts and the
Intersection of Race, Gender & Class."[55] The course promises to
teach students to analyze legal disputes "from the perspective of
groups of subordinate status," a category that Professor Austin
subdivides into "race, ethnicity, gender, sexual orientation, age,
religion, or class."[56] The intention of "Advanced Torts" is to
encourage students, especially minority students, to regard the

law not as a body of rules applicable equally to all citizens but rather as a malleable concept, subordinate to one's perceived identity interests. If the testimony of Austin's former students is any measure, the course has been successful on this score. One student who took "Advanced Torts" enthused that it "took a different, more cultural look at Torts," one that "resonated personally with me especially as a Latina."[57]

Central to Professor Austin's "Advanced Torts" course is her claim that minority status confers the privilege of interpreting the law as one pleases. In her published articles Professor Austin has exhorted the black community to reject the distinction between lawful and unlawful activity, regarding this distinction as one of the imposed strictures of an oppressive white society. Accordingly, Professor Austin pours scorn on such "traditional values" as "conformity to the law," which she insists will "intensif[y] divisions within the black community."[58] Austin has called on African Americans to engage in outright lawbreaking, which she calls "hustling," but which in fact amounts to any number of acts of thievery licensed by Professor Austin's demands for social justice. Thus, "clerks in stores [who] cut their friends a break on merchandise, and pilfering employees [who] spread their contraband around the neighborhood," are encouraged by Professor Austin to occupy the "good middle ground between straightness and more extreme forms of lawbreaking."[59]

Asked in a 1999 interview to describe how she views her role as a legal scholar, Professor Austin answered that it "should start with the premise that black people are at the center of the universe and go on from there."[60] This view, Professor Austin explained, was the "common characteristic of the body of scholarship that is classified as critical race studies," which she has long promulgated in her academic writings. "I rely fairly heavily on culture as being the base on which you begin to build so that your authorities come from the culture and not outside of the culture," Professor Austin explained. So extreme is Professor Austin's insistence on the primacy of culture over law that she claims minority communities require an "alternative source of [legal] authority."[61]

Still another salient feature of Professor Austin's courses is their rejection of any pretense of scholarly objectivity, in favor of an aggressively political agenda. Such is the case with her seminar, "Environmental Racism." The seminar's official description discloses that it "will explore the problems and principles that fuel the environmental justice movement."[62] Among the political agendas of the course listed by Professor Austin are "supporting the environmental racism claim" and championing "environmental/occupational health issues such as pesticide poisoning and sweatshop conditions." Students are to take trips to sites "which have been impacted by environmental injustice."[63]

The powerful Marxist core of Critical Race Theory surfaces in Professor Austin's lament at the way "resources are removed from access by the market," resulting in "lesser quality environments" for minorities and the poor. Professor Austin's solution is to ensure that the privatization of wealth is "unraveled in a way that produces privatization or quasi-privatization for people who are the least well off." Toward this end, Professor Austin sees "law [as] useful as a supplement to activism. . . . I'm an institutional actor."[64]

Professor Austin concedes that her activist teaching style and preference for political opinion over legal doctrine has not always been well received. Asked whether she had encountered resistance to her approach, Professor Austin allowed that she had, and proceeded to enumerate some of the grievances raised by disaffected students: "Much too liberal, much too loose, not doctrinal, policy is empty, it's all very confusing."[65]

See also: Professors Bell, Berry, D. Cole,
            Dohrn, Dyson, hooks, Matsuda
Research: Jacob Laksin

Professor Bill Ayers
University of Illinois, Chicago

— Distinguished professor of early childhood education and senior university scholar, University of Illinois, Chicago campus

— A leader of the domestic terrorist group The Weathermen in the 1970s

— "I don't regret setting bombs. I feel we didn't do enough." (Ayers statement 2001)

Along with his wife Bernardine Dohrn, Bill Ayers was a 1960s radical and leader of the "Weatherman" faction of Students for a Democratic Society, which in 1969 went underground to become America's first terrorist cult. Named from a Bob Dylan song lyric, Weatherman has been described by Ayers as "an American Red Army." In 1969, the Weather Underground issued a formal "Declaration of War on AmeriKKKa" and attempted to incite white student radicals to engage in terrorist activities that would provoke a race war in AmeriKKKa (always spelled with three capitalized "K's"). White radicals would shed their "white skin privilege" to aid Third World peoples in plundering the ill-gotten wealth of the United States. Ayers summed up the nihilism of Weathermen's ideology as follows: "Kill all the rich people. Break up their cars and apartments. Bring the revolution home, kill your parents."[66]

The Weather Underground managed to bomb the U.S. Capitol building, New York City Police Headquarters, the Pentagon, and the National Guard offices in Washington, D.C., among many other targets. In 1970, three of their members blew themselves up in a Manhattan townhouse where they were making a bomb they planned to set off at a social dance for young military recruits and their dates at Fort Dix, New Jersey.

The FBI was unable to catch Ayers, Dohrn and their cohorts who were protected by the networks of the "progressive" Left, including their expensive lawyers, for five years until the organization dissolved through internal conflicts.[67] They surfaced in 1980 and received no serious jail time for their crimes, being let off on a technicality that they had been "improperly" surveilled.

Both went back to college, where their political comrades, now tenured faculty, helped them to embark on new careers. Dohrn became a law professor at Northwestern University and a prominent member of the American Bar Association. Ayers became a professor of early childhood education and a senior university scholar at the University of Illinois, Chicago. Neither of them modified their political views one iota.

Professor Ayers has written a series of books about parenting and educating children, including: *To Become a Teacher*; *City Kids*; *City Teachers*. His most recent book, *Fugitive Days*, however, is a memoir of his Weatherman exploits. In a chaotic text, Professor Ayers recounts his life as a 1960s radical, his role as an organizer of the 1969 "Days of Rage" riots in Chicago, his tenure as a Weatherman leader, his terrorist campaign across America, and his hatred for the United States. "What a country," Ayers once said. "It makes me want to puke." When interviewed shortly after surfacing from the terrorist underground in a kindergarten where he was already teaching, Ayers commented, reflecting on his fortunes: "Guilty as hell, free as a bird! America's a great country."[68]

A substantial portion of Professor Ayers's book *Fugitive Days* discusses his activities in building bombs and deploying explosives, as though he were writing lessons for radicals to come. Professor Ayers boasts that he participated in all the above-mentioned bombings with the exception of the fateful townhouse explosion in which his girlfriend Diana Oughton was killed. Recounting his bombing crusade, Ayers states, "There's something about a good bomb...Night after night, day after day, each majestic scene I witnessed was so terrible and so unexpected that no city would ever again stand innocently fixed in my mind. Big buildings and wide streets, cement and steel were no longer permanent. They, too, were fragile and destructible. A torch, a bomb, a strong enough wind, and they, too, would come undone or get knocked down."[69] So the terrorists who flew planes into the World Trade Center also calculated.

On September 11, 2001—the day of the terrorist attacks—the *New York Times* ran a profile of Ayers to mark the publication of his book. In an unintended irony, the *Times* quoted Ayers to this effect about his own terrorist career: "I don't regret setting bombs. I feel we didn't do enough." Ayers and the Weathermen were responsible for 30 bombings aimed at destroying the defense and security infrastructures of the United States. Of the day he bombed the Pentagon, Professor Ayers wrote in his memoir: "Everything was absolutely ideal...The sky was blue. The birds were singing. And the bastards were finally going to get what was coming to them." When reflecting on whether or not he would use bombs against the U.S. in the future, the Senior University Scholar writes, "I can't imagine entirely dismissing the possibility."[70]

To summarize the academic career of Professor Ayers: An ex-commander of the terrorist Weather Underground was hired, out of all possible candidates, for a faculty position in the Department of Education at the University of Illinois. This required a vote of the entire department. Ayers was then promoted to Associate Professor, a tenured position, and then again to full Professor, each requiring a vote of the entire department. Finally, he was made "Distinguished Professor and Senior University Scholar," an appointment reflecting the endorsement of the University's central administration, and an honor not widely shared. This occurred at a time when, as he made clear to the

New York Times, Professor Ayers was unrepentant about his former terrorist activities and wished he had planted more bombs. Not surprisingly Professor Ayers's "scholarship" reflects these sentiments. Professor Ayers has become honored among peers at Northwestern for books such as *A Kind and Just Parent* (1998), in which he argues that we must overcome our "prejudices" concerning violent juvenile offenders. In another book, *Zero Tolerance: Resisting the Drive for Punishment in Our Schools* (2001), Professor Ayers argues against expelling disruptive children from classrooms, especially if they are black or Latino. In *Teaching Towards Freedom: Moral Commitment and Ethical Action in the Classroom* (2004), the unrepentant former terrorist lectures us on "the evocative lessons about education and humanity of Pablo Neruda [a Communist bureaucrat] and Malcolm X," in order to explain what students should be for—"and what they should be against." This pattern suggests either that Northwestern University officials could find no better qualified candidate than an unrepentant terrorist to teach early childhood education and to join the ranks of its tenured faculty (and then to be honored as first among his peers) or that there is an affirmative action program at Northwestern for political radicals.

See also: Professors Berlowitz, Dohrn, LeVine
Research: John Perazzo

Professor Ihsan Bagby
University of Kentucky

— Professor of Islamic studies, University of Kentucky

— General Secretary of the Muslim Alliance of North America

— A black convert to Islam, Ihsan Bagby is an associate professor
  of Islamic studies at the University of Kentucky. Born in
  Cleveland, Ohio, he attended Oberlin College for his
  undergraduate degree and then earned his Masters and PhD in
  the field of Near Eastern studies from the University of
  Michigan.

Professor Bagby is an Islamic fundamentalist who has declared,
"Ultimately we [Muslims] can never be full citizens of this
country [the U.S.], because there is no way we can be fully committed to the institutions and ideologies of this country."[71] In
2001, Professor Bagby published the results of his comprehensive study, *The Mosque in America: A National Portrait*, which
purported to show that American Muslims were political and
religious moderates. In April 2004, he wrote *A Portrait of Detroit
Mosques: Muslim Views on Policy, Politics and Religion*, which
interpreted the findings of a survey conducted by a Detroit-area
Islamic organization, the Institute for Social Policy and Understanding. According to Bagby's reading of the data, and despite
his view that Muslims cannot assimilate, "The vast majority of
Muslim Americans hold 'moderate' views on issues of policy,
politics and religion."[72] In a newspaper interview, Professor
Bagby stated that the results showed that "the mosque community is not a place of radicalism."[73]

But as scholar of Islam Daniel Pipes writes, Professor Bagby's
interpretation amounts to "a case of survey research being distorted by its sponsors to hide the actual results. This is intellectual fraud and political deception."[74] In fact, the survey found

that among the Muslim respondents: fully two-thirds believed that "America is immoral"; four-fifths advocated the application of *Shari'a* (Islamic law) in Muslim-majority nations. [75]

In addition to his professorial duties and research ventures, Professor Bagby is the General Secretary of the Muslim Alliance of North America (MANA), a predominantly African-American organization, which is headed by Siraj Wahhaj, a suspected co-conspirator in the 1993 bombing of the World Trade Center. MANA's director of governmental affairs, Johari Abdul Malik, compassionately described Sheik Ahmed Yassin, then-leader of the terrorist group Hamas, as "a poor paraplegic in a wheelchair" at an April 2004 anti-Israel rally.

Professor Bagby is also a board member of the Council on American-Islamic Relations (CAIR). In 1998, CAIR co-sponsored a rally at Brooklyn College, where militant speakers advocated *jihad* and characterized Jews as "pigs and monkeys."[76] In November 1999, CAIR board chairman Omar Ahmad told a Chicago audience, "Fighting for freedom, fighting for Islam, that is not suicide. They kill themselves for Islam."[77]

Professor Bagby also sits on the advisory board of the Islamic Society of North America, which is responsible for enforcing Wahhabi theological writ in American mosques. The Islamic Society of North America views the Patriot Act as an affront to Muslim Americans and advocates that it be overturned; the organization also chose not to endorse or participate in the May 14, 2005 Free Muslims March Against Terror.[78]

> *See also:* Professors Algar, Brand, LeVine,
> Mazrui
> *Research:* John Perazzo

Professor Amiri Baraka

Rutgers University, Stony Brook

— Formerly LeRoi Jones
— Anti-white, anti-Semitic writer
— Former poet laureate of New Jersey

Amiri Baraka was born Everett Leroy Jones in 1934 to a middle-class family in Newark, New Jersey. He later changed his name to LeRoi Jones while attending Howard University in the early 1950s, then adopted the name Amiri Baraka after his conversion to Islam in 1968.

Jones launched his literary career with the 1961 publication of his Beat-influenced poetry collection, *Preface to a Twenty Volume Suicide Note.* He gained national prominence from the 1964 New York production of *Dutchman,* a play focusing on the flirtatious interactions between a black man and a white woman on a subway train at whose climax the white woman stabs the black man to death.

The following year Jones wrote "American Sexual Reference: Black Male," an essay that includes insights like this: "Most American white men are trained to be fags. For this reason it is no wonder their faces are weak and blank. . . . The average ofay [white person] thinks of the black man as potentially raping every white lady in sight. Which is true, in the sense that the black man should want to rob the white man of everything he has. But for most whites the guilt of the robbery is the guilt of rape. That is, they know in their deepest hearts that they should be robbed, and the white woman understands that only in the rape sequence is she likely to get cleanly, viciously popped."[79] In leftist circles, such writings gained Jones a reputation as a courageously candid genius, which paved his way for an academic career.

The 1965 assassination of Malcolm X by Black Muslims caused Jones to confront his own hypocrisy as a black racist living in a white world. He decided to leave the white world he inhabited for a black environment. "When Malcolm was murdered," Jones wrote, "I began to hold all white people responsible, even though in some part of my mind I knew better. But it was this heinous act...that made me pack up and move to Harlem and sever all ties with most of the white people I knew, many of whom were my close friends."[80] Among the close friends Jones left behind were his Jewish wife and two young daughters, abandoning them in a self-aggrandizing quest to fill Malcolm's vacated leadership position. Exculpating his betrayal of wife and children, Jones explained, "I was caught downtown with white people, and left. As simple as that. Like one day you got pubic hairs."[81]

Following this episode, Jones's writings took on an increasingly anti-Semitic tone. In his poem "For Tom Postell, Dead Black Poet," Jones refers to his ex-wife as a "fat jew girl." The poem also contains these sentiments: "Smile, jew. Dance, jew. Tell me you love me, jew. I got something for you now though....I got the extermination blues, jewboys. I got the hitler syndrome figured." In another poem, he writes, "Atheist Jews double crossers stole our [black people's] secrets.... They give us to worship a dead Jew and not ourselves .... Selling fried potatoes and people, the little arty bastards talking arithmetic they sucked from the arab's head."[82]

In Harlem, Jones helped found the Black Arts Repertory Theater/School, which produced plays emphasizing blackness as the central identifying characteristic of African-Americans. Outdoor performances of his plays—including one that featured a black man murdering his white employers—drew considerable public attention during the summer of 1965. Toward the end of that year, however, Jones realized that he would be unable to fill Malcolm's empty shoes and moved back to Newark.

In 1967, Jones published *Black Magic*, a collection of poems describing his recent exit from white society. That same year, he denounced blacks who enjoyed European classical music as traitors to their race. Such people, he said, were too "connected up with white culture. They will be digging Mozart more than James Brown. If all of that shit—Mozart, Beethoven, all of it—if it has to be burned now for the liberation of our people, it should be burned up the next minute."[83]

One year later, Jones became a Muslim and changed his name to Amiri Baraka, meaning "Blessed Prince." As Amiri Baraka, his literary and academic careers continued to thrive even as his ideological poisons took full possession of his writing. His 1969 poem "Black Art," reads, in part: "Poems are bullshit unless they are teeth or trees or lemons piled on a step.... We want poems like fists beating niggers out of Jocks, or dagger poems in the slimy bellies of the owner-jews. Black poems to smear on girdle-mamma mulatto bitches whose brains are red jelly stuck between 'lizabeth taylor's toes. Stinking Whores! We want poems that kill. Assassin poems. Poems that shoot guns. Poems that wrestle cops into alleys and take their weapons leaving them dead with tongues pulled out and sent to Ireland." This same poem later celebrates "cracking steel knuckles in a jew-lady's mouth."[84]

Another Baraka poem, "Black People," descends even further into venomous racism: "[The white man] owes you anything you want, even his life. All the stores will open if you say the magic words. The magic words are: Up against the wall mother-fucker this is a stick up!...Let's get together and kill him my man."[85] In another poem, Baraka writes, "Rape the white girls. Rape their fathers. Cut the mothers' throats."[86]

In case any reader missed the genocidal message of his text, Baraka spelled it out for them: "We [blacks] must eliminate the white man before we can draw a free breath on this planet"[87] When a white woman asked Baraka what whites could do to help the black cause, he replied, "You can help by dying. You are a cancer. You can help the world's people with your death."[88]

These sentiments were apparently a credential for Baraka to receive a series of academic appointments at the New School for Social Research in New York, the University of Buffalo, Columbia University, San Francisco State University, Yale University, George Washington University, and the State University of New York at Stony Brook.

They also qualified him to receive a host of academic and literary honors, including fellowships from the Guggenheim Foundation and the National Endowment for the Arts, the Langston Hughes Award from The City College of New York, the Rockefeller Foundation Award for Drama, the PEN/Faulkner Award, a lifetime achievement award from the Before Columbus Foundation, and induction into the American Academy of Arts and Letters.

To be fair, Professor Baraka has encountered some academic resistance. In 1990, his outspoken racism caused him to be denied a tenured position by the Rutgers University English department, which had previously hired him. This was a positive decision by the faculty partly compensating for the fact that he had been hired in the first place. Professor Baraka blamed "Europhilic elitists and white supremacists" for blocking his appointment. "The power of these Ivy League Goebbels [on the tenure committee] can flaunt, dismiss, intimidate and defraud the popular will," said Baraka. "We must unmask these powerful Klansmen. These enemies of academic freedom, people's democracy, and Pan American culture must not be allowed to prevail. Their intellectual presence makes a stink across the campus like the corpses of rotting Nazis."[89]

In October 2001, Professor Baraka capped his anti-Semitic furies with a screed called "Somebody Blew Up America," pointing his finger at the Jews, while repeating a disproved canard: "Who knew the World Trade Center was gonna get bombed?" reads the poem. "Who told 4,000 Israeli workers at the Twin Towers to stay home that day? Why did Sharon stay away?"[90]

In the same poem, Professor Baraka attacks the U.S. government for reflexively blaming "some barbaric A Rab" and refers to whites and Jews as "the gonorrhea in costume, the white sheet diseases that have murdered black people, terrorized reason and sanity, most of humanity, as they pleases." He further characterizes whites and Jews as those "who cut your nuts off, who rape your ma, who lynched your pa . . . who own the oil, who do no toil, who own the soil . . . who killed the most niggers . . . who believe the confederate flag need to be flying. . . . who [are] the biggest terrorist[s] . . . [who] only do evil . . . [and who] invented AIDS."[91]

In July 2002, Professor Baraka was named poet laureate of New Jersey, thereby becoming only the second person to hold that position, which paid a $10,000 stipend funded by taxpayer dollars. When the appointment produced a national scandal, New Jersey officials avoided firing Professor Baraka by eliminating the position entirely. Professor Baraka responded by vowing to sue the state for slander and the violation of his First Amendment rights.

In April 2005, the Middle East Studies Program at Columbia University advertised a gala celebration for Professor Baraka's 70th birthday, and encouraged students to attend.

> **See also:** Professors Anidjar, Dabashi, hooks, Jeffries, Karenga
>
> **Research:** John Perazzo

Professor David Barash
University of Washington

— Professor of psychology, University of Washington
— Co-author of *Peace and Conflict Studies*, a text widely used in Peace Studies courses
— Describes his textbook as "frankly anti-war, anti-violence, anti-nuclear, anti-authoritarian, anti-establishment, pro-environment, pro-human rights, pro-social justice, pro-peace and politically progressive."

David Barash has been a professor of psychology at the University of Washington (Seattle) since 1973. He currently teaches three psychology courses: "Comparative Animal Behavior"; "Ideas of Human Nature"; and "Psychology of Peace."

"Since the early 1980s," writes Professor Barash "I have been active in researching, promoting, and practicing the field of Peace Studies." Professor Barash, who has "a long-standing interest in . . . Buddhism and existentialism,"[92] believes that "animal behavior, evolutionary psychology and Peace Studies are fundamentally linked, especially since they all involve questions of how biology affects behavior, including male-female differences, reproductive strategies, and the troubling problem of violence in living things generally."[93]

Professor Barash is the co-author, along with Berkeley Professor Charles Webel, of *Peace and Conflict Studies* (Sage Publications, 2002), a text that is widely used in peace studies classes in American universities. In the preface to their book, Professors Barash and Webel write: "The field [of Peace Studies] differs from most other human sciences in that it is value-oriented, and unabashedly so. Accordingly we wish to be up front about our own values, which are frankly anti-war, anti-violence, anti-nuclear, anti-authoritarian, anti-establishment, pro-environ-

ment, pro-human rights, pro-social justice, pro-peace and politically progressive."[94]

Peace and Conflict Studies makes no pretension to being an
academic exploration of the complex issues of war and peace. It
does not explore the many possible views of world problems
that might lead to conflict, or the various assessments that might
be made of the history of peace movements. It is, in fact, a left
wing screed whose clear purpose is to indoctrinate students in
the radical view of the world shared by "progressives" like Noam
Chomsky, Howard Zinn, and Michael Moore. No indication is
provided to the uninformed student that these might be
extreme views, nor is there any indication that there are other
possible ways to view these issues. None of this is surprising
since Professor Barash is not a trained historian, economist, or
sociologist but a psychologist, while his co-author Professor
Webel is a philosopher. Consequently, the text they have written is not only ideologically one-sided, it is professionally incom-
petent. This has not prevented its widespread use in "Peace
Studies" programs across the country.

Peace and Conflict Studies discusses the problems of poverty
and hunger as causes of human conflict exclusively through the
eyes of Marxist writers such as Andre Gunder Frank and Frances
Moore Lappe. The text's view of these problems is socialist: "To
a very large extent, the problem of world hunger is not so much
a production problem, so much as it is a *distribution* problem."[95]
What the authors mean by this is that poverty is caused by the
private property system and free market capitalism which
results in economic inequality and that its cure is socialism
which redistributes income. This would be news to people in
socialist North Korea, where recent famine caused by their government's economic redistribution policies has killed more than
a million people. It would be equally surprising to citizens of the
former Soviet Union, whose Marxist leaders attempted to make

economic equality the center of their economic policy with the result that a country that had been the breadbasket of Europe was transformed into a nation of chronic food shortages until the general economic breakdown caused the system to collapse.

The *Peace and Conflict Studies* text relentlessly condemns the economic inequalities that characterize market systems, even though these systems are responsible for prodigious agricultural surpluses and for raising billions of people out of poverty, facts the authors systematically ignore. The authors also ignore the question of whether providing economic incentives to the creative and the productive, which results in this inequality isn't therefore worth the cost. Instead, the authors identify the culprits responsible for world poverty (and thus for the conflicts this suffering causes) in terms that would have pleased Marx and Lenin: "The greed of agribusiness shippers and brokers, plus control of land by a small elite leaves hundreds of millions of people hungry every day."[96] No wonder terrorists hate rich countries like the United States.

Since the authors believe that the greed of the ruling class is solely responsible for world hunger, *Peace and Conflict Studies* does actually endorse one kind of violence, and one kind alone. Not surprisingly this is revolutionary violence. Here is Professor Barash and Professor Webel's example of revolutionary violence that has led to good results:

> Consider the case of Cuba. In the aftermath of the Cuban Revolution of 1959, despite more than 40 years of an American embargo of Cuban imports and exports, infant mortality in Cuba has declined to the lowest in Latin America; life expectancy increased from 55 years in 1959 to 73 years in 1984; health care was nationalized and made available to all Cuban citizens at no or little cost; literacy exceeded 95%; and although prostitution, begging, and homelessness returned to

Cuba in the 1990s (almost entirely for economic reasons due to the embargo and to the loss of support from the former Soviet Union), Cuba still has far fewer of these problems than virtually all other countries in Latin America. *While Cuba is far from an earthly paradise, and certain individual rights and civil liberties are not yet widely practiced, the case of Cuba indicates that violent revolutions can sometimes result in generally improved living conditions for many people.*[97]

This is an extraordinary statement from authors who claimed to be peace activists and it is also the entire portrait provided by the text of Cuba's Communist dictatorship. No mention is made of the fact that Cuba is a totalitarian dictatorship in which every citizen is a prisoner in his own country, spied on by the ruler's secret police. No indication is given that Castro is the longest surviving dictator in the world with a legendary record of sadism against his own supporters. Cuba's wretched medical system is not evaluated; nor is the fact that while literacy is impressive Cubans can now read only materials approved by government censors. In 1959, when Castro seized power, Cuba was the second richest nation per capita in Latin America. After nearly fifty years of socialism it ranks near the bottom of Latin America's 22 nations, above Haiti, but below Honduras and Belize.[98] When the authors feel compelled to mention a deficiency in Cuba's achievement—whether political or economic—it is invariably blamed on the United States and its embargo, even though Cuba trades with every other nation in the world and its economic woes are attributable to the crackpot economic policies of its dictator. This one-sided promotion of a Communist dictatorship is typical of the text and an accurate sampling of the authors' ideological point of view.

Throughout *Peace and Conflict Studies*, the authors justify Communist policies and actions and put those of America and

Western democracies in a negative light. This one-sided tilting to America's totalitarian enemies is evident in its treatment of the Cuban Missile Crisis, for example. In 1962, the Soviet dictator Nikita Khrushchev precipitated an international crisis and brought the world to the brink of nuclear war by secretly placing nuclear missiles in Cuba and lying to President Kennedy when confronted over them. In *Peace and Conflict Studies*, however, the Cuban Missile Crisis is discussed without the authors ever mentioning the cause of the crisis—the Soviet missiles. Instead, the crisis is described as having been caused by the American president's alleged psychological insecurity and his consequent desire to act tough. This created a dilemma from which the world was rescued by the Soviet dictator. Here is the entire account of the Missile Crisis in this college text:

> The Cuban Missile Crisis—the closest humanity has apparently come to general nuclear war—was brought about in part because John F. Kennedy had felt browbeaten by Soviet Premier Khrushchev at their 1961 summit meeting in Vienna and felt humiliated by the debacle of the failed American-supported invasion of Cuba at the Bay of Pigs. The following year, Kennedy was determined that he wouldn't be pushed around again by the Soviet leader; fortunately for the world, Khrushchev was able (perhaps due largely to insufficient military strength) to be willing to back down."[99]

Nor is this positioning of the Soviet Union on the side of peace when it is the aggressor unique. In its account of the Cold War generally, *Peace and Conflict Studies* treats the Soviet Union as a sponsor of peace movements and the United States as the militaristic and imperialist power that peace movements—and thus the students of peace in the Peace Studies program—are supposed to keep in check.

A brief section of *Peace and Conflict Studies* is devoted to the 9/11 terrorist attack on the United States. It provides troubling insight into the impact courses like this may be having on American college students as their country faces the terrorist threat. The authors begin by telling students that, "Terrorism is a vexing term." From the "peace studies" perspective, the moral aspects of the term are purely relative: "Any actual or threatened attack against civilian noncombatants may be considered an act of 'terrorism.' In this sense, terrorism is as old as human history."[100]

Far from being criminal or evil, terror (according to Barash and Webel) is a last resort of the weak as a means of self-defense: "'Terrorists' are people who may feel militarily unable to confront their perceived enemies directly and who accordingly use violence, or the threat of violence, against noncombatants to achieve their political aims." If you're weak, then apparently it's all right to murder women and children if it advances your cause. Terrorism, according to the authors, is also "a contemporary variant of what has been described as guerrilla warfare, dating back at least to the anti-colonialist and anti-imperialist struggles for national liberation conducted in North America and Western Europe during the late 18th and early 19th centuries against the British and French Empires."[101] In other words, the American Founders were terrorists, and the terrorists in Iraq can be viewed as patriots (as radicals like Michael Moore have actually described them).

So that no one will miss the point, the progressive authors of *Peace and Conflict Studies* explain: "Placing 'terrorist' in quotation marks may be jarring for some readers, who consider the designation self-evident. We do so, however, not to minimize the horror of such acts but to emphasize the value of qualifying righteous indignation by the recognition that often one person's 'terrorist' is another's 'freedom fighter.'"[102] The terrorists who killed 3,000 innocent civilians from eighty countries in the heinous attacks of 9/11 can thus be viewed as "freedom fighters" striking the oppressor.

Peace and Conflict Studies continues: "After the attacks on the World Trade Center in New York City and the Pentagon in Washington, D.C., many Americans evidently agreed with pronouncements by many senior politicians that the United States was 'at war' with 'terrorism.' Yet, to many disemboweled [sic] people in other regions, 'Americans are the worst terrorists in the world' (according to a 1998 TV interview with the American Broadcasting Company). Following the attacks, President George W. Bush announced that the United States 'would make no distinction between terrorists and the countries that harbor them.' For many frustrated, impoverished, infuriated people— who view the United States as a terrorist country—attacks on American civilians were justified in precisely this way: making no distinction between a 'terrorist state' and the citizens who aid and abet the state."[103] In other words, America is a terrorist state and the terrorists are liberators of the world's oppressed.

> *See also:* Professors Berlowitz, Coy, Eckstein,
> Fellman, Haffar, Targ, Wolfe
> *Research:* David Horowitz[104]

Hatem Bazian
University of California, Berkeley

— Lecturer at UC Berkeley

— Calls for an *"Intifada"* in America

— "...the Day of Judgment will never happen until you fight the Jews...and the stones will say, 'Oh Muslim, there is a Jew hiding behind me. Come and kill him!'"

Hatem Bazian is a native Palestinian who is currently a lecturer in the Near Eastern Studies and Asian American Studies Departments at UC Berkeley. During his academic career, he has taught courses on Islam, Islamic law, Sufism, Arabic, and the Politics of the Middle East at Berkeley, San Francisco State University, Berkeley Graduate Theological Union, and Diablo Valley College. He is also a co-host and assistant producer of "Islam Today," a weekly California radio program devoted to Muslim issues around the world.

At an April 10, 2004 rally in San Francisco against the war in Iraq, Professor Bazian called for an *"Intifada"* in America. At the demonstration, signs proclaimed, "Support Armed Resistence [*sic*] in Iraq and Everywhere." One smiling student carried a sign saying "Long Live Fallujah," the stronghold of Abu Musab al-Zarqawi and his terrorists; another held a Bush effigy aloft on a noose. Professor Bazian declared to the cheering crowd, "we're sitting here and watching the world pass by, people being bombed, and it's about time that we have an *Intifada* in this country that change[s] fundamentally the political dynamics here."[105] He concluded his call to violence with a promise of more to come: "They're gonna say, 'some Palestinian being too radical'—well, you haven't seen radicalism yet!"[106] In his book *American Jihad: The Terrorists Living Among Us*, Steven Emerson describes Professor Bazian's appearance at the American Muslim Alliance conference held in May 1999 in Santa Clara, California. Professor Bazian was promoting the Islamic State of Palestine: "In the Hadith [a narration about the life of the Prophet Mohammed], the Day of Judgment will never happen until you fight the Jews... and the stones will say, 'Oh Muslim, there is a Jew hiding behind me. Come and kill him!'"[107] When a Students for Justice in Palestine rally at UC Berkeley resulted in the arrest of 79 protesters in 2002, Professor Bazian spoke at a follow-up rally protesting the arrests. "If you want to know where the pressure on the university [i.e., to prosecute the trespassers who were arrested] is coming from, look at the Jewish names on the school buildings," he said.[108]

Typically, there was no response to Bazian's publicly-expressed crude racism from a UC Berkeley central administration that is famous for its extraordinary sensitivity to "othering" and racial harassment.

In May 2002, Professor Bazian was the sole speaker for a two-day event at San Francisco's George Washington High School. The event was so inflammatory it generated formal letters of apology from the school administration to the public. Advertised as a Middle Eastern "cultural assembly," the gathering featured a student singing a rap song comparing Zionists to Nazis while other students paraded with Palestinian flags. Student and faculty observers described the speeches as "pure pro-Palestinian propaganda."[109]

In February 2004, Bazian gave a Muslim Student Association-sponsored lecture at McGill University in Montreal titled, "The New American Empire and its Adventures in the Middle East." In this address, he cited neo-conservative think tanks, "Israel-centric" public officials, the Christian Right, and the oil industry as the four forces behind American foreign policy. "The New York conservatives wanted to make the Middle East a safe neighborhood," said Professor Bazian "but not for Arabs; they wanted to make it a safe neighborhood for Israel."[110]

See also: Professors Algar, Armitage, Christiansen, Massad

Research: Jonathan Calt Harris[111]

Professor Marc Becker

Truman State University

— Associate professor of Latin American history at Truman State
University
— Organizer and media developer for "Historians against the War"
— Protests the celebration of Columbus Day

An associate professor of Latin American history at Truman
State University, Marc Becker is an organizer and media developer for Historians against the War, which defines itself as an
anti-war group of "radical scholars and intellectuals... deeply
concerned about growing repression [in the United States] and,
in particular, its impact on critical thought and expression." In a
joint effort with the radical Center for Constitutional Rights,
Historians Against the War strives to expose "U.S. war crimes
and government deception," including "the destruction of antiq-
uities allowed by the U.S. forces in Iraq."[112] Historians Against
the War has developed a nationwide "virtual speakers bureau" of
members prepared to disseminate the group's anti-American
message to the crowds attending anti-war demonstrations anywhere in the country—all in an effort to derail what it calls "the
current empire-building and war-making activities of the United
States government at home and abroad."[113]

Professor Becker has a long history of radicalism and antipathy toward the United States. At age 18, he refused to register
for the draft and fled to Canada to avoid prosecution. As part of
his classroom lectures, he recounts to students stories of his participation in protests against free trade talks in Latin America,
including his numerous trips to condemn "Western intrusion" in
Ecuador, one of Latin America's most stable democracies. Of his
experience at one such protest in 2002, where his fellow

demonstrators got out of control and were tear-gassed by Ecuadorian police, Professor Becker has said, "For me, the impact of having been tear-gassed was such that I lost my fear. They can do this, but they can't kill us, and we come back even stronger."

Professor Becker condemns American capitalism and "militarism." He has protested the celebration of Columbus Day, because "Columbus's actions launched an era of modern colonialism, rape, pillage, genocide, cultural destruction, slavery, economic and environmental devastation." "Christopher Columbus," Professor Becker elaborates, "is a classic grade school hero—and one that is built on a very tall pile of lies. We are told that he proved that the world was round, even though people had known this for millennia and the only astounding thing about Columbus's ideas was how completely wrong he was (the earth was much larger than he thought). We are told that Columbus discovered America, but yet with people living in this hemisphere for tens of thousands of years he discovered it only in the sense that a robber might be said to 'discover' cash in a bank vault."[114]

Professor Becker views the contemporary issues of free trade and globalization through the same ideological prism: In 2003, he said, "Five hundred and eleven years after [Columbus] sailed the ocean blue, globalization in the form of the FTAA, the WTO, and the IMF continues to devastate the Indigenous peoples of the Americas."[115]

See also: Professors Ensalaco, Williams

Research: John Perazzo

Professor Joel Beinin
Stanford University

— Middle Eastern history professor at Stanford University

— Former president of Middle East Studies Association

— Supported Saddam Hussein's aggression against Kuwait

— A former Zionist, Professor Joel Beinin now refers to *jihadist* suicide bombers as "martyrs" and denounces American "imperialism" on Al-Jazeera Television.

Professor Joel Beinin teaches Middle East history at Stanford University and is a former president of the Middle East Studies Association. Born in 1948 to Labor Zionist parents, he experienced an ideological transformation at age 22 while living on Kibbutz Lahav. Professor Beinin joined the "New Left" at Hebrew University, then migrated to Trotskyite anti-Zionism and finally to Maoism. A Marxist ever since, he received his BA, MA, and PhD from Princeton, Harvard, and the University of Michigan, respectively. He has received Ford Foundation grants, and has taught in France, Britain, Israel and Egypt.

In 1991, Professor Beinin dismissed U.S. concerns over Iraq's invasion and attempted annexation of Kuwait as "patently ridiculous," insisting that the real American goal was not to stop Saddam's aggression but to maintain weak, unstable "ministates" in the region, thereby assuring cheap oil and generating demand for U.S. weapons.

Just before the 2003 Iraq War, Professor Beinin appeared on Al-Jazeera to condemn U.S. "imperial" policy in the Arab world, despite the fact that the United States never had a Middle East colony, and in 1956 famously supported Egypt's defense of the Sinai against its own allies, the colonial powers Britain and France. This history didn't impress Professor Beinin anymore than the fact that his fellow countrymen were about to step into harm's way to liberate 30 million Iraqis from a monstrous tyrant. Instead, Professor Beinin told the Al-Jazeera's Arab audience that President Bush planned to establish "a puppet regime" in Baghdad to benefit U.S. oil interests and force "Israeli dictates" on the Palestinians.

Once the war began, Professor Beinin accused Deputy Secretary of Defense Paul Wolfowitz and other U.S. policymakers of colluding with "Israel's Likud Party," and asserted that the United States and Israel had collaborated with Arab regimes to block "democracy and economic development in the Arab world." Professor Beinin insisted that the United States was bent on displaying its "overwhelming military power... to make and unmake regimes and guarantee access to oil."[116] American conservatives, in his opinion, wanted to provoke "Islamist forces" so that they would "forsake legal political action and engage in armed struggle."[117] In other words, the aim of the United States was to spread terror throughout the Middle East.

Professor Beinin rejects the idea that the terrorism of the War on Terror is the creation of fanatical Islamicists themselves. He mocks the view that radical Islam is the source of terror with a term he coined: "terrorology." A year after 9/11, Professor Beinin congratulated fellow members of the Middle East Studies Association for their "great wisdom" in refusing to recognize Islamic terrorism as a threat, because this would have been to succumb to imperialistic prejudices against oppressed peoples.[118] Even al-Jazeera has described Islamic terrorism as a threat.

Professor Beinin's ideological hostilities are directed not against the terrorist enemy, but against the state of Israel and its citizens, including those who were refugees from persecution in Arab countries. Professor Beinin denies that the exodus of Jews from Arab lands after 1948 was caused by the historic persecution of Jews in Arab countries, intensified by the creation of

Israel. According to Professor Beinin, this exodus of hundreds of thousands of Jews from countries they had lived in for millennia was the result of "provocative actions by Israeli agents."[119]

After September 11, Professor Beinin focused not on Osama bin Laden's *fatwas* calling for global *jihad* against the West, but on "Israel's disproportionate use of force" against Palestinians as a root cause of the conflict. This was to ignore the obvious, since the agenda of Islamic militants like Hamas and al-Qaeda is the elimination of Israel, regardless of the force it uses to defend itself, and Palestinian grievances were low on the list in Osama bin Laden's 1997 *fatwa*. In the face of the explicit programs of Hamas, Hizbollah, Palestinian Islamic Jihad and other Islamic groups calling for the "liberation of Palestine from the Jordan to the sea," Professor Beinin denies that Palestinian terrorism "pose[s] an existential threat to Israel."

The *Stanford Review*, a conservative campus newspaper, describes Professor Beinin's courses as "expensive training for the Marxist press corps."[120] When students in his class rejected his request to attend an anti-Iraq war protest *in lieu* of the class, Professor Beinin trumped them by holding his lecture at the protest itself.[121]

Professor Beinin conducts an online course sponsored by Oxford, Stanford, and Yale Universities, called "Palestine, Zionism and the Arab-Israeli Conflict." The "Zionist lobby" in Washington, he informs students, has the power to induce Washington to adopt an "uncritically pro-Israel foreign policy." For "serious" reading, he recommends Egypt's state-run *Al-Ahram*, a newspaper that routinely features anti-Semitic conspiracy theories and endorses Holocaust denial, likens Israeli leaders to Nazis, and praises suicide bombings.

In 2002, Professor Beinin initiated a petition that charged Israel with plotting the "ethnic cleansing," which would commence with the war in Iraq. He predicted that Israeli premier

Ariel Sharon would use the war as an opportunity "to push the Palestinians into Jordan." Actually this is the opposite of what happened: Sharon proposed the withdrawal of Israelis from Gaza instead.

See also: Professors Anderson, Andijar, Brand,
J. Cole, Dabashi, Haddad, Massad

Research: Alyssa Lappen[122]

Professor Derrick Bell
New York University

— Professor at New York University School of Law

— Pioneer of "Critical Race Theory"

— "Slavery is, as an example of what white America has done, a constant reminder of what white America might do."

Derrick Bell is a professor at the New York University School of Law. Born in 1930, Professor Bell may be considered the founder, or at least the godfather, of "Critical Race Theory," an academic tradition in which race plays the same role as class in the Marxist paradigm. In the mid-1970s, Professor Bell was, along with Alan Freeman, a pioneer in the field. Professor Bell was not only angered by what he viewed as the slow progress of racial reform in the United States, but also held that the gains brought about by the civil rights laws of the 1960s were being eroded in the 1970s. He believed, as he does to this day, that whites would support civil rights protections for blacks only if those protections would also promote white self-interest and social status.[123] Since racial minorities, in Professor Bell's view, are a permanently oppressed caste—and racism is a normal, permanent aspect of American life—equality before the law is oppressive to African Americans, whose moral claims are superior to those of whites. The perspective around which Professor Bell has built his academic career is the endless repetition of the claim that whites and white institutions are irremediably racist. He has endorsed a journal dedicated to the "abolition of whiteness," called *Race Traitor*, whose motto is "Treason to the white race is loyalty to humanity."

According to Professor Bell and his fellow Critical Race theorists, existing legal structures are, like American society at large, racist in their very construction. Critical Race Theory suggests that to combat this "institutional racism," oppressed racial groups have both the right and the duty to decide for itself, which laws are valid and are worth observing. Critical Race Theory also promotes the use of storytelling narratives in law-review articles to better reflect the "oral traditions" of black experience.[124] Professor Bell has used the technique of placing legal and social commentary into the mouths of invented characters extensively in his writings. He acknowledges that this "style of storytelling" is "less rigorous than the doctrine-laden, citation-heavy law review pieces" that law professors traditionally publish,[125] but he and his disciples employ it nonetheless.

Derrick Bell earned a bachelor's degree from Duquesne University in 1952 and a law degree from the University of Pittsburgh in 1957 (he was the school's only black graduate that year). The first job of his legal career was in the Civil Rights Division of the Justice Department. He left that position after a short time to work as an attorney for the NAACP Legal Defense Fund, where he became a protégé of Thurgood Marshall.

In the immediate aftermath of Dr. Martin Luther King, Jr.'s 1968 assassination, members of Harvard University's Black Law Students Association pressured their school to hire a minority professor; this led eventually to Bell's hiring in 1971 as the first black faculty member in the law school's history. From the very outset of his stay at Harvard, Professor Bell was acutely aware of the fact that he lacked the qualifications that had traditionally been prerequisites for an appointment at Harvard: he had neither graduated with distinction from a prestigious law school, nor clerked for the Supreme Court, nor practiced law at a major firm. Yet he mocked such criteria as being nothing more than the exclusionary constructs of a racist white power structure that had traditionally sought to deny African Americans an opportunity to teach at the nation's elite schools.

In 1980, Professor Bell left Harvard to become the dean of the University of Oregon School of Law. He resigned from that position in 1985, ostensibly as an act of protest against the fact that the school had failed to grant tenure to an Asian female professor. A number of Professor Bell's colleagues at Oregon, however, viewed this as a contrived, face-saving pretext for leaving a position from which he was about to be fired. They believed that Professor Bell, who had largely become an "absentee dean" known for spending more time on the lecture circuit than at Oregon, was slated for imminent termination.[126]

Professor Bell joined the faculty of Stanford Law School in 1986 and immediately became a source of controversy. Many of his students there complained that he was not using his lecture time to teach principles of law, but rather as a platform from which to indoctrinate his captive audience to his left-wing theories and worldviews. Cognizant of Professor Bell's glaring deficiencies as a teacher but afraid to openly address them, Stanford quietly instituted a lecture series designed to help his students learn the course material that Professor Bell was not teaching them. Perceiving this as a racial affront, Professor Bell left Stanford and returned to Harvard in the fall of 1986.[127]

In April 1990, Professor Bell demanded that Harvard Law hire a black woman—specifically the visiting Professor Regina Austin—as a tenured faculty member. A critical race theorist herself, Professor Austin was of the view that as an oppressed race, African Americans could decide what laws they would be justified in breaking and what crimes they would be justified in committing.[128] Though Harvard had a longstanding policy that forbade the hiring of visiting professors during the year of their residence at the school, Professor Bell made Professor Austin's hiring a "non-negotiable demand."

When the law school would not cave to Professor Bell's pressure, he protested by taking a leave of absence from his $120,000 per year teaching post. He explained that black female law students were in desperate need of "role models" with whom they could identify. Although 45 percent of Harvard Law's faculty appointments since 1980 had gone to minorities and women, none of them were both black *and* female—hence Professor Bell's objection. But even if Harvard had agreed to grant tenure to Professor Austin, Professor Bell would not have been satisfied. As he would later write in a law review article condemning schools for hiring "token" minorities: "The hiring of a few minorities and women—particularly when a faculty is under pressure from students or civil rights agencies—is not a departure from, or an adherence to, this power-preserving doctrine" of white male supremacy.[129]

Left-wing students staged two sit-ins in the office of the dean of the law school to demonstrate their support for Professor Bell's position. The relatively small supply of credentialed black professors, coupled with the intense competition among so many colleges to secure their services, was apparently irrelevant to the Harvard protesters.

In 1990-91, Professor Bell taught a civil rights course at Harvard without pay, though he later acknowledged that he had gotten himself placed on the payroll of a "major entertainment figure" as a "consultant." To express his displeasure with Harvard in definitive terms, in the spring of 1991 Professor Bell announced that he would take a one-year visiting professor's position at New York University Law School. He later extended this to two years, and later still announced that he would spend a third year at NYU. This third year would require not only NYU's waiver of time limits on visiting professorships, but also Harvard's waiver of its firm policy forbidding professors to be on leave for more than two years. Harvard dean Robert Clark stated that if Professor Bell did not return to his post, he would lose his place on Harvard's faculty. Professor Bell refused to return and thus lost his job.[130] He has taught at NYU ever since.

A few of Professor Bell's more notable quotes (all of them from his 1992 book *Faces at the Bottom of the Well*) on the subject of race include the following:

"Unable or unwilling to perceive that 'there but for the grace of God, go I,' few whites are ready to actively promote civil rights for blacks."

"[D]iscrimination in the workplace is as vicious (if less obvious) than it was when employers posted signs 'no negras need apply.'"

"We rise and fall less as a result of our efforts than in response to the needs of a white society that condemns all blacks to quasi citizenship as surely as it segregated our parents."

"Slavery is, as an example of what white America has done, a constant reminder of what white America might do."

"Black people will never gain full equality in this country.... African Americans must confront and conquer the otherwise deadening reality of our permanent subordinate status."

> *See also:* Professors Austin, hooks, Michael
> Dyson, Thomas
> *Research:* Joseph Wilson, John Perazzo

Professor Marvin Berlowitz
University of Cincinnati

— Director, the Urban Center for Peace Education and Research,
University of Cincinnati
— Marxist, anti-war activist

Marvin Berlowitz is professor of educational foundations at the University of Cincinnati and the director of the Urban Center for Peace Education and Research. A committed Marxist, Professor Berlowitz teaches "resistance" as in, "Privatization must be resisted," although only a Marxist could make the connection between resisting privatization and peace. The center is in effect a collective of left-wing professors who are intent on indoctrinating students in Marxist ideology and hostile to other views.

The course offerings of the Peace Education Certificate program, available to both graduate and undergraduate students, are a testament to Professor Berlowitz's educational philosophy: all avoid academic rigor in favor of *de rigueur* left-wing dogmas. Courses in Berlowitz's program cover the range from Marxist dialectics to radical environmentalism, feminist theory, identity-politics, multiculturalism, and "Educational Sociology," which is described in the catalogue this way: "Courses in Educational Sociology concentrate on Marxist, feminist and other classic and social transformation theories in education as well as on research on social issues related to schooling and educational inequities."[131] The only possible connection to peace research in this smorgasbord would be if one made the assumption that capitalism and private property, along with the American culture that is founded on them, were the root causes of war. This is precisely the assumption that Berlowitz makes.[132] In Berlowitz's seamless totalitarian web everything is interconnected

and—where the market system is involved—negative: "The capitalist concentration in the pop culture industry," he says, "has
given rise to a genre which systematically desensitizes our youth
to violence in much the same manner that the U.S. military has
utilized to increase the kill ratio of our troops in fire fights. Perhaps such 'culture' is equally useful to desensitize our civilian
population to the human costs of neo-liberal [capitalist] ideology. We must also keep in mind that the U.S. pop culture industry saturates the world market with its toxins to an even greater
extent than Mc Death sows metabolic destruction by extending
its arches to every hemisphere. In the sociopathic language of
our leaders, I suppose that Columbine & Santee would be
viewed as 'acceptable collateral damage.'"[133]

A faculty biography describes Berlowitz's interests in these
terms: "His most recent publications have been in the area of
educational reform including a broad based critique as well as
specific works on the expansion of JROTC [officer's training]
and also magnet schools as examples of neo-liberal ideology in
educational reform."[134] Neo-liberal is a neo-Marxist term for
"capitalist." Professor Berlowitz's objects of disdain range from
the McDonald's hamburger chain to the two-party system and
the world market:

- "We're limited to a choice between the party of the rich
  and a party of the wealthy. We have the only major industrial capitalist country in the world that does not have a
  labor party."
- "Structural changes because of globalization have led to
  increasing economic disparities between the wealthy and
  the poor. As a result, the highest concentration of poverty
  is found among urban school children and racially
  oppressed groups."

Professor Berlowitz's educational reform zeal is inspired in part by his contempt for the Junior Reserve Officer Training Corps (JROTC). He claims that the program is part of a pernicious Pentagon plan to convert underachieving schools into boot camps. "The Defense Department seeks 'at risk' schools to transform into military academies for the purpose of future recruitment," he explains.[135]

One of Berlowitz's educational reform missions is to expunge "Eurocentricity" from the curriculum. Working in partnership with Professors Nathan Long of the University of Cincinnati and Eric R. Jackson of Northern Kentucky University, Professor Berlowitz has authored a 17-page paper arguing for peace education courses to take up the concept of "Eurocentricity." The paper states that "the dominance of Eurocentricity in peace education leads to the exclusion and distortion of African American perspectives and this restricted focus undermines the status and viability of peace education as a component of educational reform."[136] As the authors see it, current programs are characterized by (1) a failure to represent accurately the African American emphasis on positive peace, the role of trade unions, anti-imperialism, solidarity with socialist nations, and internationalism in general; (2) the vanguard role of African Americans in the struggle against nuclear proliferation and conscription; (3) a tendency to minimize the role of African Americans in the development of non-violent philosophy as merely being eclectic; and (4) a tendency to under-represent the leadership role of African Americans in anti-war movements and white peace organizations.

With an eye toward overcoming potential academic opposition to their proposed focus on "Eurocentricity," the authors point to the success of left wing feminists in making the university receptive to their radical agendas. "Peace educators can learn

from the successes of feminists in overcoming the contradictions
of sexism and patriarchy in the field," they note. Thus the professors conclude that the surest way of adding yet another dose
of left wing politics into the curriculum is to portray peace as a
fight for racial equality. The paper even includes a racial slogan
to this effect: "Peace cannot be achieved in a white skin while
the black is branded."[137]

Professor Berlowitz's radical evangelizing is not confined to
the Peace and Education program or to the university. As the
director of the university's in-house research institution—the
Center for Peace Research, Implementation, Development and
Education (UC PRIDE)—Professor Berlowitz has designed several "educational" initiatives aimed at transporting his politics
into high school classrooms. In 2001 under the direction of Professor Berlowitz and several students and former students in the
University of Cincinnati's Peace Education department, UC
PRIDE unveiled an online course offering credit at the university, and targeting elementary school teachers in Ohio.[138] At the
core of the course, which has been offered since the fall of 2001,
was Professor Berlowitz's distinctly radical approach to education.

As Professor Berlowitz himself explained the course in
March 2001, "This is an alternative to school metal detectors
and the software that is aimed at profiling students at risk for
violence."[139] Professor Berlowitz's alternative, in keeping with
his Marxism-inspired contempt for the white middle class, was
to alert teachers to the role of suburban whites, presumed to be
biased against minority students, in allegedly driving these students to violence. "The bias awareness component of the course
is especially significant to those who are working with youth
who have grown up in historically homogeneous white suburbs,
which are now experiencing conflicts associated with an influx
of ethnically and racially diverse populations," Professor

Berlowitz explained.[140] The course offered teachers no solution for alleviating violence among troubled students in urban schools. Instead, it urged them to be "more culturally sensitive to the needs of urban schoolchildren."[141]

Such efforts are complemented by the peace education department's attempts to instill anti-war views in the University of Cincinnati student body. For instance, a running "Peace News" feature on the department's website reads like a one-stop directory for anti-war protests in the Cincinnati area. The department also makes regular financial contributions to on-campus anti-war groups.[142]

See also: Professors Coy, Eckstein, Fellman, Haffar, Schwartz, Targ, Wolfe

Research: Jacob Laksin

Professor Mary Frances Berry

University of Pennsylvania

— Geraldine R. Segal professor of American social thought and professor of history, University of Pennsylvania

— Chairman, Civil Rights Commission 1993-2004

— "Civil Rights laws were *not* passed to give civil rights protection to *all* Americans."

Born in 1938 in Nashville, Tennessee, Mary Frances Berry has been the Geraldine R. Segal professor of American social thought and professor of history at the University of Pennsylvania since 1987. In 1990-91, she was president of the Organization of American Historians, one of the two principal professional associations of American historians, both of which have been dominated by the Left for nearly two decades. She has also held administrative posts at the University of Maryland and served as the Chancellor of the University of Colorado at Boulder.

Professor Berry is the holder of an endowed chair at an Ivy League university, one of the most prized positions in American higher education. Yet she has almost no traditional academic credentials for holding such a position. According to her official bibliography,[143] in the course of her university career, Professor Berry has authored no scholarly books (merely a series of texts whose titles reveal their ideological agendas) and only two peer-reviewed academic articles. The first article was published in 1991 in the *Journal of American History*.[144] The second is a five page article "Vindicating Martin Luther King, Jr.," which appeared in the *Journal of Negro History* in 1996. A third article appeared in a student-edited law school journal and is not even sourced. Professor Berry's *Journal of American History* article, "Judging Morality: Sexual Behavior and Legal Consequences in the 19th Century South," begins in the following fashion: "The legal system supports our capitalist economic system. Because capitalism requires inequality, the only real question is who will be the repositories of the inequality. To date, black people have disproportionately been those repositories." This is a representative sample of her work.

As a member of a Department of History—and despite her lack of actual peer-reviewed scholarship—Professor Berry votes on all the hires and promotions of scholars in the department. As a full professor, her vote carries special weight. Thus Professor Berry will be shaping historical studies at the University of Pennsylvania for a long time to come.

Apart from her academic career, Professor Berry has had a long career in government, which she began as an Assistant Secretary of Education in the former Cabinet Department of Health, Education, and Welfare under then-President Jimmy Carter. After Dr. Berry returned from a trip to China and stated that Americans had no right to criticize Communist China's education system for requiring students to "develop what they call socialist consciousness and culture," Carter transferred her to the U.S. Civil Rights Commission. As Berry critic and head of the Center for Equal Opportunity, Linda Chavez points out,[145] "China's higher education system was still reeling from the devastating effects of Mao's bloody Cultural Revolution, which forced millions of intellectuals, ordinary teachers and students into forced labor on collective farms, or sent them to re-education camps where they faced torture and death. Berry, then the government's top-ranking official in higher education, nonetheless praised China's education system as a model for the United States and publicly criticized the press for printing 'false' reports about the Chinese system." Practicing what she preached, Professor Berry was accustomed to carrying Mao Zedong's *Little Red Book* of Communist *dicta* in her purse.[146]

Denouncing America's systemic flaws, while comparing it unfavorably to Communist states, has been a longstanding practice for Professor Berry. She complained, for instance, that the U.S. media's "massive barrage of propaganda" had made black Americans blind to the Soviet Union's virtues, including its "safeguards for minorities," "equality of opportunity," and "equal provision of social services to its citizens."[147] With perfect consistency, Professor Berry characterized the 1960s as an era when blacks in America lived under a "threat of genocide'" that was "roughly comparable" to what Jews faced in Hitler's Germany.[148] This absurdity is belied by the national support Martin Luther King's crusade for civil rights in the South received, while the Civil Rights Acts themselves passed by 85% and 90% majorities in the Congress. In an interview on National Public Radio in April 2005, Professor Berry dismissed United States complaints of human rights violations in Cuba as examples of "the pot calling the kettle black."[149] In other words, Professor Berry—a person with a six-figure salary, holder of a prestigious post at a famous American university, and being interviewed respectfully on the national government funded radio network—believes she is oppressed and living in a dictatorship.

Professor Berry served on the Civil Rights Commission from 1980 until 2004. Ronald Reagan, early in his presidency, attempted to fire Professor Berry from the Commission, arguing that as a political appointment she served at the pleasure of the president. But Professor Berry sued and eventually won in federal district court the right to keep her post. She said, "I decided to sue him [Reagan] because he shouldn't be allowed to fire a commissioner just because he doesn't like the commission reports. Then you could only do reports that people liked, and why have a civil rights commission at all?"[150] President Clinton made her the chair of the Civil Rights Commission in 1993, a position she held until President George W. Bush eventually dismissed her in 2004 despite her determination to stay on past her constitutional term.

In Professor Berry's radical perspective, white racism is an intractable and pervasive crisis in America fifty years after the civil rights revolution. "The primary explanation for racially motivated violence against blacks," according to the professor, "has been the need of a segment of the white population to preserve [its] belief in the inferiority of blacks, and to maintain the social and political subordination of an historically outcast group by any means, including violence."[151]

Professor Berry is a strong advocate of racial preferences in employment and education. In his book *The End of Racism*, scholar Dinesh n'tsouza quotes Berry's response to the idea that racial preferences are inconsistent with the mandates of civil rights laws: "Civil rights laws were *not* passed to give civil rights protection to *all* Americans," she said. Professor Berry opposes the concept of race-neutrality in hiring and college admissions, because she believes white America has an ongoing desire to relegate blacks to subservient roles. She does not explain why white Americans support affirmative action policies for black Americans if their desire is to keep blacks subservient.

Professor Berry condemned President Reagan and his administration as people who "never met a civil rights law they liked."[152] The laws to which she was referring were all laws encompassing race-based preferences, precisely what Martin Luther King's civil rights movement had been created to oppose.

In Professor Berry's opinion, Republican appointments of African Americans such as Clarence Thomas, Condoleezza Rice, and Colin Powell to the highest positions of authority and

power in government were anti-black in intention. Their purpose was to fool African Americans into thinking that they lived
in a nation where they could in fact succeed on merit, where
whites were not plotting collectively to keep them in their
place. This delusion causes blacks to accept complacently a status quo that is far more oppressive and discriminatory than they
realize. Says Professor Berry: "The reason there is no agitation
among blacks—I don't see any—is because the symbolism is
such that you could tell yourself—until something happens to
you—that nothing is wrong. You could say, 'Look at Colin Powell. Blacks are everywhere. We can just do anything.' Our people
don't draw a distinction between what people are doing."[153] In
other words, blacks who do not carry around Mao's *Little Red
Book* like Professor Berry are too dumb to understand the difference between appearance and reality.

> *See also:* Professors Dyson, Foner, Hall, hooks,
>   Marable
> *Research:* John Perazzo

Professor Michael Berube

Penn State University

— Professor of English, Penn State University
— Self-described "progressive educator"
— Believes in teaching literature so as to bring about "economic transformations."

Michael Berube is a professor in the English Department at Penn State University. He teaches undergraduate courses in "American and African-American literature," as well as graduate courses in such fashionably Marxist-cum-post-modernist programs as "cultural studies."

A leftist and self-proclaimed "progressive educator," Professor Berube is candid about the political character of many university English departments. In a 2003 commentary in the *Chronicle of Higher Education,* he acknowledged that "it's widely understood that English departments are well stocked with liberals, and I've often wished we leftists had less of a presence in literature departments and more of a presence in state legislatures."[154] Professor Berube supported the war in Afghanistan and came under heavy critical fire from more radical leftists for doing so. In September 2002, Professor Berube wrote that the U.S. military intervention in Afghanistan was "laudable" for having overthrown the Taliban, one of "the worst regimes on the planet." He questioned the morality of "the anti-imperialists who opposed the war in Afghanistan in stark and unyielding terms," and who argued "to their shame, that the U.S. military response was even more morally odious than the hijackers' deliberate slaughter of civilians."[155] With the onset of the Iraq War, Professor Berube resumed an orthodox anti-war position.

As Professor Berube himself acknowledges, his literature classes often have little to do with literature. For instance, a class that he has taught for years, "Postmodernism and American Fiction," is merely a forum for the professor to dilate on the "anti-foundationalist philosophy" of radical philosopher Richard Rorty, a philosophy which among other things leads to moral relativism. Professor Berube regards Rorty's views as the only views a "sane" person could hold. By the same token religious people were to be regarded simply as irrational. "In the class," Professor Berube wrote in May 2000, "we talk about what it means to be an 'anti-foundationalist'—that is, one of those sane, secular people who believe that it's best to operate as if our moral and epistemological principles derive not from divine will or uniform moral law, but from ordinary social practices."[156]

That Professor Berube's class promoted his anti-religious prejudices under the guise of "postmodernist theory" and did so at the expense of the literature he had been hired to teach, did not trouble him. On the contrary, "The problem is with the fiction: It just isn't postmodern enough." In this context, Professor Berube chastised "accomplished novelists" for failing to "write the kind of stuff that fits into college seminars on postmodernism." According to Professor Berube, "The important question for cultural critics, is also an old question—how to correlate developments in culture and the arts with large-scale economic transformations."[157] In the old Marxist days, for which Professor Berube is obviously nostalgic, this was called the "base-super-structure" question—to what degree a society's economic base allegedly determined its cultural productions. The idea that Marx's discredited "science" of human development is "post-modern" rather than pre-modern is one of the quainter notions of academic leftists, which Professor Berube obviously shares.

Professor Berube is more than prepared to defend his idea that a university literature curriculum should be subordinated to his left-wing politics. In a 2002 article for the Association of

Departments of English *Bulletin,* Professor Berube took exception to one professor's claim that university English departments
had become "laughingstocks" because of their overt political
agendas. Conceding that English departments had been steadily
losing students over the years, Professor Berube was impatient
with the notion that the blame for this lack of interest rested
with the left wing character of the departments themselves, and
their jettisoning of the traditional literary canon in favor of modish political subspecialties under the guise of "literary theory." By
Professor Berube's lights, the only corrective to the "laughing-
stock" reputation attached to university English departments
should be the introduction of *more* theory. "If we want to think
seriously about graduate programs as institutions of professional
training, we should be concentrating on the current status of literary theory," he explained. "I mean, more or less, the history of
Twentieth-Century theories of literature and of textuality,
beginning with the work of Viktor Shklovsky and his fellow
Russian formalists... and running through Marxism, psycho-
analysis, New Criticism, structuralism, poststructuralism-decon-
struction, feminism, reader-response, new historicism,
postcolonialism, and queer theory..."[158]

In a 1998 essay called "The Abuses of the University,"[159] Professor Berube described the university as "the final resting place
of the New Left," and the "progressives' only bulwark against the
New Right." Critics of this definition—in particular those who
failed to regard "feminist or queer theory as a legitimate area of
scholarship"—were only perpetuating "ignorance and injustice,"
he wrote. The idea that a university might be an institution dedicated to the pursuit of knowledge rather than the imposition of
left wing fashions would seem to professors like Michael Berube
an idea from a galaxy far away.

> **See also:** Professors Gitlin, Holstun, Jameson,
> Shortell
>
> **Research:** Jacob Laksin

Professor Laurie Brand
University of Southern California

— Professor of international relations, University of Southern California
— Former president of the Middle East Studies Association

Before joining the faculty at the University of Southern California, Professor Laurie Brand was at the Institute for Palestine Studies, an Arab organization set up to promote the Palestinian view of the Middle East conflict. Not surprisingly, Professor Brand's academic work is indistinguishable from political activism in behalf of the Palestinian cause.

Professor Brand blames the Israeli-Palestinian conflict on Israel alone. "There is no peace without justice, and there is no justice under [Israeli] occupation,"[160] she has written, ignoring the fact that Israel's military presence in Gaza and the West Bank stems from three invasions by Arab states through those same corridors. In 2002, as Israel moved to defend itself from a series of suicide bombings and terrorist attacks during the Second Intifada, Brand joined a group of anti-Israel academics in signing a notorious letter imputing to Israel, without evidence, the intention to drive the Palestinians from the disputed territories: "Americans cannot remain silent while crimes as abhorrent as ethnic cleansing are being openly advocated. We urge our government to communicate clearly to the government of Israel that the expulsion of people according to race, religion or nationality would constitute crimes against humanity and will not be tolerated."[161] This was an anticipation of fact that failed to materialize (Israel announced its unilateral withdrawal from Gaza instead), which revealed the ideological nature of the authors' positions.

Professor Brand's attitude towards her own country is hardly more balanced. In the run-up to the war in Iraq, Professor Brand, then temporarily working in Lebanon, took to the streets to protest the planned effort to remove Saddam Hussein from power. She even drafted a letter of protest to then-Secretary of State Colin Powell, which she promptly dispatched to the U.S. embassy in Beirut. Signed by 70 Americans, the letter claimed to speak on behalf of "Americans living in Lebanon," listing a number of anti-war arguments ranging from the tendentious ("'regime change' imposed from outside is itself completely undemocratic"), to the ludicrous in charging that in excess of one million Iraqis could die because of damage to Iraq's water supply resulting from the war. It concluded: "We refuse to stand by watching passively as the US pursues aggressive and racist policies toward the people around us. We reject your claim to be taking these actions on our behalf. Not in our name."[162]

At a conference at the German embassy in Beirut in July 2003, Professor Brand rejected the notion that the United States intended to foster democratic government in Iraq. To the extent that the American administration was concerned with democracy, she said, it was to destroy it in the United States. The administration, she said, was guilty of "systematic disregard for democratic institutions and values."[163] Professor Brand's fury at the Bush administration had not appreciably mellowed in October 2004 when she joined a "nonpartisan group of foreign affairs specialists" in signing an open-letter claiming that "the war in Iraq is the most misguided one since the Vietnam period." The letter argued that, "[e]ven on moral grounds, the case for war was dubious" and the "results of this policy have been overwhelmingly negative for U.S. interests."[164]

The following month Professor Brand delivered an address to the Middle East Studies Association, the professional association of academic scholars of the Middle East. It was called "Scholarship in the Shadow of Empire." In it she insisted that the Bush administration's policies in Iraq were "dismal failures," a claim she sought to substantiate by invoking the authority of Paul Krugman, the left wing columnist for the *New York Times*. Although she was conspicuously silent about Islamist terrorism generally and dictators like Saddam Hussein specifically, Brand could scarcely contain her rage at what she held to be the real source of strife in the Middle East: the United States. "Given the current situation in the region, especially, but far from exclusively, in Iraq and Palestine/Israel, and the US's role in these conflicts, I cannot remember when I have been more continuously outraged," she said.[165]

Her outrage? "What greater abdication of responsibility, as both citizen and scholar, than to remain silent in the face of Guantánamo, Abu Ghrayb, and Fallujah?"[166] Evidently, Brand has outrage only for the alleged terrorist "victims" of American actions. As for the actual innocents in Fallujah whom the terrorist Zarqawi condemned to death and beheaded, Professor Brand maintains a discreet silence.

> *See also:* Professors Anderson, Andijar, Beinin, Massad
>
> *Research:* Jacob Laksin

Professor Elizabeth M. Brumfiel
Northwestern University

— Professor of archaeology and anthropology at Northwestern University

— President of the American Anthropological Association

— Called on anthropology scholars to take a leading role as anthropologists against the Iraq War

Elizabeth Brumfiel is a professor of Archaeology and Anthropology at Northwestern University. Her teaching career includes twenty-five years as a faculty member of Albion College, where she chaired the Anthropology and Sociology Department. Brumfiel is also the current president of the American Anthropological Association, the world's largest organization of anthropologists.

Professor Brumfiel received her PhD from the University of Michigan where her work focused on "the dynamics of gender, class, and factional politics in ancient Mexico and the changes in resource exploitation that accompanied Aztec expansion."[167] She teaches a course in the "Archaeology of Inequality in America." Professor Brumfiel has received grants from the National Endowment for the Humanities, the National Science Foundation, and the H. John Heinz III Charitable Trust. She has presented both the Distinguished Lecture in Archaeology for the Archaeology division of the American Anthropological Association, and the David L. Clarke Memorial Lecture at the University of Cambridge in 1997. She has edited four books and has written a number of scientific papers, though she has authored no books on her own, unusual for a full professor.

Professor Brumfiel has also been a featured speaker at the annual conference of the Radical Archaeology Theory Seminar (RATS), a "conference which stresses the ability of archaeology to challenge existing, received and constructed assumptions about the past and the present."[168] The promotional literature for one such conference includes the following agenda: "As radical archaeologists we should be committed to political action against class and gender oppression, racism and discrimination. Yet how does the pursuit of social justice and solidarity play out in our work? Within our critiques and actions against colonialist/imperialist policies and practices, how does the archaeological endeavor fit in? This RATS session will discuss the nature of social activism in archaeology, the goals we should pursue, and how to connect our research interests with our political struggle."[169] In short, Radical Archaeology Theory views "science" as a means of advancing radical political agendas, as though scholarship and politics were one and the same.

In 2004, Professor Brumfiel and the American Anthropological Association injected themselves into a labor conflict between the Hilton Hotel in San Francisco, where the organization planned to hold its annual meeting, and hotel union workers, who were protesting the lockout of unionized employees during a labor dispute. "Management has locked workers out of their jobs in order to pressure them into accepting terms favorable to the hotels," Professor Brumfiel said. "Anthropologists cannot, in all good conscience, meet in facilities whose owners are using the lockout of low-wage workers as a bargaining tactic."[170] In point of fact, management had only initiated the lockout after union workers had already stopped working and begun a picketing campaign, which was in its third week. Moreover, the dispute was not about low wages, but rather the length of worker contracts. Brumfiel and her organization refused to cross the picket line in order to show "solidarity" with the left-wing union, which had launched the strike. The American Anthropological Association annual meeting was moved to Atlanta.

Under Professor Brumfiel's leadership, the Anthropological Association has also refused holding meetings in Louisiana, because of that state's laws against sodomy, and has pledged that its boycott will remain in effect as long as those laws are on the books.[171] The Association has also opposed proposals for a Constitutional amendment defining marriage as a union solely between partners of opposite sexes.[172] According to Professor Brumfiel, states which support the amendment may be disqualified from consideration as possible venues for future American Anthropological Association meetings.

In fact, under Professor Brumfiel's leadership, one of the American Anthropological Association's principal campaigns in 2004 was public support of same-sex marriage. In an official statement, the Association claimed, "The results of more than a century of anthropological research on households, kinship relationships, and families, across cultures and through time, provide no support whatsoever for the view that either civilization or viable social orders depend upon marriage as an exclusively heterosexual institution. Rather, anthropological research supports the conclusion that a vast array of family types, including families built upon same-sex partnerships, can contribute to stable and humane societies. The Executive Board of the American Anthropological Association strongly opposes a constitutional amendment limiting marriage to heterosexual couples."[173] Whatever the impact of introducing same-sex marriage into advanced technological societies in whose predecessor cultures it has been absent for thousands of years, this American Anthropological Association statement was obviously not based on any scientific grounds, but merely expressed the fashionable left-wing position of the moment. Whatever the merits of the position, the statement itself was an abuse of scholarship, which was being used to make claims it could not sustain.

As a self-conscious leftist working within the tradition of political Marxism, Brumfiel obviously has no problem with blurring the distinction between scholarship and politics. As president of the Association she jettisoned any idea that scientists should strive for neutrality in the professional roles and exhorted her fellow anthropologists to use their academic platform as a bully pulpit from which to preach anti-war advocacy: "In what contexts will scientists be willing to develop weapons of mass destruction and to test them on human subjects without their knowledge or consent, as they did during the Cold War? And how do economic pressures, political pressures and a climate of patriotism discourage scientists from engaging in anti-war and anti-weapons advocacy? The contextual nature of human action and the impact of politics and economics on science are important messages for anthropologists to communicate to scientists and to the public. With increased participation by anthropologists...these messages can reach a wider audience, which would benefit science, public policy, and anthropology."[174]

> *See also:* Professors Berlowitz, Berube,
> De Genova, Richards, Saitta
> *Research:* Tom Ryan

Professor Thomas Castellano
Rochester Institute of Technology

— Professor of criminal justice, Rochester Institute of Technology
— Deplores the "Dirty Harry" syndrome in American justice
— Claims the 9/11 attacks were a result of America's "imperialist" policies

Thomas Castellano has been a professor of criminal justice at Rochester Institute of Technology since 2003. Prior to that, he spent nearly twenty years teaching in the criminal justice department at Southern Illinois University. While there, he also directed the Center for the Study of Crime, Delinquency, and Corrections, and was a member of the Illinois Governor's Commission on Hate Crimes.

Professor Castellano claims that Americans are victims of a "Dirty Harry syndrome," in which society glorifies vigilante justice at the expense of individual rights. According to Professor Castellano, this is evident not only in America's law-enforcement policies, but also in entertainment industry trends that have turned Clint Eastwood, Sylvester Stallone, and Arnold Schwarzenegger into icons. Moreover, President Bush, who Professor Castellano says was not elected in 2000 but *appointed*, has himself fallen under the spell of this "syndrome," causing him to implement "cowboy justice" in the war on terror.[175]

According to Professor Castellano, in implementing the Patriot Act the Bush-Ashcroft team was more concerned with seizing power and suppressing civil liberties than securing the nation against terror. The professor claims that Section 802 of the Patriot Act, which gives the government power to investigate and prosecute people performing acts of civil disobedience (i.e., breaking the law), was written solely with the intent of

silencing political opponents of the Republican Party and allowing FBI and CIA to infiltrate into political organizations. He further claims that the Patriot Act will put an end to Fourth
Amendment protections against illegal search and seizure.

In Professor Castellano's view, the prisoners held in Guantanamo Bay—who were captured as enemy combatants captured on the field of battle—are living proof of the Bush
administration's disregard for the Constitutional rights of American citizens; military tribunals are an affront to due process; the
many immigrants who have been detained or deported under
stricter immigration controls have been deprived of their rights;
and the Department of Homeland Security will do nothing to
improve Americans' safety, but is designed to give the president
more power over organized labor.

Professor Castellano blames the United States and its
allegedly unjust foreign policies for having provoked the 9/11
horrors in the first place. The reason the United States was
attacked, according to Professor Castellano, was not poor security measures against terrorists, but America's "imperialist" policies.[176]

Professor Castellano teaches the administration of justice,
and in this role he presides over the training of students for
careers as police officers and FBI agents. His chief area of interest is "the impact of crime control policies on people's lives." He
questions the ethics of prison privatization, which he says causes
inmates and staff to be treated as commodities, which in turn
results in prison overcrowding. For this trend, Professor Castellano blames conservative politicians and their ability to promote
fear through the media. "We have this machine—the criminal
justice prison industrial complex—that generates value to a certain segment of the population," he says. "The machine won't go
away unless there's a sea change in how we think of crime and
punishment." To accomplish this change, Professor Castellano,

who is a former member of the Southern Illinois Restorative Justice Action Committee, advocates alternatives to the incarceration of criminals. Professor Castellano wants responses to crime that are "restorative" rather than "retributive." In other words, Professor Castellano, a professor of criminal justice at one university and former head of an entire program in criminal justice at another university, does not believe that criminals should be punished with jail.[177]

See also: Professors Dunkley, Richards, Shortell

Research: John Perazzo

Professor Noam Chomsky
Massachusetts Institute of Technology

— Professor of modern languages and linguistics at the
    Massachusetts Institute of Technology

— Prolific pamphleteer and academia's most influential leftist

— "The so-called War on Terror is pure hypocrisy, virtually without
    exception"

Noam Chomsky has taught at the Massachusetts Institute of
Technology since 1955. In 1961, he was appointed full professor
in the Department of Modern Languages and Linguistics (now
the Department of Linguistics and Philosophy). From 1966 to
1976, he held the Ferrari P. Ward Professorship of Modern Languages and Linguistics. In 1976, he was appointed Institute Professor.

Professor Chomsky's most recent book, *Hegemony or Survival*, is an attack on America as a threat to global survival. Its
dust jacket calls the author "the world's foremost intellectual
activist," which might be suspect as publisher's hyperbole, but
exists in an echo chamber of similar sentiments. According to
the *Chicago Tribune*, Professor Chomsky is "the most cited living
author" and ranks just below Plato and Sigmund Freud among
the most cited authors of all time. While acknowledging that he
is reviled in some quarters for his ferocious anti-Americanism
and cavalier relationship with the factual record, a recent *New
Yorker* profile calls Chomsky "one of the greatest minds of the
20th century."[178]

Professor Chomsky is without question the most politically
influential academic among other academics and their students
alive today. He is promoted by rock groups such as Rage Against
the Machine and Pearl Jam at their concerts the way the Beatles

once promoted the Guru Maharaji, solemnly reading excerpts from his work in between sets and urging their followers to read him too. *Manufacturing Consent*, a documentary adapted from one of Professor Chomsky's books with the same title, has achieved the status of an underground classic in university film festivals. And at the climactic moment in the Academy Award-winning *Good Will Hunting*, the genius-janitor, played by Matt Damon, vanquishes the incorrect thinking of a group of sophomoric college students with a fiery speech quoting Professor Chomsky on the illicit nature of American power.

Professor Chomsky became a national figure through a series of influential articles that appeared in the *New York Review of Books* in the 1960s attacking supporters of the Vietnam War. In Communist Hanoi, Professor Chomsky found a radical version of the Eternal City, when he traveled there with other revolutionary tourists, like Jane Fonda, to make speeches of solidarity with the Communists, whose heroism he believed revealed "the capabilities of the human spirit and human will."[179]

Professor Chomsky never made a cerebral return to Indo-China to rethink the consequences of his anti-war activities. Instead, he was one of the chief deniers of the Cambodian genocide, which took place in the wake of the Communist victory and American withdrawal, directing his vitriolic attacks towards the reporters and witnesses who testified to the human catastrophe that was taking place. Initially, Professor Chomsky tried to minimize the deaths (a "few thousand") and compared those killed by Pol Pot and his followers to the collaborators who were executed by resistance movements in Europe at the end of World War II. By 1980, it was no longer possible to deny that some 2 million of Cambodia's 7.8 million people had perished at the hands of the Communists. But Professor Chomsky continued to deny the genocide, proposing that the problem may have been a failure of the rice crop. As late as 1988, when the skulls were piled too high to ignore any longer, Chomsky returned to the subject and insisted that whatever had happened in Cambodia, the United States was to blame.[180]

This conclusion is the principal theme of what may be loosely termed his intellectual *oeuvre*. Whatever evil exists in the world, the United States is to blame. His intellectual obsession is America and its "grand strategy of world domination." In 1967, Professor Chomsky wrote that America "needed a kind of denazification." The Third Reich has provided him with his central metaphor for his own country ever since.

Professor Chomsky has denounced every president from Wilson and FDR to Ronald Reagan and Bill Clinton as the front men in "four year dictatorships" by a ruling class (Professor Chomsky has in mind American corporations and their directors which he has described as "evil"). In his view, the United States, led by a series of lesser Hitlers, picked up where the Nazis left off after they were defeated (primarily by the Soviet Union of course) in 1945. According to Professor Chomsky, a case could be made for impeaching every president since World War II because "they've all been either outright war criminals or involved in serious war crimes."[181]

Professor Chomsky's other hate affair is with the state of Israel, a country he regards as playing the role of Little Satan to the American Great Satan and functioning strategically as an "offshore military and technology base for the United States." Of a pattern with this animus is Professor Chomsky's involvement with neo-Nazis and holocaust revisionism. This strange and disturbing saga began in 1980 with Professor Chomsky's support of a French crank named Robert Faurisson, a rancorous anti-Semite who was fired by the University of Lyon for his hate-filled screeds. ("The alleged Hitlerite gas chambers and the alleged genocide of the Jews form one and the same historical lie.")[182] Professor Chomsky wrote a preface to a book by Faurisson defending his "free speech" and explaining that Faurisson was an "apolitical liberal" whose work was based on "extensive historical research." Professor Chomsky added that he saw "no hint of anti-Semitic implications" at all in Faurisson's work.

In the post-9/11 political ferment, Professor Chomsky's reputation, which had suffered because of his support of Pol Pot and his dalliance with figures like Faurisson, was revived by the anti-war left. His following has grown, particularly in Europe and Asia, where his views have helped inform an inchoate anti-Americanism, and on the university campus, where divesting from Israel (a cause he has championed) and attacks against the War on Terror are de rigueur. *The New York Times* and *Washington Post*, which had for the most part ignored the dozens of Professor Chomsky books that had appeared clone-like over the past few years, both treated *Hegemony and Survival* as a significant work, with Pulitzer Prize winner Samantha Power writing in the *Times* that Professor Chomsky's work was "sobering and instructive."

While bodies were still being pulled out of the rubble of the Twin Towers, Professor Chomsky was dismissing the atrocity as dwarfed in magnitude by Bill Clinton's missile attack on a factory in the Sudan following the bombings of two U.S. embassies by al-Qaeda, in which no one was injured. Charging to an M.I.T. audience of 2,000 that the U.S. military response against the terrorists in Afghanistan was a calculated "genocide" that would cause the deaths of 3-4 million Afghans, Professor Chomsky also denounced America as "the world's greatest terrorist state." Not content to do this before a collegiate audience whose response would only be protests in a democracy, Professor Chomsky traveled to the Muslim world to repeat the charges of U.S. genocide and terror to millions in Islamabad and New Delhi whose reactions would not take such innocent and non-violent paths. Despite Chomsky's hysterical predictions made in front of inflamed Muslim mobs, no such "genocide" or "famine" occurred in Afghanistan, thanks to $350 million in food shipments supplied by the United States. Chomsky himself was aware of these shipments even as he made his reckless charges.[183]

Professor Chomsky sees the 9/11 attack on the World Trade Center as a turning point in history when the guns that were historically trained on the Third World by imperialist powers like America, have been turned around. And that is a good thing, because in Professor Chomsky's eyes unless American "hegemony" is destroyed, the world faces a grim future. Now, as throughout his long career, America's peril is Noam Chomsky's hope.

See also: Professors Bill Ayers, Dohrn, Kirstein, Richards, Zinn

Research: Peter Collier[184]

Kathleen Cleaver

Emory University

— Senior lecturer in law at Emory University
— Former Communications Secretary for the Black Panther Party
— Teaches that "racist and white supremacist and exploitative practices are engrained" in American society and government

Kathleen Cleaver is a senior lecturer in law at Emory University in Atlanta, Georgia and a former Communications Secretary for the Black Panther Party, though her faculty biography notes only that she "spent most of her life participating in the human rights struggle." Cleaver herself describes the group—whose leaders committed numerous felonies, including murder, and tortured members accused of "informing"[185]—as a "liberation" movement. The author of a hagiographic introduction to a book of photographs of the party, called *Black Panthers 1968*, Cleaver maintains that the party was a righteous resistance group framed by the FBI for crimes it did not commit.[186] In Cleaver's telling, the Black Panther Party cannot reasonably be described as a violent group because it used violence only as a means of "self-defense." "The only way you can reach a conclusion that the Party was violent is that blacks are not entitled to defend themselves," Cleaver has said.[187] She did not explain how self-defense covers arson, rape, and the shotgun assassinations of local club owners, all documented Panther crimes.[188]

Cleaver still harbors hopes of the revolution she sought to bring about during her days with the Panthers. "Have I changed my views on how society needs to be changed? No. It needs fundamental root-and-branch improvement, not plastering over," she told an interviewer from PBS in 2004.[189] Cleaver has used her authority as a member of Emory's law faculty to promote the radical cause. In March of 2004, for instance, Cleaver took part in a special screening of a promotional documentary on *The Weather Underground*, about the eponymous terrorist outfit. Cleaver joined former Weatherman and convicted terrorist Laura White-horn for a panel discussion, during which the group's members were described as idealistic youths who had courageously spoken out against the Vietnam War and racism in America.[190]

Cleaver's understanding of American history and law fairly bristles with her political views. Even today, she has written, "racist and white supremacist and exploitative practices are engrained" in American society and government. According to Cleaver, the "inability to treat Black people in a humane fashion" has "become part of the identity of the United States."[191]

> White supremacy is a function of the colonial or imperial domination of peoples of color. When you use these Europeans as the rulers of Indians and Africans in creating a society based on a plantation system of slavery, in which the majority of the workers are Black or Brown, and all the owners are completely white and European and speaking a different language, then the core of the development of a society is white supremacy: white economic and political and military supremacy over the people of color, who are your laborers, your indigenous, your servants, your slaves. So that particular institutional complex was built in North America, and it still operates in what they're talking about as globalization.[192]

These extreme ideas make up the substance of Cleaver's seminar on the law of slavery and anti-slavery.[193] They also fig-ure in her other courses at Emory, most prominently her course "American Legal History: Citizen and Race."

In November 2001, Cleaver convened a conference of schol-ars at the Emory law school whose express purpose was denouncing the Patriot Act. Among the participants were Ward Churchill and his wife Natsu Saito. No less loathsome to Cleaver is the U.S.-led war in Iraq. Asked by an interviewer whether she saw similarities between the war in Vietnam and Iraq, Cleaver lamented that the terrorist insurgents in Iraq were not making greater efforts to reach out to American antiwar radicals:

> I wish there were, in the sense that the Vietnamese made a very conscientious effort in their foreign and military policies to include Americans opposed to the government. They made a big distinction between what the government and the people did. Therefore, they were able to engage, discuss, and talk with American citizens and the antiwar movement. I don't see that type of communication happening in the case of Iraq.[194]

Cleaver has no patience for the notion that terrorism poses a threat to the United States. Instead, she has claimed that terrorism is a propaganda invention of the U.S. government. "They're using the whipping boy of terrorism the way they used the whipping boy of communism to get their own sordid little corporate war programs in place."[195]

Cleaver has not one scholarly book or even article to her name. Her only publication in a legal journal is an article that appeared in the *Yale Journal of Law and Humanities* (1998): "Mobilizing in Paris for Mumia Abu Jamal," but this is a memoir, not legal scholarship. In her academic bibliography[196] she lists op-ed columns in the *Los Angeles Times*, an "Open Letter to Julius Lester" printed in the *National Guardian* and an article she wrote in the 1960s for the New Left magazine *Ramparts*, "On Eldridge Cleaver." She has no qualifications to teach at a major law school.

See also: Professors Ayers, D. Cole, Dohrn,
            Kirstein, Matsuda

Research: Jacob Laksin

Professor Dana Cloud
University of Texas, Austin

— Associate professor of communication studies

— Member of the International Socialist Organization, a self-styled
revolutionary Communist Party

— The day after 9/11, Cloud stated: "the United States military has,
in recent years, been the most effective and constant killer of
civilians around the world."

Dana Cloud is an associate professor of communication studies at the University of Texas, Austin. Professor Cloud "specializes in the analysis of contemporary and popular and political
culture from feminist, Marxist and Critical Race Theory perspectives," as described in the University of Texas official website. Professor Cloud is a member of the International Socialist
Organization, a Leninist vanguard that considers itself part of
the Fourth Communist International. Formed in 1977, the
International Socialist Organization describes itself as the largest
"revolutionary" socialist group in the United States; actually the
Communist Party is probably somewhat larger.

Professor Cloud was quick to blame American policies for
having provoked the 9/11 attacks, singling out the United States
as the world's number one terrorist state. On September 12,
2001—just one day after the atrocity in which three thousand
innocent Americans perished—Professor Cloud wrote that she
felt "outrage at the hypocrisy of President Bush, Vice President
Cheney, and all of the politicians and pundits who last night
rushed to declare war on the still-unidentified perpetrators of
this tragedy."[197] Targeting civilians, she conceded, was "despica-
ble. But it is worth pointing out that the United States military

has, in recent years, been the most effective and constant killer of civilians around the world. The 1991 Persian Gulf War left more than two hundred thousand civilians dead as a direct consequence of the war. Ongoing economic sanctions in Iraq have killed more than 1.5 million more, including hundreds of thousands of children."[198]

Like many anti-American radicals, Professor Cloud routinely repeats the propaganda of the Saddam regime, ignoring the fact that the United States and its allies had provided more than $50 billion in food aid to Iraqi civilians under the Oil for Food program, whose proceeds were diverted by Saddam to his own agendas and who, with the collusion of U.N. officials, stole more than $20 billion for themselves.

"Many Americans don't stop to think," Professor Cloud added, "about why Palestinians and others in the Middle East have cause to be extremely angry with the United States for its support of Israel in its decades-long campaign of terror against Palestinian civilians. Few people I have spoken with have thought about the role that the U.S.'s refusal to participate in the U.N. World Conference Against Racism in Durban, South Africa, (where questions of Israeli racism against Palestinians arose) may have played in intensifying Arab anger at the United States."[199] The planning session of the conference Professor Cloud refers to was convened in the compassionate state of Iran under the watchful eyes of the mullahs who barred Jews, Americans, and members of the Baha'i faith from attending. Conference participants demonstrated in the streets, distributing flyers that portrayed Jews "with fangs dripping blood and wearing helmets inscribed with Nazi swastikas," a display of ethnic hatred described by one reporter as "a venomous carnival of incitement." A yarmulke-wearing bystander was confronted by Arab and South African demonstrators chanting "Kill the Jews."[200]

Lord Greville Janner, a British MP, characterized the events in Durban, including the official proceedings, as "the worst example of anti-Semitism that I have ever seen."[201]

Professor Cloud also warned against "the scapegoating of Arabs and the hasty and predictable attempt to blame the attacks on Osama bin Laden and his supporters." Professor Cloud further spoke about her fear of "the curtailing of our civil liberties in the wake of this crisis." She had a specific fear in mind: "Already we are hearing about tightening airport security."[202] Like other leftists, Professor Cloud was determined to find the root causes of the unprovoked 9/11 attacks in something the country she already condemned as a dedicated Leninist had done: "Why would someone target the U.S.? Why would people feel so desperate that they would want to kill themselves and innocent civilians in these kinds of attacks? We need to address these questions if we are to prevent the kind of devastation that happened yesterday from happening ever again."[203]

Professor Cloud's antipathy for the United States is expressed in her disdain for the *Pledge of Allegiance*—"It seems very strange to pledge loyalty to a scrap of cloth representing a corrupt nation." In July 2002, she decided to write a new *Pledge*—not to America, but to those people worldwide who are the alleged victims of American greed, exploitation, and aggression: "I pledge allegiance to all the ordinary people around the world, to the laid off Enron workers and the WorldCom workers, the maquiladora workers and the sweatshop workers from New York to Indonesia, who labor not under God but under the heel of multinational corporations; I pledge allegiance to the people of Iraq, Palestine and Afghanistan, and to their struggles to survive and resist slavery to corporate greed, brutal wars against their families, and the economic and environmental ruin wrought by global capitalism. I pledge allegiance to building a better world where human needs are met and with real liberty, equality and justice for all."[204] As in the world that Lenin built.

See also: Professors Bell, Christiansen, hooks,
Dohrn, Fellman, Jagger, Zinn

Research: John Perazzo

Professor David Cole
Georgetown University

— Professor of law at Georgetown University

— Radical attorney-activist who has defended terrorists and their supporters

— Believes "greatest threat to our freedoms is posed not by the terrorists themselves but by our own government's response."

David Cole is professor of law at Georgetown University and a prominent attorney-activist in the ranks of the anti-war Left. At Georgetown, Professor Cole is best known for his course "National Security and Civil Liberties." The course proposes to address such issues as "the respective roles of Congress, the president, and the courts in times of emergency"; "the targeting of foreign nationals"; and "preventive detention, surveillance standards, enemy combatants, military tribunals, the role of international tribunals, and regulation of speech and association."[205]

On all these issues Professor Cole's views are no secret. He is a staff attorney at the Center for Constitutional Rights, a radical "civil liberties" group which has specialized in the past in using legal means to oppose American foreign policy in regard to Cuba and other Communist regimes and which regards current American security measures in the War on Terror as an "assault" on the Constitution. Of the War on Terror, Cole wrote in 2002, "it appears that the greatest threat to our freedoms is posed not by the terrorists themselves but by our own government's response."[206] Professor Cole signed the "statement of conscience" condemning the war, sponsored by Not in Our Name, a Maoist antiwar group that lists Cole as an advisory board member. The statement pledges "to do everything possible to stop" the war and calls on "all Americans to RESIST the war and repression that has been loosed on the world by the Bush administration."[207]

Professor Cole and the Center for Constitutional Rights garnered media coverage in 2005 when the Center elected to represent one of its colleagues, attorney Lynne Stewart, during her trial for abetting the terrorist activities of the blind sheik, Omar Abdel Rahman, the spiritual leader of the "Islamic Group" which bombed the World Trade Center in 1993 and plotted to blow up the Holland and Lincoln tunnels during rush hour. Stewart was accused of defying a Justice Department order and helping the sheik communicate instructions to his terrorist agents in Egypt to break a truce with other groups. After a highly publicized eight-month trial, Stewart was found guilty on all counts against her, including providing material support for terrorism, conspiracy, and defrauding the government.[208] Immediately after Stewart's February 10, 2005 conviction, Professor Cole wrote a post-trial column for *The Nation*, where he is legal affairs correspondent, denouncing the decision: "This case illustrates how out of hand things have gotten in the 'war on terrorism.'"[209] (Note the scare quotes around the war on terrorism.) Professor Cole claimed that Stewart had committed no crime, and the charges against her "were a stretch."[210] Professor Cole concluded that if anyone could credibly be accused of terrorism, it was the Justice Department.

Previously, in 2002 Professor Cole had delivered a lecture to students at the University of South Florida, entitled "Freedom and Civil Liberties in the Wake of September 11," in which he mounted a vigorous defense of Sami al-Arian, a university professor who had been exposed as the North American leader of Palestinian Islamic Jihad, a terrorist group that had killed more than a hundred civilians in suicide bombings in the Middle East. A videotape of al-Arian calling for "Death to Israel" had been aired on FOX News Channel's *O'Reilly Factor*. Within months,

Professor al-Arian was arrested on the basis (among other evidence) of wiretaps conducted over a ten-year period of his conversations with terrorists in America and the Middle East, organizing payments for specific suicide bombings, ordering bomb making materials and recruiting terrorists. Calling Professor al-Arian "the victim," Cole contended, "People cannot be punished for advocating criminal activity unless the Supreme Court has said their speech is intended and likely to incite imminent lawless actions."[211] This was true, but it was not speech that was the basis of al-Arian's indictment.

Professor Cole was familiar with the charges against Professor al-Arian and his terrorist group because he was the counsel for Professor al-Arian's brother-in-law, Mazen Al-Najjar, whom the Justice Department had been attempting to deport for years in connection with these activities. In his speech Professor Cole referred to Mazen al-Najjar's case as a routine instance of the unjust targeting of foreign nationals by U.S. authorities, and asserted, on no evidence, that Al-Najjar was being "held under conditions which are far worse than any convicted murderers."[212] Cole did not see fit to note the evidence that identified Mazen al-Najjar as a fundraiser for the terrorist group Palestinian Islamic Jihad.

One of the focal points of Professor Cole's attack on the Patriot Act is its provision criminalizing "material support" for terrorism, the provision which has enabled federal authorities to close down many "charitable" foundations that fund terrorist activities. Professor Cole argues that this provision is an unconstitutional infringement on free speech and "imposes guilt by association."[213] Writing in the Winter 2002 issue of *Human Rights*, a journal of the American Bar Association, Professor Cole protested: "The Patriot Act also resurrects ideological exclusion, the practice of denying entry to aliens for pure speech. It excludes aliens who 'endorse or espouse terrorist activity,' or who 'persuade others to support terrorist activity or a terrorist organization,' in ways that the secretary of state determines undermine U.S. efforts to combat terrorism. It also excludes aliens who are representatives of groups that 'endorse acts of terrorist activity' in ways that similarly undermine U.S. efforts to combat terrorism.... Excluding people for their ideas is flatly contrary to the spirit of freedom for which the United States stands."[214] In other words, Professor Cole is in favor of admitting foreigners into the United States who explicitly support terrorist groups. This, apparently, is an inalienable right.

See also: Professors al-Arian, Dohrn, Matsuda, Shallah

Research: Jacob Laksin

Professor Juan Cole
University of Michigan

— Professor of history, University of Michigan
— President of the Middle East Studies Association
— Believes that a "pro-Likud" cabal controls the American government from a small number of key positions within the Executive Branch

A professor of modern Middle East and South Asian history at the University of Michigan, Juan Cole has many impressive titles. In addition to his professorship, he is the editor of the *International Journal of Middle East Studies*, and the author of a weblog focusing on U.S. foreign policy in the Middle East. In 2003, he emerged as a sought-after Middle East expert for the major media (including *The New York Times, Washington Post*, and National Public Radio). In November 2004, Juan Cole was elected president of the Middle East Studies Association, the foremost professional association representing academics working in this field. Once a gathering of respectable scholars, the Middle East Studies Association has become so ideological that it is more properly viewed as a political rather than an academic organization. Its annual conferences can appear to be more like a political rally of Marxists and Muslims than a symposium of academic specialists.

Professor Cole's views are shaped by his fundamental belief in a conspiracy of Jewish "neo-conservatives" that runs U.S. Middle East policy. His recurrent theme is that a nebulous "pro-Likud" cabal controls the American government from a small number of key positions in the Executive Branch. He never names the leaders or organizations behind this fabulously clever and utterly secret conspiracy, but vaguely associates it with organizations like the American Israel Political Action Committee (although the AIPAC is estimated to be 80% Democratic) and any prominent Jew in the Bush administration.

Here are some examples: "The Neocons wanted to knock down Saddam, Khamenei and al-Asad in hopes that those countries would be so weakened and preoccupied with internal power struggles that Sharon would have an unimpeded opportunity to pursue his dreams of Greater Israel."[215] "It may be that the powerful Likudniks inside the U.S. government are deliberately engineering a diplomatic rift in NATO, so as to ensure that Paris and Moscow cannot position themselves to influence Washington's position (usually supine) toward Sharon's excesses."[216] Paul Wolfowitz's attitude to NATO allies is "so gratuitous and immature that one can only guess something else lay behind it;" in Professor Cole's view, that "something else" is a wish to create bad blood between the U.S. government and states that are, in Professor Cole's terms, "no longer a knee-jerk supporter of Israeli militarism and expansionism."[217]

When Karen Kwiatkowski, a retired U.S. Air Force Lt. Colonel sponsored by the political Left, analyzed the war aims of the Neocon network, Professor Cole berated her for *not* pointing to a Jewish conspiracy. "I am surprised," said Professor Cole, "she left out what surely was the Neocons' major concern, which is that Iraq, Iran and Syria stood in the way of Ariel Sharon's continued theft of Arab land in the Occupied territories and potentially elsewhere."[218]

Professor Cole has also made such fact-stretching statements as, "[m]uch of the Arab world has a formal peace treaty with Israel,"[219] and "[c]hemical weapons are not weapons of mass destruction."[220] Showing a typical contempt for evidence that even CBS accepted, Cole states that "Saddam Hussein never gave any real support to the Palestinian cause, and he did not pay suicide bombers to blow themselves up."[221] In fact Saddam not only provided $25,000 per suicide bomber but $74 million directly to the terrorist organization Hamas. And even if Saddam did pay money to the families of these murderers, Cole insists, "[s]upporting orphans [of dead suicide bombers] is, in any case, not the same as funding terrorism."[222] One must wonder whether *making* orphans is, in Professor Cole's eyes, terrorism.

Professor Cole is capable of dangerous sophistry regarding his own chosen subject of study. "Are there Muslims who are fascists?" says Professor Cole. "Sure. But there is no Islamic fascism, since 'Islam' has to do with the highest ideals of the religion."[223] He applies a particularly brazen double standard, decrying the term "Islamo-fascist" as a "thoroughly abhorrent" form of bigotry, even as he routinely brands Zionism (without any hyphen) "racist"[224] and "fascist."[225]

When a February 2004 poll revealed that 51% of Americans believed Iraq had WMDs at the start of the war—a belief shared by every major intelligence agency in the world, including the French and Jordanian—Cole responded that "Half the American public is terminally stupid."[226]

See also: Professors Anderson, Beinin, Brand, Cloud, J. Cole, Esposito, Joseph Massad

Research: Jonathan Calt Harris [227]

Professor Miriam Cooke
Duke University

— Professor of Asian and African languages and literature, Duke University

— President of the Association for Middle East Women's Studies

— Blames 9/11 on Israel

Miriam Cooke is a professor of modern Arabic literature and culture at Duke University's Center for the Study of Muslim Networks, a leftist entity that is strongly opposed to the U.S. War On Terror. She is also president of the Association for Middle East Women's Studies, an international organization staunchly opposed to what it calls the "new imperialism," by which it means the imperialism spearheaded by the United States.

The author of nine books, Professor Cooke cited America's alleged unjust foreign policies and its very way of life as the root causes of the September 11, 2001 terrorist attacks. "9/11 has a long history going back through the Gulf War to the establishment of Israel in 1948," she said. "It is a history that spans the length of the Cold War and is witness to the growing suspicion and fear of U.S. policies in the region. . . . Too far for U.S. citizens to see, Afghanistan seethed and suffered. It became the mirror to the U.S. of the dangerous outcome of its policies. . . What we saw on 9/11 was the return of the repressed. Afghans . . . directed their anger and hatred against the centralized state apparatus. Products of the twin discipline of religion and militarization, they easily transformed capitalist ideology into its religious underside and wrapped it in the rhetoric of Islam."[228] Despite Professor Cooke's analysis, none of the terrorists who attacked on 9/11 were from Afghanistan, and they were mainly Saudis.

Professor Cooke condemns the war on terror for "link[ing] humanitarian and political rhetoric to military action." "Is the goal of this total war the establishment of the peace of Terror through the annihilation of all these nomads?" she asks rhetorically, as though the United States were a genocidal nation.[229]

Professor Cooke is a proponent of academic Marxism's theory of "post-colonialism." This is just an updated term of art for "neo-colonialism," preferred by Maoists and other sixties Marxists to make the claim that while there may no longer be formal colonies anymore, there are still informal, economically exploitative imperialisms which are impoverishing and destroying the Third World.

Professor Cooke is a strong proponent of "Islamic feminism," which establishes a double standard that lets Islamic countries off the hook for their oppression of women. Islamic feminism holds that Muslim women should enact social change from within the confines of their own culture and religion. Western powers are viewed as having purely imperialistic designs and, as a result, their intervention, even if it benefits Islamic people including women, is unwelcome. Such is the logic that caused Professor Cooke—a longtime proponent of Muslim women writers, activists, and intellectuals—to oppose the U.S. overthrow of Afghanistan's Taliban government (one of the most oppressive regimes on earth, particularly with regard to women) and the democratization of the Middle East. Although empowering women would seem to be an obviously positive development for someone like Professor Cooke who also teaches courses in Womens Studies, she evidently believes that if Western efforts are involved in the liberation of women, then it is no longer liberation but a form of "post-colonial" oppression. Consequently, Professor Cooke and her fellow activists were more opposed to U.S. military intervention than they were in favor of getting rid of the Taliban, even if it meant that Afghanistan's women remained in a state of perpetual slavery.

During a talk at a forum on the future of Iraq at the John Hope Franklin Center on March 26, 2003, Professor Cooke rejected the liberation of Afghan women as a legitimate reason to go to war. Rather than being grateful for calling attention to the suffering of women, she castigated First Lady Laura Bush for her radio address supporting those women. Professor Cooke accused Mrs. Bush of furthering "the imperial project in her highly gendered appeal to a world conscience."[230] In Professor Cooke's eyes, America's leaders are damned if they do and damned if they don't. Regarding the al-Qaeda terrorist training camps dotting the Afghanistan countryside, Professor Cooke said nothing. She was equally silent on the ten million Afghans who registered to vote—40 percent of them women—in the October 2004 election.

Professor Cooke disparages "the campaign to democratize the Middle East,"[231] because it is a campaign spearheaded by the West. Professor Cooke opposed the war in Iraq for the same reason, fatalistically predicting that Iraqi women would end up "like the Shiite women who were driven out of their homes in southern Iraq in March 1991, to enter refugee camps in Saudi Arabia and then went on to exilic futures outside the Middle East."[232] In fact, none of this happened and the numbers of asylum seekers from Iraq and Afghanistan have been drastically reduced from pre-war levels. No longer are Iraqi women captive to Saddam Hussein's rape rooms, or to having their husbands taken away in the middle of night. The presence of six female ministers in the new Iraqi government formed in the spring of 2004 demonstrated that women are making strides in that country. But for Professor Cooke, none of this matters as much as fighting the war against American "imperialism."

Throughout her career, Professor Cooke has written extensively about the idea of a "women's *jihad*." During a lecture at
Wellesley College in November 2003, she elaborated on this
concept. This *jihad*, she maintained, is not for an "Islamist state,"
but rather for an "Islamic community." She insists that women's
role within the Islamic world should be "drawing attention to
the consequences of war, not advocating violence." Yet her paci-
fism is reserved for her own democratic country. For the Islamic
terrorists she is understanding of the need for violence, or as she
puts it "the defense of the community when attacked by out-
siders."[233]

Israeli civilians, naturally, are also appropriate targets for Professor Cooke's "women's *jihad*." When Wafa Idris, a 27-year-old
Palestinian woman, perpetrated a suicide bombing that killed an
80-year-old man in January 2000, Professor Cooke's thesis about
women and war were put to the test. But Professor Cooke justified this atrocity by falling back on her "blame the imperialists"
worldview. She said, "For those of us who really are concerned
with women's role in the Arab public square, in the way in
which women have been trying to empower themselves vis-à-vis
the U.S., vis-à-vis old colonial powers, vis-à-vis their own men,
the situation has become so desperate that now women's participation in war is a mark of absolute hopelessness."[234] Of
course the profile of suicide bombers is quite the opposite of
hopelessness: They aspire to paradise through their homicidal
acts. Wafa Idris was indeed desperate but not because of the
Israelis. She had been banished from her husband's bed and then
divorced because her first child was a stillbirth. With no future
in society in which women are the chattel of their husbands,
Wafa Idris was indeed without hope, but this had nothing to do
with the colonial powers old or new.

Beyond teaching her own courses, Professor Cooke is very
active in Duke's Islamic Studies Department. She is co-director

of the university's Center for the Study of Muslim Networks, and was involved in the 2003-2004 Carolina Seminar on Comparative Islamic Studies. She accompanied a group of students on a trip to Lebanon in 2002 and has taken part in various local film festivals in recent years. As such, Cooke wields considerable influence over the way Duke students experience Islamic culture and particularly its relationship to women. But her students, instead of learning about women's liberation, are receiving lessons in women's oppression—opposing oppression allegedly prevalent in the United States, and supporting oppression in the Islamic world.

See also: Professors Brand, Cloud, Dabashi
Research: Cinnamon Stillwell[235]

Professor Patrick Coy

Kent State University

— Associate professor at Kent State University's Center for Applied Conflict Management

— Condemns America's "imperial policies in a globalized economy"

— "It is not just Saddam Hussein whose actions threaten UN credibility. George W. Bush may be the greater long-term threat."

Patrick Coy is a radical leftist whose consuming scholarly interest is the socialist Catholic Worker movement.[236] A disciple of the Italian Communist Antonio Gramsci, he nurses a deep resentment of America's "hegemony" in world affairs. Writing in 2003 in the quarterly leftist journal *Peace Review*, Coy despaired of the "United States' placement as the world's lone military superpower" and raged against its "imperial policies in a globalized economy." Professor Coy has condemned every American military campaign in recent history. In recent years, he has emerged as Kent State's foremost opponent of the Bush administration's war on terror, which he has described as "rallying support for a policy of a permanent war economy, aggressive military retaliation, preemptive attacks abroad and civil liberty suppression at home."[237]

Professor Coy was not only opposed to the war in Iraq, but to any attempt by the United States to hold the regime of Saddam Hussein accountable for its violations of 16 UN resolutions, including those that constituted the truce in the first Gulf War. In an October 2002 column for the *Catholic Reporter* about President Bush's appearance before the United Nations on September 12, Professor Coy wrote that under his theory of conflict management the very attempt by the United States to make Saddam adhere to international law and to agreements he had signed, *even through the United Nations*, was merely "exploitation" of a weaker power by a stronger one. "It is not just Saddam Hussein whose actions threaten UN credibility. George W. Bush may be the greater long-term threat."[238]

In a June 2004 op-ed in the *Akron Beacon Journal*, Professor Coy reflected on the War on Terror thus far. According to Professor Coy, most Americans were "ashamed of the sexual war crimes being committed in their name in Iraq, Afghanistan and Guantanamo Bay."[239]

The Professor's abrasively anti-war views are also the subject of his research. In August 2004, he received a grant for $110,460 from the National Science Foundation for a research project called "Harnessing and Challenging Hegemony during Three Wars: The U.S. Peace Movement, 1990–2004." Teaming up with two other radical professors, Gregory Maney and Lynne Woehrle, Professor Coy plans to investigate ways to expand the anti-war movement in the United States, or, as the project's mission statement puts it, to "highlight cultural obstacles to generating mass dissent as well as the strategic choices and dilemmas facing activists in responding to these obstacles."[240] The project was inspired by the work of Italian Communist Antonio Gramsci, who defined "hegemony" as the means by which society's ruling class compels the oppressed classes into accepting its views about society. At Kent State, evidently things work in the opposite direction. Several Kent State students will work as research assistants on this highly political project, to avail themselves of the benefit of engaging in "broader study of social movements, conflicts, and social change," and presumably joining them and advancing their agendas afterwards.

> **See also:** Professors Berlowitz, Eckstein, Fellman, Haffar, Shortell, Schwartz, Targ, Wolfe
>
> **Research:** Tom Ryan

Professor Hamid Dabashi

Columbia University

— Professor of Islamic studies, Columbia University

— Chair of the Department of Middle East and Asian Languages and Culture

— Describes Israel as "a military base for the rising predatory empire of the United States"

Hamid Dabashi is Columbia University's Hagop Kevorkian Professor of Iranian Studies, chair of the Department of Middle East and Asian Languages and Cultures, and director of graduate studies at the Center for Comparative Literature and Society. The author of nine books dealing with Islamic and Iranian culture, he received a dual PhD in Islamic Studies and the Sociology of Culture from the University of Pennsylvania in 1984.

The defining characteristic of Professor Dabashi's scholarship is his aversion to the United States and Israel. Professor Dabashi portrays the Middle East as a historically hapless victim of Western colonialism, explaining that the current political realities of the Middle East are reducible to the paradigm of the "abuse of labor by capital."

Exempt from this view of Middle East history as unrelieved victimhood by the West is the state of Israel. Professor Dabashi regards Israel as "a military base for the rising predatory empire of the United States" rather than an independent nation.[241] In a 2004 article for the Egyptian weekly *Al-Ahram*, Professor Dabashi condemned all Israelis (men, women and children) as cold-blooded and physically repulsive oppressors. "[A] half century of systematic maiming and murdering of another people [that] has left its deep marks on the faces of these people, the way they talk, the way they walk, the way they handle objects, the way they greet each other, the way they look at the world."[242] Professor Dabashi claimed that Israeli Jews have a congenital predisposition toward brutality: "There is an endemic prevarication to this machinery, a vulgarity of character that is bone-deep and structural to the skeletal vertebrae of its culture."[243] This is crude and overt racism. Yet there has been no Columbia University administrative response to Dabashi's publication of such views about Jews. This is a striking double standard for a university administration that otherwise is ready to act quickly and harshly against any violations of "sensitivity towards others."[244]

By the same token, Professor Dabashi has denounced supporters of Israel's right to exist as "warmongers" and "Gestapo apparatchiks," calling the Jewish state a nest of "thuggery," as well as a "ghastly state of racism and apartheid" which "must be dismantled."[245] When critics suggest that these blanket and historically baseless attacks on Israelis are tantamount to anti-Semitism, Professor Dabashi claims he is guilty of nothing more than critiquing the Israeli government. As he told an interlocutor in June of 2003, "We have to always be careful that a legitimate criticism of the Israeli government is not identified with . . . anti-Semitism."[246] This statement lacks any credibility, as Dabashi's grotesquely anti-Semitic article in *Al Ahram* attests.

It is a measure of Professor Dabashi's anti-Israel fervor that he has, on more than one occasion, cancelled classes he was scheduled to teach at Columbia in order to take part in anti-Israel political rallies.[247] In April 2002, when Israeli troops entered the town of Jenin, which was a base for terrorist attacks on Israeli citizens, Professor Dabashi suspended classes and urged his students to attend the rally protesting the Israeli defense measures. Professor Dabashi was a featured speaker at the rally, where he likened Israel's presence in Jenin to the Nazi conduct of the Holocaust. When a student objected that classes had been cancelled so that Dabashi could engage in a political cause, the professor retorted: "I apologize if canceling our class in solidarity with [Palestinian] victims of a genocide... inconvenienced you."[248] Similarly, when Rabbi Charles Sheer, the director of Hillel at Columbia, criticized Dabashi's role in the rally, the professor responded by condemning Sheer in the campus newspaper for launching a "campaign of terror and disinformation reminiscent of the Spanish Inquisition" against him simply because he—Dabashi—had "publicly spoken against the Israeli slaughter of innocent Palestinians in refugee camps."[249] Subsequently, in an October 2003 article in *The Times Higher Education Supplement*, Professor Dabashi insisted that he had been spurred to action by "evidence pointing to a massacre" of Palestinians in Jenin by Israeli forces.[250] There was in fact no such evidence, and the entire Israeli operation against the terrorists was conducted on a house-to-house basis to minimize civilian casualties (while greatly increasing the risks to the Israeli Defense Forces).

In May of 2003, Professor Dabashi once again cancelled class in deference to an anti-Israel teach-in that afforded him the opportunity to rage at the U.S.-led war in Iraq. "Because there are no answers to our questions about this war, we just get angrier and angrier" the *Columbia Spectator* quoted Professor Dabashi. "But this is where the blessed thing called 'teach-in' comes in handy."[251] In an apparent reference to President Bush, Professor Dabashi claimed that the teach-in was a "Revenge of the nerdy 'A' students against the stupid 'C' students with their stupid fingers on the trigger."[252]

In opposing America's war on terror, the Iranian-born professor has claimed that the United States is actually more oppressive than the dictatorial Middle Eastern regimes it opposes. Of domestic counter-terrorism legislation, Professor Dabashi has said that American civil "liberties have been systematically corroded [sic] to the point that the combined effects of the Home-land Security Act, the USA Patriot Act, and the specter of Patriot Act II are devastating and create political conditions worse than those found in the Islamic Republic [of Iran]."[253] Professor Dabashi also believes that Iran's theocratic regime is more democratic than the United States government. "In [Iran]," he has said, "there is a democratically elected government. If you ask me, [President] Khatami has more clear legitimacy than Bush does."[254]

Regarding it as his duty to expose the ugly truth about American "imperialism" in all its "horror," Professor Dabashi has compared Defense Secretary Donald Rumsfeld to Attila the Hun as "a destroyer of civilization." "After this catastrophe of the looting of cultural heritage [by U.S. troops in Iraq]," comments Professor Dabashi, "you realize that for the people in Washington, there is no culture, there is no civilization, there is no heritage, there is no need for domestically cultivated institutions of democracy in Iraq or elsewhere. There are just oilfields with flags on them."[255] In April 2003, he assured the *Boston Globe* that, "The Shiites are horrified [by America's brutality]. Not only are their fellow Shiites and, in fact, their fellow Muslims maimed and murdered right in front of their eyes by the Americans, but the most sacrosanct sites in their collective faith are now invaded by foreign armies. The next time the British and Americans ask themselves, 'Why do they hate us?' they [had] better remember the horrid scenes of their armies trampling on the sacred sites."[256] But Professor Dabashi is obviously wrong. Two years after these comments were made, Iraq's Shiites became a pillar of the new Iraqi government.

In a moment of candor, Professor Dabashi acknowledged that his fanatical hatred of the United States and Israel, coupled with his political activism, has taken its toll on what reputation he once enjoyed as a serious scholar. "I used to be a very respectable scholar, and I tend to think I am still a half-decent one," he lamented to an interviewer in 2003, "but my academic credentials become overshadowed by the reputation I have acquired as a public intellectual."[257] As well they should.

See also: Professors Anderson, Eckstein,
                    LeVine, Massad
Research: Jacob Laksin

Professor Angela Davis
University of California, Santa Cruz

— Professor of the history of consciousness at the University of California, Santa Cruz

— Recipient of the Lenin "Peace Prize"

— Leader of a movement to free all criminals who are minorities claiming that they are political prisoners of the racist United States

Angela Yvonne Davis is a tenured professor in the "history of consciousness" program at UC Santa Cruz. She has also taught at UCLA and the State University of New York at Stony Brook. She is a former Black Panther and was an active member of the Communist Party until 1991, when she was expelled for opposing the coup against Gorbachev. She then formed the "Committees of Correspondence," to carry on the Communist mission with other Party members, including Bettina Aptheker, also a professor at Santa Cruz, Conn Hallinan who is Provost at Santa Cruz[258] and Professor Harry Targ, chair of the "Peace Studies" program at Purdue.

Her professorship is in the history of consciousness program at the University of California, Santa Cruz—a program that awarded a doctorate to her Black Panther comrade—rapist, crack addict, and murderer Huey P. Newton. (The "Dr. Huey P. Newton Papers are archived at Stanford.) Professor Page Smith, the eccentric creator of the history of consciousness program, told an interviewer inquiring about Newton's degree that he had created the program "to demonstrate that PhD is a fraud."[259] In this endeavor, he was only half successful, since the program is still going forward.

Born into a middle-class family in Birmingham, Alabama in 1944, Davis attended segregated elementary schools in that city until she was selected for a special life of radical privilege, going to live with Communist Party leader Herbert Aptheker's family in New York and attending the Little Red Schoolhouse and Elizabeth Irwin High, both institutions of the Communist left.

In 1961, Davis enrolled at Brandeis University, where she majored in French and came under the influence of Marxist Herbert Marcuse, author of the theory of "repressive tolerance." Widely influential in the academic left, this theory held that conservative thought should be repressed wherever possible because it expressed the view of the dominant class. In 1968, Davis was hired to faculty at UCLA. As Soviet tanks rolled into Czechoslovakia to crush the "Prague spring," Professor Davis joined the Communist Party, voicing her belief that "the only path of liberation for black people is that which leads toward complete and radical overthrow of the capitalist class."[260]

In September 1969, Professor Davis was fired from UCLA when her membership in the Communist Party became known. This resulted in a celebrated First Amendment battle that made Angela Davis a national figure and forced UCLA to rehire her.

In 1970, Professor Davis was implicated by more than 20 witnesses in a plot to free her imprisoned lover, fellow Black Panther George Jackson who was awaiting trial on a murder charge. The plot involved hijacking a Marin County, California courtroom and taking the judge, the prosecuting assistant district attorney, and two jurors hostage. Professor Davis supplied a group headed by Jackson's younger brother with a small arsenal of weapons she had purchased two weeks earlier. In an ensuing gun battle outside the court building, Judge Harold Haley's head was blown off by a sawed-off shotgun owned by Professor Davis. Three other people were killed. To avoid arrest Professor Davis fled California, where she used aliases and changed her appearance to avoid detection. Two months later the FBI apprehended her in New York City.

At her trial, Professor Davis could not be cross-examined, since she acted as her own attorney. She presented a number of alibi witnesses, almost all Communist friends, who testified that she had been with them in Los Angeles playing Scrabble at the time of the Marin slaughter. Witnesses who placed her in Marin were dismissed by Professor Davis and her attorneys as being unable to accurately identify blacks, because they themselves were white. A friendly jury acquitted her. Following the verdict, juror Ralph DeLange faced news cameras and gave the revolutionary clenched-fist salute. He laughed at the justice system, saying that prosecutors had been mistaken to expect that the "middle-class jury" would convict Professor Davis.[261] Along with most of the jurors he then went off to a victory party for the defendant.[262]

While she was still a fugitive, Angela Davis was an official hero to her first loyalty, the Moscow dictatorship, which had imprisoned tens of millions in the Soviet Union without trial, whose only crime was to be out of step with the regime. Aleksandr Solzhenitsyn, the author of the *Gulag Archipelago* who spent eight years in Stalin's concentration camps and chronicled the suffering had this to say about Professor Davis in a speech he delivered to the AFL-CIO on July 9, 1975 in New York City:

> There's a certain woman here named Angela Davis. I don't know if you are familiar with her in this country, but in our country, literally, for an entire year, we heard of nothing at all except Angela Davis. There was only Angela Davis in the whole world and she was suffering. We had our ears stuffed with Angela Davis. Little children in school were told to sign petitions in defense of Angela Davis. Little boys and girls, eight and nine years old, were asked to do this. She was set free, as

you know. Although she didn't have too difficult a time in [America's] jails, she came to recuperate in Soviet resorts. Some Soviet dissidents—but more important, a group of Czech dissidents—addressed an appeal to her: "Comrade Davis, you were in prison. You know how unpleasant it is to sit in prison, especially when you consider yourself innocent. You have such great authority now. Could you help our Czech prisoners? Could you stand up for those people in Czechoslovakia who are being persecuted by the state?" Angela Davis answered: "They deserve what they get. Let them remain in prison." That is the face of Communism. That is the heart of Communism for you.[263]

In 1979, Professor Davis was awarded the International Lenin Peace Prize (formerly named the International Stalin Peace Prize) by the Soviet police state. Professor Davis ran for vice president of the United States on the Communist Party ticket in 1980 and 1984.

Angela Davis is currently a "University Professor," one of only seven in the entire University of California system, which entitles her to a six-figure salary and provides her with a research assistant. This income is supplemented by speaking fees ranging from $10,000 to $20,000 per appearance on college campuses, where she is an icon of radical faculty, administrators, and students, and invariably presented as a "human rights activist." The speaking bureau that represents her describes her as "known internationally for her ongoing work to combat all forms of oppression in the U.S. and abroad." A lounge is named in her honor at the University of Michigan.

Professor Davis opposed America's war against terror in Afghanistan, and during the months preceding the 2003 war in Iraq, she was a frequent guest speaker at anti-war rallies. She is also the leader of her own movement against what she calls the

"Prison-Industrial Complex," claiming that all minorities in jail are actually "political prisoners" and should be released. Says Professor Davis, "My question is, 'Why are people so quick to assume that locking away an increasingly large proportion of the U.S. population would help those who live in the free world feel safer and more secure?... how difficult is it to envision a social order that does not rely on the threat of sequestering people in dreadful places designed to separate them from their communities and their families?'"[264] Pretty difficult, actually. Especially for the victims of such predators.

A political apparatchik through and through, Professor Davis has never really made a scholarly contribution or written a serious academic work, despite the expansive university honors she has received. Her political tracts include: *If They Come in the Morning: Voices of Resistance* (1971) *Women, Race, and Class* (1981); *Violence Against Women and the Ongoing Challenge to Racism* (1992); *Resisting State Violence: Radicalism, Gender, and Race in U.S. Culture* (1996); *Global Critical Race Feminism: An International Reader* (1999); *Are Prisons Obsolete?* (2003). Yet she is a "University Professor"—a very prestigious post in the California system, normally awarded on the basis of extraordinary contributions to scholarship.

> *See also:* Professors Aptheker, Davis, Furr,
> Marable, Targ
> *Research:* Larry Cott, John Perazzo

Professor Gregory Dawes
North Carolina State University

— Associate professor of Latin American and world literatures,
North Carolina State University

— Marxist

— Believes communist China and Cuba have been "successful in
instituting political and economic democracy."

Gregory Dawes is an associate professor of Latin American and
world literatures at North Carolina State University. A self-proclaimed Marxist, Dawes's political views color his courses. For
instance, a syllabus for "Contemporary World Literature I," features only left-wing and Communist poets—Garcia Lorca,
Bertolt Brecht, Pablo Neruda, Nazim Hikmet and Muriel
Rukeyser. For reference, students are provided with two lists of
poets who were political and lived in the same period, One list
contains a dozen other leftist and Communist poets; the other
contains four allegedly "fascist" poets including T.S. Eliot (who
was only referred to as a fascist by the Communist Left) and
William Butler Yeats, who was an Irish nationalist (the other
two, Ezra Pound and Giuseppe Ungaretti, were actually fascists).
No liberal or conservative or un-political poets are provided.[265]

Dawes edits a journal titled *A Contracorriente*, which
approaches the social history and literature of Latin America
from "gender and Marxist" perspectives.[266] As he explained in an
article in the journal's inaugural issue in 2003, Dawes founded
the journal to combat what he regarded as the neglect by academic literature departments in the United States and Europe of
the tenets of Marxism. The problem with modish academic theories like postmodernism, in Dawes's judgment, was that they
"all diverge to some degree or another from class, gender and

race analyses of concrete socio-historical events and, as I see it, from Marxism as the explanatory model for the fundamental critique of capitalism per se and for its transcendence in more egalitarian social systems (socialism and communism)."[267] By "diverting attention away from the class struggle and analysis," such theories hindered "attempts to overcome capitalism and imperialism," Dawes wrote.[268] In the same essay, Dawes chastised Latin American studies programs in American universities for their "political accomodationism" to "metropolitan imperialist centers" like the United States.[269] By contrast, Dawes proclaimed, *A Contracorriente* would serve as a "venue for earnest leftists writing on literature and history who will not accept the world as it is."[270]

This suture of radical politics to literary criticism is a recurrent theme of Dawes's academic writings. In the journal *Postmodern Culture*, Dawes noted approvingly in 1991 that "[o]ne of the major contributions to literary studies in recent years has been the recognition that political consciousness is invariably fused with aesthetic practice."[271] Dawes also had praise for China's "Cultural Revolution" and the Castro dictatorship of Cuba, both of which, he contended, had "been successful in instituting political and economic democracy."[272] Consequently, Dawes is particularly enamored of writers whose works, as he sees them, celebrate the revolutionary vision. Examining the work of Kurt Vonnegut in a 1998 essay Dawes felt compelled to point out what he described as Vonnegut's observation "that capitalism is a monstrous creation of humankind that should be replaced by humanist socialism."[273]

Marxist revolution provides the aesthetic unity of Dawes's academic work. His 1993 book, *Aesthetics and Revolution: Nicaraguan Poetry, 1979–1990*, based on his doctoral dissertation, dwells on the Marxist themes of Nicaraguan Sandinista verse. His most recent book, *Verses Against the Darkness:*

Neruda's Poetry and Politics, is a tribute to Pablo Neruda, the Chilean Stalinist and lifelong Communist apparatchik. In the book, Dawes lavishes praise on Neruda for his communist beliefs, in particular for "equating himself with the destiny of the class which can potentially put an end to class society."[274]

In addition to his work as a professor, Dawes is a prominent activist on the North Carolina State campus, speaking out against American foreign policy and free-market capitalism. In March of 2003, Dawes participated in a panel opposing the war in Iraq. He even delivered a lecture for the occasion, entitled "U.S. Imperialism and the Case of Iraq."[275] Imperialism had also been on Dawes's mind one year earlier. At an October 2002 panel convened by North Carolina State's Africana Studies department, Dawes, whose expertise is literature, delivered a lecture on "Globalization as Imperialism."[276]

See also: Professors Aptheker, Davis, Foster, Furr, Targ

Research: Jacob Laksin

Professor Nicholas De Genova
Columbia University

— Assistant professor of anthropology at Columbia University

— Called for a "million Mogadishus"—the 1993 military ambush in Somalia that killed 18 Americans

— "The only true heroes are those who find ways that help defeat the U.S. military."

An assistant professor of anthropology at Columbia University, thirty-five-year-old Nicholas De Genova briefly entered the spotlight at an anti-Iraq War teach-in at Columbia in 2003 when he called for "a million Mogadishus,"[277] a reference to the 1993 military debacle in Somalia that took eighteen American lives. "U.S. patriotism," Professor De Genova told three thousand Columbia students, "is inseparable from imperial warfare and white supremacy. U.S. flags are the emblem of the invading war machine in Iraq today. They are the emblem of the occupying power. The only true heroes are those who find ways that help defeat the U.S. military."[278]

Professor De Genova had made controversial statements before. At a 2002 teach-in at Columbia, he said, "The heritage of the Holocaust belongs to the Palestinian people. The State of Israel has no claim to the heritage of the Holocaust. The heritage of the oppressed belongs to the oppressed, not the oppressor."[279] Evidently, the simultaneous invasion of the new-born state of Israel by all of its Arab neighbors in 1948, and the state of war subsequently maintained against Israel by the Palestinians and backed by other Arab states, does not, in Professor De Genova's reading of the political situation, constitute oppression.

After both comments, Professor De Genova attempted in interviews to explain and soften his remarks, without notable success. He explained his "million Mogadishu" remark as a hope that U.S. forces would become bogged down in a Vietnam-style guerrilla war. After his remarks on Israel and the Palestinians, Professor De Genova explained that what he meant was the State of Israel was not the "legitimate inheritor" of the legacy of Nazi oppression.

In a 2004 panel discussion at Columbia, Professor De Genova demanded the inclusion of a Native American Studies component at Columbia's Center for the Study of Ethnicity and Race, despite the fact that Columbia had only a dozen Native American students. "We continue to be embroiled in the social relations that make racism a central part of U.S. society," said De Genova, whose page on the Anthropology Department's website states that his current research focuses on the "Homeland Security State" and the "so-called 'War on Terrorism.'"

See also: Professors Cloud, Brumfiel, Jensen,
Kirstein, Meranto
Research: Joseph Wilson

Professor Bernardine Dohrn
Northwestern University

— Professor of law at Northwestern University

— Director of the Legal Clinic's Children and Family Justice Center of Northwestern University

— Leader of the 1970s domestic terrorist group the Weather Underground

Bernardine Dohrn was a 1960s radical and the leader of the "Weatherman" faction of Students for a Democratic Society, which in 1969 went underground to become America's first terrorist cult. At a 1969 "War Council" in Flint, Michigan, Dohrn gave her most memorable and notorious speech to her followers. Holding her fingers in what became the Weatherman "fork salute," she said of the bloody murders recently committed by the Manson Family in which the pregnant actress Sharon Tate and a Folgers coffee heiress and several other inhabitants of a Benedict Canyon mansion were brutally stabbed to death: "Dig it! First they killed those pigs, then they ate dinner in the same room with them. They even shoved a fork into the victim's stomach! Wild!"[280] The victim of the fork attack was Sharon Tate. The "War Council" ended with a formal declaration of war against "AmeriKKKa," always spelled with three K's.

Professor Dohrn expresses no real regret over her radical past. Though she has distanced herself from the Manson remark (insinuating falsely that it was a "joke"[281]) her political views are as extreme as ever. Currently she is an associate professor of law at Northwestern University. She is the director of the Legal Clinic's Children and Family Justice Center at Northwestern and sits on important committees and boards of the American Bar Association and the American Civil Liberties Union.

Professor Dohrn has said of her Weatherman past, "We rejected terrorism. We were careful not to hurt anybody."[282] This is doubly false. The Weatherman agenda was terrorism (which is why Charles Manson was her hero), and war (its career was launched with a formal "declaration of war") and Dohrn periodically issued "war communiqués" to the public at large. The intention of the group was to shed their "white skin privilege" and launch a race war on behalf of Third World People. Professor Dohrn and her comrades did harm people. A Chicago district attorney named Elrod was paralyzed during the riot the Weatherman staged during their Chicago "Days of Rage." Dohrn led a grotesque celebration of his paralysis by leading her comrades in a parody of a Bob Dylan song—"Lay, Elrod, Lay."[283] Three soldiers in the Weatherman's self-styled "red army" were blown up attempting to manufacture an "anti-personnel" bomb that was to be set off at social dance at Fort Dix, where young draftees and their dates would be innocently having a good time. Police are still investigating a bombing in San Francisco that killed a policeman. Professor Dohrn is one of the suspects.[284] Moreover, Professor Dohrn has not dissociated herself from the views of her husband, Professor Bill Ayers, expressed to a reporter for the *New York Times* and reported in that paper on September 11, 2001, that "we didn't bomb enough."[285]

Professor Dohrn spent most of the 1970s with her accomplices running from the FBI, which had placed her on its "Ten Most Wanted List." In 1980, she and her cohorts surrendered, but all charges against them were subsequently dropped on the grounds that they had been illegally surveilled.

Justifying her actions, Professor Dohrn has said, "We organized both against war and racism. We also taught that all human life is equally valid, not just the body count of the United States."[286]

Professor Dorhn has been a commencement speaker at several graduations, including California's prestigious Pitzer College. At Pitzer, she told the graduating youngsters, "During your student years here, the shredded economy and loss of jobs, the consequences of deregulation and devolution that bankrupted state and local governments, the relentless punishment and imprisoning of over two million people in America, flagrant corporate plunder and criminality, rolling blackouts, the apparently permanent war on terrorism, the shock and awe occupation of Iraq, systematic and degrading detention without trial, torture and extra-judicial assassinations, and the establishment of a crescent of new U.S. military bases across the Middle East and South Asia—all have transformed whatever blissful illusions were harbored as you entered college."[287]

One cannot help wondering how Bernadine Dohrn of all people was chosen over all other candidates, presumably in a national search, to get this prestigious job at Northwestern University Law School. Was there no one else available but an ex-terrorist? Since Professor Dohrn was hired specifically in law as it relates to families and children, did the search committee not realize that in the 1970s she had engaged in stealing credit card numbers from parents shopping at a children's store where she worked to help finance Weather Underground terrorist activities?[288] This wasn't held against her in seeking a job as professor of law, and especially of family and childhood law? To be sure, since her appointment to the law faculty Professor Dohrn has published numerous articles in academic journals. On the other hand, most of her output seems focused on arguing against the punishment of juvenile offenders who commit violent crimes. Thus she is still pursuing a focused ideological agenda in which the perpetrators of violence (like herself) are somehow actually victims.

See also: Professors Austin, Ayers, D. Cole, Bell, Matsuda

Research: John Perazzo

Professor Robert Dunkley

University of Northern Colorado

— Assistant professor of criminology, University of Northern Colorado

— Gives final exams that require students to "Make the case for gay marriage" and to explain why the United States liberation of Iraq is "criminal"

Professor Robert Dunkley is an assistant professor of criminology at the University of Northern Colorado. Professor Dunkley teaches Sociology 346, which is described in these words in the UNC Course catalogue for 2002–2003:[289] "SOC 346—Criminology. Survey criminal behavior generally, including theories of causation, types of crime, extent of crime, law enforcement, criminal justice, punishment and treatment." On May 5, 2003, barely three weeks after American troops marched into Baghdad, Professor Dunkley gave his Sociology 346 students a take home exam whose final essay question required students to write an essay declaring that their country's war in Iraq was "criminal."

A student taking the exam answered the "question" by writing that Saddam Hussein was a war criminal. According to her account, she received an "F" for her grade in the exam. She then took it through the appeals process provided by the school, as a result of which her final grade in the class was changed to a "B." During the formal inquiry Professor Dunkley revealed that he had destroyed all copies of the exam and the exam questions, which was a violation of university regulations. For the purposes of the inquiry he reconstructed the exam questions from memory.

The student had claimed publicly that the original exam question required students to "Make the case that George Bush is a war criminal." When the students' claim appeared in the press, Professor Dunkley disputed her version of the exam question and said that it was "Make the argument that the military action of the U.S. attacking Iraq was criminal." Legally, of course, this would amount to the same claim, since the president is the commander in chief. The student contends that Professor Dunkley altered the exam question when he supplied his copy to the appeals committee. In any case, a perusal of all four questions— as supplied by Professor Dunkley and approved by university officials—shows how far the university culture has gone in accepting ideological indoctrination as a norm.

The "questions" supplied by Dunkley require students to: 1) demonstrate their knowledge of two left wing theories ("power control theory" and "Integrated-Structural Marxism"); 2) demonstrate their knowledge of, and justification for, feminist law theory; 3) Make the case for gay marriage; and 4) Make the argument that the military action of the U.S. attacking Iraq was criminal.

Did Professor Dunkley rewrite the fourth question (which is not really a question) after the fact, as his student claimed? Dunkley gave the exam to his students on May 5, 2003, three weeks after the fall of Baghdad on April 13, 2003. The exam claims that President Bush, referring to missing Weapons of Mass Destruction, had said "we may never find such weapons." Here is what President Bush actually said to reporters on May 31, 2003, three weeks after the exams were handed in: "You remember when Colin Powell stood up in front of the world, and he said Iraq has got laboratories, mobile labs to build biological weapons. . . . They're illegal. They're against the United Nations resolutions, and we've so far discovered two [the labs were later judged to not contain any such weapons, that they most likely were used for weather balloons]. And we'll find more weapons as time goes on, but for those who say we haven't found the banned manufacturing devices or banned weapons, they're wrong. We found them."

Professor Dunkley's questions[290]

The following questions are essay. Answer as completely as possible. Be thorough and concise, but make a solid argument and logical case for your answer. Make sure you answer all questions sought. All students must answer questions 1 & 2. Select one question from 3 & 4 to answer. The minimum number of pages per question is three (3) typed, double spaced, and stapled to the test questions.

1. Compare and contrast Power Control Theory and Integrated-Structural Marxism. How do they analyze the family in terms of social class? How does this class discussion relate to crime? Which family members are essentially excluded in their analysis? What are the weak points of both theories and what are their strengths? Which theory do you support?

2. The Feminist movement of the 1980s offered a significant "new way" in looking at law and its affect on women. The idea of equality is an issue still unresolved. Explain what the equality doctrine is. How should women define and respond to sexual differences? Can the claim of special treatment for women be considered problematic? Why? How can this be neutralized? What do feminists mean by "Doing Law?"

3. The taboo (deviance) society places on homosexual relationships and gay lifestyles today is beginning to subside. Attempts are being made to allow gay marriages, which appears right around the corner. Make an argument that would support gay marriages and gay families and explain

how this additional type of family could help prevent crime (use one of the above theories from question #1 in your discussion and Shaw and McKay's analysis of social ecology).

4. The American government campaign to attack Iraq was in part based on the assumptions that the Iraqi government had "Weapons of Mass Destruction." This was never proven prior to the U.S. police action/war and even President Bush, after the capture of Baghdad, stated "we may never find such weapons." Cohen's research on deviance discusses this process of how the media and various moral entrepreneurs and government enforcers can conspire to create panic. How does Cohen define this process? Explain it in-depth. Where does the social meaning of deviance come from? Argue that the attack on Iraq was deviance based on negotiable statuses. Make the argument that the military action of the US attacking Iraq was criminal? [sic]

See also: Professor Castellano
Research: David Horowitz

Professor Michael Eric Dyson
University of Pennsylvania

— The Avalon Professor in the Humanities at the University of
   Pennsylvania

— Wrote a book about the violent rapper Tupac Shakur, lauding
   him as a black Jesus

— Believes that the 9/11 attacks were "predictable to a degree due
   to America's past imperialistic practices, and how it is viewed by
   other countries"

Michael Eric Dyson is an ordained Baptist minister and The
Avalon Professor of the Humanities at the University of Pennsylvania. He has also taught at the University of North Carolina,
Columbia University, and DePaul University and is one of the
highest paid and most honored professors in America.

Professor Dyson's scholarship and teaching are infused with
references to hip-hop music and its notoriously violent and
misogynist "gangsta rap" form. In 1996, Professor Dyson published the book *Between God and Gangsta Rap*, which opens
with a letter to his brother, who was convicted of second-degree
murder in the 1980s. Dyson maintains that his brother was
legally innocent, attributing his fate to the "miserable plight of
black men in America." According to Professor Dyson, Gangsta
rap, which is a notoriously misogynist and brutal genre that glorifies criminals actually addresses this plight. "Gangsta rap's in-
your-face style may do more to force America to confront
crucial social problems than a million sermons or political
speeches."[291]

In 2001, Professor Dyson published *Holler if You Hear Me:
Searching for Tupac Shakur*. This example of professorial scholar-
ship is an attempt to lionize a gangster and musician named
Tupac Shakur, who had the tattoo "Thug life" imprinted on his

abdomen. Dyson lauds Tupac as a black Jesus figure. In fact, Tupac Shakur lived up to his tattoo, embracing a life of drugs and violence. In October 1993, he got into a fight and shot two off-duty police officers. A year later he was convicted of having participated in the 1994 gang rape of a young woman and was sentenced to four-and-a-half years in prison. That same year, Shakur was shot five times during a robbery attempt. Finally, in September 1996, he was fatally shot in a drive-by shooting in Las Vegas. In Professor Dyson's estimation, on the other hand, the rapper "was more than the sum of his artistic parts."

In April 2005, Professor Dyson published *Is Bill Cosby Right? Or Has the Black Middle Class Lost its Mind?* The book attempts to introduce the class war in into the black community. In 2004, Cosby, an immensely popular cultural figure as the head of TV's model "Huxtable family" lamented the failure of many African American parents to look after their children, the majority of whom are raised in single-parent households. Cosby urged the black community to embrace education more passionately, become more law-abiding, and learn to speak proper English. Professor Dyson's book dismisses Cosby as a member of the black ruling class betraying the oppressed.

In May 2005, Professor Dyson was invited to speak about his book on the *Today Show*, where he was interviewed by Al Roker, a black commentator. When Roker asked Dyson whether or not Cosby's statements had any validity, the professor replied, "Oh sure... there's validity always. Tim[othy] McVeigh [the master-mind of the deadly April 1995 terrorist bombing in Oklahoma City] had a point. The state is over-reaching. But the way you do it, dropping bombs and castigating of human beings, that's terri-ble. .... Let's hold the larger society accountable for creating the conditions that lead to some of the downfalls of the poor peo-ple."[292] In Professor Dyson's view, Cosby had detonated a ter-rorist bomb against innocents in the black community.

During the same interview, Roker read to Dyson some statements by Cosby[293]:

"Those people are not Africans; they don't know a damn thing about Africa. With names like Shaniqua, Shaliqua and Mohammed and all of that crap, and all of them are in jail."

"All this child knows is 'gimme, gimme, gimme.' These people [black parents] want to buy the friendship of a child...and the child couldn't care less....These people are not parenting. They're buying things for the kid. Five-hundred-dollar sneakers, for what? They won't...spend $250 on *Hooked on Phonics*."

"You can't land a plane with 'why you ain't'....You can't be a doctor with that kind of crap coming out of your mouth."

Dyson responded: "...Black people have always been creative in naming their children. Africans name their kids after the days of the week, after conditions of their birth. Black people in [the] 1930s gave their kids names after consumer products, Cremola, Listerine, Hershey Bar. So black naming has always been creative. I'm not worried about Shaniqua and Taliqua, I'm worried about Clarence [Thomas] and Condoleezza [Rice], who can hurt us in high places of power in America."[294]

In an interview conducted shortly after 9/11, Professor Dyson was asked, "What do you think about the terrorist attacks on the World Trade Center and the Pentagon?" He answered, "It is predictable to a degree, due to America's past imperialistic practices and how it is viewed by other countries....What I am against is the hypocrisy of a nation [the U.S.] that would help train Bin Laden by funneling millions from the CIA to Afghan rebels to put down the Soviets, and now switching sides to funnel money to the Soviets to stop the spread of fundamentalism."[295] Dyson is simply wrong about the CIA and bin Laden. The CIA neither trained nor paid bin Laden. The CIA only supported Afghan resisters, not foreign fighters. It was the Saudis who trained and paid all foreign fighters, such as bin-Laden (who was never actually in battle).

When asked how Tupac Shakur would have viewed the 9/11 attacks, Professor Dyson replied: "I think that Tupac would say, 'What business do we have being in Arab nations when the tentacles of colonialism and capitalism suck the lifeblood of native or indigenous people?'... America has forfeited its duty as global policeman, by virtue of its own mistreatment of black people."[296]

In short, here we have a professor of humanities who views a crude and violent "gangsta-rapper," a convicted rapist, as an apex of culture, and who views the flying of airplanes filled with women and children hostages into buildings filled with ordinary office workers as morally justified.

See also: Professors Baraka, Berry, hooks,
Karenga, Thomas
Research: Thomas Ryan

Professor Rick Eckstein
Villanova University

— Associate professor of sociology, Villanova University

— Instructor in Villanova's Center for Peace and Justice Education

— Leninist who teaches that terrorism is a product of capitalist
imperialism

Rick Eckstein is an associate professor of sociology at Villanova University, and is an instructor in the University's Center for Peace and Justice Education, an interdisciplinary program that offers students both a minor and a concentration in issues of, "world peace and social justice."

Professor Eckstein's trained expertise is in the sociology of American sports and stadium-building in American cities. He is the co-author of *Public Dollars, Private Stadiums: The Battle Over Building Sports Stadiums*. This is about as far from international relations as one can get. Nevertheless, this has not stopped him from venting his personal political passions on his students in a course titled, "War, Imperialism and Terrorism." In the syllabus for this class, Professor Eckstein makes clear his belief that terrorism is not a product of radical Islamic organizations and ideas, but of the oppressions inflicted by American capitalism. His syllabus explains: "In this class we will explore war, imperialism, and terrorism as reflections of national and international social inequality. As the U.S. wages its seemingly endless 'war against terrorism,' and its episodic wars on other nation-states, it is increasingly important that we look beyond slogans and good/evil dichotomies to understand why so many people are dying (and will continue dying) in the name of peace and freedom. I think of this course as an antidote to our cultural emphasis of reducing complex social phenomena (such as war, imperialism, and terrorism) to moral dichotomies and/or personalities. There is a lot more to these social phenomena [than] 'good vs. evil' and crazy people. However, you should be warned that these more complex explanations often indict *us* as co-conspirators in the institutionalized violence so prevalent in our world."[297] [emphasis in original]

As should be obvious, this is a completely one-sided approach to the subject. As one might expect from an amateur unfamiliar with the vast quantity of scholarly research conducted over the last century in the fields of History and Political Science regarding the complexities of imperial expansion and its causes, Professor Eckstein's principal text is a political pamphlet that is both outdated and primitive: V.I. Lenin's *Imperialism: the Highest Stage of Capitalism*. Other readings include, Gore Vidal's rhetorical broadside, *Dreaming War: Blood for Oil and the Cheney-Bush Junta*; and Noam Chomsky's polemic, *Media Control*, nothing remotely resembling a scholarly text. In his course summary, Professor Eckstein implores students to "start reading Lenin right away."[298] The readings, he warns, are "not optional and there are no Cliff Notes to steer you through Lenin's classic on imperialism."

So that students will not mistake his course for an academic exploration of ideas, Professor Eckstein provides guidelines for the topics he expects students to pursue: "I want YOU to suggest certain topics for our collective consideration. For example, I know at least two of you took trips last year that raised a lot of questions about the United States' imperialistic actions with other countries. Therefore, I am going to leave the course outline vague at this time except for the first topic. During the next several weeks, we will explore the nature of capitalism and how the internal logic of this political economic system makes war, imperialism, and terrorism seem perfectly normal; kind of like economics and politics by other means!"[299]

Professor Eckstein sees Villanova as a political institution that can strengthen the opposition to American imperialism: "Institutionally," he writes,[300] "[Villanova] can make it more comfortable for people to question official policy. They can lend... institutional support to certain student groups, by having a speaker series and bringing in prominent people, who are, if not necessarily against the war, asking questions about the war."[301]

Incredible as it may seem, given so intellectually one-sided a syllabus as described above, Professor Eckstein has been appointed to the Arts & Sciences advisory board for the Villanova Institute for Teaching and Learning. In 2000, Eckstein was awarded Villanova's Lindback Award for Teaching Excellence. This pattern of academic amateurs teaching courses for which they have no qualification is of course not confined to Villanova.

See also: Professors Armitage, Aptheker,
Barash, Coy, Ensalaco, Fellman,
Haffar, Schwartz, Wolfe

Research: Thomas Ryan

Professor Paul Ehrlich
Stanford University

— Professor of population studies and biology at Stanford University

— Author of the 1968 book *The Population Bomb*

— "We've already had too much economic growth in the United States. Economic growth in rich countries like ours is the disease, not the cure."

Paul Ehrlich is currently a professor both of population studies and biological sciences at Stanford University. He is best known as an environmentalist who gained notoriety in the 1960s and 1970s, most notably with his 1968 book *The Population Bomb*, co-authored with his wife Anne Ehrlich, by predicting an impending ecological apocalypse. Among Professor Ehrlich's predictions which turned out to be false were the following:

— "The battle to feed humanity is over. In the 1970s the world will undergo famines...hundreds of millions of people (including Americans) are going to starve to death." (1968)

— "Smog disasters" in 1973 might kill 200,000 people in New York and Los Angeles. (1969)

— "I would take even money that England will not exist in the year 2000." (1969)

— "Before 1985, mankind will enter a genuine age of scarcity...in which the accessible supplies of many key minerals will be facing depletion." (1976)

— Falling temperatures will cause the ice caps to sink into the ocean, producing "a global tidal wave that could wipe out a substantial portion of mankind, and the sea level could rise 60 to 100 feet." (1970)

— After switching from predicting an impending Ice Age to its logical opposite, Global Warming, Ehrlich said, "The population of the U.S. will shrink from 250 million to about 22.5 million before 1999 because of famine and global warming."

In *The Population Bomb*, Paul Ehrlich decreed, "We must have population control at home, hopefully through a system of incentives and penalties, but by compulsion if voluntary methods fail." He suggested adding "temporary sterilants" to the water supply but thought "society would probably dissolve" before the government could do that. Ehrlich called China's policy of forced abortion "vigorous and effective," a "grand experiment in the management of population." Ehrlich's predictions snared a generation of gullible reporters and Green activists in the 1970s, who gave his totalitarian prescriptions serious consideration.

Ehrlich also authored the books *Human Natures: Genes, Cultures, and the Human Prospect; Betrayal of Science and Reason: How Anti-Environment Rhetoric Threatens Our Future*; and *The End of Affluence*.

Over the years, Paul Ehrlich has made the following preposterous statements, none of which has affected his tenured position and lifetime job at one of America's most prestigious universities:

— "Actually, the problem in the world is that there is much too many rich people." (Associated Press, April 6, 1990)

— "Giving society cheap, abundant energy would be the equivalent of giving an idiot child a machine gun." (Quoted by R. Emmett Tyrrell in *The American Spectator*, September 6, 1992)

— "We've already had too much economic growth in the United States. Economic growth in rich countries like ours is the disease, not the cure." (Quoted by Dixy Lee Ray in her book *Trashing the Planet*, 1990)

Paul Ehrlich's career is a testament to the fact that in the current university, outside the hard sciences, there is no bottom line for bad ideas and no consequence for wrong ones.

Professor Ehrlich is also a relentless critic of American foreign and domestic policies. In the immediate aftermath of 9/11, he theorized that a central cause of the attacks against the United States was the unequal distribution of wealth worldwide; that American affluence was resented and viewed as unjust by much of the human race; and that it was incumbent upon the United States—which had just seen 3,000 of its citizens murdered by Muslim fanatics—to convince foreign onlookers that in declaring war against the terrorists' patrons, it was not seeking "to wage war on Islam." Ehrlich advocated that the U.S. respond not with a military strike against the Taliban, but rather with charity and financial aid for the people of Afghanistan; the Taliban, in his view, should have been permitted to remain in power.[302]

In a November 2002 article titled "Getting at the Roots of Terrorism," Professor Ehrlich attacked the Bush administration for "its utter failure to take any steps to reduce the factors that inspire terrorists to attack us," and its "apparent plans to take control of Iraq's vast petroleum reserves." "Oil," he claimed, "also explains the presence of American troops in Saudi Arabia, which enrages some Muslims, especially Osama bin Laden."[303] American troops were placed in Saudi Arabia in 1990 at the request of the Saudis after Saddam Hussein's invasion and attempted annexation of Kuwait.[304]

Research: Ben Johnson[305] and John Perazzo

Professor Marc Ellis

Baylor University

— Professor of Jewish studies at Baylor University
— Director of the Center for American and Jewish Studies at Baylor
— Anti-Israel activist and propagandist

Marc H. Ellis is director of the Center for American and Jewish Studies at Baylor University, a Baptist University in Waco, Texas. Like Norman Finkelstein, Ellis is honored and cited as a Jewish anti-Jewish and anti-Israel authority by Holocaust Deniers,[306] including on the web site[307] of recently deported Canadian Nazi Ernst Zundel. Unlike Finkelstein, however, Ellis has never endorsed Holocaust denial. But Ellis has hosted Finkelstein on numerous occasions,[308] such as at the 2nd Dallas Palestinian Film Festival; in addition, the two sit together on the boards of a number of anti-Israel propaganda organizations, such as the *Deir Yassin Remembered Organization*,[309] which also includes among its members PLO spokeswoman Hanan Ashrawi and convicted Israeli spy, Mordecai Vanunu.

Ellis has publicly endorsed Finkelstein's book, *The Holocaust Industry*, and also Finkelstein's scurrilous *ad hominem* attacks on Nobel Prize winning writer and concentration camp survivor Elie Wiesel. Ellis is proud of his collaboration with Finkelstein and also endorses Finkelstein's activities against Israel.

Ellis holds a PhD from Marquette University, a Jesuit institution in Milwaukee, also no one's idea of a serious research center on Jewish thought. His first position after graduation was at the Maryknoll School of Theology in New York, a Jesuit institution that is not accredited as a research university but is a center of "liberation theology," which is Marxized Christianity and was also the center of the solidarity movement for Central American Communists in the1980s. Ellis moved to Baylor University in 1998 as a full professor, where he directs "Jewish Studies," all by himself, the sole faculty member in the program. The Center web site lists endorsements by a "Christian feminist theologian," but not by a single Jewish scholar.

Professor Ellis has published a series of books, all largely promoting liberation theology mixed with his thoughts about the Holocaust and Israel's endless record of "inhumane crimes." Most of his books have been published with Fortress Press, a non-academic church publisher associated with the Evangelical Lutheran Church. Ellis seems to have succeeded in getting virtually no Jewish audiences, publishers or journals anywhere in the world to take his scholarship seriously with one exception. Ellis sits on the editorial board of *Tikkun* magazine, a leftist, pro-drug, sixties-fixated magazine, which promotes Marxism and New Age liberation theology dressed up in Jewish garb and is antagonistic to Israel's policies. Professor Ellis is a regular on the lecture circuit, especially before Christian audiences before whom he attacks Israel. He is naturally a speaker in demand for Palestine "solidarity" events.

Professor Ellis repeatedly insists that Jews have abandoned "prophetic ethics." But there is little in his books to indicate that he has the slightest idea of which ethics the Prophets of the Bible really promoted, nor that he has even read the prophets. Ellis's idea of promoting the ethics of the Hebrew Prophets is to write attacks on Israel for the same al-Ahram Egyptian daily that regularly prints blood libels about Jews and cites the *Protocols of the Elders of Zion* as an authoritative source.[310]

In Professor Ellis's opinion, Israel's existence is not justified by Jewish suffering during the Holocaust. The only massacres of any Holocaust-relevance are those Israel perpetrates. Jenin and Deir Yassin (neither of which was in fact a massacre) are the moral equivalents of the Holocaust of the Jews, Professor Ellis insists over and over. But in Jenin, fewer than twenty civilians died in the midst of a military operation by Israel against terrorists hiding in the town. Deir Yassin was the scene of a battle in which some civilians got killed in the fighting but no massacre took place.[311] One cannot imagine a more obscene distortion than to compare these Arabs killed in military operations with the Jewish victims of the Nazi Holocaust, especially when the person doing the comparison has never had a word to say against Arab aggression and Arab anti-Jewish terrorist atrocities, nor against Arab calls for genocide.

Professor Ellis is openly contemptuous of any talk about Jews being in need of any national empowerment. Such things constitute "Constantinian Judaism," to use Ellis's favorite terminology, a malapropism picked up—one suspects—after spending too much time misrepresenting Judaism at Christian theological institutions. National empowerment for the Jews is nothing more than conscripting religion to serve the agenda of the militarist state—Professor Ellis uses it to describe Jews who support either Israel or the United States. Jews can only fulfill their proper ethical role in history, which—Professor Ellis is persuaded—is to promote socialism and leftist fads, if they are stateless and suffering. While crying his eyes out over the "inhumane" treatment of Arabs by Israel, Professor Ellis never finds time in all his discussions of the theological implications of the Holocaust to consider the mass murder of Jewish children by the Palestinian terrorists.

Professor Ellis is a passionate endorser of the "One-State Solution," in which Israel will simply be eliminated as a Jewish state and will be enfolded within a larger Palestinian-dominated state that stretches from the Jordan to the sea. This, insists Ellis, is the ultimate realization of the Jewish mission and the only permissible lesson that Jews may learn from the Holocaust.

See also: Professors, Christiansen, Finkelstein, LeVine, Mazrui

Research: Steven Plaut[312]

Professor Mark Ensalaco
University of Dayton

— Professor of political science at the University of Dayton

— Teaches a course on Western Imperialism for which he has no academic qualifications

— Has called for an investigation of Iraq's gassing of Kurds during the Iran-Iraq War, because "the United States gave the Iraqis the principal agents on which to build chemical weapons"

Mark Ensalaco is an associate professor of political science at the University of Dayton, a faculty he joined in 1989. He also directs the university's International Studies and Human Rights Studies programs. Ensalaco earned an M.T.S. in Theological Studies at Harvard Divinity School in 1984, and a PhD in Political Science from the State University of New York in 1991.

Much of Professor Ensalaco's teaching before 9/11 centered on Latin America. But following the attacks, he focused his efforts heavily on a seminar course titled "Human Rights and Terror," and a class called "Political Violence." Of the latter, Ensalaco said, "I see that our students are angry and hurt about what happened in New York and Washington [on 9/11], and as important as it is for us to promote learning here at the University, I think it's also important to promote tolerance."[313] By tolerance, Professor Ensalaco meant tolerance for those who appear to be America's enemies. Professor Ensalaco regards the United States as responsible for the 9/11 attacks on itself. "I'd like our students to understand the historical context of the attitudes that caused the attacks. If the students understand the complexities involved, perhaps they'll avoid the conception that all people of Islam or all Arabs are terrorists."[314]

Professor Ensalaco says he "would like to see a truth commission investigate the United States' support for Iraq during the Iran-Iraq war." He has also called for an investigation of Iraq's gassing of the Kurds during that war, in which American policy was directed towards preventing the Islamic revolutionary regime of Iran from dominating the Gulf, because, as he asserts, "the United States gave the Iraqis the principal agents on which to build chemical weapons."[315] In other words, if Iraq builds chemical weapons and commits war crimes, in Professor Ensalaco's view, the United States is culpable.

In the "Human Rights and Terror" course, Professor Ensalaco assigns students *Through Our Enemies' Eyes: Osama Bin Laden, Radical Islam & the Future of America*. This tract was penned by an anonymous author who is described as a "senior U.S. civil servant with nearly two decades of experience in the U.S. intelligence community's work on Afghanistan and South Asia." The book's author explains that Osama bin Laden's overriding personality traits are not unlike those of many revered American heroes: "I . . . will use several analogies from . . . Anglo-American history that are meant to show that bin Laden's character, religious certainty, moral absolutism, military ferocity, integrity, and all-or-nothing goals are not much different from those of individuals whom we in the United States have long identified and honored as religious, political, or military heroes, men such as John Brown, John Bunyan, Thomas Jefferson, Patrick Henry, and Thomas Paine."

Professor Ensalaco, who lacks professional training in the areas he has chosen to teach, is now listed on the University of Dayton website as a university "terrorism expert."

See also: Professors Barash, Becker, Berlowitz, Fellman, Wolfe

Research: Thomas Ryan[316]

Professor John Esposito
Georgetown University

— Professor of Islamic studies at Georgetown University

— Defended suspected (then indicted) terrorist Professor Sami al-Arian as a "consummate professional"

— "September 11 has made everyone aware of the fact that not addressing the kinds of issues involved here, of tolerance and pluralism, have catastrophic repercussions."

The *Wall Street Journal* once described John Esposito as "America's foremost authority and interpreter of Islam." The former president of the Middle East Studies Association, he currently teaches at Georgetown University, where his dual titles are professor of religion and international affairs, and professor of Islamic studies. He also heads Georgetown's Center for Muslim-Christian Understanding.

Esposito received his PhD in Islamic studies from Temple University in 1974. He went on to become a professor at the College of the Holy Cross, a small Jesuit school in Massachusetts, where he spent the first twenty years of his professional academic career. From there, he moved to Georgetown. He has written more than two-dozen books focusing on Islam's relation to politics and human rights. He was named editor-in-chief of the *Oxford Encyclopedia of the Modern Islamic World*, and has served as a Muslim affairs consultant to the Department of State, as well as to corporations and universities worldwide.

Averting his scholarly eyes from the study of Islamist violence on grounds that it "reinforces stereotypes," Professor Esposito contends that the Muslim world is steadily advancing toward democratic reform, toward an "Islamic democracy that might create an effective system of popular participation unlike the

Westminster model or American system," the latter of which he disparages as "ethnocentric." Forecasting a trend of ever-increasing freedom and democracy in Muslim lands, Professor Esposito wrote in 1994 (a year after the first attack on the World Trade Center): "democratization in the Muslim World proceeds by experimentation and necessarily involves both success and failure. The transformation of Western feudal monarchies to democratic nation states took time... Today we are witnessing a historic transformation of the Muslim world."[317] In the decade prior to 9/11, Professor Esposito predicted that fundamentalist Islamic groups and governments in Arab nations would reject violence and thus would present no threat to the United States. "The [very] term 'fundamentalism,' he warned, "is laden with Christian perceptions and Western stereotypes. More useful terms are Islamic revivalism and Islamic activism, which are less value-laden and have roots within a tradition of political reform and social action."[318]

Impugning those who equate Islamist movements "with radicalism and terrorism," Professor Esposito claims that such thinking merely "becomes a convenient pretext for crushing political opposition."[319] Islamist movements, he explains, "are not necessarily anti-Western, anti-American, or anti-democratic."[320] Moreover, he minimizes the fact that those nations that have adopted Islamic law (such as Afghanistan, Iran, Saudi Arabia, and Sudan) are, for the most part, totalitarian states that export terrorism and egregiously violate the human rights of their inhabitants. "Contrary to what some have advised," he writes, "the United States should not in principle object to implementation of Islamic law or involvement of Islamic activists in government."[321]

Professor Esposito subscribes to the Edward Said school of thought, which holds that Middle Eastern attitudes toward Israel can never be understood from an "American colonialist perspective." In other words, they should be viewed from the point of view of Israel's alleged role as a base of American imperialism. Ignoring Hamas's program of creating an Islamic radical state to replace Israel—a genocidal agenda—Professor Esposito has characterized the Palestinian terror group as a community-focused organization that, in addition to its violence, does a considerable amount of societal good via such productive activities as "honey [production], cheese-making, and home-based clothing manufacture." Professor Esposito described Yasser Arafat's calls for jihad as social initiatives not unlike the launching of a "literacy campaign" or a fight against AIDS.[322] He has defended Professor Sami al-Arian, then a suspected terrorist (now indicted) as a "consummate professional." At the time of this remark, al-Arian was running Palestinian Islamic Jihad from the campus of the University of South Florida, and his activities had been exposed in the press.

Professor Esposito serves on the board of advisors for the Institute for Islamic Political Thought, a London-based foundation run by Azzam Tamimi, a Palestinian academic who has openly proclaimed his support for Hamas and the Taliban, and who has praised the 9/11 attacks on the World Trade Center. Tamimi considers Esposito his "*ustadh,*" or teacher.[323]

Professor Esposito traces the root causes of the 9/11 attacks not to fanatical Islamic extremism, but directly to the doorstep of the United States and what he regards as its exploitation of Muslim nations. "September 11," says Professor Esposito, "has made everyone aware of the fact that not addressing the kinds of issues involved here, of tolerance and pluralism, have catastrophic repercussions."[324] He advises Americans "to look at the proximate grievances, not to justify what terrorists do, but to be able to address, when one can, those conditions which foster the growth of radicalism and extremism in societies overseas. There are real grievances; it is not as though we are dealing with a bunch of crazies. As we all know now, a lot of the so-called terrorists involved in 9/11 were people who came from good families, were educated, etc. One needs to ask why there was this attraction for these people. And why, for a while, did someone like Osama bin Laden acquire something of a cult following? He did because some of the things he appealed to were real issues that exist in the Muslim world and real sources of anti-Americanism as well."[325]

See also: Professors al-Arian, Beinin, Cole,
Cooke, Haddad, LeVine, Matsuda,
Mazrui, Massad

Research: John Perazzo

Professor Larry Estrada

Western Washington University

— Associate professor of comparative cultures and ethnic studies,
  Western Washington University

— President of the National Ethnic Studies Association

— Founding member of the separatist radical organization MEChA,
  which seeks to establish an independent Hispanic state,
  "Atzlan," in the American Southwest

Lawrence "Larry" Estrada is associate professor of ethnic studies and both the creator and director of the American Cultural
Studies program at Fairhaven College. An interdisciplinary liberal arts college within Western Washington University,
Fairhaven has adopted a number of heterodox approaches to
education, including rejecting letter grades in favor of "narrative
evaluations."[326]

Described as a unique "interdisciplinary program," American
Cultural Studies features a curriculum designed around identity
politics, with course titles like "The Native American Experience" and the "Lesbian, Gay, Bisexual, and Transgender Experience."[327] Such courses are in keeping with the program's aim to
encourage "students and faculty to address issues such as race,
ethnicity, social and cultural theory, social economic class, gender and sexual orientation." A website for the program informs
the inquisitive that it "[e]mpowers [students] to examine and
question such deep concepts as privilege, silence and voice."[328]

Professor Estrada is a former chair of the Washington State
Commission for Hispanic Affairs. He teaches a course called
"The Hispano/a-American Experience, which focuses on "the
development of the Hispano/a-American community," placing a

special emphasis on "continuing immigration and economic stratification."[329]

Listed among Professor Estrada's academic interests is the "U.S./Mexican Border." During the summer Professor Estrada teaches a course in Mexico, called "Contemporary Cultures of Mexico." After traveling to Oaxaca students are offered "training" that is "inclusive of seminars" on several subjects, evidently chosen for their compatibility with Professor Estrada's political views, especially with respect to the environment. Thus students can learn about "Mexican sustainable agriculture," and research "environmental justice issues in Mexico."[330]

Since 2002, Professor Estrada has served as president of the National Association for Ethnic Studies, a self-described forum of "scholars and activists" that promotes an educational curriculum geared toward "ethnic studies" to supplant a traditional curriculum of higher education. In October 2003, Professor Estrada gave a talk to Hispanic students at Yale under the auspices of MEChA—the Chicano Student Movement of Atzlan—a militant Chicano separatist group he helped found.[331] On its official website, MEChA describes itself as "part of the intercontinental Indigenous Struggle of the Americas."[332] Its stated goal is the "liberation of Atzlan, meaning self-determination of people in this occupied state and the physical liberation of our land."[333] In his Yale presentation, Professor Estrada urged his student listeners to campaign for the expansion of ethnic, and specifically Chicano, studies on campus and warned that unless students pressed for, and universities implemented, affirmative action policies, "We're going to see a disproportionate amount of Latino students unable to continue on to a higher education."[334]

Appearing at an April 2004 National Association of Ethnic Studies conference, Estrada claimed, "We are in a state of denial about how segregated our education system is. Segregation is rampant in public schools, although it has been legally outlawed. It's residential segregation but it's still segregation."[335] According to Professor Estrada, a "hundred thousand lower income students cannot begin or continue their education because of tuition increases and reduction of state support."[336]

Professor Estrada, a radical ethnic separatist who believes that "Aztlan" should secede from the United States, has naturally used his position as the National Association of Ethnic Studies head to defend Colorado professor Ward Churchill. Asked in a February 2005 interview to comment on widespread condemnation of Churchill—whose notorious essay likened the victims of September 11 to Nazis and blamed American foreign policy for the terrorist Islamist attacks—Professor Estrada lashed out at Churchill's critics. "Churchill," he explained, "is really getting a bad rap for what he was trying to do, which was to explain why events like 9/11 transpired."[337] Professor Estrada had no patience for claims that Churchill's statements were extreme or that his academic record was questionable. Churchill's critics, Professor Estrada claimed, are motivated merely by McCarthyism. "The far right media are trying to create a domestic scare," Estrada claimed. "If we can't find terrorists, we'll create terrorists in our midst."[338]

Besides his role as the director of the American Studies program, Professor Estrada has served as Western Washington University's vice provost for diversity, and its director of affirmative action and equal opportunity.

Among his accomplishments is the creation of the Ethnic Student Center, a student-run "cultural/ethnic" organization that assists students in "being active in social justice," and provides them with a forum to advance "social change."[339] Past events organized by the center include a "MEChA social,"[340] presentations on "Colonialism in Native North America,"[341] and

"Environmental Justice." Members of the Ethnic Student Center also regularly accompany Professor Estrada on his visits to other colleges, where they support his claims that university curricula are insufficiently multicultural and urge administrators to make "diversity" a top priority on campus.[342]

See also: Professors Gutierrez, Navarro, Perez

Research: Jacob Laksin

Professor Matthew Evangelista
Cornell University

— Professor of government, Cornell University
— Director of the Peace Studies Program
— Took part in anti-war teach-in and signed letter urging Cornell faculty to speak out against Iraq war in class

Matthew Evangelista is professor of government and the director of the Peace Studies Program at Cornell University. Professor Evangelista's academic writings have dealt with the peace movement during the Cold War and the conflict itself. In a compendium of academic writings called *Ending the Cold* War, Evangelista claims that "Soviet reformers" like Gorbachev pursued arms control negotiations "despite" such Reagan administration policies as the Strategic Defense Initiative, rather than because of them, as is the consensus among many historians.[343] In his view, the Soviet dictator Michael Gorbachev is to be credited with bringing an end to the Cold War.

The same theme is prominent in Professor Evangelista's book, *Innovation and the Arms Race: How the United States and the Soviet Union Develop New Military Technologies*, which disparages American efforts to develop a missile defense system, and alleges that the commercial pressures of arms suppliers in the "military-industrial complex" propelled the Cold War arms race more than any Soviet threat. Professor Evangelista has predicated an entire course around his idiosyncratic account of the Cold War's end.[344]

Other courses taught by Professor Evangelista draw on such standbys of the ideological academy, namely identity politics. Typical is Evangelista's course, "Gender, Nationalism, and War," which takes as its subject the "relevance of gender to nationalism, conflict, and war," and explores the "political formation of gender identity."[345]

Upon assuming the directorship of the Peace Studies Program at Cornell in July 2002, Professor Evangelista vowed to turn his "attention to how the war against terrorism relates to questions of just war theory and international law."[346] Instead, Professor Evangelista directed his energies simply toward opposing the war on terror.

In November 2002, as both political parties authorized the use of force to remove Saddam Hussein as a threat to the peace, Professor Evangelista published an article blaming the United States for Saddam's criminal regime: "If Saddam Hussein is a monster…then the United States is in many respects his Dr. Frankenstein."[347] In the same article, Professor Evangelista explained that "the United States intends to continue its military domination of the world,"[348] and warned "that other major powers should be concerned about U.S. pretensions to act independently of any international legal constraints."[349]

The following month, Professor Evangelista took part in a teach-in to protest America's policy in Iraq, sponsored by Cornell's "Anti-War Coalition." Professor Evangelista's contribution to the teach-in was a lecture titled "Living in a State of Perpetual War."[350] Dismissive of any rationale for military action against Iraq, Professor Evangelista likewise had little sympathy for the war against terror. Instead he suggested that the terrorists were avenging the grievances of the oppressed: "We should separate those who sympathize with some of the same concerns of terrorists from those who are actually willing to carry it out," Professor Evangelista insisted.[351]

In February 2003, Professor Evangelista played a key role in organizing a series of anti-war events called "Week against War." To mark the event, Professor Evangelista lent his signature to an anti-war declaration by Cornell faculty members. Called "An

Appeal to Cornell Faculty, Staff and Graduate Students in a Time of War," it urged "Cornell faculty and instructional staff to make class time available during the week of February 10-14 to discuss issues relating to the war in Iraq." Whether the academic disciplines of the faculty members had any connection to war and foreign policy was irrelevant, according to the signatories. All that was important was that the professors impress upon their students the "ramifications of the current crisis."[352] As if to justify this flagrant appeal to the stern inculcation of one-sided political advocacy in the classroom, the signatories explained that "we are not only academic professionals but citizens with a conscience and a voice."[353] Whether the classroom was the equivalent of a public square was a question the appeal did not address.

That same month, during a discussion of Iraq with Cornell faculty members, Professor Evangelista declared that the planned American bombing attacks would make American forces look like "war criminals."[354] He further claimed that the United States planned "to launch one war after another; first Iran, then North Korea, then Pakistan and Colombia,"[355] and that American foreign policy was premised on "a future of wars without end." Like other overwrought predictions about American intentions, this prediction of Professor Evangelista has not come to pass nor is it likely to—not that it hurts his standing on the Cornell campus. Professor Evangelista also dismissed the idea that American foreign policy supported political reform in the Middle East: "I don't see a sustained U.S. commitment to democracy in Afghanistan, and I'm concerned the U.S. will not follow-through in Iraq, even if there is a lot of good will."[356] Professor Evangelista's concern did not last long. A year and a half later in September of 2004, Evangelista's name appeared on a political advertisement in the *New York Times*, demanding an end to the "occupation" of Iraq, even as the United States was securing the formation of an independent and democratic Iraqi regime. The ad called on the U.S. to abandon its "misguided efforts to choose Iraqi leaders, impose governmental structures and enforce American-drafted laws."[357]

As well as being director of the Peace Studies Program, Matthew Evangelista is a full professor in the Department of Government at Cornell, which is one of the most important in the nation. A product himself of that department (he received his PhD there) and still relatively young, Evangelista's opinion will naturally carry great weight within his faculty, both regarding the hiring and the promotion of future scholars, for decades to come. Given the intensity of his politics and the overtly one-sided character of his teaching, it is not difficult to predict what sort of scholars he will be voting to hire and which kind he will be voting to promote.

See also: Professors Berlowitz, Fellman, Targ, Wolfe

Research: Jacob Laksin

Professor Richard Falk

Princeton University

— Milbank Professor of International Law Emeritus, Princeton
  University

— Visiting Distinguished Professor at the University of California,
  Santa Barbara

— Regards America as a "proto-fascist" state

Richard Falk is professor emeritus of International Law and
Policy at Princeton University. Following his recent retirement
from Princeton, he now serves as a Visiting Distinguished Professor at the University of California, Santa Barbara, and is chair
of the Nuclear Age Peace Foundation. Central to the theme of
his life's work, which includes the writing of more than twenty
books, is Falk's consistent opposition to American foreign policies, including the War on Terror. Falk claims that the root cause
of these terrorist attacks is that "the mass of humanity... finds
itself under the heels of U.S. economic, military, cultural, and
diplomatic power."[358] Twenty-five years earlier, Falk was an
enthusiastic supporter of the Islamic radical, the Ayatollah
Khomeni whom he hailed as a "liberator" of Iran. In 1979,
Khomeni instituted one of the bloodiest and most repressive
regimes in Iran's history and launched the current radical Islamic
jihad against the West.

Professor Falk is a longtime prominent member of the International Association of Democratic Lawyers (IADL)—a Communist front group, which at one point operated under the
direction of the International Department of the Central Committee of the Communist Party of the Soviet Union. A 1978
CIA investigation into the IADL at the request of the House
Intelligence Committee found that the group "has been one of

the most useful Communist front organizations at the service of the Soviet Communist Party. . . . In the 31 years of the IADL's existence, it has so consistently demonstrated its support of Moscow's foreign policy objectives, and is so tied in with other front organizations and the Communist press, that it is difficult for it to pretend that its judgments are fair or relevant to basic legal tenets."[359]

The IADL is closely affiliated, both through its membership and ideology, with the National Lawyers Guild, an organization created as a Soviet front, which embraces its Communist heritage. Following the 9/11 attacks, the Guild launched a national campaign to repeal the Patriot Act—arguing that its provisions trample on people's civil liberties. The Guild similarly opposes the Domestic Security Enhancement Act and the use of military tribunals for captured combatants in the War on Terror. Falk characterizes these measures to reduce terrorist threats as "sweeping powers" that represent a "slide toward Fascism."

In a 2003 article titled "Will the Empire be Fascist?" Professor Falk cites "unaccountable military power," "uncritical and chauvinistic patriotism," and "an authoritarian approach to law enforcement" as indicators of America's move toward fascism. He alleges that terror warnings and threat assessments as tools used by the government to frighten and thereby control the American people, observing that the "periodic alarmist warnings of mega-terrorist imminent attacks" have not yet been followed by any actual attacks.[360] In an interview conducted in 2003, Professor Falk stated, "Given an Attorney General like John Ashcroft, the domestic face of the American global design is revealed as a kind of proto-fascist mentality that is prepared to use extreme methods to reach its goals. Without being paranoid, this is the sort of mentality that is capable of fabricating a Reichstag fire as a pretext, so as to achieve more and more control by the state over supposed islands of resistance."[361]

Attacking the Bush administration for what he calls its "fascist conception of control," Falk writes, "America has proved to be resilient in the past, as when anti-Democratic forces were unleashed by the rabid witch-hunting anti-Communism of McCarthyism during the 1950s, but this resilience is now being tested as never before, because the proponents of this extremist American global strategy currently occupy the heights of political influence in and around the White House and Pentagon."[362]

Professor Falk's proposed antidote to what he calls the rise of American fascism is the creation of a "Global Peoples' Assembly," a governing body whose members would "represent the worldwide voice of the people in action and decision making." In practice, such an organization would be authorized to direct U.S. foreign and domestic policies, as well as the policies of other nations. In an article titled *Globalization Needs a Dose of Democracy*, which he co-wrote, Falk said, "We believe that the most promising innovation would be a worldwide grassroots campaign to establish the first Global Peoples' Assembly."[363]

Professor Falk has been particularly outspoken against the War in Iraq. In an article he co-wrote prior to the 2003 U.S. invasion, Falk stated, "Nothing in Iraq's current behavior would justify a preemptive attack against Iraq.... There are available alternatives to war that are consistent with international law and are strongly preferred by America's most trusted allies. These include the resumption of weapons inspections under United Nations auspices combined with multilateral diplomacy and a continued reliance on non-nuclear deterrence."[364]

Falk worked closely with the anti-sanctions organization Voices in the Wilderness, helping the group to formulate legal arguments against the UN-authorized, U.S.-enforced sanctions against Iraq. Members of the group met with senior Iraqi officials, and Saddam Hussein himself publicly thanked Voices for serving as a channel of information from the Iraqi regime to the

American people. Throughout its anti-sanctions crusade, Voices turned a blind eye to the human rights atrocities Saddam himself was perpetrating against his own people.

Falk is also the chair of the Nuclear Age Peace Foundation. This group's recommended strategy for combating terrorism is to increase U.S. aid to those fundamentalist countries that act as a breeding ground for terrorists. Foundation president David Krieger states that a "new approach to security [which] must be built on the power of diplomacy and aid rather than on military power. It must be built on policies that reverse inequities in the world and seek to provide basic human rights and human dignity for all. These policies must adhere to international law, and end the double standards that have helped to produce extreme misery in much of the Arab world."[365]

See also Professors Aptheker, Cole, Davis, Matsuda, Navasky, Targ

Research: John Perazzo

Sasan Fayazmanesh
Cal State University, Fresno

— Professor of economics, Cal State Fresno

— Anti-American, anti-Israel. He refers to the two countries as "Usrael"

— Apologist for terrorist groups Hamas, Islamic Jihad and Hezbollah

Born in Iran, Sasan Fayazmanesh is an economics professor at California State University, Fresno. He received his Bachelors and Masters degrees in applied mathematics from California State University, Los Angeles, and UCLA, respectively. He then went on to earn a PhD in economics at the University of California's Riverside campus.

Fayazmanesh's writings have appeared in such publications as the *Journal of the History of Economic Thought, Research in the History of Economic Thought and Methodology*, the *Encyclopedia of Political Economy*, and the *Review of Radical Political Economics*. He is currently writing a book entitled *Money and Exchange*, scheduled to be published in 2005.

Fayazmanesh detests the United States and Israel. He derides the U.S. government's classification of Hamas, Islamic Jihad, and Hezbollah as terrorist groups, asserting that the designation is unjustly based solely on the fact that those groups "are hostile to the Israeli occupation and answer violence with violence."[366]

Fayazmanesh condemns what he calls "the holy alliance" between the United States and Israel, whose names he mockingly combines as "USrael" to show that the two nations' foreign policies are interwoven, inseparable, and mutually supportive. He states, "USrael has been using the accusation of Iran developing WMD for a long time to overthrow the Iranian government. . . . The Israelis, of course, have been repeating the same charge. . . . The USraeli accusation is . . . quite hypocritical. Both countries have nuclear weapons. Both are engaged in research and development in the area of nuclear weapons technology. Both are ready to use nuclear weapons if necessary." Fayazmanesh gives no indication that he sees any unusual danger in a scenario where an Islamic theocracy, whose government has sworn death to infidels and death to America might gain access to the most potent weapons on earth.[367]

Fayazmanesh is offended by President Bush's reference to an "axis of evil," composed of Iran, Iraq, and North Korea. Says the professor, "David Frum, a former speech writer for President Bush . . . took credit for coining the phrase 'axis of evil' and including it in President Bush's 2002 State of the Union message. Frum . . . currently writes for the neo-fascistic *National Review Online*, which supports everything Israel does. . . . The expression 'axis of evil' was part of the neoconservative agenda of making the world safe for Israel."[368]

In Fayazmanesh's view, American policy toward Iran's Islamic theocracy since 1979 has been "duplicitous, irrational, and incoherent, since it was pulled in opposite directions by Israel and the US corporations."[369]

Several of Fayazmanesh's courses reveal a sharply political bent. For instance, an introductory course he teaches, "Economics 101: History of Economic Thought," features no fewer than five works on Marx, including one by Fayazmanesh himself, "Marx's Methodology of Political Economy," which he wrote for the *Encyclopedia of Political Economy*. Fayazmanesh's views on the Middle East, meanwhile, are on display in another course he teaches called "Economics 183: Political Economy of the Middle East." The course has only two required textbooks, one of which is *A History of the Modern Middle East*, written by William Cleveland, a professor of history at Simon Fraser University,

Burnaby, Vancouver, in British Columbia and an anti-Israel activist who has long decried Israel's "occupation." The book offers a politically charged chronicle of the Middle East that apportions the blame for the region's political and economic tribulations to U.S. foreign policy and Israel.

Research: John Perazzo

Professor Joe Feagin
Texas A&M University

— Professor of sociology at Texas A&M University

— Former president of the American Sociological Association

— "Every part of the life cycle, and most aspects of one's life, are shaped by the racism that is integral to the foundation of the United States."

Joe Feagin is the Ella McFadden Professor of Liberal Arts in Texas A&M University's Department of Sociology. He is also the former (1999–2000) president of the American Sociological Association.

The distinguishing feature of Professor Feagin's worldview, as expressed in his writings, is his passionately held belief that the United States is a racist nation. According to Professor Feagin, America's "systemic racism" is defined by "a diverse assortment of racist practices; the unjustly gained economic and political power of whites; the continuing resource inequalities; and the white-racist ideologies, attitudes, and institutions created to preserve white advantages and power." "One can accurately describe the United States," he says, "as a 'total racist society' in which every major aspect of life is shaped to some degree by the core racist realities."[370] "In the United States," Feagin elaborates, "racism is structured into the rhythms of everyday life. It is lived, concrete, advantageous for whites, and painful for those who are not white. . . . Every part of the life cycle, and most aspects of one's life, are shaped by the racism that is integral to the foundation of the United States."[371]

Though his primary focus is on race, Professor Feagin also focuses on America's alleged hostility to women. "[M]ost men," he states, "will not aggressively promote women's rights because of their personal and economic interest in maintaining discriminatory practices. Thus, women must take the initiative in fighting sex discrimination."[372]

America's inherent impulse to oppress African Americans has abated only scarcely, if at all, since the days of Jim Crow segregation policies. "[T]he central problem is that, from the beginning, European American institutions were racially hierarchical, white supremacist, and undemocratic. For the most part, they remain so today."[373] All that has changed since the days of segregation, he contends, is that whites have become more adept at concealing their racism: "We've learned to say the polite, nonracist thing, but that doesn't meant there has been a sharp decline in white racist attitudes. We've just learned to camouflage [racism], to hide it."[374] Explains Feagin, "Most of white America is in denial about racism, but we know just backstage it exists in extreme forms."[375] As Feagin told the Texas A&M student newspaper in October 2004, "There are two types of white Americans: racists and recovering racists."[376]

To compensate blacks for their many afflictions at the hands of America's longstanding racist traditions, Feagin advocates the payment of monetary reparations to African Americans. In the September/October 1994 issue of *Poverty & Race* magazine, he wrote: "Reparations for African Americans is an idea whose time has come. . . . Richard America's $3-trillion estimate of the reparations cost seems reasonable, given the huge amount of labor stolen from African Americans over 375 years. The logical payer is the U.S. government."[377] Since the U.S. government was created only 207 years earlier, the implication is that the United States must pay reparations for English slavery as well.

Anticipating white resistance to this idea, Feagin adds: "[T]he magnitude of the oppression of African Americans by white Americans has yet to be understood by whites. Most whites need to be educated to the past and present costs of racism for

African Americans, as well as the costs to themselves and for society generally.... Transforming white opinions and attitudes is no easy matter, but short of revolution no changes will come until whites give up their ancient prejudices and stereotypes."[378] In Feagin's view, whites who cannot see the logic and the justice of reparations are suffering from a psychological malady he calls "slavery denial."[379] Note the contradiction between these statements about the white attitude towards blacks and the very different statements made by Feagin above, where whites are portrayed as viciously and consciously racist. Now, apparently, they are merely in denial, merely ignorant of the magnitude of oppression suffered by their fellow human beings. Which is it? It cannot be both. We see here the clarity of analysis that has brought Feagin an endowed Chair in Liberal Arts and the presidency of the American Sociological Association.

Professor Feagin is a Marxist: "The Marxist tradition provides a powerful theory of oppression centered on such key concepts as class struggle, worker exploitation, and alienation. Marxism identifies the basic social forces undergirding class oppression, shows how human beings are alienated in class relations, and points toward activist remedies for oppression."[380] Ultimately, therefore, Professor Feagin blames capitalism for American racism. "The Marxist tradition has accented the way in which capitalist employers take part of the value of workers' labor for their own purposes—thus not paying workers for the full value of their work. That theft of labor is a major source of capitalists' profit. Similarly, white employers have the power, because of institutionalized discrimination, to take additional value from black workers and other workers of color. White employers can thus superexploit workers of color. This continuing exploitation of black workers not only helps to maintain income and wealth inequality across the color line but also is critical to the reproduction of the entire system of racism over long periods of time."[381]

Professor Feagin condemns the "blatant, obscene ignorance" underlying white Americans' "deep nativism and racist tradition [that] we need to get over." Claiming that most white Americans object to hearing foreign-born immigrants speak their native languages, he says, "You know in Europe, you're considered cultivated and educated if you speak two languages. Here it's just [considered] wrong."[382]

In October 2004, Professor Feagin told an audience of sociology students and professors that "the white-racist mind is the basic problem on campus and in society."[383] Expanding on this theme, he has said: "One of the ways racism plays out in colleges and universities is in a severe bias in curriculums that only examine issues in white society... a study needs to be done on mediocre white men because the term 'unqualified' never seems to apply to white men."[384] Possibly Professor Feagin is unaware of the multi-culturalist curriculum which virtually all American universities have adopted.

> **See also:** Professors Baraka, Dyson, Richards, Schwartz
>
> **Research:** John Perazzo

Professor Gordon Fellman
Brandeis University

— Professor of sociology, Brandeis University

— Chairman of Brandeis University's Peace, Conflict, and
  Coexistence Studies Program

— "If [the War on Terror] is about terrorism and terrorism is the
  killing of innocent civilians, then the United States is also a
  terrorist."

Gordon "Gordie" Fellman, a former sixties radical at Brandeis, is
the professor of sociology and chair of the Peace, Conflict, and
Coexistence Studies Program known familiarly as "PAX" at
Brandeis University.

The thesis of Professor Fellman's 1998 book, *Rambo and the
Dalai Lama: The Compulsion to Win and Its Threat to Human
Survival*, maintains that all human conflicts are fundamentally
rooted in the desire "to overcome the other," or what Fellman
calls the "adversary tendency": "The ultimate expression of the
adversary tendency is murder, and that collectively is war,"
according to Fellman.[385] Opposing this tendency, Fellman advocates a "mutuality paradigm" of universal brotherhood that
would end war and conflict once and for all.

Professor Fellman believes that responsibility for Islamic
hatred of America lies with America itself: "The only rational
way to address [terrorism] is to acknowledge the humiliations
inflicted by centuries of colonialism and imperialism . . . which
appear to underlie the complaints against the West. Some people who identify with Islam appear to be determined either to
restore the former glory of Islam somehow through force, or at
least to have the humiliations and degradations inflicted upon
Islamic cultures by the West avenged."[386] Professor Fellman

apparently forgets that the European powers did not control the Middle East "for hundreds of years" but only for a brief inter- regnum after the defeat of the Ottoman Empire from 1920 to 1950. Previously it was large and powerful Muslim states, which pursued vast imperial expansion for hundreds of years (includ- ing against Europe) before the Europeans ever got into the imperial business. Behind the facade of "peace studies" analysis, Professor Fellman seems only concerned to blame the West. Pro- fessor Fellman even justifies suicide-bombings as "ways of inflicting revenge on an enemy that seems unable or unwilling to respond to rational pleas for discussion and justice."[387] Profes- sor Fellman evidently regards the fifty-year war the Arab states have conducted against Israel and their refusal to recognize its existence as a state, as a "rational plea for discussion." In fact the only Arab states—Jordan and Egypt—who have made such a plea have been able to conclude successful peace treaties with Israel.

Professor Fellman is a leader of the protests at Brandeis against Operation Iraqi Freedom. "This war has been planned since before Bush became president," claims Fellman. "It sets a horribly dangerous example of preemptive war. It is consistent with Bush's violation of all international treaties. . . . For Bush to claim that Saddam is evil for ignoring the United Nations—if he were more self-conscious, he would be talking about himself."[388] Similarly, in a 1998 essay, Fellman likened Hussein to special prosecutor Kenneth Starr. "Saddam Hussein of course causes vastly greater damage than does Kenneth Starr," Fellman con- ceded, "but the impulse appears to be the same: destruction of the other as the highest item on one's agenda."[389] Nor can there ever be any justification for war, Fellman has argued: "I consider war the way of the weak. Making war is for the imagination challenged, it only reasserts masculinity."[390] Apparently Profes- sor Fellman views masculinity as an undesirable trait.

Professor Fellman has turned his crusade against the War on Terror into a campus-wide phenomenon, creating the Faculty Coalition Against the War and attending rallies as an "anti-war" leader. When conservative students at Brandeis organized a support the war protest on campus, Fellman confronted them and called them "freaks." Fellman is notorious for grading his students subjectively, and for making "personal evolution" in class, i.e., the assimilation of his perspective on the world, count for one-third of the grade.

See also: Professors Berlowitz, Coy, Eckstein, Haffar, Richards, Shortell, Schwartz, Targ

Research: Thomas Ryan[391]

Professor Norman Finkelstein
De Paul University

— Assistant professor of political science at DePaul University

— Asserts that the Holocaust has been exaggerated and exploited by Jews to justify Israeli human rights violations and crimes against humanity

— "The U.S. qualifies as the main terrorist government in the world today..."

Norman Finkelstein was recruited by DePaul University as an assistant professor of political science. At the time, Finkelstein had recently been fired from two New York-area adjunct teaching jobs (New York University and Hunter College) because of his pseudo-scholarship and rantings against Jews and Israel. The fact that Professor Finkelstein was hired after his anti-Semitic statements had made him notorious reflects on the university itself. An entire department voted to hire him, and the DePaul administration approved the appointment. This is the same university that fired an adjunct professor, Thomas Klocek, without a hearing because he asserted in an argument with a group of eight Palestinian students, whom he neither knew nor had ever personally taught, that Israel should not be destroyed. (That September 2004 incident occurred during a student activities fair. Klocek, who is Catholic, told the eight students who were disseminating literature for two anti-Israel groups—Students for Justice in Palestine, and United Muslims Moving Ahead—that their literature was biased against Israel; that Palestinians were Arabs who resided in the West Bank and Gaza but had no national historical identity as a people; that it was irresponsible and inaccurate to suggest that Israel was treating Palestinians in a manner similar to how Nazi Germany once treated Jews; and that while most Muslims are not terrorists, most terrorists nowadays are Muslims.[392] For making these assertions, Klocek lost his job.)

Professor Finkelstein is a disciple of discredited historian and Holocaust denier David Irving, who he claims is an authoritative scholar. Professor Finkelstein refers to the six million Jews murdered by the Nazis as the "Six Million" in quotation marks,[393] and says that nearly every self-identified Holocaust survivor is a fraud, a thief and a liar. Professor Finkelstein's own parents are Holocaust survivors and Professor Finkelstein has long tried to capitalize on this as a way to legitimize his anti-Semitism. In an interview with the German paper, *Die Welt*, he has said: "Not only does the "Six Million" figure become more untenable but the numbers of the Holocaust industry are rapidly approaching those of Holocaust deniers. . . . Indeed, the field of Holocaust studies is replete with nonsense if not sheer fraud."[394]

In his book *The Holocaust Industry: Reflections on the Exploitation of Jewish Suffering*, Professor Finkelstein wrote, "'If everyone who claims to be a survivor actually is one,' my mother used to exclaim, 'who did Hitler kill?'"[395] He added that most survivors are fraudulent and that too much money is spent commemorating the Nazi genocide. "My parents often wondered why I would grow so indignant at the falsification and exploitation of the Nazi genocide. The most obvious answer is that it has been used to justify criminal policies of the Israeli state and U.S. support for these policies." The *New York Times* has compared Professor Finkelstein's book to the old czarist forgery, *The Protocols of the Elders of Zion*.

In a December 2001 interview with *CounterPunch* Magazine, Professor Finkelstein said, "[Jewish organizations that seek compensation for Holocaust survivors] bring to mind an insight of my late mother, that it is no accident that Jews invented the word 'chutzpah.' They steal, and I do use the word with intent,

95% of the monies earmarked for victims of Nazi persecution, and then throw you a few crumbs while telling you to be grateful.... They have disgraced the memory of the Jewish people's suffering on the one hand by turning it into an extortion racket." Also: "If you understand terrorism to mean the targeting of civilian populations in order to achieve political goals, then plainly the U.S. qualifies as the main terrorist government in the world today..."[396]

When asked whether he thought that "the West was in some way responsible for the tragedy of September 11," Professor Finkelstein replied: "Let's put it this way. The so-called West, and really we're talking about the United States, and to a lesser extent its pathetic puppy dog in England, have a real problem on their hands. Regrettably, it's payback time for the Americans and they have a problem because all the other enemies since the end of World War Two that they pretended to contend with... were basically fabricated enemies.... Why should Americans go on with their lives as normal, worrying about calories and hair loss, while other people are worrying about where they are going to get their next piece of bread? Why should we go on merrily with our lives while so much of the world is suffering, and suffering incidentally not with us merely as bystanders, but with us as the indirect and direct perpetrators."[397]

See also: Professors Anderson, Armitage, Bagby, Baraka, Dabashi, Haddad, LeVine, McCloud

Research: Steven Plaut[398]

Professor Eric Foner

Columbia University

— DeWitt Clinton Professor of history at Columbia University

— Former president of the American Historical Association

— "I'm not sure which is more frightening: the horror that engulfed New York City or the apocalyptic rhetoric emanating daily from the [Bush] White House."

Columbia University history professor Eric Foner is by today's politicized academic standards one of the foremost professionals in his field. He is a former president of both professional historical associations and regarded as the leading expert on the Reconstruction period, the tumultuous era that followed the Civil War.

Professor Foner was raised in a notable Communist family—his uncle, Philip Foner, was the Party's official labor historian. Eric Foner was an anti-American sixties radical and as a historian is an apologist for American Communism. On October 4, 2001 following the attack on the World Trade Center, Professor Foner contributed to a *London Review of Books* symposium of reactions to the atrocity. In his contribution, Professor Foner focused not on the atrocity itself but on what he perceived to be the threat of an American response: "I write this in an ominous lull between the talk of vengeance and vengeance itself. The moment any such retribution is sought with bombs and guns will be the moment for the mobilisation of anti-war forces all over the world... [Terror] merely enhances and exaggerates the feeling among exploited people that the matter of protest has to be left to a few martyrs. And just as the signs were growing of a renewed confidence in the world anti-capitalist movement, the attention of the world's leaders is focused on a single, dreadful act that gives them the excuse they need to gun the engines of oppression."[399]

In March 2003, as American forces entered Iraq to overthrow the Saddam dictatorship, Professor Foner participated in an anti-war "teach in" at Columbia University, where he invoked Communist Party icon Paul Robeson as a model of patriotism. "I refuse to cede the definition of American patriotism to George W. Bush," Professor Foner declared. "I have a different definition of patriotism, which comes from Paul Robeson: 'The patriot is the person who is never satisfied with his country.'"[400] Robeson, a recipient of the Stalin Peace Prize, had made headlines in the early Cold War by proclaiming that "American Negroes" would not fight to defend America in a war against the Soviet Union. Professor Foner had been preceded on the podium by fellow Columbia professor Nicholas De Genova, who told the 3,000 students and faculty in attendance, "The only true heroes are those who find ways that help defeat the U.S. military. I personally would like to see a million Mogadishus."[401] This was a reference to the 1993 killing and public mutilation of eighteen American soldiers killed by Muslim rebels in Mogadishu, Somalia.

In Professor Foner's view hostility towards America was warranted by America's historical record. "A study of our history in its international context might help to explain why there is widespread fear outside our borders that the war on terrorism is motivated in part by the desire to impose a Pax Americana in a grossly unequal world." In a September 2004 article for the *History News Network*, Foner wrote that the hostility to the United States was "based primarily on American policies—toward Israel, the Palestinians, oil supplies, the region's corrupt and authoritarian regimes, and, most recently, Iraq."[402]

In a lengthy review of Professor Foner's academic work, the liberal intellectual historian John Diggins wrote, "[Eric] Foner... is both an unabashed apologist for the Soviet system and an unforgiving historian of America."[403] Foner's history of the United States, *The Story of American Freedom*, was caustically dismissed by historian Theodore Draper, who called it a work more accurately described as "the story of unfreedom." Writing in the *New York Review of Books*, Draper characterized Foner as "a partisan of radical sects and opinions" and described his narrative as "a tale of hopeful efforts that failed and of dissident voices that cried out in the wilderness." A distinctive feature of Foner's history was his attempt "to rehabilitate American Communism." Draper summed up: "From [Foner's] account it would be hard to understand why so many millions of immigrants should have come to the United States for more freedom."

Professor Foner has written a new introductory text to American history, *Give Us Liberty*, which was adopted by 300 collegiate institutions in its first year.[404]

> **See also:** Professors Dabashi, De Genova, Gitlin, Marable, Massad, Zinn
>
> **Research:** David Horowitz[405]

Professor John Bellamy Foster
University of Oregon, Eugene

— Associate professor of sociology

— Editor of the Marxist magazine *Monthly Review*

— Considers the collapse of the Soviet empire a setback for human progress

John Bellamy Foster has taught at the University of Oregon, Eugene campus since 1985. Among the courses Foster teachers are "Social Movements," "Marxist Sociological Theory," and "Classical Marxist Theory." Foster is a member of the American Sociological Association as well as the Union for Radical Political Economics. He has been a speaker and panelist for several years at the annual Socialist Scholars Conference in New York City and was an invited speaker at the Marxism 2002 Conference in London.

Since 1996, Foster has been an editor of the international academic journal of ecosocial research *Organization & Environment.* He has also been an editorial board member of the British Routledge journal *Capitalism, Nature, Socialism,* which describes itself as "an international red-green journal of theory and politics."

In 1992, Professor Foster became an editor of *Monthly Review,* founded by Paul Sweezy and Leo Huberman. The magazine was close to the Communist Party but independent. Its political line shifted from fellow-traveling Stalinism to Maoism after 1957. Foster was co-editor of *Monthly Review* from 2001 until 2004 with Robert W. McChesney, a professor and co-founder of the "media reform" organization Free Press. Since McChesney's departure as co-editor in 2004, Foster has been *Monthly Review*'s sole editor.

In an academic world of publish-or-perish, many Foster books and articles have been published—most of them, conveniently, by *Monthly Review* and Monthly Review Press, both under his control. These include Foster's books *The Theory of Monopoly Capitalism* (1986, MRP) and *Ecology Against Capitalism* (2002, MRP). Foster is also the editor of *Hungry for Profit: The Agribusiness Threat to Farmers, Food, and the Environment* (2000, MRP) and *Pox Americana: Exposing the American Empire* (2005). This anthology includes essays by radical Noam Chomsky, former Weather Underground domestic terrorist group leader Bernardine Dohrn, and others.

In an interview with one of his *Monthly Review* writers, Professor Foster said, "The dominant thrust nowadays is toward what might be called the privatization of nature." Foster advocates "the socialization of nature. . . . the more that nature is placed under the protection of people in general through democratic processes that determine the rules of sustainability, the better things are going to be."[406] Government, in other words, should "own" nature.

Accordingly, Professor Foster regrets the collapse of Communism. "The fall of the Soviet bloc made matters worse," wrote Professor Foster in the March 2005 *Monthly Review*, "in the sense that there were now seemingly no obstacles to the universalization of capitalism, and thus no reason for the system to present itself any longer in sheep's clothing. Beginning in the 1990s the world witnessed an even more dramatic shift toward naked capitalism, heartless both in its treatment of workers and its domination of those countries at the bottom of the global hierarchy. Both class struggle from above and imperialism were intensified in the wake of capitalism's triumph in the Cold War."[407] Never mind that with the collapse of the Soviet empire, the world discovered that government-created environmental catastrophes on a scale far worse than anything in the capitalist

West were commonplace in the "People's Democracies." The scale of ecological degradation inflicted by Soviet Communism has been known since at least the mid-1990s.[408] Professor Foster evidently has not noticed.

In the same issue of *Monthly Review*, Professor Foster revealed himself to be an adherent of the most extreme global warming scenario. "It is now rational, as Jared Diamond explains in his new book *Collapse*," he wrote, "to consider the possibility of the ecological collapse of global capitalist society, in ways analogous to earlier ecological collapses of civilizations."[409] Global warming is happening, Foster suggests, because of the end of the Cold War and collapse of Soviet socialism, which unleashed rapacious capitalism. "[T]he problem is capitalism," Professor Foster writes; "the only solution, as difficult as this may be to contemplate at the present time [March 2005], is socialism."[410]

Thomas Jefferson once observed that "to compel a man to furnish contributions of money for the propagation of opinions which he disbelieves and abhors is sinful and tyrannical."[411] It is likely that working Americans in Oregon would probably share Jefferson's disgust if they were aware of the Marxist religion of hatred for economic liberty and for America that their tax dollars subsidize at their state university.

Research: Lowell Ponte

Professor H. Bruce Franklin

Rutgers University

— John Cotton Dana Professor of English and American Studies,
Rutgers University

— Co-founder of the Bay Area Revolutionary Union, a Maoist
vanguard

— Editor of *The Essential Stalin.* ("Stalin is the opposite of what we
in the capitalist world have been programmed to believe.")

In 1969, as an associate professor of English at Stanford University, H. Bruce Franklin co-founded the Bay Area Revolutionary organization as a Maoist vanguard. His partners in creating the organization were Bob Avakian (who would later become the cult leader of the Revolutionary Communist Party) and Stephen Charles Hamilton, formerly a member of the Progressive Labor Party, also a Maoist group. Based in the San Francisco Bay area and drawing many of its members from Stanford, Professor Franklin's group embraced the ideals of armed struggle in the hopes of establishing a "dictatorship of the proletariat" in the United States.

In 1971, a factional dispute caused Professor Franklin, formerly a military intelligence officer, to leave the organization taking about half of its 500-odd members with him. The dispute centered on the issue of "armed struggle." Avakian's faction maintained that violent revolution should not begin for another fifteen years or so, while the impatient Professor Franklin and his followers wanted to begin acts of terror immediately. Avakian eventually renamed the organization the Revolutionary Communist Party, which is a campus presence today.

Meanwhile, Professor Franklin established a new organization, Venceremos (Spanish for "We will win" and a slogan of

Fidel Castro). Calling for the victory of Maoism everywhere, Venceremos demanded that its members maintain a passionate commitment to armed struggle. Venceremos supported the victory of the North Vietnamese, and voiced its commitment to violence to support the Communist side in the war. Each Venceremos member was required to own four specific types of guns. A *San Francisco Examiner* reporter who interviewed Professor Franklin at the time summarized the Venceremos agenda as Professor Franklin described it to him: Encourage young men "not to fight the draft. Go to Vietnam and shoot your commanding officer. Become an airplane mechanic and learn to sabotage planes. . . . [A]ll police and members of their families must be killed and law enforcement demoralized. All jails and prisons must be opened and inmates liberated."[412] An outgrowth of Venceremos was the notorious Symbionese Liberation Army (SLA) terrorist group that kidnapped Patricia Hearst in 1974. Venceremos provided most of the SLA's members and support.

In 1972, Professor Franklin was fired from his tenured professorship for having delivered three on-campus speeches that led to violence and rioting on campus. Only after listening to 110 witnesses testify during a six-week period did a seven-member Advisory Board vote 5–2 in favor of his dismissal. That decision was endorsed by Stanford president Richard Lyman and was upheld by the Board of Trustees by a margin of 20–2. Professor Franklin later sued the university in an attempt to regain his job, but lost in court.

In that same year, Professor Franklin edited *The Essential Stalin*. Identifying himself as a Communist, Franklin wrote, "I used to think of Joseph Stalin as a tyrant and butcher who jailed and killed millions. . . . But, to about a billion people today, Stalin is the opposite of what we in the capitalist world have been programmed to believe. . . . If we are to understand Stalin at all, and evaluate him from the point of view of either of the two major opposing classes, we must see him, like all historical figures, as a being created by his times and containing the contradictions of those times. . . . In 1952, the Soviet Union was the second greatest industrial, scientific, and military power in the world. . . . From a Communist point of view, Stalin was certainly one of the greatest of revolutionary leaders. . . ."[413]

Today Professor Franklin holds an endowed chair in the English Department at Rutgers University, implying that there was no more qualified candidate than a man who was an admirer of Stalin and had already lost a tenured position because he had incited students to acts of violence. In 2000, Professor Franklin published a book titled *Vietnam and Other American Fantasies*, which, according to one enthusiastic reviewer, "is the product of [his] long history of critical analysis of the United States' imperial arrogance." The text is widely used in college courses. According to Professor Franklin, "Countless Americans came to see the people of Vietnam fighting against U.S. forces as anything but an enemy to be feared and hated. Tens of millions sympathized with their suffering, many came to identify with their 2,000-year struggle for independence, and some even found them an inspiration for their own lives." Franklin was one of the signatories to the Historians Against the War [in Iraq] 2003 denunciation of America's effort to liberate Iraq.

See also: Professors Aptheker, Baraka, Davis, Furr, Targ

Research: John Perazzo

Professor Grover Furr
Montclair State University

— Associate professor of English at Montclair State University

— Believes it was "morally wrong" for the United States to bring about the collapse of the Soviet Union

— "What [American universities] need, and would much benefit from, is more Marxists, radicals, leftists—all terms conventionally applied to those who fight against exploitation, racism, sexism, and capitalism."

Since 1970, Grover Furr has been a professor of English at Montclair State University in Montclair, New Jersey. While his academic expertise is in medieval English literature, he presents himself as an expert on Communism, which he embraces. "Was there something morally wrong in trying to bring down the Soviet Union?" asks Furr. "I think the only honest answer possible is: Yes, it was wrong."[414]

In a speech delivered at the First Unitarian Universalist Church of Essex County in New Jersey, Furr said, "I think the reason Stalin is vilified is because, in his day at the helm of the Soviet Union, the exploiters all over the world had something to worry about! That's why I feel some kinship with Stalin and the Communist movement of his day." And not only his day: "What the majority of humanity needs today is an International like [the Communist International] to co-ordinate the fight against exploitation—just as the IMF and the World Bank, Exxon and Reebok, the U.S. and French and the other governments, coordinate the fight FOR exploitation." A copy of the entire speech appears on his academic website, which is a site his students must use as a study resource.[415]

Although not a historian, Furr frequents the "Historians of American Communism" net,[416] a scholarly forum. There he engages in arguments with actual experts, for instance denying that Stalin's government was responsible for the Katyn Massacre of 15,000 Polish Army officers during World War II (even though the Soviet government under Gorbachev admitted Soviet guilt and actually apologized to Poland), or denying Stalin's well-documented campaign to liquidate the Jews: "The mass murder of Jews, but not only of Jews, by the Nazis is very well documented. In the case of the Cold War horror stories demonizing Stalin, the shoe is on the other foot—all the evidence points in the opposite direction."[417] On another occasion, he wrote: "Of the hoary horror tales virtually taken for granted as true concerning Stalin, I have researched many at this point in my life, and have yet to find a single one that is true, or anywhere near it."[418] Scholars participating in the forum generally find Furr's positions alternately amusing and irritating, but generally absurd.

At Montclair State University, Professor Furr teaches a "General Humanities" course described on his website as "an introduction to Western European culture and society from the Ancient World through the Middle Ages." Required reading for the course includes Ronald Takaki, a prominent multiculturalist whose view of America's oppression of minorities is only a shade more moderate than Ward Churchill's; Rodney Hilton, a British Communist; and G.E.M. de Ste Croix, whose *The Class Struggle in the Ancient Greek World* is a Marxist tract. Another of Furr's courses, titled "The Great Books and Ideas,"[419] offers more radical fare. Readings for the course include works by Karl Marx, a Marxist analysis of Shakespeare by Richard Wilson, a book by Communist Party member Ted Allen, another by Marxist feminist Silvia Federici, and one by radical activist Marcus Rediker, who has worked to win a new trial for convicted cop killer and leftist icon Mumia Abu-Jamal. So much for "great ideas."

Although Professor Furr has no training or credentials either as a historian of the United States or as a historian of southeast

Asia, he is allowed by the Montclair State University central administration to teach a course on the Vietnam War. As one might expect from an amateur guided by political agendas, Professor Furr uses the course to vent his political passions on his helpless students. "The Western imperialists, the U.S. among them, are the biggest mass murderers in history. . . . The U.S. is even more guilty [of genocide] than Pol Pot. . . . It was a good thing that the U.S. 'lost' in Vietnam. . . . If the U.S. and their South Vietnamese stooges had won, South Vietnam would have been yet another place for American companies to move to. Hundreds of thousands more American workers would have lost their jobs. . . . *Under no circumstances, therefore, should we ever support the U.S. government or believe what it says.*"[420] [emphasis in original]

A number of Professor Furr's views are taken directly from *Challenge*, the Progressive Labor Party's (Maoist) newspaper. Opinion pieces written by Professor Furr, on the other hand, are published in the school newspaper, *The Montclarion*, and also posted on his Montclair University website, where he celebrates the violence that took place in Los Angeles after the 1992 Rodney King verdict as a "rebellion," accuses the U.S. of being behind the 1981 assassination attempt on Pope John Paul II,[421] and echoes the views of Ward Churchill and Noam Chomsky that on September 11, 2001 the U.S. got what it deserved.

Professor Furr is involved in the Modern Languages Association, whose recommendations are often implemented in secondary schools. Professor Furr heads the association's radical caucus,[422] which wields significant influence in the organization.

A sampling of the views of forty of Professor Furr's students is available on RateMyProfessors.com.[423] Among the comments: "I can't believe this man is teaching!" "He sends you radical left wing propaganda almost every day through email." "Pretend to be a communist and he'll think you're the greatest thing ever."

"He uses the classroom as a platform to teach his radical political views." "Hates the USA."

In Professor Furr's view, universities are not radical enough. "What [American universities] need, and would much benefit from, is more Marxists, radicals, leftists—all terms conventionally applied to those who fight against exploitation, racism, sexism, and capitalism. We can never have too many of these, just as we can never have too few 'conservatives.'"[424]

> ***See also:*** Professors Aptheker, Davis, Foster,
> Franklin, Targ
> ***Research:*** Rocco DiPippo[425]

Professor Melissa Gilbert

Temple University

— Associate professor of geography and urban studies, Temple
  University
— Favors a teaching approach that puts political "social action at
  the center of academic projects"
— Enlists students to conduct research substantiating her
  opposition to welfare reform as part of their coursework

Melissa Gilbert is an associate professor of geography and
urban studies in the Department of Ethnic Studies at Temple
University. Professor Gilbert's academic interests include such
political sub-specialties as "feminist geography" as well as "feminist and critical race theory." Also listed among Professor
Gilbert's areas of expertise are political advocacy initiatives disguised as scholarship. These include Professor Gilbert's zeal for
"labor and community organizing," and her affinity for "economic empowerment."[426]

Professor Gilbert's scholarly research is framed by her enthusiasm for political "social action." In fact, she regards the roles of
political activist and professional educator as one and the same.
Her academic website notes that "because she is interested in
social change, and the role of academics and research in this
process, she has utilized social action research as part of a
broader feminist methodology."[427] In other words, her research is
self-consciously ideological and is driven by her fervent desire to
impose her political agendas on the world.

Toward this end, Professor Gilbert is an exponent of what she
calls "service learning." In practice, this amounts to a sustained
effort to inculcate political activism in her students by providing
them with "opportunities to participate in community organiza-

tions," and exposing them to "contexts for supporting community and grassroots efforts at social transformation."[428] In a 2004 academic paper expounding the merits of this approach, Professor Gilbert explained that it "positions social action at the center of academic projects."[429]

Chief among these projects is Professor Gilbert's ongoing campaign to oppose welfare reform. In 1998, for example, Professor Gilbert attempted to establish a "service learning program" in the Department of Geography and Urban Studies at Temple "to document human rights violations related to welfare reform."[430] It is a measure of her success that the "research" that current Temple students are assigned to conduct is aimed primarily at confirming Professor Gilbert's assertion that work requirements "reduce the ability of [welfare] recipients to pursue educational goals" and, against all logic, that seeking employment makes it difficult for "poor women [to] attain economic self-sufficiency."[431]

Professor Gilbert concedes that programs that fuse academics and left-wing activism pose some "ethical problems."[432] Nevertheless, she advocates "moving beyond course by course learning approaches." The reason, according to Professor Gilbert, is that "these [activist] types of programs...help mitigate the unequal power relations between the university and the community." So important is this goal to Professor Gilbert that she asserts that politically motivated research should be a "cornerstone of [university students'] educational development."[433]

Evidence suggests it is already the cornerstone of Professor Gilbert's courses. Transparently geared toward political activism, Professor Gilbert's courses are informed by her belief that American society and its institutions are fundamentally racist and discriminatory, especially toward women. In one recent academic article, Professor Gilbert asserted that "most women are in sex-segregated occupations with the attendant low wages and lack of opportunity for advancement"[434] (a proposition that would be hard to square with any data).

Professor Gilbert's course "Urban Society: 'Race,' Class and Gender in the City," begins in tendentious fashion, with a section called "The Social Construction of 'Race': Racism and White Privilege."[435] The title reflects the fashionable view among radical social theorists that race is not a neutral biological fact but is the creation of white supremacists who use it to oppress minorities. The next section of Professor Gilbert's course propounds a feminist version of this radical social-constructivist theory, and is called the "Social Construction of Gender." Assigned readings in both these sections and throughout Professor Gilbert's syllabus are exclusively by radical advocates of these theories. A third section of the course is organized around the proposition that the "internal structure" of American cities is "institutional racism." Again, no texts critical of this conclusion are provided for students. The final section of Professor Gilbert's syllabus introduces students to a variety of radical organizations and movements working to transform society in accordance with Gilbert's own radical politics.[436]

A similarly activist spirit pervades Professor Gilbert's course "Urban Policy Analysis." The course starts from the dubious premise that unjust urban policies in the United States are responsible for the fact that "resources and power are unequally distributed by 'race,' class, gender, and geography."[437] Any scholarly discussion of public policy issues presenting a different intellectual viewpoint—liberal, libertarian, or conservative—is conspicuously absent from the course's agenda. Instead, students are expected to concentrate on a narrow political goal: designing policies that will realize Professor Gilbert's vision of a radically transformed and egalitarian society. As the syllabus for the course notes, "We will also explore what kinds of policies and/or political action might result in a more equitable distribution of power and wealth."[438]

Professor Gilbert's other course on urban policy, "Modern Urban Analysis," follows this pattern. The course is billed as an instruction in those "dominant accounts of scientific inquiry" that supposedly "explain urban processes." The course is billed as an instruction in "Marxism, feminism, critical race theory, and postmodernism."[439] A fifth perspective, "positivism," is included in addition to these four to represent views that accept the unjust status quo.

Yet another course taught by Professor Gilbert, "Poverty and Employment in the Changing Urban Economy," seeks to blame poverty on "globalization" (i.e., the spread of free market institutions) and privatization. Comprised entirely of readings opposed to welfare reform and advocates of the welfare state, the course promises to introduce students to "the ways in which poor people have been organizing against the attacks on their economic and human rights."[440] Yet another introduction to radical movements.

Professor Gilbert, now in her forties, is a tenured associate professor in her department. This means that she will be playing a significant role in both the hiring and promotion of younger scholars at Temple for decades to come. Given the ideological fervor of her views, and her deep hostility to any perspective besides her own, it is hard to imagine that her votes will encourage intellectual diversity or disinterested academic inquiry in her field.

See also: Professors Austin, Bell, Berlowitz, Schwartz, Wolfe

Research: Jacob Laksin

Professor Todd Gitlin
Columbia University

— Professor of journalism and sociology at the Columbia School of
Journalism

— Anti-war activist, author of a book on the sixties

— "The most powerful public emotion in our lives was *rejecting*
patriotism."

A former president of Students for a Democratic Society
(SDS), the largest campus organization of the New Left in the
early 1960s, Todd Gitlin is today a professor of journalism and
sociology at the Columbia School of Journalism, where he
immerses students in the obscurantist texts of leftist icons like
Jurgen Habermas so that they can understand the oppressive
nature of capitalist media. He is also an occasional contributor
to *The Nation* and the *New York Times*.

Professor Gitlin is the author of *The Sixties: Years of Hope,
Days of Rage* a standard apologia for the sixties, critical enough
to earn it credibility, but firmly committed to the view that this
was a progressive rather than a "destructive generation"[441] (the
title of a critical book on the sixties by former radicals Peter Collier and David Horowitz). As a chronicler of the events of that
decade, Professor Gitlin can hardly bring himself to acknowledge the actual crimes committed by sixties radicals like the
Black Panther Party activists who were responsible for a series of
robberies, arsons, and murders, preferring to view their thuggery
as provoked by a repressive society.

Professor Gitlin has been a strong supporter of the Iraq anti-
war movement. He has stated that the very "essence" of American policy in the war on terror is "monumental arrogance." Not
only is arrogance "the hallmark of [President] Bush's foreign

policy," Professor Gitlin writes, but "it *is* his foreign policy." Professor Gitlin participated in the infamous March 2003 Columbia University "teach-in," at which his colleague Professor Nicholas De Genova expressed his wish that American soldiers might be slaughtered *en masse* in "a million Mogadishus."

In an article titled "Varieties of Patriotism," Professor Gitlin recently reflected upon the decades he has spent harboring the belief that his country is ultimately unworthy of his respect and even allegiance. He traced the roots of that sentiment back to the fires of the Vietnam War. "For a large bloc of Americans my age and younger," he writes, "too young to remember World War II—the generation for whom 'the war' meant Vietnam and possibly always would, to the end of our days—the case against patriotism was not an abstraction. There was a powerful experience underlying it: as powerful an eruption of our feelings as the experience of patriotism is supposed to be for patriots. Indeed, it could be said that in the course of our political history we experienced a very odd turn about: The most powerful public emotion in our lives was *rejecting* patriotism."[442] Coming of age in the era of the Vietnam War, then, was the perceived cause of what Professor Gitlin described, on another occasion, as his persistent sense of "estrangement," "shame," and "anger at being attached to a nation." But of course the alienation of the Left from America long predates the Vietnam War and has outlasted it. That is because the alienation is the inevitable consequence of the analysis and agendas of the Left, which reject capitalism and individualism, the very foundations of the nation itself.

After 9/11 Professor Gitlin wrote an article critical of leftists who opposed the war against the Taliban in Afghanistan and even unfurled an American flag and hung it from his apartment window for a few weeks. But he soon re-furled it because "leaving the flag up was too easily misunderstood as a triumphalist cliché. It didn't express my patriotic sentiment, which was turning toward political opposition...."[443] This opposition quickly turned into contemptuous condemnation of his country's efforts to liberate Iraq. "By the time George W. Bush declared war without end against an 'axis of evil' that no other nation on earth was willing to recognize as such—indeed, against whomever the president might determine we were at war against,... and declared further the unproblematic virtue of pre-emptive attacks, and made it clear that the United States regarded itself as a one-nation tribunal of 'regime change,' I felt again the old estrangement, the old shame and anger at being attached to a nation—*my* nation—ruled by runaway bullies, indifferent to principle, their lives manifesting supreme loyalty to private (though government slathered) interests, quick to lecture dissenters about the merits of patriotism."[444]

See also: Professors De Genova, Foner,
              Marable, Navasky, Scheer
Research: David Horowitz[445]

Professor Lewis Gordon
Temple University

— Laura H. Carnell Professor of Philosophy, Temple University
— Director of the Institute for the Study of Race and Social Thought,Temple University
— Structured Temple's philosophy department around "genuinely radical" thinking

Lewis R. Gordon is a professor of philosophy at Temple University, Philadelphia. According to a faculty biography, his work concentrates on "Africana thought and the study of race and racism," and particularly such sub-specialties as "postcolonial thought, theories of race and racism, philosophies of liberation, philosophy in film and literature, philosophy of education."[446]

Professor Gordon is a member of the Radical Philosophy Association and was for many years the executive editor of its journal the *Radical Philosophy Review*, which bills itself as a "forum for activist scholars." In keeping with its radical agenda, the association features an "Anti-Intervention Project" whose mandate explains "What is called globalization is, in fact, global capitalism, under the cultural, political and economic hegemony of the United States." The Radical Philosophy Association proposes to play a "unique role in analyzing the various forms of intervention brought about by this new form of capitalism. As philosophers we can deconstruct the various ideological legitimations of these interventions."[447]

Professor Gordon has written several articles for *Political Affairs*, a journal that describes itself as the "theoretical organ of the American Communist Party." Gordon's most recent book, *Existentia Africana*, was dedicated to his mentor Professor William R. Jones, author of a treatise called *Is God a White*

Racist? A Preamble to Black Theology. In the preface to *Existentia Africana*, Gordon describes Jones's work as a text in which "black liberation thinkers [are challenged] to take seriously the possibility that the signs and symbols of the Western religions upon which they depended may harbor the seeds of their destruction."

According to Professor Gordon white America does not see blacks as individuals, but as a threatening "existential reality" waiting to overtake the country. "African philosophy" is Professor Gordon's remedy. It will counter the "hostility" to blacks in American public life, Gordon argued, because it is "premised on identity and liberation." Toward this end, practitioners of African philosophy have to do more than teach; they also have to "encourage the spirit of possibility" among their students, to "develop a sober conception of 'utopia.'"

In a 1998 essay based on his book *Bad Faith and Antiblack Racism*, Professor Gordon argued for an "African-American philosophy," a field of inquiry altogether different from "the traditional motivations of Western philosophy."[448] What made this racially defined discipline necessary, according to Professor Gordon, were the "humanistic anxieties" stemming from "modern slavery and racism," which in Gordon's view were "historically specific" to black Americans. Nor had these injustices been exorcised from modern American society, according to Professor Gordon. Especially outrageous was the *unwillingness* of Americans to regard African Americans in racial terms, in their "blackness." As Professor Gordon explains, "The problem is that without their blackness, they would disappear; without addressing their blackness, the ethical question of how black people should be *treated*—as all people should be treated, with respect, with dignity—would be evaded."

For Professor Gordon politics is an essential component of a philosophical education: "How seriously do we need to engage such a marriage of inquiry and politics? Consider the fact that right-wing and fascist forces are busily deploying instrumental reason in the service of their projects of a misanthropic future. Progressive education demands the construction of viable alternatives."[449] The key, Professor Gordon explains, is for professors to view their students not merely as seekers of knowledge. They should also be seen as potential agents to be deployed in the service of their "progressive" political aims. "Our students should be the optimism of possibilities," Professor Gordon writes.

An activist approach to teaching requires students ready to be activists. Before coming to Temple, Professor Gordon was a professor at Brown University and head of its Africana studies program where he specialized in "black philosophy." In the spring of 2001, the student paper at Brown printed a paid advertisement opposing reparations for slavery 137 years after the fact. When radical students protesting the ad stole and destroyed an entire issue of the *Brown Daily Herald*, Professor Gordon became their faculty spokesman and chief defender. "If something is free, you can take as many copies as you like," referring to the destruction. "This is not a free speech issue."[450]

When Professor Gordon left Brown to take up his new position at Temple in the fall of 2004, he cited as one of his motivations his view that the students in urban Philadelphia would be even more political than the traditional students of Ivy League Brown, or as he put it, were more "willing to take intellectual risks."[451] Professor Gordon's appointment at Temple coincided with that of a new and like-minded department chair, Professor Paul Taylor, a "critical race theorist."[452] Together they set about the task of reorganizing the philosophy department to ensure that it was "based on genuinely radical, genuinely critical thinking."[453]

In his first year at Temple, Professor Gordon founded a special institution, supported by Temple, to combine his twin avocations, activism and racial politics, called the Institute for the Study of Race and Social Thought. His colleague Professor Taylor is a close collaborator in shaping the programs of the Institute, which has held several conferences devoted to radical race themes. In September 2005, for example, the Institute hosted a conference on "Black Civil Society in American Political Life." Among the panels were "Politics of Race, Gender and Class," and "African Americans and American Democracy," which was led by Professor Gordon and Al Sharpton adviser and Princeton professor Cornel West.[454]

In his departmental course on "Existentialism" Professor Gordon urges students to meditate upon the theme of "liberation." Absurdly for a course about existentialism—which was exclusively the creation of European thinkers from Kierkegaard to Sartre—but wholly in keeping with Professor Gordon's Afro-centrist prejudices, his course is not limited to what he calls the "Western perspective" but includes "contributions from Africana and Eastern thought," including the work of such obscurities as "Nishtani" and "Jones."[455]

Professor Gordon's emphasis on the "liberation" of his students, especially racial minorities, is predicated on his view that minorities generally and blacks particularly are cruelly oppressed in American society. "Generally speaking, Blacks are expected to be attacked and never respond," Professor Gordon explains. "To respond often leads to attacks of either being 'too sensitive' or 'contentious.' There seems only to be room for docility."[456] His solution, besides pursuing the study of revolutionary philosophy, is to support racial preferences. In this, he cites himself as an example: "I am a very proud affirmative action recipient."[457]

Professor Gordon's mission at Temple, apparently successful so far, is to replace a traditional department devoted to academic philosophy with a department of philosophy blatantly devoted to political activism. It is the overt, indeed self-confident nature of this agenda that is both striking and troubling for the future of academic studies at Temple.

See Also: Professors Anton, Austin, Bell, hooks, Jaggar, Jeffries, Thomas

Research: Jacob Laksin

Professor Jose Angel Gutierrez
University of Texas, Arlington

— Professor of political science

— Director of the Mexican-American Studies Center at the
University of Texas, Arlington

— "We have got to eliminate the *gringo*, and what I mean by that is
if the worst comes to the worst, we have got to kill him."

A licensed attorney and a former county judge for Zavala
County, Texas, Chicano activist Jose Angel Gutierrez is a profes-
sor of political science and director of the Mexican-American
Studies Center at the University of Texas, Arlington. Gutierrez
has also served as president of the school board for the Crystal
City Independent School District, and as the Urban Renewal
Commissioner for Crystal City, Texas. He received a BA from
Texas A&M University in 1966; a master's degree from St.
Mary's University in San Antonio, Texas; a PhD from the Uni-
versity of Texas, Austin; and a law degree from the University of
Houston's Bates College of Law.

Early in his activism, in the 1960s Gutierrez worked to
reform public education, demanding equal treatment for Chicano students. By 1967, however, his call for equality had been
transformed into a doctrine of Chicano supremacy, and he
helped establish the Mexican American Youth Organization
(MAYO). For a decade, MAYO was the most important political
organization of Mexican American youth in Texas. While pro-
fessing a dedication to social justice[458] for its constituents,
MAYO stressed Chicano cultural nationalism and sought to
achieve its goals via direct political confrontation. Rejecting
diplomacy in favor of a more aggressive style, the group made its
official logo an Aztec warrior inside a circle.

According to the April 3, 1969, *Congressional Record*, Texas Democratic congressman Henry B. Gonzalez said the following about MAYO: "MAYO styles itself the embodiment of good and the Anglo-American as the incarnation of evil. That is not merely ridiculous, it is drawing fire from the deepest wellsprings of hate. The San Antonio leader of MAYO, Jose Angel Gutierrez, may think himself something of a hero, but he is, in fact, only a benighted soul if he believes that in the espousal of hatred he will find love. He is simply deluded if he believes that the wearing of fatigues...makes his followers revolutionaries....One cannot fan the flames of bigotry one moment and expect them to disappear the next."[459] Although MAYO closed its doors in the 1970s, Gutierrez's radical calls for a Chicano uprising continued.

"We have got to eliminate the *gringo*," Professor Gutierrez said, "and what I mean by that is if the worst comes to the worst, we have got to kill him."[460] Animated by this belief, Gutierrez established the militant La Raza Unida ("the Unified Race"), an association of groups formed in the late 1960s and early 1970s with chapters throughout the Southwest, especially in California, Colorado, and Texas. La Raza Unida was founded on the premise that Mexican territory was stolen by white Americans, and that large regions of the American Southwest do not rightfully belong to the United States. With calls for the seizure of U.S. land as one of the organization's chief objectives, La Raza Unida held its first convention in 1972 and continues working toward this goal today. In 2004, La Raza Unida produced an ad to publicize an August 24 rally to be held in a venue it identified as "East Los Angeles, Califaztlán." The significance of this merging of the words "California" and "Aztlán" cannot be overstated. Radical Hispanic groups such as La Raza Unida and MEChA commonly refer to a mythical place called Aztlán.[461] This is supposedly the cradle of Aztec civilization which was unjustly seized by the United States following the Mexican-American War, and which ought now be returned to its alleged rightful owners: the people and government of Mexico. La Raza Unida articulates its own—and Gutierrez's—immigration philosophy as follows: "We see no human being as 'illegal.' Those who have arrived to the U.S. with heritage indigenous to the Americas, and specifically those crossing the southern border, are migrants on their own continent."[462]

Speaking in California in 1995, Professor Gutierrez said: "The border remains a military zone. We remain a hunted people. Now you think you have a destiny to fulfill in the land that historically has been ours for forty thousand years. And we're a new Mestizo nation. And they want us to discuss civil rights. Civil rights. What law made by white men to oppress all of us of color, female and male. This is our homeland. We cannot—we will not—and we must not be made illegal in our own homeland. We are not immigrants that came from another country to another country. We are migrants, free to travel the length and breadth of the Americas because we belong here. We are millions. We just have to survive. We have an aging white America. They are not making babies. They are dying. It's a matter of time. The explosion is in our population."[463]

In April 2004, Gutierrez spoke in Kansas City at the "Latino Civil Rights Summit," where he stated, "We are the future of America. Unlike any prior generation, we now have the critical mass. We're going to Latinize this country."[464] Gutierrez is the author of a number of books about Chicano activism, including *The Making of a Chicano Militant* and *Making of a Civil Rights Leader: Jose Angel Gutierrez*. He is also the author of *A Chicano Manual on How to Handle Gringos*.

These are not scholarly books but political propaganda, the last one an example of crude racism. (One can only imagine how the University of Texas at Arlington would have reacted to a faculty member who had dared to publish a book with a reverse title, say, *An Anglo-Saxon Manual on How to Handle Chicanos.* Yet Professor Gutierrez has received tenure status from his department and his university, and is therefore authorized to pass on scholarship, hiring, and promotion of other faculty.

Professor Gutierrez once said, "Our devil has pale skin and blue eyes."[465] Notwithstanding such statements, and notwithstanding his intimate involvement with such radical organizations as MAYO and La Raza Unida, Gutierrez has received a number of awards and honors. In 2000 he was named one of the "100 Outstanding Latino Texans of the 20th Century" by *Latino Monthly.* In 1996 he was named "Distinguished Texas Hispanic" by *Texas Hispanic Magazine.* In 1995 he received the Distinguished Faculty Award from the Texas Association of Chicanos in Higher Education. And in 1994 he received the "Chicano Hero Award" from the largest Hispanic organization in the United States, the National Council of La Raza.

See also: Professor Navarro

Research: Thomas Ryan, John Perazzo

Professor Yvonne Haddad
Georgetown University

— Professor of the history of Islam and Christian-Muslim relations
— Criticized the U.S. government for closing down several Islamic
  charities funding terrorist organizations

When White House officials briefly used the word "crusade"[466]
to express American resolve in the war on terror, Yvonne
Yazbeck Haddad, professor of the history of Islam and Christian-
Muslim relations at the Center for Christian-Muslim Understanding at Georgetown University, scolded them. "It's what the
terrorists use to recruit people—saying that Christians are on a
crusade against Islam. It's as bad to their ears as it is when we
hear 'jihad.'"[467] Of course the last crusade—a response to the
Muslim invasion of the Holy Land—occurred more than seven
hundred years ago.

When the media later observed that American Muslim football teams use such names as "Mujahideen," "Intifada" and "Soldiers of Allah," Professor Haddad was quick to defend the team
titles, saying, "Who cares? Why are people so sensitive? *Intifada*
is something that Muslims and Palestinians all approve of. It
means 'just get off my back.' Is the only way we accept [Mus-
lims] is if we devalue their faith?"[468]

In fact, although Professor Haddad has made a name for herself advocating "sensitivity" in the dialogue between Orient and
Occident, hers is a one-way street, where it is only the West that
possesses a deficit of cross-civilizational understanding, contri-
tion, and deference. Haddad's double standards are embodied in
the very mission statement of Georgetown's Center for Christian-Muslim Understanding, which she helps to run, proclaiming,
"Regrettably, it continues to be imperative to counter the

misunderstanding and ignorance of Islam. The Center works to erase the stereotypes and fear that lead to predictions of Islam as the next global threat or a clash of civilizations between the Muslim world and the West."[469] In Haddad's view, as between Occident and Orient, it is exclusively the West that is in need of remedial education.

Since the World Trade Center attacks of 2001, Professor Haddad has used the language of multiculturalism and Muslim sensitivity to attack a raft of policy decisions the administration has embarked on. For example, when the U.S. intervened in Afghanistan in the fall of 2001, Haddad explained, "many Muslims were offended by the U.S. destruction of the Taliban in Afghanistan because the Taliban stood for Islam."[470] Haddad added that liberating Afghan women was counterproductive to U.S. interests, as "Muslim women have formed their opinion of American women from watching T.V. reruns of shows like *Dynasty* and as a result assume American women to be 'whores'."[471]

Professor Haddad's quest for greater sensitivity towards Muslims has prompted her to castigate virtually every domestic response to the terrorist threat. In a speech in the spring of 2004, Haddad condemned the Patriot Act, saying (falsely) "It basically lifted all legal protection of liberty for Muslims and Arabs in the United States."[472] When the FBI closed down several Islamic charities after discovering they were funding terrorist organizations, Professor Haddad protested, "In effect, the American government is perceived by Muslims to have assumed a veto power over *zakat* (tithe), one of the basic tenets of the Islamic faith."[473] Her conclusion: "The security measures adopted by the Bush Administration are perceived both overseas and among many in the Muslim community in North America not as anti-terrorism but as anti-Muslim."[474]

True to multiculturist form, Professor Haddad would have the West respond to its present security challenges not with statecraft or force, but with apologies. In a forum discussing Pope John Paul II's visit to the Holy Land in 2000, Professor Haddad fixated on what she called an "apology deficit" in the West. "It is a fact that there are some Arab Christians and Muslims who are still waiting for the Jewish people to apologize for what they have done to the Palestinians."[475] In addition, she remonstrated with the pope for apologizing to Jews for the Holocaust but not apologizing to the Palestinians for what Israel is allegedly doing to them.

> *See also:*   Professors Algar, J. Cole, McCloud, Mazrui
>
> *Research:* Jonathan Dowd-Gailey[476]

Professor Warren Haffar

Arcadia University

— Assistant professor of political science at Arcadia University, director of the International Peace and Conflict Resolution Program
— Believes Osama bin Laden should be a negotiating partner
— Likens American Revolutionaries to Islamist jihadists

Warren Haffar is an assistant professor of political science at Pennsylvania Arcadia University. He received his PhD from the University of Pennsylvania in "Conflict Resolution and Peace Science." An environmental activist, he also serves as the director of the school's International Peace and Conflict Resolution Program. The scarcely concealed aim of the program is to indoctrinate students in a left-wing understanding of international conflicts grounded in the unswervingly anti-military certitudes of the faculty. An emblem of this mission is Haffar's reaction to the terrorist attacks of September 11. The core of Haffar's argument was that Osama bin Laden was a man with genuine grievances whom the United States could do business with.

In October of 2001, Haffar warned a still-grieving American public against the folly of demonizing the al-Qaeda terrorist. Better to accept bin Laden as a permanent feature on the international landscape, Haffar advised. "Oftentimes," he explained, "these people stick around and we have to look at them, deal with them in a different capacity." Rather than hunting down the terrorist responsible for the atrocities of 9/11, Haffar urged the United States to accommodate him, to "reconstruct his identity in a way that is positive."[477] That is, the brutal deaths of 3,000 innocent Americans had somehow wrongly led the

United States to the "cultural construction" of Osama bin Laden as a savage enemy who ruthlessly killed civilians.

As the director of Arcadia's International Peace and Conflict Resolution Program, Haffar has made his perspective the underlying theme of the program's curriculum. The program was developed with the assistance of the radical anti-war group Physicians for Social Responsibility. Its staff is made up of faculty with an aversion to any existing American foreign policy direction and to any course other than one guided by the assumption that all international conflicts, irrespective of their nature or of the parties involved—even terrorists whose agenda is the killing of infidels—have non-violent solutions. "War," Haffar insisted during the lead-up to the Iraq conflict, "is the least desirable outcome. If we go to war, that means we've failed." How this attitude differs from that of appeasement, considering Saddam's many violations of international law, including the U.N. ultimatum (Resolution 1441) of November 8, 2002, Haffar does not address.

In an observation that would be unintelligible to most Americans but is nonetheless common to many peace studies programs, Professor Haffar claims there is no significant difference between the American founders and the Islamic terrorists. "Look at the strategies and tactics that were used at the time of the Revolution, and that were responsible for our winning," Haffar says. "Rebels were jumping out of the woods and using guerrilla tactics." Professor Haffar deplores the negative images in which al-Qaeda terrorists have been cast: "We look upon terrorists as savages," he laments, attributing the negative images to a biased media.[478]

While Professor Haffar has relentlessly negative views of America's international actions, he is more than willing to exculpate organizations like the United Nations and its leader Kofi Annan of any malfeasance. In the midst of the scandal in which top UN officials colluded with Saddam Hussein to steal $21 billion of the "Oil for Food" program earmarked for Iraqi children, Professor Haffar explained to the press: "Kofi Annan has not been shy about confronting the U.S. That is his role and that is why some people are going after him."[479]

In attacking America's war in Iraq, Professor Haffar claimed to be concerned about children. "If bombs are flying and troops are marching in, it's a terrible experience for kids," Haffar told an interviewer. "They might lose their parents. They might lose their house. They might lose their school. They might lose their friends. War is such a horrible option." Yet when urging Washington to appease Saddam Hussein ("To manage interethnic conflict, you can have a dictator like Saddam Hussein that holds all the power"), Professor Haffar simplify ignored Saddam's war against Iraq's children, his deportation and detainment of thousands of children during the Iran-Iraq war; his unleashing of chemical weapons on thousands more in the Kurdish regions of his country; his approval of government-run sex trafficking in children; his prison for four- to twelve-year-olds; his torturing of children in the presence of their parents to extract information from them; and his theft of the money earmarked for Iraqi children in the "Oil for Food" program.[480]

Professor Haffar is a regular speaker on the academic lecture circuit, where he bills himself as an expert on "conflict resolution" and "terrorism and anti-terrorism." Professor Haffar's view is that all anti-terrorism efforts that involve force are wrong and a "failure."

See also: Professors Alam, Berlowitz, Coy, Eckstein, Fellman, Targ

Research: Jacob Laksin

Tom Hayden
Occidental College

— Adjunct lecturer in politics at Occidental College

— Lectures that the United States seeks to establish an "empire" in the Middle East

— Calls for an antiwar "strategy" to defeat the United States in Iraq

Tom Hayden is a former New Left activist and a current adjunct lecturer in politics at the Urban and Environmental Policy Institute at Occidental College, Los Angeles. Hayden has no scholarly publications, nor does he have any training beyond a BA that would qualify him for such a post—and especially for teaching (as he does) a course on international politics (see below); his writings are merely the venting of left-wing opinions, which also describes his classes at Occidental.

A onetime leader of the 1960s-era radical group Students for a Democratic Society (SDS), Hayden has made his experiences as an activist the organizing theme of his course "Politics and Protest." The activist agenda underlying "Politics and Protest" is transparent in the course description and syllabus. Adopting the vocabulary and specific agendas of the political Left, it explains that the course "will focus on such protest issues as human rights, fair trade, racial and gender justice, the environment, immigration, war and militarism, and poverty."[481] A typical lecture is titled "The Student Anti-Sweatshop Movement." One text is assigned for the lecture: Featherstone, "Latin Sweatshops Pressed by U.S. Campus Power." No text is provided which takes a critical look at the agendas of the activists or at the underlying economic assumptions of their movement.

Other required texts follow this pattern and are drawn overwhelmingly from left-wing authors, mainly Hayden himself (e.g,

"It's Empire Vs. Democracy"). The readings hail the Marxist guerrillas in Chiapas, and incite opposition to "globalization" and "American Empire." The course even includes a special section on SDS, for which students are required to read a single article from *The Nation* magazine: "The Port Huron Statement at 40." Co-authored by Hayden with Dick Flacks in 2002, it is an exercise in nostalgia in which the two authors of the SDS manifesto celebrate their own handiwork.[482] Students are provided with no critical views of SDS, its ideology, its tactics, or its spiral downwards into terrorism—although there are several academic studies available.

Another course taught by Hayden, "The Politics of Globalization," displays the same preference for political advocacy over scholarship. A longtime activist in the radical wing of the environmental movement and as a legislator, Hayden views the course as a training ground for future activists. Although the course claims to address the "debates about free trade and fair trade," what it in fact does is settle these debates in favor of Hayden's hostility towards free market capitalism. Toward this end, the course focuses on such fashionable environmentalist causes as "sustainable communities." The course praises the "grassroots movements linking Americans and others around the world to address issues of economic justice, and issues of corporate social responsibility."[483] The movements praised are anarchist, Marxist, and other forms of radicalism.

Hayden has also leveraged his reputation as a student radical into regular speaking engagements on university campuses. Appearing at the University of Wisconsin in 2002, he delivered a lecture entitled "Saving Democracy from the Globalization and from the War on Terror." Hayden took the occasion to air a conspiracy theory, claiming that the United States had no interest in putting an end to terrorism. Rather, he asserted, the U.S. government was only using the pretext of the war on terrorism to establish an empire in the Middle East, with plans to invade Syria and Iran in the offing.[484] In this connection, Hayden has claimed that the threat of terrorism is merely a propaganda invention of "conservatives inside and outside the Bush adminis-tration [who] are seeking to take advantage of America's under-standable fears to push a right-wing agenda that would not otherwise be palatable."[485] Far from being focused on combating terrorism, according to Hayden, these conservatives simply seek to "justify the continuation of a growing military budget and an authoritarian emphasis on national security."[486]

By 2004, Hayden was openly calling for the anti-war move-ment to sabotage the U.S.-led military campaign. "The strategy," he explained, "must be to deny the U.S. occupation funding, political standing, sufficient troops, and alliances necessary to their strategy for dominance."[487] Beyond denying any further funding to American troops, Hayden insisted that "the move-ment will need to start opening another underground railroad to havens in Canada for those who refuse to serve." Hayden also called for opposition to America's "puppet regime" in Iraq and stressed the need to defeat the U.S. strategy of "Iraqization"— that is, devolving power to democratically elected Iraqi lead-ers.[488] The tactic bore striking similarities to Hayden's successful campaign during the Vietnam War to pressure Congress into suspending all aid to the anti-Communist regimes in Vietnam and Cambodia. In his autobiography, *Reunion*, Hayden momen-tarily regretted the consequences of that campaign, which led to the victory of Pol Pot and the Cambodian genocide (approxi-mately two million people were killed), but evidently this remorse was short-lived.

> *See also:* Professors, Cloud, Ensalaco, hooks,
> LeVine, Richards, Schwartz
> *Research:* Jacob Laksin

Professor Caroline Higgins
Earlham College

— Professor of peace and global studies and history, Earlham College

— Director of the Global Studies Program, Earlham College

— Her courses are premised around community activism; students are informed that they will "be working for peace and justice."

Caroline Higgins is a professor of peace and global studies and history, and director of the Global Studies Program at Earlham College, a Quaker school in Richmond, Indiana. In a review posted online for Earlham's "Peace and Global Studies Library," Professor Higgins lauded *Empire*, a polemical analysis of globalization by the neo-Marxist writer Michael Hardt and the convicted terrorist Antonio Negri, "for its vision of putting an end to capitalist exploitation and ushering in a communist society based on cooperation and community."[489]

Professor Higgins is entitled to her private political views. The professional issue is that her political views are everywhere stringently enforced in her classroom. For example, her course "Methods of Peacemaking" amounts to a for-credit blueprint for left-wing activism. A syllabus for the course notes that it is principally concerned with "social movements and initiatives which suggest new strategies for change."[490] But students are not only expected to study such movements and their strategies—they are actually expected by their professor to implement those strategies in the Richmond community. In the words of the syllabus, there is "inevitably an intersection of practice and theory." Students are informed that "we shall be working for peace and justice."[491]

The students are to begin by mapping "the thematic universe of Richmond, Indiana," in order to identify "challenges and growth points in the community."[492] Professor Higgins does not hesitate to provide an example of the types of "growth points" that students are encouraged to consider. Students are expected to "visit a factory" and meet with "labor union leaders."[493] The underlying idea of the course is for students to "refine" their own theories about "which initiatives for peace and social change are effective," in order that they may "contribute through cultural action to building peace in Richmond."[494] Assignments for the course duly reinforce that mission. For instance, students are required to write a paper meditating on "the challenges and rewards of ethnographic activity for the social activist."[495]

An analogous methodology marks "Theory and Practice Revisited," a senior seminar for peace studies students and one which is intended to be the "capstone" course of their experience at Earlham. Taught after taking the seminar, students are expected to achieve "clarity" about their "personal positions with regard to peace and social transformation." Similarly, one purpose of the course is "to work together to produce analysis of a problem, development, challenge, or approach to social change, which is enlightening for peace theorists and activists."[496] That there should be no doubt about the kind of social change that Professor Higgins finds desirable, readings for the course are comprised, without exception, of works by Marxists and other radicals, including Gore Vidal, Angela Davis, and even the Mexican Marxist guerilla leader Subcomandante Marcos. No alternative social analysis, no conflict or debate with these views, is even attempted—or wanted.

Professor Higgins's course in the "Philosophy of Social Science" is an exercise in anti-Western polemics: "Only in the twentieth century have various African, Asian, and Latin American philosophers challenged European hegemony in the field," her syllabus informs students. They are joined by "women, people of color, and other diverse groups who have also rejected what they consider to be an [sic] European, male-centered approach to philosophy."[497] Professor Higgins makes no attempt to justify the evident absence of diverse views or scholarly skepticism in her required readings: "Against the approach of this course it can be objected that students get essentially one point of view, a point of view critical of mainstream thinking. This is a valid objection," Professor Higgins notes in her syllabus.[498] Rather than remedying this unprofessional curriculum, Professor Higgins suggests that students look elsewhere for a less doctrinal discussion of philosophical issues: "My response is that rather than changing this course, I should urge all of you to take more courses and read more books," she writes.[499] Explaining her position, Professor Higgins invokes her radical belief that the function of a professor is essentially adversarial to the mainstream culture, and that she must challenge the "common assumptions of our culture."[500] In other words, if students do not want to be fed one-sided radical propaganda instead of scholarship, then her only advice is to try someone else's course.

The main theme of Professor Higgins's course "Feminism, Ecology and Peace" is her transparent aversion to Western culture. Teeming with feminist, environmentalist, and Marxist tropes, the course examines "three kinds of oppression—sexism, exploitation of the earth, and class and colonial violence."[501] In keeping with its promise, outlined in the syllabus, to offer "[a]lternatives to oppressive economic social structures,"[502] the course's required readings consist entirely of tracts from radical feminist and environmentalist ideologues.

Despite being a full professor of peace and global studies and history, and the head of an entire academic program, Professor Higgins's "scholarship" is essentially non-existent. It is limited to the editing of a book of impressionistic essays praising peace studies. Her only solo-authored book is a novel, *Sweet Country*. Written twenty years ago under her married name, Caroline Richards, it tells the story of a leftist underground movement in the wake of the 1973 coup in Chile.

See also: Professors Berlowitz, Eckstein, Fellman, Targ, Wolfe

Research: Jacob Laksin

Professor James Holstun
State University of New York, Buffalo

— Professor of English

— Faculty adviser to the Graduate Group of Marxist Studies

— Refers to Israel's 1948 creation as "The Catastrophe"

James Holstun is a professor of English at the State University of New York (SUNY), Buffalo. Though his professional training is in English literature, his departmental website informs students: "My work is generally Marxist, and I think Marxist theory and political practice are more relevant now than ever, given the global dominance of the capitalist mode of production and American imperialism."[503]

Holstun received his BA in English Literature from Georgetown University in 1977; he pursued his graduate studies at the University of California, Irvine, where he earned both a master's degree (1979) and a PhD (1983) in English Literature. Holstun began his teaching career at UCLA, where he was a lecturer in the English Department from 1983 to 1985. The following year he was hired as an assistant professor of English at the University of Vermont and in 1991 became associate professor of English at SUNY Buffalo. Since 2000, he has been a full professor of English at Buffalo.

Professor Holstun has authored two books: *A Rational Millennium: Puritan Utopias of Seventeenth-Century England and America* (1987); and *Ehu's Dagger: Class Struggle in the English Revolution* (2000). He also edited *Pamphlet Wars: Prose in the English Revolution* (1992).

Professor Holstun's extreme views on Israel have propelled him into the midst of a rising campus controversy. At issue is Professor Holstun's insistence on spreading anti-Israeli bias through both the academic and advisory positions he currently holds at Buffalo.

Beginning in 2002, Professor Holstun has taught at least one course each year on Palestinian literature, though he holds no formal academic qualifications to teach in the relevant fields, neither in Middle Eastern history nor in Arabic. His degrees are all in the field of English literature. But in a pattern that is all too common in the contemporary academy, this has not prevented Holstun from using the cover of a "literature" class to vent his political prejudices, encountering no problems with either the English Department or the Buffalo central administration for doing so. The texts for the course are Palestinian writings since the foundation of the State of Israel in 1948. According to Professor Holstun, the ensuing years have proven an unrelieved disaster for the proletarian Palestinians, who have been "occupied and exiled" by the powerful capitalist Jews.

Professor Holstun is forthright about the polemical content of his course. "We will focus on Palestinian culture and society since *Al-Nakbah* ('The Catastrophe,' which is how Professor Holstun and the Palestinian rulers at war with Israel refer to Israel's creation in 1948), during which Zionists drove 700,000 Palestinians from their homes."[504] There is no historical basis for Professor Holstun's statement. Nonetheless his syllabus continues. "We'll be looking not just at Palestine's struggles with Zionism, but . . . Joan Peters's influential attempt to erase Palestinians, and Norman Finkelstein's response." The advocacy nature of this course, wholly inappropriate to an academic curriculum, is underscored by the invidious reference to Joan Peters's scholarly work and to a notorious Holocaust denier like Professor Norman Finkelstein as the antidote. In April of 2004, the Graduate Group of Marxist Studies, at Professor Holstun's instigation, invited Professor Finkelstein to Buffalo to deliver a lecture. A *New York Times* review of Finkelstein's 2003 book *The Holocaust*

Industry described the book as "an ideological fanatic's view."[505] In an email that was reprinted on Professor Finkelstein's personal website, Professor Holstun enthused that Finkelstein's Buffalo lecture was a "particularly welcome event . . . Finkelstein was superb."

Professor Holstun's course on Palestinian literature includes such non-literary texts as *A History of Modern Palestine: One Land, Two Peoples* by Ilan Pappe, a virulently anti-Zionist professor at Haifa University, who recently backed an academic boycott of Israeli universities by English academic leftists. Professor Holstun has said he welcomes the author's conspiratorial narrative, which calls the "expulsion of Palestinians in 1948 an act of 'ethnic cleansing,' proceeding under the aegis of the Zionist 'Plan D,' which systematically drove 700,000 Palestinian Arabs from their villages."[506] The claim is pure invention.

In his class Professor Holstun also screens films such as *Jenin, Jenin,* a discredited piece of PLO propaganda, which describes as a "massacre" an attempt by Israeli military forces to root out terrorists in this Palestinian town after a series of suicide bombings of Israeli civilians. The Israeli effort was actually conducted in house-to-house attacks that minimized civilian casualties among the Palestinians while maximizing the risks to the Israelis themselves. Fifty-six people died, thirty-four of whom were armed terrorists.[507] The Israelis themselves lost twenty-three troops.[508]

In a February 2005 commentary on Buffalo's National Public Radio, located on the SUNY-Buffalo campus, Professor Holstun accused Israel of perpetrating a "land grab" against the Palestinian people, although Israelis occupy no lands that are Palestinian that were not taken as the result of Arab aggressions and as a military precaution against future aggressions; moreover, Israel has returned lands seized under these circumstances when Arab states, like Egypt, have been willing to sign a formal peace with Israel. Professor Holstun also refers to the Israeli security fence as an "apartheid wall," built to keep the Palestinian people caged in and treated as "criminals" and "livestock," ignoring (and/or denying) that the Palestinians on the other side of the fence are there because Israel was invaded by Arabs three times across those lands and has been the target of terrorist attacks from them for more than fifty years. Professor Holstun: "Our media have seen to it that Americans know more about Palestinian suicide attacks than about Israeli attacks by sniper, tank, helicopter gunship, and F-16."[509] The correct phrases would be Palestinian suicide attacks against civilians and Israeli retaliations against the terrorist attackers. But then, Professor Holstun is not an academic expert in Middle East politics, only a promoter of Palestinian propaganda.

See also: Professors Algar, Dabashi,
                    Finkelstein, Haddad, Harrar, Massad
Research: Karen Welsh[510]

Professor bell hooks
City University of New York

— Distinguished professor of English at City College in New York

— "It is difficult not to hear in standard English always the sound of slaughter and conquest."

— "My commitment to engaged pedagogy is an expression of political activism."

Gloria Watkins, better known by her *nom de guerre*, "bell hooks," (the lowercase affectation is hers) is one of the most highly regarded academics by her peers in America and a distinguished professor of English at City College in New York. Her written work, however, is virtually never about literature as such, but rather about the "patriarchy" and race and class "hierarchies" that in her view dominate every aspect of the social order and its culture. Typical of her numerous titles are *Killing Rage: Ending Racism; Outlaw Culture: Resisting Representation; Teaching to Transgress: Education as the Practice of Freedom; Art On My Mind: Visual Politics; We Real Cool: Black Men and Masculinity; Reel to Real: Race, Sex and Class at the Movies.* Her book *Killing Rage* begins with this sentence: "I am writing this essay sitting beside an anonymous white male that I long to murder."[511]

Professor hooks sees herself as an "insurgent Black intellectual voice" committed to "renewed liberation struggle." As a tenured member of the academic elite who has taught at Yale and the Sorbonne, is a highly prized and amply rewarded campus lecturer, and makes an income in the six-figure range, Professor hooks concedes some internal conflict. In a 1996 essay, "The Rebel's Dilemma," Professor hooks laments: "the academy has always been so similar to the dysfunctional patriarchal family hierarchy that hemmed me in as a child that I feel that I can never be truly healthy, well and whole in the deepest sense, without leaving it." Her conclusion however is not to leave but to use her position to confront the "structures of domination." As she puts it, "The work then is always part of our struggle for liberation."[512]

Of hooks's more famous sentence, "I am writing this essay sitting beside an anonymous white male that I long to murder," the inspiration for this malice was nothing more heinous than the occupation of an airline seat. A stewardess had given a white stranger the first-class seat previously assigned to hooks's traveling companion and moved her to coach, because her upgrade had not been entered into a computer correctly and therefore was not registered.[513] Hooks attributes this innocent contretemps to "white racism."

Professor hooks's views on education are expressed in her 1994 book, *Teaching to Transgress*, which like her other writings is a broadside against the "white supremacist capitalist patriarchy."[514] According to Professor hooks, an educator has a "right as a subject in resistance to define reality." Teaching, according to Professor hooks, "is a performative act . . . that offers the space for change, invention, spontaneous shifts, that can serve as a catalyst drawing out the unique elements in each classroom."[515] Professor hooks exhorts educators "to teach in a manner that empowers students" by converting their classrooms into incubators of "progressive" politics. "My commitment to engaged pedagogy is an expression of political activism."[516] Of English, the language of her nominal subject, Professor hooks writes: "It is difficult not to hear in standard English always the sound of slaughter and conquest."[517]

In the same text, Professor hooks provides an example of the success of her "engaged pedagogy" on one of her students at City University: "I have not forgotten the day a student came to class and told me: 'We take your class. We learn to look at the world from a critical standpoint, one that considers race, sex, and class. And we can't enjoy life anymore.'"[518] Should her teaching strategy run into obstacles, Professor hooks recommends a tract about the feminist movement: "When such conflicts arise, it is always useful to send students to read *Yours in Struggle*." In other words, Professor hooks is not engaged in the practice of teaching students *how* to think, i.e., how to think critically when confronted with complex and differentiated material; but rather is teaching them *what* to think—and she is perfectly explicit about the fact that her classroom "pedagogy" is simply an extension of her political activism.

Professor hooks's widespread popularity in the academic world has brought her invitations to give commencement speeches at collegiate graduation ceremonies. In 2002, she was the commencement speaker at Southwestern University in Texas, where she had been invited to teach as a visiting scholar-in-residence of feminist studies: "The radical, dissident voices among you have learned here at Southwestern how to form communities of resistance that have helped you find your way in the midst of life-threatening conservatism, loneliness, and the powerful forces of everyday fascism which use the politics of exclusion and ostracism to maintain the status quo," Professor hooks told the graduating class.[519] "Every imperialist, white supremacist, capitalist, patriarchal nation on the planet teaches its citizens to care more for tomorrow than today. . . . And the moment we do this, we are seduced by the lure of death. . . . To live fixated on the future is to engage in psychological denial. It is a form of psychic violence that prepares us to accept the violence needed to ensure the maintenance of imperialist, future-oriented society."[520]

Referring to terrorist attacks on the World Trade Center, she said, "Our nation's call for violence in the aftermath of 9/11 was an expression of widespread hopelessness, the cynicism that has been at the heart of our nation's ongoing fascination with death." This "moment of collective clarity," she explained, however, "was soon obscured by the imperialist, white supremacist, capitalist, patriarchal hunger to show the planet our nation's force, to show that this nation would commit absolute acts of violence that will wipe out whole nations and worlds." Her speech passed no judgment on the terrorists who carried out the attack, but decried instead "our government's declaration of its commitment to violence, to death."[521]

In sum, this is a distinguished professor with a six-figure salary, loaded with academic honors, who is given license to conduct a one-sided Marxist-feminist indoctrination of hapless students, but still believes—as she explains as an invited commencement speaker—that she is living under the tyranny of a fascist dictatorship: namely, the United States.

> *See also:* Professors Baraka, Dyson, Jeffries,
> Karenga, Marable, Schwartz, Thomas
> *Research:* Jacob Laksin

Professor Alison Jaggar
University of Colorado, Boulder

— Professor of philosophy and women's studies
— Describes herself as a "socialist feminist"
— Author of the paper "One Is Not Born a Man"

Alison Jaggar is professor of philosophy and a former chair of the Women's Studies Department at the University of Colorado, Boulder (UCB). She is the former president of the American Philosophical Association. Integrating Marxist and feminist theory, Jaggar describes herself as a "socialist feminist" and "activist," who seeks to combat "the male-dominant structure of everyday life." According to Professor Jaggar "the standpoint of women is discovered through a collective process of political and scientific struggle."

Professor Jaggar received her BA in philosophy from the University of London (Bedford College), her master's in philosophy from the University of Edinburgh, and her PhD in philosophy from the State University of New York, Buffalo. As early as 1983, UCB began offering students a major in women's studies, but the degree was granted under the umbrella of American studies. In 1995, Jaggar headed a successful campaign to extricate women's studies from the American studies program, calling the American studies designation "increasingly inappropriate."[522]

In Jaggar's view, women are analogous to the proletariat in Marx's class schema. "The political economy of socialist feminism," writes Jaggar, "establishes that, in contemporary society, women suffer a special form of exploitation and oppression.... The distinctive social experience of women generates insights that are incompatible with men's interpretations of reality and these insights provide clues to how reality might be interpreted from the standpoint of women. The validity of these insights, however, must be tested in political struggle and developed into a systematic representation of reality that is not distorted in ways that promote the interests of men above those of women."[523]

Professor Jaggar's socialist feminism is rooted in a dissatisfaction with gender-blind Marxist class analysis. In Professor Jaggar's perspective, virtually all undesirable social conditions can be traced to the doorstep of capitalism, including the oppression of women. According to Jaggar, "residual capitalism" in socialist countries is the cause of women's oppression.[524] Professor Jaggar is a totalitarian thinker: "[W]hereas the standpoint of the ruling class reflects the interests [of] only one section of the population," she writes, "the standpoint of the oppressed represent[s] the interests of the totality in that historical period."[525] In other words, the viewpoint of the revolutionary agent is unitary and coincides with historical truth.

In Professor Jaggar's view, women and men are not gender selected by nature but are social constructs. At a 1995 "Conference on Feminism, Epistemology, and Ethics," Professor Jaggar delivered a paper titled "One Is Not Born a Man." Since to her, men and women are not so by nature, their gender roles can be changed. To overcome women's oppression, Professor Jaggar believes the act of childbearing must no longer be limited to one sex. She writes: "The one solid basis of agreement among socialist feminists is that to overcome women's alienation, the sexual division of labor must be eliminated in every area of life. . . . [W]e must remember that the ultimate transformation of human nature at which socialist feminists aim goes beyond the liberal conception of psychological androgyny to a possible transformation of 'physical' human capacities, some of which, until now, have been seen as biologically limited to one sex. This transformation might even include the capacities for insemination, for lactation and gestation so that, for instance, one woman could inseminate another, so that men and non-parturitive [non-child-bearing] women could lactate and so that fertilized ova could be transplanted into women's or even into men's bodies."[526]

Professor Jaggar has taught at the University of Illinois; the University of California, Los Angeles; and Rutgers University, where she was chair of the Women's Studies Department. That a person with these bizarre beliefs was elected president of the American Philosophical Association speaks for itself about the political radicalization and intellectual decline of a major national scholarly organization.

See also: Professors Anton, Sedgwick
Research: Thomas Ryan

Professor Frederic Jameson
Duke University

— Professor of comparative literature at Duke University and
  leading academic figure

— Co-chair, "Marxism and Society" academic studies major at
  Duke

— Believes "Americans created bin Laden during the Cold War,"
  and claims 9/11 attacks are "a textbook example of dialectical
  reversal"

Of the innumerable Marxist literary critics currently plying their
craft at American universities, few enjoy the following of Frederic Jameson, an admirer of Mao, an unreconstructed Marxist,
and a longtime professor of comparative literature at Duke. Professor Jameson is also co-chair of Duke's "Marxism and Society"
studies program. He is a person of national and international
intellectual influence.

Professor Jameson's work is a mainstay of university literature departments. Among his more influential texts is his 1971
effort, *Marxism and Form*, credited by some observers with resurrecting the then-moribund study of Marxist literary theory.
Jameson's writings on criticism are embraced with equal ardor
by practitioners of post-modern Marxism. Professor Jameson's
seminal work in this regard is his 1981 tome, *The Political Unconscious: Narrative as a Socially Symbolic Art*. In this work, Professor Jameson took the forthrightly "extreme position" that the
task of a literary critic is to impose a narrow political framework
on a given text. With this end in mind, Professor Jameson argued
that "the political perspective [is] the absolute horizon of all
reading and interpretation," and urged students to approach literary texts not as works of intrinsic merit but rather as "socially
symbolic acts."[527]

Professor Jameson's conception of literary works as essentially activist—indeed revolutionary—endeavors has given rise to several courses at Duke. A writing course called "Novel Visions," offered at Duke in 2001, was expressly founded on Professor Jameson's claims. Students taking the course were urged to understand "writing as a social and political practice," a message reinforced in the course description: "This class will think seriously about how novels, in different historical moments, provide views on the social world or 'visions' for meaningful change."[528] In other words, a person with no formal training in history, under the smokescreen of a "literature" course, is teaching a primitive Marxist history of the western world.

Another class, "Globalization and Literature," draws on a comprehensive array of Marxist theories, including Professor Jameson's 1991 work, *Postmodernism or The Cultural Logic of Late Capitalism*, in which he bewailed the "baleful" spread of global capitalism and called for a "political form of postmodernism" to counteract it by stimulating the "capacity to act and struggle which is at present neutralised by our spatial as well as our social confusion."[529]

As such examples attest, Duke's comparative literature program is in many ways the brainchild of Professor Jameson's radical theories. A largely traditional program prior to Professor Jameson's arrival in 1985, the Duke program is today a nursery of "critical theory" and Marxist cultural criticism. Professor Jameson's influence at Duke extends to the university's publisher, Duke Press, on whose faculty board Jameson served for five years. Beyond publishing two books through the press, Jameson played a prominent role in influencing the kinds of writing and research selected for publication.

Now getting on in years, the seventy-one-year-old Jameson is still active in campus causes. Most prominent among these is his involvement in Duke Divest, a movement that compares Israel to apartheid South Africa, and pressures universities to withdraw their investments in companies that do business there. Jameson is one of forty faculty members in the group. A petition drafted by the group and signed by Professor Jameson states that it is "appalled by the human rights abuses against Palestinians at the hands of the Israeli government," and denounces the "continual military occupation and colonization of Palestinian territory by Israeli armed forces and settlers."[530] The petition acknowledges that attacks on Israeli civilians are "unacceptable and abhorrent," but does not call for their suspension.[531]

Several weeks after 9/11, the *London Review of Books* convened a scholarly symposium on the terrorist attacks, titled "Reflections on the Present Crisis." Professor Jameson joined twenty-nine other radical scholars in attendance. After asserting matter-of-factly that "the Americans created bin Laden during the Cold War," Professor Jameson concluded that the attacks were "therefore a textbook example of dialectical reversal."[532]

Professor Jameson evinced no sympathy for the victims of the attacks, but condemned instead "the nauseating media reception," the "cheap pathos" that "seemed unconsciously dictated" by the "White House."[533] According to Jameson, the real cause of the terrorist attacks was the "absence of any Left alternative means that popular revolt and resistance in the Third World" could pursue.[534] In Professor Jameson's view, this indicated that the Islamist rage over injustice has "nowhere to go but into religious and 'fundamentalist' forms."[535] In the spring of 2002, Professor Jameson published an article in the Duke academic journal, *The South Atlantic Quarterly*, contending that the "history of the [American] superstate is as bloody as anyone else's national history," and despairing that a "minority president [Bush] has been legitimized," and bemoaning the "sinister extension of the surveillance state...in the name of a universal revival of patriotism..."[536]

Professor Jameson is so revered by the academic community at Duke that he has been the subject of special ceremonies paying tribute to his legacy. In April 2003, Professor Jameson stepped down as chair of Duke's Literature Program, a title he had held for eighteen years. In tribute, Duke hosted a four-day conference honoring his work: "The Future of Utopia: Is Innovation Still Possible in Politics, Culture, and Theory? An Interdisciplinary Conference in Honor of Frederic Jameson."[537] The conference was attended by scores of radical academics who turned up to lavish praise on the guest of honor.

See also: Professors Berube, Holstun, hooks

Research: Jacob Laksin

Professor Leonard Jeffries
City University of New York

— Professor of black studies at City University of New York

— Believes that blacks ("sun people") are morally and culturally
  superior to whites ("ice people")

— "Jews are a race of skunks and animals that stole Africa from
  the Black Man."

Leonard Jeffries is a longtime faculty member at the City University of New York and a onetime chair of its Black Studies
Department. He is also one of the leading proponents of
Afrocentrism—a school of dubious intellectual merit that judges
Western civilization to be racist in essence and demands a corrective curriculum glorifying African peoples and culture. But
Jeffries subscribes to more than just cultural chauvinism. He is
also a black supremacist, claiming whites to be genetically infe-
rior to blacks, and an inveterate anti-Semite, apportioning to
"rich Jews" the blame for everything from the allegedly anti-
black content of Hollywood movies to the transatlantic slave
trade.

   In 1988, Professor Jeffries was appointed by then-New York
State education commissioner Thomas Sobol to help draft a
report recommending an expanded focus on "multiculturalism"
in the state's K-12 curricula. Jeffries's influence was everywhere
in evidence in the final report. Reading more like a polemic than
a scholarly assessment, the report claimed that "African Americans, Asian Americans, Puerto Ricans/Latinos, and Native Americans have all been the victims of an intellectual and educational
oppression that has characterized the culture and institutions of
the United States and the European American world for centuries."[538] The title of the report was: "A Curriculum of Inclusion."

Professor Jeffries's black supremacist views first came to public notice at this time, when a white student, writing in the campus newspaper, catalogued the host of anti-white theories that Professor Jeffries routinely advanced in one of his classes, Black Studies 101. Professor Jeffries had been teaching at the City University since 1972, when he was tapped to head the black studies department and was almost instantly granted tenure, thanks in no small part to an administration determined to appease a surging militancy among black leftists on campus. Jeffries had little or no standard peer-reviewed scholarship to his name at the time he was granted tenure—or, for that matter, since. And this was not the first time that his bigotry had been aired in public.

Nor would it would be the last. In April of 1990, the *New York Times* reported that another Jeffries class, nominally about African heritage, would have been truer to its content had it been offered under the title "Anti-Jewish Conspiracies 101." Unhistorically and irresponsibly overstating the participation of Jews in the transatlantic slave trade, Professor Jeffries taught that "rich Jews who financed the development of Europe also financed the slave trade."[539] In a similar vein, Jeffries carried on against the notion that the murder of six million Jews during World War II deserved to be recognized as a uniquely horrific act of genocide. Professor Jeffries also used his class to instruct students in his theory that humanity was divided into "sun people" (i.e., blacks) whose higher melanin content made them morally and culturally superior to the "ice people" (whites).[540]

The two reports confirmed what some students at the City University already knew: that Jeffries was using his classes as pulpits to preach bigotry against Jews and whites. At this point, Jeffries decided to aggressively go public with his hate-filled views. In July of 1991, Jeffries delivered a speech that made him nationally notorious. Speaking at the taxpayer-funded Empire

State Black Arts and Cultural Festival in Albany, New York, he asserted that there was a "systematic" and "unrelenting" "attack coming from the Jewish community" against blacks: "Russian Jewry," Jeffries claimed, "had a particular control over the movies, and their financial partners, the Mafia, put together a system of destruction for Black people."[541] Singling out his Jewish disputants in academia, Professor Jeffries claimed that they were "slick and devilish and dirty and dastardly."[542] Especially vile was Professor Jeffries's attack on then-assistant U.S. secretary of education Diane Ravitch, whom Jeffries denounced as the "ultimate, supreme, sophisticated, debonair racist" and a "Texas Jew."[543]

Professor Jeffries claimed that he had once headed a Jewish fraternity in college. Boasting that he had been known as the "King of the Jews," Jeffries claimed that the fraternity's members had relied on a "system of support" to cheat their way to academic success. Stated Jeffries: "The whole average of the fraternity was a dean's list average, even dumb Jews made it, because there was a system of support."[544] But according to the president of Greek life at the college that Jeffries attended (Lafayette College in Easton, Pennsylvania), the school has never had a Jewish fraternity.[545]

In the same speech Professor Jeffries insisted that America's first president must henceforth be known as "George Washington the slave master bastard Founding Father." Professor Jeffries then offered his distinctive account of American history. In his historical narrative, "America was founded by rich white men with property and power," whose bigoted ideals were codified in the Constitution, a "document of affirmative action for rich white folks with property and power."[546]

The response was immediate: Michele Wallace, a professor in the English department, led off the attacks, calling Jeffries a "maniac." Under public fire, the university was compelled to take action. In March of 1992, the board of trustees voted to remove Jeffries as head of the Black Studies Department. Contemptuous of his City University critics—in his Albany speech Jeffries had spoken with derision of "my Jews at City College"[547]—Jeffries refused to accept the trustees' decision, challenging it in the federal district court in Manhattan on free speech grounds. The legal battle would rage until April 1995, when an appeals court, reversing an earlier ruling, upheld Jeffries's dismissal as department head.

His legal defeat notwithstanding, it was not at all clear that Jeffries came out the loser in his fight with the college. Though he was not reinstated as the head of the Black Studies Department, Jeffries remains at the college as a tenured professor. Moreover, he continues to travel to colleges and universities, delivering speeches in which his hatred of Jews and whites reveals itself as fiercely as ever.

See also: Professors Baraka, Dyson, hooks
Research: Jacob Laksin

Professor Robert Jensen

University of Texas, Austin

— Associate professor of journalism

— "The United States has lost the war in Iraq and that's a good thing."

— "Scratch the surface of U.S. rhetoric about its quest to bring freedom and democracy to the world, and one finds the suffering of the people who must live with the reality of U.S. foreign policy."

Robert Jensen is an associate professor of journalism at the University of Texas, Austin. He has opposed American military reprisal for 9/11, the war in Iraq, minimal precautions to protect U.S. borders, and capitalism. Calling America a warlike nation, Jensen has denounced "U.S. aggression against innocent people in the rest of the world...Given the bloody record of the United States in the past sixty years, and the seemingly limitless capacity of U.S. officials to kill without conscience, I must confess I am not optimistic that such aggression will stop anytime soon, in large part because those corporate structures that drive the killing are still around.... I am hopeful about the possibilities but not optimistic that in my lifetime I will see the demise of capitalism, corporations and wage slavery."[548]

In a 2004 article in the Web publication *Alternet*, Jensen dismissed U.S. efforts to bring democracy to Iraq. He endorsed Ward Churchill's attack on the victims of 9/11 as "little Eichmanns" and has rejoiced in the setbacks the United States has experienced in Iraq, referring to the war as a "Defeat for an Empire."[549] He has urged that "God condemn America, so the world might live,"[550] though there is little evidence that he is a believer in anything but Marxism. He condemns Israel's efforts at self-defense, referring to its "brutal occupation of Palestine." He has criticized Michael Moore's film *Fahrenheit 9/11* as being "too conservative." On racial matters, he is narcissistically flagellant on the subject of "white privilege," a posture that he can use to mount attacks on merit-based hirings and school admissions, and even the economic system itself. He recites Ward Churchill's erroneous claim that the United States intentionally infected Native Americans with diseases such as smallpox (as has long since been demonstrated, Lord Amherst, an English general, considered doing this in 1763; that it was done by American forces in the 1830s has passed into leftist dogma, without foundation). Jensen is a member of the radical No War Collective and the Third Coast Activist Resource Center.

In an introduction to a recently published collection of his speeches, Jensen, expressing his contempt for America, writes: "Citizens of the United States are citizens of the empire—not an empire in exactly the same fashion as the Roman or British versions, but an empire all the same, reaching for global domination through the use of military and economic power. The consequences of this imperial project have been grim for many people around the world—those who have been the targets of U.S. military power; those who have lived under repressive regimes backed by the United States; and those who toil in economies that are increasingly subordinated to the United States and multinational corporations. Scratch the surface of U.S. rhetoric about its quest to bring freedom and democracy to the world, and one finds the suffering of the people who must live with the reality of U.S. foreign policy."[551]

Jensen's academic performance at Texas has come under fire by his colleagues as well as those outside the university. He has been accused on the Professor Watch List of using his Critical Issues in Journalism class as a forum for indoctrinating students into socialism and a denunciation of "white privilege."[552] A conservative student organization audited Jensen's Journalism 101 course in the spring of 2004 and posted this evaluation: "In a survey course about journalism, one might expect to learn about the industry, some basics about reporting and layout, the history of journalism, the values of a free press and what careers make the news machine function. Instead, Jensen introduces the unsuspecting student to a crash course in socialism, white privilege, the 'truth' about the Persian Gulf War and the role of America as the world's prominent sponsor of terrorism. Jensen half-heartedly attempts to tie his rants to 'critical issues' in journalism, insisting his lessons are valid under the guise of teaching potential journalists to 'think' about the world around them."[553]

As an associate professor who has been awarded tenure, Jensen will vote on the fates of younger faculty in the Department of Journalism at Austin, perhaps for the next thirty years. This is the major state-funded school of journalism in Texas.

See also: Professors Cloud, Gitlin, McChesney, Navasky, Scheer, Schell

Research: Joseph Wilson

Professor Ron (Maulana) Karenga
California State University, Long Beach

— Professor and chair of the Department of Black Studies
— Convicted in 1971 of falsely imprisoning and torturing two female members of his radical organization
— Creator of the African American holiday Kwanzaa

Ron Karenga is chair of the Department of Black Studies at California State University, Long Beach. Professor Karenga claims to hold two PhDs. The first is in political science, with a focus on the theory and practice of nationalism, obtained from the United States International University—an institution that no longer exists. The second is in social ethics, with a focus on the classical African ethics of ancient Egypt, obtained from the University of Southern California.

An activist and Marxist, Professor Karenga is best known for creating the African American holiday Kwanzaa. In the mid-1960s, he bestowed upon himself the title "Maulana," Swahili for "master teacher," and is now widely referred to as Maulana Karenga. Professor Karenga began his foray into black nationalism in the early 1960s, founding the militant black power organization United Slaves (US), which became notorious after a shootout between US and the rival Black Panthers in the UCLA cafeteria over a student election resulted in the deaths of two of the Panthers.

In 1971, Professor Karenga and US members Louis Smith and Luz Maria Tamayo were convicted of felonious assault and false imprisonment for assaulting and torturing two female US members, Gail Davis and Deborah Jones. According to a contemporary newspaper account of the trial, "The victims said they were living at Karenga's home when Karenga accused them of trying to kill him by placing crystals in his food and water and in various areas of his house. When they denied it, allegedly they were beaten with an electrical cord and a hot soldering iron was put in Miss Davis's mouth and against her face. Police were told that one of Miss Jones's toes was placed in a small vise, which then was tightened by the men and one woman. The following day Karenga told the women that 'Vietnamese torture is nothing compared to what I know.' Miss Tamayo put detergent in their mouths; Smith turned a water hose full force on their faces, and Karenga, holding a gun, threatened to shoot both of them. The victims Deborah Jones and Gail Davis were whipped with an electrical cord and beaten with a karate baton after being ordered to remove their clothing."[554]

Karenga was convicted of two counts of felonious assault and one count of false imprisonment. He was sentenced on September 17, 1971, to serve one to ten years in prison, and was released after four years in 1975. This history did not prevent him from securing faculty appointments, first at San Diego State and then at Cal State Long Beach following his release. Apparently a nationwide search for applicants for these positions was unable to turn up a better candidate (or alternatively, Professor Karenga's political bona fides trumped all other considerations). The US organization was temporarily disbanded during Karenga's incarceration but was reestablished by him in 1975.

In 1977, Professor Karenga devised a cultural philosophy called Kawaida, a Swahili term for tradition and reason, from which the holiday Kwanzaa arose. Professor Karenga billed Kwanzaa as an alternative to Christianity, Judaism, and Islamic holiday traditions. He asked his followers to follow the seven "principles" of Kwanzaa, known as the "Nguzu Saba," or the "Seven Principles of Blackness," which are observed during the seven days of Kwanzaa. The core principles are collectivist, including: "*Umoja* (Unity)—To strive for and maintain unity in the family, community, nation and race; *Ujima* (Collective Work and Responsibility)—To build and maintain our community together and make our brother's and sister's problems our problems and to solve them together. *Ujamaa* (Cooperative Economics)—To build and maintain our own stores, shops and other businesses and to profit from them together. *Nia* (Purpose)—To make our collective vocation the building and development of our community in order to restore our people to their traditional greatness. *Imani* (Faith)—To believe with all our heart in our people, our parents, our teachers, our leaders and the righteousness and victory of our struggle."

In a 2002 article, Ann Coulter observed that the seven principles of Kwanzaa are also the same seven principles of the 1970s domestic terrorist group the Symbionese Liberation Army. Each snake head of the SLA's emblem stood for one of the SLA's revolutionary principles: Umoja, Kujichagulia, Ujima, Ujamaa, Nia, Kuumba, and Imani—the same seven "principles" of Kwanzaa.[555]

In 1998, Professor Karenga and United Slaves issued a statement in support of the Third Annual Celebration of Cuba's Internationalism. The statement read: "The Organization US joins all freedom-loving peoples around the world in standing in solidarity with the Cuban people in their heroic and historic struggle to defend their right of self-determination and to break out of the unjust and immoral economic boycott by the U.S. government."[556]

In explaining the 9/11 attacks, Professor Karenga observes: "they did it to: (1) avenge years of state terrorism, mass murder, selective assassination, collective punishment, and other forms of oppression by the U.S. and its allies; (2) to demonstrate vulnerability of the U.S. at its crucial centers of power, i.e., financial—Manhattan, military—the Pentagon, and political— Washington, D.C.; (3) to cause the rulers of the country to fear, to be uncertain and to reverse the role of hunter and hunted; (4) to insist on being heard and considered in human, political and military terms; (5) to demonstrate a capacity to strike regardless of the superior strength and technology of the U.S.; and (6) to dramatize and underline in a highly visible way the asymmetry of suffering between the U.S. and the oppressed in the world."[557]

In an April 2003 event at his school, Professor Karenga joined faculty and students in a "Walk Out for Peace" anti-war rally organized by Students Against the War. Professor Karenga invoked his African American philosophy of Kawaida, stating, "Our ethical tradition requires several conditions for a just war, which this self-declared war against the Iraqi people doesn't meet. This is not a war of self defense, it is a war of self aggrandizement."[558] On another occasion Professor Karenga wrote, "The proposed war against Iraq is not an isolated initiative. Rather, it is part of a post-9/11 imperial offensive which carries with it racist and colonial conversations and commitments of 'crusades' to protect 'the civilized world' against 'dark and evil nations' in 'dark corners of the world.'"[559]

In 1989, Professor Karenga became head of the Department of Black Studies at Cal State Long Beach. The department, which seeks to "critically examine and understand the African experience from an Afrocentric perspective,"[560] features such courses as "Politics of Black Power" and "Racism in the American Military." As chair of the Black Studies Department, Professor Karenga is in a position to appoint the departmental search committee and influence all hires. He is also the author of *Introduction to Black Studies*, regarded as the most widely used introductory text in black studies.[561]

Research: Thomas Ryan

Professor Peter Kirstein
Saint Xavier University

— Professor of history, Saint Xavier University
— Created a national controversy by attacking an Air Force Academy cadet as a "baby killer"
— Member of Historians Against the War

Peter Kirstein is a professor of history at Saint Xavier University in Chicago, Illinois. His academic website[562] features his "teaching philosophy," which includes these edicts: "Teaching is a moral act. It is NOT a dispassionate, neutral pursuit of 'truth.' It is advocacy and interpretation." "Teach peace, freedom, diversity, and challenge American exceptionalism on every front." "Move beyond the academic concentration camp of one's 'discipline.'" The website also informs students that "the CIA is a terrorist organization," and recommends that "the agency should be abolished and its $30+ billion budget used to buttress Social Security and feed the starving poor in America!!" [emphasis in original]

The accent on advocacy is on prominent display in Kirstein's courses at Saint Xavier. For instance, his introductory course "United States History to 1877" centers on the "European invasion of America," while his follow-up course, "United States History Since 1877," engages with the "[t]hemes of war, racism, civil rights, and economic issues," through the prism of a "non-elite, multicultural social history" and unaccountably ends its survey with the Vietnam War. Vietnam is also the subject of another Kirstein course, "Vietnam and America." Of particular concern to the course is the war's "impact on domestic protest and peace movements." Another Kirstein course, "Socialism and Capitalism," invites students to ponder the "socialist alternatives" to "unregulated" free-market capitalism.[563] On Kirstein's personal website, the course listing is embedded with a link to a special page, created by Kirstein, paying tribute to Karl Marx.[564]

In November 2002, Professor Kirstein created a national controversy after receiving the following email in late October from an Air Force Academy cadet:

Dear Sir or Ma'am,

The Air Force Academy is going to be having our annual Academy Assembly. This is a forum for mainly but not only Political Science majors, discussing very important issues dealing with politics.

Right now we are in the planning stage for advertising and we would appreciate your help in the follow [sic] areas. Do you know of or have methods or ways for interschool advertising and or communications? What would be the best way for us to advertise at your school whether it is sending you the fliers and you making copies or by perhaps putting an advertisement in your local publication? We would appreciate your input and the cost of what you recommend. Thank you for your time and consideration.

Very Respectfully,
Cadet Robert Kurpiel

On October 31, 2002, Kirstein sent this email to Cadet Kurpiel:

You are a disgrace to this country and I am furious you would even think I would support you and your aggressive baby killing tactics of collateral damage. Help you recruit. Who, top guns to reign [sic] death and destruction upon nonwhite peoples throughout the world? Are you serious sir? Resign your commission and serve your country with honour.

No war, no air force cowards who bomb countries without AAA [anti-aircraft artillery], without possibility of retaliation. You are worse than the snipers. You are imperialists who are turning the whole damn world against us. September 11 can be blamed in part for what you and your cohorts have done to Palestinians, the VC, the Serbs, a retreating army at Basra.

You are unworthy of my support.
Peter N. Kirstein

When Kirstein's letter became public, it set off a national controversy, becoming the subject of radio and TV talk shows and Internet chatter. The History News Network reported the flap in a November 17, 2002, article titled, "The Historian Who Denounced the Military for 'Baby-Killing' Tactics."[565] (There are of course no such tactics.) In the debate that followed, Kirstein provided further insight into his beliefs: "One of the great achievements of Communism, rarely recognized in the West," he wrote, "is its relatively successful containment of American power from the early 1950s through the demise of the Soviet state in 1991."[566] America's rejection of the World Court, he sneered, was because of its "concern that its senior-national leadership might be tried for war crimes and crimes against humanity."[567]

While conceding he may have committed an indiscretion in his email to the cadet, Kirstein escalated his attack on his country and its military: "Vietnam was a disgrace, a war crime and an event far worse than the crimes of President Saddam Hussein."[568] Kirstein's use of the honorific "president" to describe Saddam is instructive. Saddam did get 100 percent of the votes in the election he staged, but he was the only candidate. Moreover, the penalties for voting *against* him were a dip in one of his acid baths, or a stint in the plastic shredders he used for his opposition, or silent burial in one of the mass graves into which 300,000 "no" votes had already disappeared.

Despite his apology for his indiscretion, Kirstein was obviously unrepentant: "I welcome the controversy that I have caused and I am in this for the duration. I will not be silenced or intimidated by talk shows, *Wall Street Journal* editorials, Internet campaigns to destroy me and take away my livelihood, or pressure from militants who play the New McCarthyism game of patriotism and blind allegiance to an immoral foreign policy."[569] In a 2003 talk sponsored by the Center for Educational Practice, Kirstein urged his fellow educators to follow his example and condemn the American military. Likening his email to the struggles of Martin Luther King, Jr. and Gandhi, Kirstein said: "I crossed the line, through an e-mail, when I also protested against a military institution that trains its students to kill other human beings with high-tech, invulnerable flying machines. I ask you to consider peacefully crossing the line. If enough people cross the line, I guarantee you, they will have to remove the line." In the same speech, Kirstein said, "The militarization of American society and its incessant military crusades pose a greater threat to our freedoms than the putative enemies that we slaughter on the battlefield or even worse in their homes or hospitals in distant lands."[570]

Professor Kirstein's academic website[571] commemorates *"Vietnam Liberated 30 Years Ago: April 30, 1975,"* ignoring the reality that Vietnam is still a Communist police state. It also features a shrine to Karl Marx, with Kirstein proudly posing at Marx's gravesite and a link to an ironically named speech by Fidel Castro, one of Marx's last surviving dictator disciples, "History Will Absolve Me."

Of the U.S.-led intervention in Iraq, Kirstein has claimed that "American motives were not self-defense but dreams of hegemony: namely the control of oil, a permanent military force that could virtually eliminate any geostrategic competition in the Gulf and an encirclement and ultimate invasion of Iran."[572] Kirstein hastened to add that even if Saddam Hussein was in possession of illicit weapons of mass destruction, this would not justify his ouster since both the United States and Israel had nuclear weapons arsenals. From Kirstein's perspective, the distinction between dictatorship and democracy was seemingly one without difference.

To mark the one-year anniversary of the U.S. army's entry into Baghdad, Saudi Arabia's *Arab News* published comments by several American radicals, including Professor Kirstein: "Images remain. The image of the American flag being draped over a statue of Saddam Hussein as the invaders conquered Baghdad. The Oil Ministry alone being guarded as vandals stole precious artifacts from Baghdad museums and other facilities. Innocent Muslims being whisked away in chains to Guantanamo Bay. The president of the United States referring to non-white, non-Western nations as an axis of evil..."[573] Professor Kirstein regards the United States as "the leading terrorist and criminal nation in the world today."[574]

Among his colleagues at St. Xavier, Professor Kirstein is by no means regarded as a fringe radical. In 1997, he won St. Xavier University's Teaching Excellence Award.[575]

See also: Professors Chomsky, Lembcke, Zinn

Research: Michael Bauer

Professor Vinay Lal
University of California, Los Angeles

— Associate professor of history
— Regards the war on terror as fraudulent
— Views America as a threat to mankind

Vinay Lal has been on the faculty of UCLA since 1993. He teaches courses in Indian history, comparative colonial histories, subaltern history, and Indian historiography. In addition, he teaches graduate-level seminars on the contemporary politics of knowledge, "postcolonial theory," and the politics of culture. In 1992–93, just prior to his arrival at UCLA, he was a William R. Kenan Fellow, Society of Fellows in the Humanities, and lecturer in history at Columbia University.

Among the courses Professor Lal teaches is one titled "Fiat Lux Seminar: Honors Collegium 98," which is subtitled "Re-Reading Democracy in America: Politics Before and After 9/11." According to the UCLA catalog, there are "two requirements" for students to complete the course—a paper on one of the two class texts, and an in-class presentation. Here is how the requirement is described:

> A presentation might focus on what the election to California's governorship of a movie star who has been charged by a dozen women with sexual molestation, drives perhaps the most environmentally unfriendly vehicle in the world, and appeared not to have a single idea about governance says about American 'democracy.' Other presentations can focus on corporate ownership of the media, the rise of Fox News, the MTA and grocery chain strikes in Los Angeles, the trade union movements, the presence of African-Americans and Latinos in

the US army, the film 'Bowling in [sic] Columbine', the assault on civil liberties, the indefinite detention of hundreds of Muslims without any accountability to notions of justice, or thousands of such phenomena.[576]

The course description shows that Professor Lal's seminar is a course in political propaganda, not academic inquiry. Unsurprisingly, the text assigned for the Fiat Lux Seminar is *Vietnam and Other American Fantasies* by H. Bruce Franklin, a radical who in the past has edited (and provided a favorable introduction for) a collection of writings by Joseph Stalin. Professor Lal explains the importance of Franklin's text in this way: "Though many commentators have unthinkingly rehearsed the cliché that after 9/11 all is changed, our other principal text comes from one of the most respected scholars of American history [Franklin is in fact a professor of English literature], whose relatively recent inquiry into the meaning of the Vietnam War in American life suggests that nothing has changed, insofar as the U.S. remains on course in exercising its ruthless dominance over the rest of the world."[577]

Professor Lal sees many similarities between George W. Bush and Osama bin Laden, characterizing both as rogues who egotistically invoke divine blessings for their unworthy causes. "Bush and bin Laden have much more in common," he wrote. "If anything, bin Laden's parochialism is slightly less offensive: whereas Bush concludes his addresses to the nation with 'God bless America,' as though God should care about nation-states or has earmarked America as especially deserving of His approbation, bin Laden is content to observe, 'God is great, may pride be with Islam.' The fundamentalism of fanatical conviction knows no boundaries; rogues do understand each other."[578]

Professor Lal regards the horrors of 9/11 as a type of karmic justice visited upon the United States for its past transgressions.

He sneers at "America's discovery that it is no longer inviolable, and that it may be susceptible to the very suffering that it has so cavalierly visited upon others."[579]

Professor Lal's view of the United States is of a nation obsessed with violence and conquest, always in search of new pretexts for making war—in large part, the professor claims, because war is a lucrative enterprise for corporate America. "War is the reigning metaphor of American experience, it dominates the idioms of speech and conduct: in the last decade alone, the airwaves have been full of the 'war on cancer,' the 'war on crime,' the 'war on drugs.' The largest hoaxes are bathed in the language of war: thus all types of crime have declined, but with two million Americans in jail, the country has the largest prison population in the world. If Palestinians could be locked away, doubtless Israel would be entitled to declare success in its war on the aspirations of a people. . . . No modern power has so consistently been at war with such a wide range of political regimes; no other culture has so elaborate a mythology of guns, so profound an affection for the right to own guns. . . Politicians and the much-feted 'American public,' whose 'compassion' and 'values' are tirelessly trotted out at every turn, recognize that war is good for America. That, alone, raises the most terrifying prospects for the future of humankind."[580]

As an associate professor, Vinay Lal will be voting on who is hired and promoted in the UCLA history department for the next twenty-five years.

See also: Professors Eckstein, Holstun, Reich
Research: John Perazzo

Professor Jerry Lembcke
Holy Cross College

— Associate professor of sociology, Holy Cross College

— Socialist and anti-war activist

— Believes post-traumatic stress disorder was invented to discredit the anti-war movement

Jerry Lembcke is an associate professor of sociology at Holy Cross College in Massachusetts, where he is regarded as a "nationally recognized expert on the Vietnam War and Vietnam veterans."[581]

For the socialist Lembcke, the Vietnam War is a consuming interest, but hardly a scholarly one. Professor Lembcke's mission is to persuade students to accept his inflexible view that the Vietnam War, along with all the wars of the United States, are "neo-imperialist" manifestations of America's capitalist foundations and are to be opposed.

Professor Lembcke's views are made explicit in his 1998 book, *The Spitting Image: Myth, Memory, and the Legacy of Vietnam*. The book is required reading in several sociology classes at Holy Cross and advances two arguments that are equally tendentious. The first is that the stories of Vietnam veterans returning from the war only to be spit upon by angry anti-war activists are nothing more than a "myth" invented, Professor Lembcke argues, by the Nixon administration. The documentation of spitting incidents is an interesting scholarly challenge, but Professor Lembcke claims that the only documented instances of spitting actually involved belligerent Vietnam veterans unloading on those of their disillusioned comrades who joined forces with the anti-war movement. Professor Lembcke's claims are undermined by the testimony of countless veterans who have reported the disrespectful treatment they received from anti-war activists, which reflects the general attitude of a movement that burned flags and draft cards, poured blood on draft files, conducted "Days of Rage" in major cities, was responsible for more than a thousand bombing incidents, and relentlessly accused the president and the troops he commanded of being "baby killers." Nevertheless, Professor Lembcke's book was well received by mainstream media outlets upon its release, and many credulous journalists persist in recycling its claims.[582]

The second and even more preposterous thesis advanced by Professor Lembcke in *The Spitting Image* is that post-traumatic stress disorder (PTSD) was a political invention. Specifically, Professor Lembcke argues that PTSD was created with the aim of discrediting returning veterans who protested the Vietnam War. "PSTD functioned to help erase the memory of the war as an act of U.S. aggression that we lost because the Vietnamese beat us, by rewriting it as a war we lost because we defeated our-selves, i.e. our military was stabbed in the back, our soldiers spat on, etc."[583] According to Professor Lembcke, "the image of the dysfunctional PTSD-stricken victim-veterans" replaced the "his-torical reality" that the Vietnam War "empowered a generation of GIs who revolted against the war and joined the movement to stop it."[584]

In fact, the number of veterans who protested the war was miniscule compared to the number who served. Professor Lem-bcke was himself one of those few. A former chaplain's assistant in the war, Lembcke returned home to join the radical group Vietnam Veterans Against the War. As Professor Lembcke him-self conceded in a 1999 article for *Holy Cross Magazine*, he hopes with his book to burnish the "image of anti-war warriors," which, he claims, is at odds with the "militarism that dominates our culture." In the same article, Professor Lembcke darkly warned that "reclaiming our memory of the Vietnam era entails a struggle against very powerful institutional forces that toy with our imaginings of the war for reasons of monetary, political, or professional gain." For Professor Lembcke, "Vietnam symbolizes popular resistance to political authority and the dominant images of what it means to be a good American."[585]

It is these themes, informed more by Professor Lembcke's political inclinations than scholarly research into Vietnam-era history, that dominate his lectures at Holy Cross. For instance, in 1998 Professor Lembcke gave a sociology lecture called "Men, Women, and Medicine," making the case for the "social construction of post-traumatic stress disorder"—i.e., its invention to serve political ends. On another occasion, delivering a guest lecture for a sociology course called "Abnormal Psychology," Lembcke warned students to beware of the supposedly sinister political motivations behind "the mental labeling of Vietnam vets."

During the 2004 presidential election, Professor Lembcke deployed his revisionist theories in the service of the John Kerry campaign. The attacks on Kerry, Professor Lembcke explained in an October 2004 op-ed, were "premised on a widespread discontent about Vietnam. On the surface, Kerry is targeted because he came home from the war and joined the anti-war movement, but the gendered lexicon of the barbs themselves points to an unarticulated angst in the American subconscious that is about something more serious than Kerry's fidelity or even the defeat in Vietnam."[586] What this something was, according to Professor Lembcke, was the "American character and its struggle to confront the neo-imperialist impulses common to the U.S. invasions of both Vietnam and Iraq."[587]

See also: Professors Berlowitz, Eckstein, Fellman, Shortell

Research: Jacob Laksin

Professor Mark LeVine

University of California, Irvine

— Associate professor of history

— Blames the U.S. and Israel for provoking Islamic terrorism

— Rock musician and Marxist

Mark LeVine is a radical activist and guitar-playing associate professor of history at the University of California, Irvine. His academic website explains: "My scholarship, activism and music are all tied to my commitment to struggles for social justice in the United States and around the world." He is an advisory board member to Occupation Watch, an organization set up by radicals to incite American soldiers in Iraq to request "conscientious objector" status and leave their posts. Professor LeVine is an academic known for his steady stream of anti-American and anti-Israel diatribes that depict Washington and Jerusalem as aggressors in a war against Islam.

Professor LeVine has performed musically with Mick Jagger, Johnny Copeland, Chuck D, Albert Collins, and Ben E. King. He considers himself, with his long blond hair and rock persona, a "disgruntled ex-hippie" who renounced his Jewish faith in his late teens after—as he puts it—witnessing his father's death as well as "a lot of suffering and injustice." A left-wing anti-war activist who frequently guest-stars at "peace" rallies, Professor LeVine views globalization, capitalism, and any form of nationalism—or at least especially American and Israeli nationalism—as forces of evil that promote war and misery.

Professor LeVine's hipster persona is on ample display at his website.[588] Casting himself as a latter-day Renaissance man, he describes how he "interviewed senior international political figures, reported from Beirut's green line, taught the Qur'an to

Muslim Brothers, performed from Woodstock to Paris to Damascus Gate, lived next door to Hamas mosques, stood against bulldozers, dodged terrorist bombs, and uncovered damning files in dusty archives. [He knows] the history, politics, religions—and most important, the peoples—of the region as a friend, but with a highly critical eye." LeVine also claims a "long history of blending art, scholarship, and activism" and being "uniquely positioned to offer such analysis in a manner that will be especially appreciated by members of generations of X and Y."

Beneath this trendy exterior, LeVine, who has degrees from Hunter College and New York University, is an utterly unoriginal incarnation of very old and discredited intellectual ideas. His worldview encompasses a quasi-communist utopia, a classless future, where all racial, nationalist, and cultural identities are dissolved. In other words, the discredited vision of Marx that led to the deaths of one hundred million people while bankrupting whole continents in the last century.

To bring this socialist millennia to fruition, he claims, it is necessary to "dig beyond the easy symbolism of 'freedom,' 'democracy,' 'Zionism equals racism,' and other mantras and challenge a matrix of discourses—modernity, colonialism, capitalism and nationalism; what I call the 'modernity matrix'—that are each based on the creation of zero-sum oppositions between (individual or collective) Selves and Others, us and them, and which together have supported a five-hundred-year-old world system that supports slavery in the Sudan and Mauritania and IMF bailouts, organized terrorism and *'le peuple du Seattle'* alike."[589] For someone claiming to be a historian to suggest that modernity consists simply of "oppositions" is as preposterous as lumping together slavery, terrorism, and the International Monetary Fund (not to mention *le peuple* of Seattle or anywhere else). In LeVine's view, there is only one cause of global evil—capitalism. This is thought worthy of a rock musician.

When the UN Development Program and the Arab Fund for Economic and Social Development released the Arab Human Development Report 2002, a devastating account of the failures of the Arab world written by Arab intellectuals, Professor LeVine criticized the Western media for their enthusiastic acceptance of its chief premise, which was to hold Arab states accountable for their plight, instead of blaming the United States and Israel. For LeVine, the report was an inherently flawed document because it failed to address the external "issues of money and power" that prevent Arabs from instituting substantive reform. It is the capitalist West, according to LeVine, that is responsible for the Arab world's inability to create economic prosperity.[590]

When an Israel Defense Forces bulldozer inadvertently killed pro-Palestinian activist Rachel Corrie as she tried to prevent it from destroying a tunnel used for weapons smuggling, Professor LeVine praised her "spirit and courage" and extolled the International Solidarity Movement, a pro-terrorist organization which had recruited Corrie to her fatal occupation. "As America's war on Iraq grows bloodier, we would do well to reflect on the meaning of Rachel's life and death, and the powerful message of the International Solidarity Movement," LeVine wrote at the time. "She and the other human shields, like their colleagues in Iraq, are true soldiers of peace."[591] The remark about "colleagues in Iraq" is a reference to American "anti-war" volunteers who went to Iraq before hostilities in 2003 began, in order to protect the Saddam dictatorship from being overthrown. They soon left.

Professor LeVine's view of the war on terror boils down to a single point: if Islamic terrorists harbor murderous rage against America and Israel, then America and Israel are responsible for that fury. The causes of terrorism are capitalism and American and Israeli imperialism, and have nothing to do with social and religious issues within Islam: "without both an acceptance of responsibility for past policy and the transformation of future policy toward the Islamic regions of our planet, there will be no solution to terrorism, only continued violence and war."[592]

"[W]ar and occupation," Professor LeVine writes, in a series of Marxist clichés unanchored in any observable reality, "are wonderful opportunities for corporations to make billions of dollars in profits, unchecked by the laws and regulations that hamper their profitability in peace time... Because of this, in the postmodern global era, global corporations and the government elites with whom they work have great incentive to sponsor global chaos and the violence it generates."[593] Exaggerated reports of widespread civilian casualties in Iraq prompt the professor to hysterical responses, calling the United States "a criminal nation that must be stopped."[594]

See also: Professors Algar, Dabashi, Haddad, Massad

Research: Tzvi Kahn[595]

Professor Robert McChesney
University of Illinois, Urbana-Champaign

— Research professor of communications
— Founder of left-wing "media reform" organization Free Press
— A current director of the Marxist *Monthly Review* Foundation

In 1999 Robert McChesney was hired as a research associate professor at the Institute of Communications Research, Graduate School of Library and Information Science at the University of Illinois, Urbana-Champaign. He was also appointed a senior research scientist at the school's National Center for Supercomputer Applications. In 2000, McChesney was promoted to research professor. From 1988 until 1998 he taught journalism and mass communication at the University of Wisconsin, Madison, where he became friends with local radical journalist John Nichols, now Washington correspondent for *The Nation* magazine. McChesney has co-authored three books with Nichols: *It's the Media, Stupid!*; *Our Media, Not Theirs: The Democratic Struggle Against Corporate Media*; and *Tragedy & Farce: How Media Warps Elections and Democracy*.

Professor McChesney is the founder of the left-wing "media reform" organization Free Press, and a board member of the left-wing Institute for Public Accuracy. He is a former editor and current board member of the Marxist magazine *Monthly Review*, which has a fifty-year history of supporting Communist movements and regimes.

Professor McChesney blames the media for having "helped anoint a president" in 2000.[596] He refers to President Bush as "the moronic child of privilege."[597] Professor McChesney writes, "[C]onsider the manner in which the press reported President Bush's 'victory' in the 2000 election. It is now clear that the majority of the people in Florida who went to vote for president in November 2000 intended to vote for Al Gore. . . . But Al Gore isn't president. Why is that? Or to put it another way, why didn't the press coverage assure that the true winner would assume office?. . . The primary reason is due to sourcing: throughout November and early December of 2000, the news media were being told by all Republicans that the Republicans had won the election and Al Gore was trying to steal it. The Democrats, on the other hand, were far less antagonistic and showed much less enthusiasm to fight for what they had won. Hence the news coverage, reflecting what their sources were telling them, tended to reflect the idea that the Republicans had won and the Democrats were grasping for straws. . . . Once the Supreme Court made its final decision, the media were elated to announce that our national nightmare was over."[598]

Elaborating further on this theme, Professor McChesney writes, "No one should be surprised by the polls showing that close to 90 percent of Americans are satisfied with the performance of their selected president, or that close to 80 percent of the citizenry applaud his Administration's seat-of-the-pants management of an undeclared war. After all, most Americans get their information from media that have pledged to give the American people only the president's side of the story."[599] This "analysis" by an alleged expert in research was made in the spring of 2003, just after a short, almost casualty-free, successful war. When consolidating victory proved more difficult and a domestic opposition developed, the president's poll numbers fell dramatically. How would Professor McChesney's analysis, which presumes a pliant corporate media eager to do the government's bidding and possessing a determining influence on citizen opinion, explain this dramatic shift?

In Professor McChesney's view, the American media are largely shills for conservatives and the Bush administration, and willing abettors of his unjust wars. In a 2003 article titled "The Media Crisis of Our Times," McChesney writes: "What is most striking in the U.S. news coverage following the September 11 attacks of 2001 is how...the very debate over whether to go to war, or how best to respond, did not even exist. Tough questions were ignored. Why should we believe that a militarized approach will be effective? Moving beyond the 9/11 attacks, why should the United States be entitled to determine—as judge, jury, and executioner—who is a terrorist or a terrorist sympathizer in this global war? What about international law? Most conspicuous was the complete absence of comment on one of the most striking features of the war campaign, something that any credible journalist would be quick to observe:... There are very powerful interests in the United States who greatly benefit politically and economically by the establishment of an unchecked war on terrorism. This consortium of interests can be called...the military-industrial complex. It blossomed during the Cold War when the fear of Soviet imperialism—real or alleged—justified its creation and expansion. A nation with a historically small military now had a permanent war economy, and powerful special interests benefited by its existence."[600]

> **See also:** Professors Foster, Gitlin, Navasky, Scheer
>
> **Research:** Lowell Ponte

Professor Aminah Beverly McCloud
De Paul University

— Professor of Islamic studies
— Director of the Islamic World Studies Program at DePaul
— Follower of Nation of Islam leader Louis Farrakhan

Aminah Beverly McCloud is the director of the Islamic World Studies Program at DePaul University, America's largest Catholic college. Launched in September 2004, the program offers both a major and minor in the subject of Islamic religion and culture. A member of the Nation of Islam and a disciple of its anti-Semitic, anti-white leader Louis Farrakhan, Professor McCloud helped DePaul develop the program in response to what she considers Americans' widespread ignorance about the Islamic world.

Professor McCloud teaches the courses "Islam in the United States" and "Islam in Global Contexts." One of the texts she requires students to read in both classes is Seyyed Hossein Nasr's *The Heart of Islam: Enduring Values for Humanity*. This text turns a blind eye toward the darker sides of fundamentalist Islam and likens Muslim terrorists to the American founders who fought for independence from Britain. Nasr writes, "When some people attack Islam for inciting struggle in the name of justice, they forget the Boston Tea Party and the American Revolution."[601]

Another required text is the novel *Nisanit* by Fadia Faqir. A *Publishers Weekly* review of this book states, "Mired in political rhetoric, this alarming first novel by a Jordanian native tracks a Palestinian terrorist, his girlfriend, and his Israeli interrogator. The subject matter—a terrorist's thought processes, his lethal acts (including the murder of nine Israeli settlers), capture, torture and attendant plunge into madness—is potentially gripping, but Faqir repeatedly proffers graceless, simplistic agitprop instead of careful plotting or characterizations."[602] In the book, Israelis are portrayed as sadists, and the protagonist of the story, a terrorist named Shadeed, ponders the prospect of peace, observing, "It would never spread over their country until these aggressors [the Israelis] stopped polluting their air."[603]

As a Black Muslim, Professor McCloud has often found herself at odds with Middle Eastern Muslim immigrants. "In their pursuit of the American dream and whiteness," she says, "the new arrivals have largely ignored African-American Muslims, and have assumed that they can impose their own understanding of Islam on African-Americans."[604] In an interview with the house organ of Farrakhan's movement on the seventieth anniversary of the organization created by Elijah Muhammad, Professor McCloud said "The Nation of Islam must define what Islam is within the American Culture."[605]

Professor McCloud has denounced the Patriot Act and protested the State Department's decision to bar Tariq Ramadan from entering the United States to join the faculty of Notre Dame University. Ramadan—the grandson of Hasan al-Banna, who founded the terrorist Muslim Brotherhood—was denied a visa because of his connections to al-Qaeda and other terrorist groups.

Professor McCloud's in-class treatment of students has been the subject of complaints on the website RateMyProfessors.com, where students post their evaluations of their teachers. Commented one student, "It's amazing that someone like this is allowed to teach. If you're ready to be her toady, agree with everything she says and fall all over yourself by extolling her self-proclaimed 'genius,' then I guess you would love her. Anyone with half an independent brain will resent her enormously."[606]

In addition to her teaching career, Professor McCloud has been a consultant to the Ford Foundation's "Civil Rights and Muslims in America" project; and a consultant and affiliate to Harvard University's Pluralism Project. These prestigious appointments indicate that Professor McCloud is not viewed as a fringe in American academic life.

See also: Professors Bagby, Finkelstein, Mazrui

Research: Thomas Ryan[607]

Professor Manning Marable
Columbia University

— Professor of history and political science, Columbia University

— Director of the Institute for Research in African American
  Studies, Columbia University

— Marxist, member of the Communist Party faction, "The
  Committees on Correspondence"

Manning Marable is professor of history and political science
and director of the Institute for Research in African American
Studies at Columbia University. A lifelong Marxist and member
of the Communist Party faction called "The Committees on
Correspondence," of which professors Angela Davis, Bettina
Aptheker, and Harry Targ are also members, Professor Marable
advocates black "resistance" as the only antidote to the "inherent
racism" of American society. Needless to say, Professor Marable
makes no attempt to distinguish between political activism and
education.

In an April 2004 lecture called "Living Black History," Professor Marable denounced the "master narrative" of American history espoused by "white Americans," which conceives America
as a pluralistic society. He regarded such a view as indefensible.
America, according to Professor Marable, was "organized around
structural racism" and "the ongoing racial stigmatization and systematic exploitation of a significant segment of the population."
The only possible solution, according to Professor Marable, was
"the subversion of the master narrative itself, which must
involve to a great extent the deconstruction of the legitimacy of
white racial identity, and the uncovering and examination of
massive crimes against humanity that have been routinely sanc-
tioned and carried out by corporate and state power."[608]

This is the mission of Columbia's Center for Contemporary Black History,[609] which Professor Marable established in 2002. The center, according to Professor Marable, seeks the "advancements of political projects that actively challenge structural racism and the consequences and effects of discrimination." No pretense to academic or scholarly inquiry here. In 2003, working in concert with the NAACP and the Mississippi Legislative Black Caucus, the Center created a project called "Freedom Summer 2004." Its purpose was to mobilize 250 "college-aged" students in Mississippi to register new voters in support of "social justice,"[610] and in particular the repeal of "repressive voter laws," which allegedly diminished the Democratic vote. The "repressive" laws in question were those barring convicted felons from casting a vote. In Professor Marable's ominous telling, the project was a vital front in the battle for "black liberation." He has sounded similar themes in the pages of *Souls*, a quarterly journal of "African American Studies" produced by his Columbia CBH Center. Serving as a platform for Marable's political causes—reparations for American slavery 140 years after the fact being prime among them—the journal lists the anti-Semitic poet Amiri Baraka among its contributing editors.

Professor Marable's center is supported financially by George Soros's Open Society Institute, no doubt in part because it fits Soros's agenda of unseating Republicans. Under Marable's direction, the center has also launched the Africana Criminal Justice Project. The undisguised mission of the project, "distinguished by its forthright commitment to the pursuit of social justice,"[611] is to radicalize black studies departments in universities across the country. As Marable has put it, "To enrich the black intellectual tradition, we must push the boundaries of what has become 'Black Studies' well beyond Black Studies." Toward this end, the program promulgates a "black theory of justice," maintaining that the American criminal justice system is irredeemably racist,

because American society is "defined by rigid racial hierarchies."[612] The "academic" sources for these tendentious conclusions are the works of "black scholars, artists, and public
intellectuals," including convicted cop-killer Mumia Abu-Jamal.

A revealing scholarly inquiry of the Center for Contemporary
Black History is the "Malcolm X Project," which proposes to
"critically explore" the assassination of the Nation of Islam
leader, of whom Professor Marable is an outspoken devotee. In
practice, the project attempts to advance the conspiracy theory,
to which Professor Marable has long subscribed, that police and
government officials colluded in Malcolm's assassination. This
conspiracy theory is so extreme that it was even rejected by Malcolm X's film biographer, Spike Lee, as well as by reputable
scholars in the field. Nation of Islam leader Louis Farrakhan had
pronounced a death sentence on Malcolm for betraying the
Nation and its leader and two members of the Nation were convicted of the crime.

But according to Professor Marable, the project seeks to
answer the "lingering question of what those in law enforcement
and government actually knew and did in this crime [the assas-
sination]," and proposes a "reconstructed history" to "bridge the
distance between the divided racial past and the present." This
"reconstructed history," Professor Marable explains, "could be
incorporated into the curricula of public schools," and function
as "educational resources for a proposed memorial honoring
Malcolm X" at Columbia University. "The goal is not just to educate and inform, but to transform the objective material and cultural conditions that perpetuate the status of marginalized
groups," and ultimately to "reconstruct America's memory about
itself."[613] The result, Professor Marable hopes, will be the emer-
gence of "new social movements," and "spontaneous insurrec-
tions." The Columbia Center for Contemporary Black History's

website features a photograph of rapist, drug dealer, and con-victed felon Huey Newton brandishing a clenched fist, taken during the Black Panther leader's incarceration for killing a police officer.

Clearly the purpose of this project is not to find out, objec-tively, whether there was some sort of passive police conspiracy ("let it happen") or even an active one ("urge them on") behind Malcolm X's death. Instead, the conspiracy is assumed, despite all the evidence tested in a court of law pointing to the Nation of Islam. But since the obvious culprit is politically unacceptable to Professor Marable, the facts of the courtroom conviction of two Nation of Islam members for murdering Malcolm are ignored, the obvious masterminds Elijah Mohammad and Far-rakhan are ignored—even though Farrakhan himself has apolo-gized in public to Malcolm X's family for fostering a climate of hate against Malcolm that led to his death—and what remains is a paranoid "research project," where the answer is already assumed, on the basis of no evidence. And this from a professor of history.

Professor Marable is convinced, of course, that there are ene-mies of his project, chief among whom he identifies as the white middle class, which he also believes to be the source of the inequities of American society that inflame his radical passions: "Part of the historic difficulty in uprooting racial and gender inequality in the United States is that whites generally—and especially white middle and upper-class males—must be taught to how the omnipresent structures of white privilege perpetuate inequality for millions of Americans."[614] The remedy lies in indoctrinating students "of privileged backgrounds," in Professor Marable's view, of "the meaning and reality of hunger and poverty," to "create and nourish" in them "a commitment to a society committed to social justice...and foster impatience with all forms of human inequality, whether based on gender, sexual orientation, or race...and empower those without power."

See also: Professors Aptheker, Baraka, Davis, Targ

Research: Jacob Laksin

Professor Joseph Massad

Columbia University

— Assistant professor of modern Arab politics and intellectual history at Columbia University

— Calls for the destruction of "the Jewish State" and denies that the Jews are a nation

— Teaches an introductory course at Columbia on Israeli politics

Joseph Massad is assistant professor of modern Arab politics and intellectual history in the Department of Middle Eastern Languages and Cultures at Columbia University. Among a faculty distinguished more for its militancy and political activism than its scholarship, Professor Massad is in a radical class of his own. A self-described "Palestinian-Jordanian," Professor Massad routinely condemns Israel as a "racist state," and calls for its destruction. In April 2002, he delivered a characteristically venomous public lecture describing Israel as "a Jewish supremacist and racist state."[615] Taking this charge to its logical conclusion, Professor Massad explained that "every racist state should be destroyed."[616] A month earlier, Professor Massad had said "the Jews are not a nation" and the "Jewish state is a racist state that does not have the right to exist."[617]

"It is only by making the costs of Jewish supremacy too high that Israeli Jews will give it up," Professor Massad said on another occasion.[618] Jewish supremacists, he believes, are those Jews "not confined to [Prime Minister Ariel] Sharon and the Israeli Jewish right wing which is anyway a majority in Jewish Israel, but also to liberal and leftist Jews." In short, all Jews are "Jewish supremacists."[619]

In common with Palestinian terrorists, Professor Massad does not distinguish between civilian and military targets. He stresses that the "resistance of Palestinians," must extend to Israeli "civil institutions" (that is, ordinary people walking on the street, women, children), and hails as "anti-colonial resisters" those Palestinian terrorists who undertake to murder Jews inside the so-called Green Line demarcating Israel's pre-1967 border.[620]

If Professor Massad's hostility toward Israel is formidable, his knowledge of the Jewish state is significantly wanting. Speaking no Hebrew, Professor Massad has a demonstrably feeble grasp of Israeli history and his books contain numerous errors prompted by his animus towards the Israeli state. In his 2001 book, *Colonial Effects: The Making of National Identity in Jordan*, for example, Professor Massad makes reference to a November 1966 Israeli raid and "massacre" that took place in Samu, Jordan. Yet not even the Jordanians, who suffered the casualties to which Professor Massad is referring, depicted Israel's action as a "massacre." Samir Mutawi, who authored the semiofficial account of Jordan's involvement in the 1967 war, wrote that "eighteen Jordanians" were killed in the raid. In fact, Professor Massad, himself provides an identical casualty figure later in his own text—fifteen soldiers and three civilians killed—thereby contradicting his prior claim that a "massacre" had occurred. Professor Massad also writes that in the March 1968 battle of Karamah, the Israeli army "could not escape unscathed (as it had during the 1967 war and on many other occasions). For the first time in its history, it received heavy damages in personnel and material." But while Israel lost twenty-eight soldiers at Karamah, it had lost some eight hundred in June 1967. Moreover, in the 1948 war against its Arab attackers, Israel lost a combined six thousand of its soldiers and civilians.[621]

An observer uninitiated in the rituals of the modern university might suppose that Professor Massad's savage enmity towards Israel, his expressed rejection of its right to exist as a nation, his support for violence against Israeli civilians, and his many egregious errors in scholarship—to say nothing of his biased view of the Israeli-Palestinian conflict—would be sufficient to disqualify him from teaching about the Jewish State. Not at Columbia. After all, Professor Massad teaches in a program in which one of the senior members, Professor Hamid Dabashi, has publicly written that the physical bodies of Israeli Jews are in their very structure evil.[622]

Besides vilifying Israel in public, Professor Massad acts out his aggressions in an introductory course on the Israeli-Palestinian conflict. The course description for "Palestinian and Israeli Politics and Society" itself notes: "The purpose of this course is not to provide 'balanced' coverage of the views of both sides but rather to provide a thorough yet critical overview of the Zionist-Palestinian conflict."[623]

To appreciate what is meant by "critical," it is worthwhile to reflect on Professor Massad's use of the word "Zionist." In Professor Massad's view, Zionism—that is, the political and religious movement advocating the right of the Jewish people to an independent state—is inherently "anti-Semitic." On its face, the claim is absurd: Zionism has never defined itself with reference to biological or racial traits, accenting only affiliation to the Jewish faith; moreover, Israel boasts a considerable diversity of races and grants more rights to its Arab citizens than does any Arab state.

Writing in the Egyptian newspaper *Al-Ahram* in January of 2003, in the course of attacking "Israel's racist nature," Professor Massad alleged an "ideological and practical collusion between Zionism and anti-Semitism since the inception of the movement."[624] Professor Massad concretized this "collusion" with the following example: "Zionism's anti-Semitic project of destroying Jewish cultures and languages in the diaspora in the interest of an invented Hebrew that none of them spoke, and in the interest of evicting them from Europe and transporting them to an

Asian land to which they had never been, is never examined by these intellectuals."[625]

By urging the migration of the Jewish people "to an Asian land to which they had never been,"[626] (an obvious falsehood) Zionism intended to safeguard the Jewish people from the perennial depredations visited on them in Europe. Far from "destroying Jewish cultures and languages,"[627] Zionism aspired to save them. But this account, though more faithful to the historical record, had the disadvantage of voiding Professor Massad's claim that "Zionism has always been predicated on anti-Semitism and on an alliance between Zionists and anti-Semitic imperialists."[628] It also conflicted with Massad's view of the "European Jew as a coloniser [sic] who has used racist colonial violence for the last century against the Palestinian people."[629]

But it did not preclude Professor Massad from condemning Israel in the most extreme terms. In one representative passage of the *Al-Ahram* article, Professor Massad, citing no evidence, derided "the racist curricula of Israeli Jewish schools, the racist Israeli Jewish media representations of Palestinians, the racist declarations of Israeli Jewish leaders on the right and on the left, and the Jewish supremacist rights and privileges guiding Zionism and Israeli state laws and policies."[630]

In a December 2002 article for *Al-Ahram*, Professor Massad provided perhaps his most bizarre definition of Zionism to date: "All those in the Arab world who deny the Jewish holocaust are in my opinion Zionists," he explained.[631] Lest one think that he harbored any genuine sympathy for the victims of the Holocaust—a word he specifically refused to capitalize—Professor Massad immediately likened the murder of six million Jews to "Zionist attempts to play down the number of Palestinian refugees."[632] He then asserted that modern-day Arabs and Muslims were suffering from an equally horrific holocaust, one perpetrated by, *inter alia*, Jews: "Today we live in a world where anti-Arab and anti-Muslim hatred, derived from anti-Semitism, is everywhere in evidence. It is not Jews who are being murdered by the thousands by Arab anti-Semitism, but rather Arabs and Muslims who are being murdered by the tens of thousands by Euro-American Christian anti-Semitism and by Israeli Jewish anti-Semitism."[633]

Equally striking is Professor Massad's repeated equation of Israel and its leaders with Nazis. There are "stark" similarities, he claims, between the plight of Jews in Nazi concentration camps and Israeli prisons' treatment of Palestinian terrorists (or "the children and young men of the stones and Molotov cocktails," as Massad—echoing a phrase coined by the Unified National Leadership of the Uprising—euphemistically dubs them[634]). In Israeli prime minister Ariel Sharon, meanwhile, Professor Massad sees the incarnation of Nazi propaganda minister Joseph Goebbels.[635]

But Professor Massad is not a stickler for the Israel-as-Nazi-Germany typology. It is enough to confront him with his statements to this effect—as a group of Columbia students did in their critical documentary, "Columbia Unbecoming"—for Massad to issue outraged denials. Writing in the stoutly anti-Israel website the *Electronic Intifada* in November of 2004, Professor Massad stated, "The lie...that I would equate Israel with Nazi Germany is abhorrent. I have never made such a reprehensible equation."[636]

As Professor Massad's reaction to the above-mentioned charges suggests, he does not take criticism well. Or at all, for that matter, when his alleged abuse of students in his classes led to a university-mandated investigation in the spring of 2005. Upon being confronted with two incidents in which he was alleged to have screamed at pro-Israeli students, his response was to declare that he did not remember the incidents. The investigatory committee concluded, however, that these incidents did indeed occur. And, of course, it would be unlikely for a faculty member to forget screaming at a student who disagreed with him (unless, of course, he did it all the time). Massad's colleague Professor George Saliba, when confronted with similar allegations, had a similar failure of memory, and the investigatory committee concluded that these incidents had also occurred. It is instructive that nevertheless no action at all was taken against Massad for dissembling to the university committee.[637] Instead, Massad was allowed to dismiss his critics as being "pro-Israel." He then claimed it was his Jewish critics who were anti-Jewish. They had targeted him, he said, for being *pro*-Jewish. Explained Professor Massad: "What galls them most is that I'm a pro-Jewish Palestinian critic of Zionism."[638]

> *See also:* Professors Anderson, Andijar,
>   Dabashi, Haffar, LeVine
> *Author:*   Jacob Laksin

Professor Mari Matsuda

Georgetown University

— Professor of law at Georgetown University

— Leading legal architect of politically correct speech codes in universities

— Matsuda's courses emphasize "social justice" activism over study of the law

A self-described "activist scholar," Mari Matsuda is a professor of law at the Georgetown University Law Center. There she specializes in "feminist theory" and "critical race theory." Professor Matsuda is an architect of the legal rationale behind campus speech codes, which attempted to outlaw "fighting words" in American universities in the late 1980s and early 1990s before they were declared unconstitutional.

Along with left-wing law professors Richard Delgado, Charles Lawrence, and Kimberly Crenshaw, Professor Matsuda contributed to the volume *Words That Wound: Critical Race Theory, Assaultive Speech, and the First Amendment*, a 1993 text that would become the legal cornerstone of the movement to restrict campus speech. Among other claims, the book argued that "areas of law ostensibly designed to advance the cause of racial equality [like the First Amendment] . . . often benefit powerful white men."[639] Judging the First Amendment to be too lenient with respect to "hate speech"—a category that evidently included all statements offensive to groups other than white males—Professor Matsuda argued that such speech was "qualitatively different" from other varieties of offensive speech.

Arbitrary censorship of hate speech, according to Professor Matsuda, was therefore preferable to the potentially devastating effects it might otherwise have on its ostensibly defenseless targets. Racist speech, Professor Matsuda wrote, "is best treated as a *sui generis* category, presenting an idea so historically untenable, so dangerous, and so tied to perpetuation of violence and degradation of the very classes of human beings who are least equipped to respond that it is properly treated as outside the realm of protected discourse."[640] Not all hate speech was actionable, however: "Expressions of hatred, revulsion, and anger directed against members of historically dominant groups by subordinated-group members are not criminalized by the definition of racist hate messages used here."[641] Hence, hate speech leveled by black Americans against whites may be "troubling," Professor Matsuda explained, but, in view of the latter's "historically dominant" role, permissible.

Many of the speech code laws advocated by Professor Matsuda were later struck down as unconstitutional. But they remain preserved at schools like Professor Matsuda's own Georgetown, which is a private institution beyond the reach of constitutional protections. At Georgetown, a broad ban is in effect on any "offensive act which is intentional or persistent" and "which is directed at specific individuals or groups of individuals, in such a way as to make an individual or group feel intimidated or unwelcome because of their actual or perceived color, disability, ethnicity, gender, national origin, race, religion, and/or sexual orientation."[642]

Speech codes are not the only mark that Professor Matsuda has left on the Georgetown campus. In fulfillment of the scholarly half of her "activist scholar" dual identity, Professor Matsuda also teaches three courses at Georgetown—all of them distinguished by their unmistakable preference for activist recruitment over legal instruction.

This preference is perhaps most transparent in a course called "Organizing for Social Change: Anti-Subordination Theory and Practice," co-taught by Professor Matsuda and adjunct law professor Marilyn Sneiderman, who is the director of field organization for the AFL-CIO and a winner of the "Harrington-Thomas-Debs Award" from the Democratic Socialists of America.[643] "This class is designed for the lawyer as change agent," explains the course description in the Georgetown catalogue. The course is concerned less with educating a new generation of lawyers than with honing "the strategies of professional organizers."[644] Having absorbed "readings from Critical Race Theory, feminist legal theory, anti-colonial theory, peace studies, and other social justice traditions," each student "is expected to complete a social change organizing project as part of the course requirements."[645] There are no alternatives to activism, for as the course description cautions: "Students who take this class should have in mind a social justice project that includes some form of public outreach, education, or institution building."[646]

A similarly activist methodology prevails in Professor Matsuda's course on "Peacemaking." In her course description Professor Matsuda explains that it "evolved from conversations with students who are interested in taking peacemaking seriously" in the aftermath of 9/11. "Peacemaking," however, is a highly misleading title for a course that aspires to train a new generation of lawyer-activists in the fundamentals of opposing American military intervention: "How have lawyers participated in peace movements, from draft resistance to Constitutional challenges?" asks the course description.[647] But although wars usually have two contending sides, any "peacemaking work" Professor Matsuda's course considers worth undertaking is directed solely at one side, the United States.

Professor Matsuda's views on war and peace are clarified in a 2003 letter to the *Boston Review*. With respect to anti-American terrorism, Professor Matsuda writes, "Our job is to ask how we [the United States] participated in its creation, and how we feed it still by choosing militarism and global inequality over peace and global justice."[648] Any discussion of the war on terror, Professor Matsuda declares, must be above all a discussion of American "militarism." "Militarism—choosing arms and battlegrounds and dead bodies before we ask how a coming war will position us yet again as the target of someone else's unchecked fury—is the big story of how we came to this place of danger in which, we are told, the Bill of Rights is a luxury."[649]

Even Professor Matsuda's one course with a discernible connection to law—an "Asian Americans and Legal Ideology Seminar"—places "particular emphasis" on "political theory."[650] Presented as an exploration of the "Asian American experience," the course is focused on the "relationship between law and social change, and the limits of liberal legal ideology."[651] Students enrolled in the seminar also examine how Asian Americans have fared within the American legal system—a subject on which Professor Matsuda has been conspicuously outspoken. In an address to the Asian Law Caucus in 1990, Professor Matsuda described twentieth-century America as a "land where racism found a home," and where anti-Asian hatred is fueled by the "real villains—the corporations and politicians who put profits before human needs."[652]

See also: Professors Cole, Falk, hooks
Research: Jacob Laksin

Professor Ali al-Mazrui
State University of New York, Binghamton

— Professor of humanities at the State University of New York

— Formerly the North American spokesman for the Islamic extremist group Al-Muhajiroun

— Defended terrorist professor Sami al-Arian as a "victim of prejudice and of popular ill will"

Ali al-Mazrui is a professor of humanities and director of the Institute of Global Cultural Studies at the State University of New York, Binghamton. Professor Mazrui is also chairman of the board of directors of the Center for the Study of Islam & Democracy, which defines its mission as "the production and dissemination of rigorous research into Islam and democracy." But in fact, the center has been closely linked to the radical American Muslim Council, whose leadership has declared its support for terror organizations such as Hamas and Hezbollah. Its executive director has suggested that the 2003 downfall of the space shuttle *Columbia* was an act of divine retribution against Israel—given that the deadly explosion took place "over a city named Palestine [in Texas], while on board was the first Israeli astronaut, who also happened to have been the pilot that bombed several years ago an Iraqi nuclear facility."[653] In addition to his center duties, Professor Mazrui has sat on the American Muslim Council's board of directors.

In 1986 Professor Mazrui hosted a PBS series called *The Africans: A Triple Heritage*, and authored an accompanying book of the same title. One insistent point of *The Africans* was the horror, and the continuing cost to the continent, of the history of European slave-trading. Professor Mazrui failed to mention, in this context, that he himself is descended from the leading slave-trading family of Mombasa (their conduct was suppressed by the British). Professor Mazrui's family sold slaves into the Muslim lands, including Saudi Arabia—another geographical goal of "the terrible heritage of slavery" that Mazrui failed to mention. In the book version, Professor Mazrui also supported the expansion of Islam south through the Sudan as a natural development not to be resisted by the Christian South. That is, he explicitly supported the genocidal conduct of the Sudanese Islamic government.[654]

In April 2002, Professor Mazrui co-authored an article titled "Is Israel a Threat to American Democracy?" The article depicts Osama bin Laden's anti-Americanism as a response to "massive economic aid from the United States to Israel" and the "provision of sophisticated American weapons to Israel."[655] This is historically untrue, however. Bin Laden's fatwa of 1998 was not greatly concerned with "Palestine," which ranked low on his list of grievances. Bin Laden was concerned with the presence of American forces "polluting the land of the Two Mosques" (i.e., Saudi Arabia) and the impact of sanctions on Iraq.

In Professor Mazrui's view, however, Arab terrorism is a reasoned reaction to unjust American and Israeli policies: "Israeli militarism, occupation of Arab lands and repression of Palestinians are the main causes of not only anti-Israeli terrorism but also anti-American terrorism. . . . Israeli repression and militarism provokes suicide bombers" and gives "rise to movements like Hamas and al Qaeda. . . . If Israeli atrocities and repression cause terrorism in the United States, and terrorism in turn threatens civil liberties in America, a chain of causation is established. The behavior of the state of Israel threatens not merely democracy within the Jewish state. Israel threatens democracy in America as well."[656]

Professor Mazrui and his co-authors accuse Israel of promoting a doctrine of Jewish racial superiority and, mirroring the atrocities of Nazi Germany, instituting policies of apartheid and genocide: "Israeli neo-Nazism reversed the scale of genetic values favored by German Nazis. Both forms of extremism exaggerated the impact of the Jewish factor. The Nazis thought the Jewish impact was negative. The Israeli extremists erred the other way."[657] "As for the trend towards militarization, Israel has indeed become the most efficient war machine since Nazi Germany."[658] "Perhaps Israel ought never to have been created. Millions of Jews were opposed to its creation in the first place. Those Jews have now been vindicated."[659]

See also: Professors Brand, LeVine

Research: John Perazzo

Professor Oneida Meranto

Metropolitan State College, Denver

— Associate professor of political science, Metropolitan State
  College, Denver

— Says that America has been and always will be racist and sexist
  because of "Capitalism, Christianization and Civilization."

— Contends that the only contributions the "Euro-American"
  Founders brought to the New World were "cultural genocide,"
  "racial hierarchy," and "gender politics."

Feminist Oneida J. Meranto is an associate professor of political
science at Metropolitan State College, Denver. In 2003, she
became the self-described "poster child for liberal leaning professors" after she was accused of throwing the College Republicans out of the Political Science Association, a student club she
supervised, because she suspected them of plotting to get her
fired.[660]

Before Professor Meranto became an academic, she was a
potter and art gallery director in Colorado. She received her BA
from Metropolitan State College in 1985, her MA from the University of Colorado (UC) in 1987, and, at age forty, earned her
PhD in political science from UC in 1991. Professor Meranto,
who is a Navajo, designed a minor in Native American Studies
at Metro State. She has served as faculty advisor to Students for
Social and Economic Justice and currently advises the Metropolitan American Indian Students for Empowerment (originally
called "Native American Students for Un-American Values").

Professor Meranto was married to the late political science
professor and anti-capitalist activist Philip J. Meranto, whose
books include: *School Politics in the Metropolis* (1970); *The Per-
sistence of Institutional Racism in Higher Education* (1981); and
Guarding the Ivory Tower: Repression and Rebellion in Higher

Education (1985), which, after his death, Oneida Meranto completed.

Guarding the Ivory Tower helped form the intellectual foundation of Professor Meranto's leftist politics, which she herself describes as "very raw."[661] The book embodies the Merantos' belief that "progressive" professors are entitled to use the classroom to foment social rebellion against capitalist, Anglo-Saxon America. The book tells the story of radical faculty who were "purged" during the 1970s "due to their political beliefs and activities" (as radical Michael Parenti observed in a review of the book). Philip Meranto himself was forced to resign from both the University of Illinois and then the University of Washington as a result of his radical activism, which involved collision with the law and subsequent arrests. After his resignation from the latter, he was unable to secure another regular academic appointment.

Professor Meranto views the United States as a nation in which racism and "sexism" are rampant. Over a decade ago, she went on record in *The Metropolitan* saying that she was fed up with the "white mind-set" of America. On February 24, 2004, she gave a speech at a protest, on Metro State's campus, against the sexual assault and rape allegations that had recently been made against a number of players on the University of Colorado football team. In her speech, Professor Meranto claimed that the only reason the allegations became a scandal was because the victims were white:

"Take a look at how we've rewarded white women or women in general that claim sexual harassment. They receive sympathy as they well should; they're accommodated; they're sometimes given their own talk shows; they receive a TV series; they write books; in essence they become famous. And if they join the reactionary right as Paula Jones did, they even get a makeover… Let me give you a few assumptions about race and rape. These two [race and rape] should always be intertwined as long as the parties are mixed race. Now number one, nonwhite women can't be raped. See, we've been socialized at a very young age, even at the age of five, that we can't be raped since rape is about power and since nonwhite women don't have power our voices are automatically suppressed. Two, nonwhite men, whether black, brown or red, desire white women. There is a history to sex, power and race in America and I suggest you understand it. Obviously some white men in great power have a nonwhite partner, but overall we as a society still have in our minds an overall sexual connotation of nonwhites. Let me give you an example. Nonwhites are closer to nature. Those that are closer to nature are more animalistic. Thus, animals are less capable of curbing their basic animalistic tendencies. The favorite movie of a white professor here on campus is *Black Robe*. Why? He said it was because the Christians taught the natives how to have sex in a more loving way."[662]

In an article written in 2001 titled "From Buckskin to Calico and Back Again," Professor Meranto claims that America has been and always will be racist and sexist because of "Capitalism, Christianization and Civilization." According to Professor Meranto, American history is all about "sex, power and race;" the only contributions the "Euro-American" Founders brought to the New World were "cultural genocide," "racial hierarchy," and "gender politics."

To judge from her own website, Professor Meranto has almost no published scholarly work to her credit—perhaps one peer-reviewed article in 2001. She also has three or four polemics in obscure left-wing venues. It is an open question as to how someone with these poor credentials ever became an associate professor with tenure, when the normal requirement for that status, which confers a lifetime appointment, is at least a scholarly book and perhaps several peer-reviewed articles. The only book

Meranto ever published was in 1986, and that was her husband's book, which she completed after his death, long before she earned a PhD. A perusal of the Department of Political Science website for Metro State College reveals the vast difference between Meranto's negligible scholarly accomplishments and those of the other members of her department.

This raises the question as to how a political fanatic like Meranto was hired in the first place, and on what possible basis did she get her promotion to a tenured position, where she will sit in judgment over all new hires and promotions to tenured rank.

See also: Professors Ensalaco, Gutierrez, Jaggar, Matsuda, Zinn

Research: Lisa Makson

Professor Armando Navarro

University of California, Riverside

— Professor of ethnic studies

— Chair of the Ethnic Studies Department

— Advocates the overthrow of the U.S. government by Latinos, and reclamation of the southwestern United States by Mexico

Armando Navarro is the chair of the Ethnic Studies Department at the University of California, Riverside. Professor Navarro earned his doctoral degree in political science at UC Riverside. He spent the 1970s and 1980s teaching and working with the group La Raza Unida, which contends that the mythical land of "Aztlán" was stolen from Mexico by the United States. He is author of *Mexican American Youth Organization: Avant-Garde of the Chicano Movement in Texas*; and *La Raza Unida Party: A Chicano Challenge to the U.S. Two Party Dictatorship*. Professor Navarro was promoted to the status of full professor on the basis of these two books—which are not actually works of scholarship, but pure political advocacy for two groups with which he is personally associated. Professor Navarro's teaching specialties include social movements and American and Latino politics. Among the items adorning Professor Navarro's office are a drawing of Che Guevara, and a photograph of himself with Cuban dictator Fidel Castro.[663]

Professor Navarro believes that Mexicans "were victims of an imperialism by which Mexico lost half of its territory."[664] He predicts that by the year 2050, the Latin population in the United States will reach 100 million, and that in states like California, New Mexico, and Texas, Mexicans will comprise the majority of the population. Says Navarro, "The Latin vote has the potential of 'tipping the balance' of U.S. elections, especially the presidential elections. . . . Imagine the possibility that Mexico recovers the lost territories, or that a new Republic of Aztlán is established; imagine that what happens is similar to the separatist movements in the province of Quebec and Puerto Rico."[665] Professor Navarro advocates the reclamation of the southwestern United States by Mexico, the overthrow of the U.S. government, and the "liberation" of the ancestral Mexican homeland of "Aztlán."

One way that Professor Navarro hopes to "[tip] the balance of U.S. elections," and "recover the lost territories of Mexico" is by supporting policies that weaken America's ability to secure its borders against illegal immigration. Professor Navarro fervently opposed California's Proposition 187, which sought to bar state and local agencies from providing social services and public education to illegal aliens. In January 1995, speaking at the Latino Summit Response to Proposition 187 conference at UC Riverside, Professor Navarro declared:

> We're in a state of war. This Proposition 187 is a declaration of war against the Latino/Chicano community of this country! They know the demographics, they know that history and time is on our side, as one people, as one nation within a nation as the community that we are, the Chicano/Latino community of this nation. What that means is a transfer of power. It means control. It means who's going to [have] influence. And it is the young people that are going to be in a position to really make the promise of what the Chicano movement was all about in terms of self-determination, in terms of empowerment, even in terms of the idea of an Aztlan![666]

In March 2001, Professor Navarro led a national delegation of Chicanos and Mexicans at the Zapatista March into Mexico City. "Our purpose of joining the march along with the Ejercito

Zapatista de Liberacion Nacional (EZLN)," he said, "is to demonstrate our solidarity with the indigenous people of Mexico. It is important for us on this side of the border to continue our friendship and unity with our brethren in Mexico."[667] The EZLN is a Marxist guerrilla group that seeks to unite the "workers, farmers, students, teachers, and employees...[and] the workers of the city and the countryside," in an effort to create a socialist revolution.

In April 2005, Professor Navarro led a group of some forty activists to Arizona to oppose the Minuteman Project, a volunteer group, which has tried to bring attention to the problem of illegal immigration by aiding the U.S. Border Patrol in monitoring the porous U.S./Mexico border. Despite the Minutemen's adherence to principles of non-violence, Professor Navarro has mendaciously depicted the group as a violent domestic terrorist outfit. But Navarro himself has not explicitly ruled out violence as a means himself. "We have a number of strategic scenarios that we can implement very quickly depending upon the circumstances," he says. "Believe me, they will be very assertive, very aggressive."[668] "We will adjust to the situation," he adds, "and obviously some of us have experience in the military...so there will be maybe some elements of surprises in terms of activities, and that is a warning to the militias."[669]

In October 2002, Professor Navarro spoke out against the impending war with Iraq, and organized a demonstration in front of Representative Joe Baca's district office in San Bernardino, California, exhorting the Democratic representative to vote against military action. In Professor Navarro's view, the Bush administration "seeks war at the expense of peace"[670] for the purpose of gaining control over Iraq's oil reserves.

Professor Navarro is active in a number of groups that share his views. He is head of the National Alliance for Human Rights (NAHR), an organization of immigrant rights activists who promote open borders and demand increased rights for illegal aliens. In 2002, Navarro was also sworn in as a new member of the State Central Committee for the Party of Democratic Revolution, a socialist party in Mexico.[671]

See also: Professors Gutierrez, Karenga,
Meranto, Thomas

Research: Thomas Ryan

Professor Victor Navasky
Columbia University

— Delacorte Professor of Journalism, Columbia University

— Chairman of the *Columbia Journalism Review*

— Chief after-the-fact defender of Alger Hiss and the Rosenberg spies

Victor Navasky is the Delacorte Professor of Journalism at Columbia University's School of Journalism, which administers the Pulitzer Prizes. He is also the director of the George Delacorte Center for Magazine Journalism at Columbia, and publisher and editorial director of *The Nation* magazine, which has long been the leading left-wing journal in America, and an apologist for every Communist regime and American military adversary since before the onset of the Cold War.

In September of 2002, Professor Navasky was named by Columbia president Lee Bollinger to serve on a special "task force," to investigate, in Bollinger's words, "how future journalists should be taught." The "task force" made no attempt at ideological inclusiveness, and members included such stars of the left-wing firmament as Columbia journalism professor Todd Gitlin, *Newsweek* columnist Anna Quindlen, and Professor Navasky himself.

Professor Navasky has a similar role as the chairman of the *Columbia Journalism Review*, a bimonthly magazine that styles itself as "America's premier media monitor," and in fact has no rival in setting standards for American journalists. For months his control and his bankrolling of the *Review* were kept quiet by the magazine, which commonly cited Professor Navasky on its pages as if he were an independent commentator whose views it had solicited.[672] The journal ran one piece in which the writer identified him as "Columbia journalism professor Victor Navasky," never informing readers that Professor Navasky now controls the magazine.[673]

Professor Navasky's views of the journalism world are discernibly colored by his left-wing politics, specifically his aversion to the trend of corporate ownership of media outlets. With an obvious reference to conservative media mogul Rupert Murdoch, Professor Navasky has inveighed against this trend as the "Murdochization" of the media, as he put it during one journalism workshop.

Professor Navasky is also director of the George Delacorte Center for Magazine Journalism at Columbia University. Several times per month, the center hosts lectures by prominent journalists, and attendance is required for students with a concentration in magazine journalism. In past years, the center has played host to a diverse slate of lecturers. Under Professor Navasky's guidance, the slate of invitees has narrowed dramatically to the political Left. In February of 2005, for instance, three of the four lectures were by prominent leftists: *The American Prospect*'s Michael Tomasky; *The New Yorker*'s Hendrik Hertzberg; and Navasky himself.

In the *Nation* world he inhabits, Professor Navasky is best known for his after-the-fact defenses of Alger Hiss and the Rosenberg spies, and for his skepticism about the veracity of the Venona decrypts—the communications between Soviet intelligence controllers and their American agents, many of whom were members of the American Communist Party. Professor Navasky has written long articles on each of these subjects. Professor Navasky, whose own background has deep roots in the Communist and fellow-traveling Left, equates anti-Communists with the followers of the late Senator Joseph McCarthy. According to

Professor Navasky the real agenda of anti-Communists is not to oppose Communism—which in his mind was never a threat—but "to discredit the left-liberal project today."

The Soviet archives have now been opened, however, and the Venona intercepts have been released. As a result, it is now known, except for holdouts like Professor Navasky, that McCarthy underestimated the extent of Soviet infiltration in the American government and that virtually all individuals called before congressional committees were involved in a conspiratorial network controlled by the Kremlin. The head of the Communist Party, Earl Browder, himself ran an espionage operation for the Soviets. Alger Hiss and Julius Rosenberg were guilty as charged.[674]

Like many who grew up reading pro-Soviet articles in *The Nation*, Professor Navasky is reluctant to acknowledge that the martyrs of the Left were actually guilty. To do so would mean admitting their right-wing opponents were actually *right*. If the Left were to concede error, the confession might lead to questions about whether they should be taken seriously today (and in this sense, Professor Navasky's aversion to anti-Communists is a sound one from his point of view). Professor Navasky and other longtime apologists for Communism have never acknowledged their role in enabling a movement that in the last century killed one hundred million innocent people.

Professor Navasky's political prejudices are evident in his pronouncements on journalism bias. Describing the animating values of anti-Communist magazines like *National Review*, Professor Navasky has used the terms "jingoistic" and "supernationalistic" (Navasky has written about his unease with concepts like patriotism).[675] By contrast, *The Nation* in his view draws on "human rights values and humanist values."[676]

From the platform that his academic employment provides, Professor Navasky has labored to disseminate *The Nation*'s far-left agendas throughout the American education system. By Navasky's own calculation, *The Nation* has special representatives on 160 college campuses, where they distribute copies of the magazine to students and urge them to purchase subscriptions. Under Professor Navasky's stewardship, *The Nation* has run an ongoing campaign to expand its influence on college campuses, sponsoring speakers and debates and even launching a radio program, called "Radio Nation," which airs on forty college radio stations. Professor Navasky has also revealed that the magazine intends to put its agendas into a special "text," supplemented by computer programs, and geared toward colleges and high schools. Professor Navasky has described this politically motivated form of outreach as an "auxiliary teaching tool."

Professor Navasky has been a Guggenheim Fellow, a visiting scholar at the Russell Sage Foundation, and Ferris Visiting Professor of Journalism at Princeton. Navasky also serves on the boards of the Authors Guild, the writers' association known as PEN, and the Committee to Protect Journalists.

See also: Professors Foner, Jensen, McChesney, Marable

Research: Lowell Ponte, Jacob Laksin

Professor Priya Parmar
Brooklyn College

— Assistant professor of education, Brooklyn College

— Teaches that rap music is an effective tool for teaching English literacy to school children, and that proper English is the language of white "oppressors"

— Required students to view Michael Moore's *Fahrenheit 9/11* on the eve of the presidential election

Priya Parmar is an assistant professor of education at Brooklyn College, where she teaches both graduate and undergraduate courses in childhood education to aspiring teachers. She received her MA and PhD degrees in "Curriculum and Instruction" at Penn State University.

Rap music is of special interest to Pamar, whose doctoral dissertation is entitled "KRS-One Going Against the Grain: A Critical Study of Rap Music as a Postmodern Text." No mere enthusiast of the genre, Parmar holds that it is an unappreciated tool for imparting English literacy to young children: A 2003 Brooklyn College faculty newsletter reports that Parmar's scholarly writing "focuses on using hip-hop culture as a tool to increase literacy skills" in elementary and secondary schools.[677]

Those critics who question whether rap music, with its crude, violent, and misogynistic lyrics and its reliance on inner-city vernacular ("Ebonics"), is an effective medium for teaching literacy are dismissed by Parmar as craven apologists for bourgeois hegemony. "Rap music causes moral panic in many because of its 'threat' to existing values and ideologies held by the dominant middle class," asserts Parmar.[678] According to Parmar the sexual lyrics and violent subject matter of rap make perfectly appropriate learning aids for young children:

From my experience in the classrooms—and that of my students who are practitioners in the field—we've learned that kids—even as young as third grade—are very sophisticated about the homophobic, violent and sexual messages from some mainstream rap artists. If you give students an opportunity to deconstruct the lyrics and then compare them with those of more social and political consciousness raising artists, such as [rap groups] The Roots or Dead Prez...youth are capable of distinguishing between reality and false perceptions and stereotypes perpetuated in commercialized rap.[679]

Rap, Parmar teaches, is more than a means of teaching literacy. It is also a vehicle for social engineering. In addition to teaching children grammar and sentence structure, Parmar maintains, the "critical examination and deconstruction of rap lyrics becomes a method to get students to critically examine such issues as race, class, culture, and identity." Parmar calls this mode of instruction an "an empowering, liberating pedagogy." She notes with approval that one of her former students used rap to "explore economic social and political issues" in a middle school.[680]

Parmar's controversial course at Brooklyn College, "Language Literacy in Secondary Education," typifies the professor's preference for politicized pedagogy. Required of all students who intend to become secondary-school teachers, the course is designed to teach students to draft lesson plans that teach literacy. Parmar's syllabus informs students that the principal focus of these lesson plans must be "social justice."[681]

Another theme animating Parmar's course is her aversion to proper English usage. To insist on grammatical English, Parmar believes, is to exhibit an intolerable form of cultural chauvinism—a point reinforced by the preface to the requirements for her course, which adduces the following quotation from the South

African writer Jamul Ndebele: "The need to maintain control over English by its native speakers has given birth to a policy of manipulative open-mindedness in which it is held that English belongs to all who use it provided that it is used correctly. This is the art of giving away the bride while insisting that she still belongs to you."[682] Students are expected to share Parmar's antipathy toward grammatical rule-based English, since she does not countenance dissent: In December 2004, for instance, several disaffected Brooklyn College students wrote letters to the dean of the School of Education taking issue with Parmar's hostility toward students who dared voice their support for correct English usage.[683]

Nor was this the only confrontation between Parmar and her students. Evan Goldwyn, a Brooklyn College student who took Parmar's course, caused a campus furor when he wrote a lengthy critique of the course for the *New York Sun*, detailing his objections to Parmar's teaching methods. Topping Goldwyn's list of grievances were Parmar's pronounced bias against English and her bigotry towards white students. "She repeatedly referred to English as a language of oppressors and in particular denounced white people as the oppressors," Goldwyn wrote. "When offended students raised their hands to challenge Professor Parmar's assertion, they were ignored. Those students that disagreed with her were altogether denied the opportunity to speak."[684]

Students also charged that Parmar's insistence on bringing politics into the classroom went beyond issues relating to English literacy. A week before the 2004 presidential election, Parmar screened Michael Moore's anti-Bush documentary, *Fahrenheit 9/11* in class.[685] Students were required to attend the screening, even if they had already seen the film. "Most troubling of all," Goldwyn wrote, "she has insinuated that people who disagree with her views on issues such as Ebonics or *Fahrenheit 9/11* should not become teachers."[686]

> *See also:* Professors Baraka, Dyson, hooks, Shortell, Thomas
>
> *Research:* Jacob Laksin

Professor Emma Perez
University of Colorado, Boulder

— Associate professor of history

— Appointed chair of the Ethnic Studies Department after Ward Churchill's resignation

— Expressed "full and unconditional support of Ward Churchill and his First Amendment rights" during the controversy over Churchill's expressed desire to see the United States destroyed

Emma Perez is associate professor of history at the University of Colorado, Boulder. She was named chair of Boulder's Ethnic Studies Department after Ward Churchill resigned the position amid extreme controversy in February 2005. Prior to joining the Boulder faculty, Professor Perez taught at the University of Texas, El Paso, where she served as chair of the History Department, assistant vice president for graduate studies, and director of the Institute of Oral History. Perez earned her doctoral, master's, and bachelor's degrees at UCLA. She lists her teaching and research interests as: Chicana/Latina Studies in the United States and Mexico, gay/lesbian history, cultural studies, history and theory, feminist theory, postcolonial theory, women of color in the United States, and creative writing.[687]

Professor Perez has made it her mission to draw attention to what she regards as the paucity of information that history books have traditionally provided about Chicana women. (The terms "Chicana" and "Chicano" were appropriated by Mexican American activists in the Brown Power movement of the 1960s and 1970s in the American Southwest.)[688] To address her concern, Perez authored the 1999 book *The Decolonial Imaginary: Writing Chicanas into History*—a text she describes as "an archaeology of discursive fields of knowledge that write

Chicanas into histories."[689] Depicting history as a male-dominated discipline whose works are written largely from a male perspective (and focus heavily—and unfairly—on the deeds of men), Professor Perez writes, "I am more concerned with taking the 'his' out of the 'story,' the story that often becomes the universalist narrative in which women's experience is negated."[690]

According to Professor Perez, those women whose names do appear in history books are, for the most part, caricatured and misrepresented. "Voices of women from the past, voices of Chicanas, Mexicanas, and Indias, [sic] are utterances which are still minimalized, spurned, even scorned. And time...has not granted Chicanas, Mexicanas and Indias much of a voice at all. We are spoken about, spoken for, and ultimately encoded as whining, hysterical, irrational, or passive women who cannot know what is good for us, and who cannot know how to express or authorize our own narratives."[691]

Professor Perez writes of the anger she feels whenever "a white man was trying to persuade me to forget a history of brutality and move on."[692] White mistreatment of Chicanos is, in Professor Perez's view, by no means a thing of the past, but rather "a history that still brutalizes."[693] She lauds the author Antonia Castaneda for pointing out "how incoming Euro-americans sexualized Mexican women in their diaries and travel logs"—which both Perez and Castaneda cite as evidence of "the intimate bond between sexual violence and colonization."[694]

Regarding American culture as hostile to Mexicans, Professor Perez is less than enthusiastic about the efforts of "Chicanos/as" to assimilate into white society, though she empathizes with the emotions and the pragmatic concerns that she believes compel them to do so. "Few have probed how assimilation may be a tactic, an interstitial move for survival," writes Professor Perez. "Why must we call upon assimilation at all?...To say yes to speaking English, to say yes to an American education, to say yes to participation in organizations like the YWCA—these were interstitial moves for survival. The contradictions women faced forced them to accept existing structures and to create their subjecthood within those structures."[695]

Professor Perez identifies what she considers her personal and scholarly mission as follows: "[T]o invert all power... to love myself and other Chicanas and women of color, to revere the Chicana... is the revolution I speak of now.... I prefer to think of myself as one who places women, especially Third [W]orld and lesbians, in the forefront of my priorities."[696]

In February 2005, Professor Perez was among the most passionate defenders of Professor Ward Churchill when he faced public criticism for having described the victims of 9/11 as "little Eichmanns." "We as faculty in ethnic studies stand in full and unconditional support of Ward Churchill and his First Amendment rights," she said, explaining that Churchill's comments had been "misconstrued in virulent terms."[697]

Writing in the conspiracy-minded webzine *Counterpunch* in February 2005, Professor Perez argued that the criticism of Churchill's statements was rooted in a neo-conservative effort to establish ideological control over the University of Colorado: "We've done some preliminary research and analysis," wrote Professor Perez, "and it's become clear exactly what's at stake and what we're up against. CU-Boulder has been made the national frontline of the neocon battle for dominance in academe. CU-Boulder has likely been made their 'test case,' their break-the-mould moment in a national strategy. Their local resources and troops (think tanks, legislative, rank-and-file followers) are already fully mobilized and their national resources are mobilizing in our direction. This is much, much bigger than an individual attack on Ward [Churchill]. What we're looking at is a carefully developed, pre-existing national strategy that has been searching for exactly the right breakthrough 'test case.' It has found extremely favorable conditions in Ward's situation and in the post-911 climate. As they've been doing already in other areas, they want to dismantle the structural footholds (academic freedom/tenure, ethnic studies) that social movements gained for people of color and liberal and progressive intellectuals inside academe during the 60s & 70s."[698] Perez further hinted that criticism of Churchill was motivated by racism, asserting that "There are faculty who have problems with his being American Indian."[699]

This statement is an example of the quality of "scholarship" that has propelled Professor Perez to the chairmanship of a Department of History and now a Department of Ethnic Studies—since Ward Churchill is not an American Indian, and this has been public knowledge for some time; his false claims in this respect (which earned him his original appointment in ethnic studies) are part of the scandal.

As chair of ethnic studies, and even after she steps down, the fact is that Professor Perez will be having a large influence for the next two decades on the type of scholar this department hires, and on that person's fate at the University of Colorado. One can imagine the results in terms of, say, the creation of variety of ideological viewpoints in this department at a major university.

See also: Professors Ensalaco, Gutierrez, Meranto, Navarro

Research: John Perazzo

Sam Richards
Penn State University

— Senior lecturer in sociology at Penn State University
— Co-Director, Race Relations Project
— "I'm open about bringing my ideology into this classroom."

Dr. Sam Richards received his PhD in "political sociology and development with an emphasis on Latin America and Africa" from Rutgers University in 1985.[700] Liberation theology, which is a Christianized form of Marxism, was the topic of both Richards's master's thesis and his doctoral dissertation. According to Penn State's *The Collegian* "[he] worries about the future, because he believes the world is on an unstoppable path toward totalitarianism."[701]

On his academic website Dr. Richards concedes that "I never seriously studied race or ethnicity while in college, and I never took an undergraduate or graduate course in the topic." Yet he is now the co-director of the Race Relations Project at Penn State and teaches Sociology 119, which is "Race and Ethnic Relations." In Dr. Richards's courses, which include topics such as "Racial Inequality," "Genocide and the Holocaust," "International Racism and Foreign Policy," and "Global Inequality," students learn that the "real" story of the United States is not just the "official" one of "bravery and hardship, of sharing and community," but more importantly the story of "death and carnage, or murder and theft."[702]

According to Dr. Richards, a mendacious ruling class controls America's masses and directs the nation towards these malign ends. "Dominating groups control the means of ideological persuasion (e.g., mass media, culture mores, ethical principles)," and "[if] the dominant group/class can convince the masses to believe in some truth that benefits that dominant group, then the masses are less likely to object to the rule of that group."[703] This is crude even for a follower of Che Guevara. Nor does it explain how a primitive Marxist such as Richards can have been teaching for two decades at a major university.

When an interviewer questioned Dr. Richards about the evident lack of ideological balance in his lectures on foreign policy, he conceded that he makes no attempt to provide one. "My take on matters related to foreign policy," he explained, "was always to show a different side than the side that the American people are taught to believe since they start breathing."[704] And just who is teaching them?

For someone supposedly concerned with oppression and injustice, Dr. Richards also spends no class time on the despotisms that America opposes, like the Castro regime in Cuba. Instead he focuses on America's alleged oppression of Marxist dictatorships like the one in Nicaragua during the 1980s. After labeling U.S. actions in Nicaragua as "terrorist," he asks, "What does this example tell us about how we approach terrorism?"[705]

In his course "Genocide and Holocaust," Dr. Richards similarly ignores communist genocides and instead offers his students several alleged U.S. examples. His students learn that "the killing of the 'native' peoples in the Americas was genocide"; the U.S. military was directly or indirectly responsible for killing more than a million Vietnamese during the Vietnam War; and the killing of the East Timorese people by Indonesia from 1975 to the present has occurred with "direct assistance from the U.S. taxpayers."

Among Dr. Richards's in-class teaching materials are four pictures of President Bush juxtaposed with pictures of monkeys, under the heading, "some evolutionary mysteries are not quite so clear." Dr. Richards's class lessons are reinforced with "out-of-class' assignments that include the viewing of left-wing propaganda films such as *The Oil Factor*, from which students learn that the "war in Afghanistan has turned into a bloody quagmire,"[706] and that the war on terror is really all about controlling Iraqi and Central Asian oil reserves. *Occupation 101* is a propaganda film about the horrors of Israel's "occupation" of Palestinian territories that features interviews with such leftist luminaries as Noam Chomsky and Ramsey Clark, lawyer for the Communist torturers of American POWs, the Ayatollah Khomeni, Slobodan Milosovec, and Saddam Hussein. Dr. Richards also includes a hagiographic documentary called *You Can't Be Neutral on a Moving Train: Life and Times of Howard Zinn*, a Marxist historian who like Chomsky and Clark has written that America is the world's greatest terrorist state.

Dr. Richards's lecture notes for the first class of each semester inform students that, "It is not possible to keep our ideologies out of the classroom or any other place where ideas are shared. SO I'M OPEN ABOUT BRINGING MY IDEOLOGY INTO THIS CLASSROOM BECAUSE I SEE THAT ALL EDUCATIONAL SYSTEMS ARE IDEOLOGICAL TO THE CORE."[707] [emphasis in original] This is a pretty frank admission that his agenda is to indoctrinate students, not educate them.

Research: Thomas Jocelyn[708]

Professor Gayle Rubin
University of Michigan, Ann Arbor

— Assistant professor of anthropology, ethnology

— Recipient of the Woman of the Year Award from the National Leather Association, a sadomasochist, fetish, BDSM (Bondage & Discipline / Domination & Submission / Sadism & Masochism) organization

— Proponent of pedophilia. Argues that the government's crackdown on child molesters is a "savage and undeserved witch hunt"

Gayle S. Rubin is an assistant professor of anthropology at the University of Michigan, Ann Arbor, in the College of Literature, Science, & Arts. It was at that same university that in the 1970s, Rubin became the first women's studies major in the school's history. As a graduate student in anthropology at the University of Michigan, Professor Rubin rewrote her senior thesis, "The Traffic in Women: Notes on the 'Political Economy' of Sex," for the book *Toward an Anthropology of Women* (1975), a collection of essays edited by Rayna Rapp. For several years thereafter, that essay was the most cited text in the entire field of cultural anthropology.[709]

The essay[710] draws heavily on the writings of Karl Marx and Frederick Engels, as well as anthropologist Claude Levi-Strauss and the psychoanalysts Sigmund Freud and post-modernist Jacques Lacan. Professor Rubin's aim in this essay is to expose and condemn what she calls the "set of arrangements" that relegate women to a subordinate position in their relations with men. She believes that gender is a social and historical construct (i.e., man-created) that is neither natural nor essential, and that one of the chief goals of feminism is to liberate both sexes from the patriarchy-created "strait-jacket of gender."[711]

Professor Rubin is an enthusiastic advocate of "queer theory," which rejects the view that sexuality is a universal human impulse. It says that sexual desire does not exist apart from history and culture; that nothing is "natural," including heterosexuality. Professor Rubin further asserts that there are no natural differences between men and women. Her views on this topic are discussed by professors Micaela di Leonardo and Roger Lancaster in their article "Gender, Sexuality, Political Economy": "Gayle Rubin's 1975 'The Traffic in Women,' for example, a *tour de force* of Marxism, structuralism, and Freudo-Lacanian theory, draws on analogies with political economy to hypothesize a universal 'sex-gender system.' Rubin associates the universal presence of gender asymmetry with a system of compulsory heterosexuality. The one implies and mandates the other: the taboo on same-sex behavior both bars women from phallic power and mandates heterosexual alliance—the traffic in women. At the same time, the system of gender inequality requires an enforced and coercive production of dichotomous gender differences—an equilibrium that can only be enforced by a strict taboo on homologous couplings. Although overstated in their universalist scope, such arguments were mainstays of lesbian feminism, and signaled early on the possibilities of collaboration between feminism and gay/lesbian studies."[712]

Impressed by Marx's explanation of class oppression (despite its refutation by historical events), Professor Rubin sees capitalism as a powerful agent of the oppression of women, though by no means the only one. She defines capitalism as "a set of social relations in which production takes the form of turning money, things, and people into capital. And capital is a quantity of goods or money which, when exchanged for labor, reproduces and augments itself by extracting unpaid labor, or surplus value, from labor into itself."[713] She views women's housework as a critical component of the amount of unpaid labor that capitalists can squeeze out of the working class. An outspoken advocate of gay relationships, Professor Rubin further writes, "Suppression of the homosexual component of human sexuality, and by corollary... oppression of homosexuals, is... a product of the same system whose rules and relations oppress women."[714]

According to the University of Michigan website, Professor Rubin's research interests include "histories, theories, social constituents, and durable inequalities of sexualities and genders." Professor Rubin is currently working on a book on the gay male sadomasochist community in San Francisco.[715]

Professor Rubin has made her mark both as an academic and as an activist. On the one hand, her academic works like "The Traffic in Women," "The Leather Menace," and "Thinking Sex" have been published in scholarly books and academic journals. Such writings are mandatory reading in universities throughout the United States, including University of California, Santa Barbara, Harvard, Columbia, and MIT. She will soon publish, through the University of California Press, a collection of essays entitled *Deviations: Essays in Sex, Gender, and Politics*.

Professor Rubin has also written for non-academic publications such as the *Cuir Underground*, which published from 1994 to 1998 and is described as "a San Francisco-based magazine for the pansexual kink communities."[716] In her article "Old Guard, New Guard," Rubin writes: "In the 1950s there were those who eroticized and engaged in very formal interactions based on strict codes of courtesy in the military model, and others who preferred the look of dirty bikers and a more orgiastic kind of buddy sexuality. Of course, there were spit and polish bikers too, and others who looked like greasy bikers but preferred formal SM sex... In the mid-1960s, classic leather styles began to give way to a kind of 'hippie leather.' People grew their hair, took psychedelic drugs, became less invested in 1950s formality and created new subgroups organized around different sexual styles, for example fistfucking. At one point, dope smoking leather guys and fistfuckers were in effect a kind of 'New Guard' . . ."[717]

Professor Rubin was the founder of Samois,[718] the first ever women-on-women sadomasochism group, and its successor organization, the Outcasts. The latter takes pride in "proud and principled perversions."[719] In 1988 Professor Rubin received a Woman of the Year Award from the National Leather Association,[720] a sadomasochistic, fetish, BDSM (Bondage & Discipline/ Domination & Submission/Sadism & Masochism) organization.

Among Professor Rubin's more controversial positions has been her support for the practice of adults engaging in sex with minor children. Her endorsement of pedophilia was evident as early as 1978, when she wrote in "Leaping Lesbian":

> The recent career of boy-love in the public mind should serve as an alert that the self-interests of the feminist and gay movements are linked to simple justice for stigmatized sexual minorities. . . . We must not reject all sexual contact between adults and young people as inherently oppressive.[721]

In 1984, Professor Rubin refined and repeated her stance in "Thinking Sex." One commentator wrote of that article: "Rubin pursues her apology of pornography, prostitution, sado-masochism, and all dissident sexual minorities; she concentrates especially on the defense of pedophilia by refusing to see in it a form of sexual exploitation. For her, any law aiming at governing sexuality constitutes "a sexual apartheid," intended to strengthen the structures of power."[722]

Professor Rubin's views on pedophilia remained relatively restrained until the 2003 publication of *The Lesbian and Gay Studies Reader*, to which Rubin contributed a chapter openly endorsing pedophilia. In that chapter, she defended her claim that the government's pursuit of child molesters was "a savage and undeserved witch hunt"—reflective of a prejudice that has "more in common with ideologies of racism than with true ethics."[723] Professor Rubin wrote, "Boy lovers are so stigmatized that it is difficult to find defenders for their civil liberties, let alone erotic orientation. Consequently, the police have feasted on them. Local police, the FBI and watchdog postal inspectors have joined to build a huge apparatus whose sole aim is to wipe out the community of men who love underaged youth."[724] To Rubin, even pedophiles who prey on helpless children are the victims of captalism and the terrorist American State.

See also: Professors Brumfiel, Sedgwick, Warner

Research: Garin Hovannisian

Professor Dean Saitta
University of Denver

— Professor and chair of the Anthropology Department at the University of Denver

— Editorial board member of the journal *Rethinking Marxism*

— Supporter of Colorado professor Ward Churchill

Dean Saitta is chair of the Anthropology Department at the University of Denver and director of the university's Museum of Anthropology. His disparate research interests in North American archaeology and labor history are linked by his commitment to Marxist ideology. In 1993 and 1995 Professor Saitta received the Mortar Board, which is the "Top Prof" award at the University of Denver. In 1994, he received an award for Outstanding Support to the Office of Admissions and says that he "loves the opportunity to work with citizens and other educators in disseminating knowledge for the benefit of Colorado's citizenry." His idea of disseminating knowledge, however, is often indistinguishable from promoting radical political agendas and propaganda of an extreme nature. Professor Saitta has served six years on the board of directors at the Colorado Endowment for the Humanities and in 1998 he won the United Methodist Church University Scholar-Teacher of the Year Award.

In a March 2005 statement titled "Thoughts on Academic Free Speech," Saitta defended the beliefs and actions of Ward Churchill. Expressing concern about the future of radical political expression in the classroom, Professor Saitta wrote, "My main concern about the Churchill affair is what it portends for the future of informed, provocative speech in classrooms that are already being monitored by conservative thought police." Of course Churchill was not attacked for his comments in the classroom, which have neither been monitored nor reported. He was attacked for public statements, for fraudulent representations to the committee that hired him, for plagiarism and for shoddy scholarship.

Professor Saitta was also incorrect in asserting that University of Colorado professors—particularly those in the Ethnic Studies Department—felt they had to be careful about the political statements they made, lest they be characterized as too "liberal" by "conservative thought police." For example, Professor Jualynne Dodson of Colorado University's Ethnic Studies Department—an ardent supporter of Communist Cuba—publicly declared that "the world needs Cuba to go on fighting and demonstrating a viable alternative to the globalization of the capitalist system."[725] There were neither reactions nor consequences for her remarks.

On the other hand, Professor Saitta does not extend his calls for "provocative speech" on campus to individuals whose views differ from his. Early in 2005, fellow University of Denver professor Richard Lamm (a liberal Democrat and former Colorado governor) tried unsuccessfully to place an article in the university newspaper, *The Source*. Titled "Two Wands," the piece described a fanciful scenario where racism could be wiped out with the wave of a magic wand, and where minority neighborhoods could acquire, with the aid of a second wand, the intellectual and educational tools they would need in order to improve their lives without public assistance. Said Professor Lamm, "we must recognize that all the civil rights laws in the world are not going to solve the problem of minority failure. Ultimately Blacks and Hispanics are going to have to see that the solution is largely in their own hands."[726]

In Professor Saitta's view, *The Source*'s refusal to publish Lamm's article was not an example of academic censorship. "Governor Lamm sought to publish his essay in an inappropriate place," wrote Saitta. "... [T]here's no controversy here, and certainly no infringement of Governor Lamm's academic free-dom."[727]

Scientific papers and journal articles Professor Saitta has written include: "Communal Class Processes and Pre-Columbian Social Dynamics"; "Politics and Surplus Flow in Communal Societies"; "Dialoguing with the Ghost of Marx: Mode of Production in Archaeological Theory"; "Marxist Theory and Tribal Political Economy"; "Marxist Models of Chacoan Pre-history"; and "Marxism, Prehistory, and Primitive Communism." He is also the author of a forthcoming book titled *Marxism and Archaeology*. Professor Saitta is a member of the editorial board of the journal *Rethinking Marxism*, which "aims to stimulate interest in and debate over the explanatory power and social consequences of Marxian economic, cultural, and social analy-sis."[728]

See also: Professors Brumfiel, De Genova, Foster, Furr, Richards

Research: Thomas Ryan

Dean Orville Schell
University of California, Berkeley

— Dean of the Graduate School of Journalism
— Co-founder and longtime editor-in-chief of Pacific News Service

Orville Schell is dean of the Graduate School of Journalism at the University of California, Berkeley. Schell earned a master's degree in Chinese studies at UC Berkeley in 1967. Before becoming dean he had a long career as a radical intellectual, expressing views that have not significantly changed over the years. In the late sixties he became a researcher for sociology and history professor and anti-Vietnam War activist Franz Schurmann, who was head of the school's Center for Chinese Studies. In 1969 Schell and his mentor Schurmann co-founded radical Pacific News Service as a vehicle for creating and distributing news and commentary that undermined, criticized, and helped mobilize activism against United States policies during the Vietnam War. (Now retired from teaching, Schurmann continues to write a Left-syndicated column distributed by the Pacific News Service called "Politics of Empire.") Schell remained editor-in-chief of Pacific News Service until 1996.

In 1974, Schell was living on a factory commune in the People's Republic of China during the last years of its Communist dictator, Mao Zedong, who died in 1976. Schell's sorrow at the failure of Mao's socialist politics was evident in what for Schell was an unusually self-revealing winter 1988 interview with the counter-cultural Left magazine *Whole Earth Review*: "China was one model in the '60s and '70s for Westerners looking for new credos and new alternative belief systems. . . . It turned out that China consumed itself. It did not necessarily disprove that certain socialist models are completely inappropriate for Third

World developing countries. Rather it simply showed that the extremism of the Maoist experiment sabotaged that model.... It's a great shame that Mao screwed up. His megalomania over-powered his efforts to see if China could be the first country that would find some different way to put itself together and to develop."[729]

Mao's "screw up" led to the murder of more than a million human beings and the enslavement of many hundreds of millions more. Like others on the far Left, Schell blames Mao or Stalin for evils committed under Communist regimes—but never Communism or Marxism, whose totalitarian outlook makes megalomaniacal dictatorship and the mass violation of human rights inevitable. No such sympathy is in evidence when Schell describes the democratic capitalist alternative: "There isn't much I'd recommend anybody imitate in China now," Schell told *Whole Earth Review* in 1988, "because China is becoming an imitation of us.... Now among the young there's enormous amounts of crime and disaffection and skepticism and cynicism, along with disillusionment, and its analogue, a greed for money. People always reach for money when everything else fails."[730]

When the People's Republic of China was dogmatically Communist, Schell wrote of it as a beacon of hope and idealism. But the more China has inched towards capitalism, the more negative and even nasty towards it Schell's rhetoric has become. In 2004, for example, he described China as practicing "Leninist capitalism." In a September/October 1997 interview with the American socialist magazine *Mother Jones* (on whose masthead Schell is listed as a "contributing writer"), he described China's pro-free market reform ruler Deng Xiaoping as "the counterrev-olutionary *par excellence* in history."[731] He described the nation's minority of Communist Party leaders as "using their positions both in the party and in the government to make money."[732]

About China, Schell has written *In The People's Republic: An American's First-Hand View of Living and Working in China* (1976, Random House); *Watch Out for the Foreign Guests: China Encounters the West* (1981, Pantheon); *To Get Rich Is Glorious: China in the 1980's* (1984, Pantheon); *Discos and Democracy: China in the Throes of Reform* (1988, Pantheon); *Mandate of Heaven: A New Generation of Entrepreneurs, Dissidents, Technocrats, and Bohemians Grasp for Power in China* (1994, Simon & Schuster); *The China Reader: The Reform Years* co-edited with David Shambaugh, (1999, Vintage); and *Empire: Impressions of China* (5 Continents Press, 2004).

Schell is an environmental activist who lives in Bolinas, California, and wrote about its counterculture activists' efforts to thwart private property development in *The Town That Fought to Save Itself* (1976, Pantheon). He is a pig farmer with his own small meat business and has written about that as well in *Modern Meat: Antibiotics, Hormones and the Pharmaceutical Farm* (1983, Random House).

After twenty-five years as a "progressive" journalist, Schell was selected as the new dean of the Graduate School of Journalism at UC Berkeley, a post he has held for the last ten years. Dean Schell's selection was not without controversy. The head of the search committee, Berkeley Marxist Troy Duster, refused to even interview the one qualified conservative journalist who applied for the job. A lawsuit filed by the Individual Rights Foundation contended that Schell's appointment constituted political patronage, illegal under California labor laws. It also argued that a political litmus test for the deanship illegally denied public employment and First Amendment rights to a conservative applicant because of his political ideas. The lawsuit was dropped after the conservative applicant abandoned the fight.

In 2000, Dean Schell published *Virtual Tibet: Searching for Shangri-La from The Himalayas to Hollywood* (Holt/Metropolitan

Books). It discussed the construction, and deconstruction, of what this ancient nation now under brutal Communist Chinese occupation has meant in the Western world view. To his credit, Dean Schell has urged the People's Republic of China to grant autonomy to Tibet and to re-admit its traditional leader, the Dali Lama.

Nevertheless, Dean Schell has made the UC Berkeley Journalism School a hothouse culture of left-wing exotics. Among his faculty appointments are Barbara Ehrenreich, an editor at *Mother Jones* and other Left publications and an officer of Democratic Socialists of America, the largest American wing of the Socialist International; anti-Iraq war activist of *The New Yorker*: veteran Berkeley radical and book editor Steve Wasserman; and Tom Engelhardt, author of the Left blog *TomDispatch* at The Nation Institute. Perhaps the closest Dean Schell has come to including a non party-liner teaching fellow in recent years is left-wing maverick Christopher Hitchens.

When asked by the *California Monthly* if there is "a liberal bias in the media," Dean Schell replied: "I don't know. I could ask you another question: Is there a liberal bias amongst educated people?"[733]

> **See also:** Professors Jensen, McChesney, Navasky
>
> **Research:** Lowell Ponte

Professor Michael Schwartz
State University of New York, Stony Brook

— Professor of sociology

— Director of the Undergraduate College of Global Studies
   at Stony Book

— "We as Americans have to hope America will lose [the war in
   Iraq]. If we win, we have to expect more wars, more
   destruction."

Throughout his thirty-year career at the State University of
New York, Stony Brook, Professor Michael Schwartz has cultivated a colorful array of radical interests. A contributor to Marxist journals such as *Science & Society*, Professor Schwartz has
authored books on radical theory (*Radical Politics and Social
Structure, 1976*), assaults on the American business community
(Power Structure of American Business, 1985), and polemics
against his ideological opponents *(Social Policy and the Conservative Agenda)*.

In an ostensible show of solidarity with the working class, the
Harvard-educated Schwartz (PhD 1971) is also listed as an affiliate faculty member with the Center for Study of Working Class
Life, a Stony Brook facility that promotes "multiple forms of
scholarship, teaching, and activism related to working-class life
and cultures."[734] The center is headed by the Marxist economist
Michael Zweig. In addition, Professor Schwartz regularly lends
his signature to causes espoused by labor union activists. In September of 2001, for instance, Professor Schwartz's name
appeared on a statement authored by New York City labor
activists that opposed the U.S.-led intervention in Afghanistan
on the grounds that the "United States and its allies have already
inflicted widespread suffering on innocent people in such places

as Iraq, Sudan, Israel and the Occupied Territories, the former Yugoslavia and Latin America."[735]

Over the years, Professor Schwartz has been well compensated for this output. In 1986, he was awarded a $125,000 grant by the National Science Foundation. The grant allowed him to bring his Marxist insights to bear on the study of the "causes of industrial decline." Perhaps unsurprisingly, many of the sociology courses offered at Stony Brook bear the imprint of Professor Schwartz's Marxist obsession with class conflict and ruling class oppression. A course called "Stratification" purports to investigate the "causes and consequences of the unequal distribution of wealth, power, prestige, and other social values in different societies."[736] Special seminars in the Stony Brook sociology department regularly take as their subject issues like "Advanced Topics in Marxist Theory," as though the decline and fall of all Marxist societies of such economic basket cases as North Korea and Cuba never happened.

Professor Schwartz's Marxism has guided him to the other side in the war on terror, towards which his interests are anything but academic. In November of 2004, just as U.S. troops were laying siege to the terrorist stronghold of Fallujah, Professor Schwartz was leading a crowd of anti-war protesters rooting for an American defeat. "We as Americans have to hope America will lose," Professor Schwartz declared. "If we win, we have to expect more wars, more destruction. Iran is next, Syria is next, and this is only the beginning."[737] The remarks, which echoed similar comments by professors Nicholas DeGenova, Robert Jensen, John Pilger, Ward Churchill, and others, were hardly spontaneous. Writing in the *Asia Times* in late September 2004, Professor Schwartz entreated the "international community" to side with terrorists in Iraq in opposing the then incipient U.S. offensive in Fallujah. Cautioning that "even the most ferocious Iraqi resistance may not be sufficient to deter the coming November offensive," Professor Schwartz wrote, "the Iraqis need and deserve the support of the international community; the best (and least destructive) deterrent against this impending onslaught would be the threat of uncontrollable worldwide protest, should the U.S. attempt to level either Fallujah or Sadr City."[738]

In defense of this forthrightly anti-American position, Professor Schwartz sought to portray the terrorists beheading Iraqi, American, and other foreign infidels in Fallujah as gallant "revolutionaries" fighting a rearguard action against "brutal" American tactics. Professor Schwartz repeated terrorist propaganda, dismissing the "cover story" that U.S. military forces were targeting legitimate terrorist targets, a charge he purportedly substantiated by noting that "hospitals report daily that the vast majority of the casualties are civilians."[739] Professor Schwartz declined to note that the majority of those casualties were caused not by U.S. forces but by the terrorist "insurgents" whose cause he urged the world to embrace.

This too was not a novel argument for Professor Schwartz. In August of 2004, writing in *TomDispatch.com*, a site run under the auspices of The Nation Institute, Professor Schwartz inveighed against the U.S. offensive in Najaf, condemning the "agony" of the American campaign against the Shiite guerrillas of radical cleric Muqtada al-Sadr, and bemoaning "the death and destruction it is wreaking on an ancient and holy city."[740] The overheated rhetoric was a logical leap from Professor Schwartz's claim, in June of 2004, that the "Bush administration plans to remake Iraq as an agent of American policy in the Middle East."[741]

Professor Schwartz now has his own taxpayer-funded personal pulpit at Stony Brook: he serves as the faculty director of a Stony Brook institution called the Undergraduate College of Global Studies. Informing students that its function is "preparing you to be a citizen of the world," the College of Global Studies has its own unique conception of proper citizenship. A November 2004 conference sponsored by the College of Global Studies was called "Could You Be Drafted? Forum on the Draft." The conference featured a gallery of left-wing speakers. Among them was Michael Foley, a professor of history at the City University of New York and the author of *Confronting the War Machine: Draft Resistance During the Vietnam War;* Brother Clarke Berge, an activist and Protestant chaplain at Stony Brook; and Anita Cole, a member of the Center on Conscience and War, a non-profit group that champions the "rights of conscientious objectors."

In typically tendentious fashion, Professor Schwartz began the forum by asserting that the introduction of a military draft was not only possible but, indeed, imminent. So desperate was the beleaguered American military for additional manpower, according to Schwartz, that the U.S. government intended to enact a draft—which Schwartz called a "ticking time bomb"—in the spring of 2005. "This ticking time bomb will go off next spring," Professor Schwartz declared.[742] However, spring came and with it the first free elections in Iraq in half a century—elections that U.S. victories made possible, and without a draft.

See also: Professors Aronowitz, Berlowitz,
Cloud, Eckstein, Fellman, Haffar,
Richards, Shortell, Targ
Research: Jacob Laksin

Eve Kosofsky Sedgwick
City University of New York

— Distinguished professor of English at the City University of New York

— Leading "queer theorist"

— Believes that literary texts are little more than embodiments of radical political causes

Eve Kosofsky Sedgwick is a distinguished professor of English at the City University of New York, but her specialty is really queer studies. It is a measure of her prominence in this field that she has bred countless imitators and earned the nickname the "queen of queer theory."[743]

Professor Sedgwick explains her academic campaign on behalf of queer theory as a necessary response to what is, to her mind, a reactionary American culture that harbors a murderous antipathy toward homosexuals. "Seemingly, this society wants its children to know nothing; wants its queer children to conform or (and this is not a figure of speech) die; and wants not to know that it is getting what it wants." So Sedgwick claimed in her 1993 book *Tendencies*.[744]

Courses taught by Professor Sedgwick seek to confine literary achievements—and even entire literary eras—in a rigidly ideological harness. In the spring of 2002, Sedgwick presided over a seminar titled "Victorian Textures." After readings in Victorian fiction, prose, and poetry, students were expected to gain some insight into the "material world of the Victorians."[745] But they were to gain these insights in Professor Sedgwick's own ideological terms: "class," "imperial relations," "spirituality," and "gender and sexuality."[746]

Professor Sedgwick's interest in portraying Victorian-era writings as vessels of radical theory has been a recurring theme throughout her career. In 1989 Sedgwick, then the Newman Ivey White Professor of English at Duke, taught a graduate course called "Gender, Sexuality, and Power in Victorian Fiction." Topping the list of issues discussed in the course were "female and male homosocial, homosexual, homophobic, and cross-gender relations."[747] Sedgwick's efforts to write queer theory into the Victorian era are also encapsulated in her 1985 work, *Between Men: English Literature and Male Homosexual Desire*. Among the claims advanced in this book is Professor Sedgwick's belief that the aristocratic men of nineteenth century England were drawn to a "homosexual role and culture."[748]

An analogous methodology operates in the course Professor Sedgwick teaches yearly on Marcel Proust. The course focuses on Proust's *A la recherche du temps perdu* (*Remembrance of Things Past*). But students anticipating an introduction to the grand themes of childhood memory and unrequited love that infuse Proust's classic novel are destined for disappointment. As a course description illustrates, the issues of primary interest to Sedgwick are of an altogether different variety. These include the "complicated relation to the emerging discourses of Euro-American homosexuality," "the vicissitudes of gender," "the relations between Jewish diasporic being and queer diasporic being within modernism," and "phallic and non-phallic sexualities." Professor Sedgwick expresses the hope that the course will become a discussion forum for her distinctly radical "preoccupations."[749]

Proust is by no means the only author to be drummed out of the closet by Professor Sedgwick's politically motivated theories. A self-described "sexual pervert,"[750] Professor Sedgwick interprets Henry James's diary entries as "an invocation to fisting-as-écriture"[751] and has ransacked James's writings for evidence of the suppressed homosexual desires in which she claims they abound. Other writers afforded the Sedgwick treatment include Jane Austen, the subject of a 1989 lecture before the Modern Language Association titled, "Jane Austen and the Masturbating Girl."[752]

Professor Sedgwick also teaches classes in "Non-Oedipal Psychologies: Psychoanalytic Approach to Queer Theory," and "Queer Performativity." A course description for "Queer Performativity" observes that the "theatrical and deconstructive meanings of 'performative' seem to span the polarities of, at either extreme, the extroversion of the actor vs. the introversion of the signifier; the supposedly total efficiency of liturgy, advertising, and propaganda vs. the self-referential signifier's dislinkage of cause from effect."[753] Infinitely less opaque than these theoretical references is the course's declared interest in "identity-based political activism."[754]

Professor Sedgwick's influence over young academics has been considerable. Inspired by her certitudes as to the broadly homophobic and progress-averse nature of American society, a central theme of her 1990 *Epistemology of the Closet*, disciples of the "queen of queer theory" have wreaked observable havoc on the field of literary studies. Hostile to the enduring literary themes of their subjects, the dilemmas of life and death and the complexities of human conflict, they instead engage in "queering" the texts, i.e., reducing them to palimpsests in which they read the evidence of sexual repression and homophobia that reaffirms their political choices.

See also: Professors Berube, Dawes, hooks, Rubin

Research: Jacob Laksin

Professor Timothy Shortell
Brooklyn College

— Associate professor of sociology, Brooklyn College
— Writes about religious people as "moral retards"
— Characterizes America as a "fascist state"

Timothy Shortell is an associate professor of sociology at Brooklyn College, a campus of the City University of New York. He earned a BS degree in psychology from Washington State University in 1987, and a PhD in social psychology from Boston College in 1993. Despite having published only one peer-reviewed article (and not a single book) since joining the Brooklyn College faculty in 1998, the school's Sociology Department elected Shortell to a three-year term as its new chairman in May 2005. This was a significant move, since department chairs are very powerful in the CUNY system. Chairs like Shortell make tenure and termination decisions about other professors, raising the issue as to whether a man so prejudiced against religious people, whom he had referred to as "moral retards,"[755] could ever countenance the hiring of one to his faculty. Professor Shortell's election as chairman sparked a public controversy because of his radical, and oftentimes crudely expressed, views on a number of matters. Those who voted for him could not have been unaware of his published comments when casting their ballots, but a majority voted for him anyway. Eventually public reaction, coming in the wake of the Ward Churchill affair, was so strong that it caused the administration at Brooklyn College to successfully seek his withdrawal.

Most notably, Professor Shortell had proclaimed himself a passionate hater of organized religion and its practitioners. Characterizing religion as a portal to inevitably dangerous and contemptible extremism, he wrote: "... [R]eligion without fanaticism is a logical impossibility. Anyone whose mind is trapped inside such a mental prison will be susceptible to extreme forms of hatred and violence. Faith is, by its very nature, obsessive-compulsive. All religions foment their own kind of holy war. (Those whose devotion is moderate are only cowardly fanatics.) In a world in which individuals and events are controlled by magical forces (symbolized by spirits, angels, ghosts, gods, etc.) fear will be the equilibrium state. There is no way to understand how such a world functions; one will be in awe of those who, through their mystifications, appear to have a special understanding of supernatural mechanics. Faith is, therefore, a child-like rationality."[756]

Sneering at those who believe in divinity and attempt to live according to the tenets of their faith, Professor Shortell characterized religious people as intellectually immature and consequently "incapable of moral action, just as children are." Professor Shortell continues: "On a personal level, religiosity is merely annoying—like bad taste. This immaturity represents a significant social problem, however, because religious adherents fail to recognize their limitations. So, in the name of their faith, these moral retards are running around pointing fingers and doing real harm to others. One only has to read the newspaper to see the results of their handiwork. They discriminate, exclude and belittle. They make a virtue of closed-mindedness and virulent ignorance. They are an ugly, violent lot."[757]

Christians are inherently violent in Professor Shortell's view. "American Christians," he has written, "like to think that religious violence is a problem only for other faiths. In the heart of every Christian, though, is a tiny voice preaching self-righteousness, paranoia and hatred. Christians claim that theirs is a faith based on love, but they'll just as soon kill you."[758] On the other hand, Professor Shortell gives no indication that he considers contemporary Islamic fundamentalism, which underpins the most hateful and murderous terrorist movements of our time, to be of any special concern.

Along with religion, Professor Shortell despises America's economic system: "Weakness," he writes, "is demanded of us by religion and consumer capitalism."[759] The categories of Professor Shortell's hatreds goes on. He describes President Bush as America's "war-criminal-in-chief"[760]—and compares the Bush administration to Hitler's. "Someone really ought to do a comparative study of this administration and the propaganda techniques of Nazi Germany," Professor Shortell writes. "Karl Rove [the Republican political strategist] owes a lot to Joseph Goebbels [Hitler's minister of propaganda]."[761]

Professor Shortell loathes the United States, which he regards as an aggressive, oppressive nation that is quite content to sacrifice countless numbers of innocent lives as it lustfully pursues its quest for empire and dominion. "Just as any fascist state," he writes, "the megalomania of the ruling elite is paid for in working class blood."[762]

Professor Shortell's view of America as the incarnation of evil is on display in a poem he wrote called: "Brownshirts."

I have seen the next generationof brownshirts.They are aroused by the smellof blood in the airintoxicated by the power of intimidation.Old fascists lead them around by the nosesfeeding them worms and lies.[763]

Despite the controversy provoked by his views and despite his lack of substantial published scholarship, Professor Shortell enjoys the complete confidence of Brooklyn College's chief academic officer Roberta Matthews. Not surprisingly, her motto is: "teaching is a political act."[764]

Research: John Perazzo

Professor Harry Targ
Purdue University

— Professor of political science and international relations, Purdue University
— Director of Peace Studies program
— Member of the executive committee of the Communist Party faction called the Committees of Correspondence for Democracy and Socialism

Harry Targ is a professor of political science and international relations at Purdue University and the director of the school's Peace Studies program. He is a member of the National Executive Committee of the "Committees of Correspondence for Democracy and Socialism," a faction of the Communist Party USA that includes UC Santa Cruz professors Angela Davis and Bettina Aptheker, Columbia professor Manning Marable and UC Santa Cruz provost Conn Hallinan. The faction was expelled from the Party by leader Gus Hall in 1991 for opposing the hard-liner coup against the Soviet Union's last dictator Mikhail Gorbachev.

Professor Targ's views on the questions of war and peace are standard Communist doctrine. Addressing himself to "the power of the people"[765] in an April 2003 email, Professor Targ called for concerted opposition to "U.S. imperialism,"[766] making it clear that he viewed the United States specifically, and capitalism more broadly, as the greatest threats to international security: "We need to clarify the connections between U.S. capitalism, global conquest, and visions of empire... we need to discover where multinational corporations and international financiers stand, whether the oil and/or military industries are driving the doctrine of preemption, and which, if any, sectors of the ruling class regard unilateralism, globalism, and militarism as a threat to global trade, production, investment and speculation."[767] Professor Targ also condemned the U.S.-led war against Iraq, on the grounds that it represented the "U.S. drive toward global hegemony." To the extent that Professor Targ evinced any concern for the suffering of Iraqis, he placed the blame squarely on American intervention in the early 1990s to oppose Iraq's aggression against Kuwait. In one February 2003 interview with a local Indiana newspaper, Professor Targ dismissed the "war option" as "grotesque and inhumane," adding, "The Iraqis never recovered from the first Gulf War."[768] That same month, Professor Targ condemned any attempt to liberate Iraq by proclaiming, "If there's one Iraqi who's killed as a result of this [war], it's criminal."[769]

Professor Targ has no hesitation about using his classroom as a megaphone for the one-sided promulgation of his political ideas. The Peace Studies program at Purdue is designed to indoctrinate undergraduates in Professor Targ's political views. In his preferred approach to Peace Studies, Professor Targ employs two strategies: First, as noted earlier, he says, "we need to clarify the connections between U.S. capitalism, global conquest, and visions of empire." Second, "we need to discern whether the imperial superpower is homogeneous or riddled with factional disagreements that can be used for our purposes."[770] To this end, the Peace Studies program features such courses as "Persuasion in Social Movements," "America in Vietnam," and "Classical and Contemporary Marxism." The last is a course in applied Marxist doctrines, which includes two propaganda films that reflect the range of the course. One "illustrates the trajectory from Marx's Manifesto to anti-globalization movements," while the second lionizes the terrorists in Chiapas, Mexico, showing how their activities "intertwine" so-called "post-colonial" theories of liberation with "liberation theology," which is a religious coating for Marxist agendas.[771]

"Persuasion in Social Movements" meanwhile is a practical training course for radical activists. As described in the course catalogue, it "focuses on six essential functions persuasion serves for social movements."[772] Among these are: "transforming perceptions of reality; altering self-perceptions of protesters; [and] legitimizing the social movement."[773] Professor Targ himself instructs the required lecture course for Peace Studies, called "Introduction to the Study of Peace," in which he draws on the views he has developed in tracts like *International Relations in a World of Imperialism and Class Struggle* and *Cuba and the United States: A New World Order?* Professor Targ is also the co-editor of *Marxism Today: Essays on Capitalism, Socialism, and Strategies for Social Change.*

In addition to his duties as a professor, Targ serves as the coordinator and administrator of Purdue's "Committee on Peace Studies." In keeping with the activist nature of the Peace Studies program, the committee organizes public propaganda sessions whose recent focus has been devoted to condemning the Bush administration, the war in Iraq, and the greater war on terror, and brings radical speakers to campus. Among the speakers that have been invited to Purdue are the anti-American British journalist Robert Fisk. In November of 2002, Fisk delivered a lecture at Purdue entitled "September 11: Ask Who Did It, But for Heaven's Sake Don't Ask Why." A report in the campus newspaper recorded that Professor Targ "turned Fisk's visit into homework for 140 students in his classes on U.S. foreign policy and introduction to peace studies."[774] In January 2003 the Purdue Peace Studies Committee screened a film assailing the looming war to liberate Iraq. Professor Targ is a longtime enthusiast of left-wing propaganda films. He wrote a review of Michael Moore's *Fahrenheit 9/11*, in which he cheered its portrayal of the "brutal and bloodthirsty consciousness of young American fighting men and women at the outset of the [Iraq] war," warning that the "film is the one that can help people understand that defeating George Bush is a necessary but not sufficient condition to create a just society."[775]

The Peace Studies program at Purdue also includes a trip to the terror-sponsoring state of Cuba. In a course titled "Experiencing Cuba," co-taught by Professor Targ, students are given the opportunity to tour Fidel Castro's Communist police state. For eighteen days in May 2004, Professor Targ chaperoned students to Cuba, where they were "educated" at a Cuban university and visited factories and farms to learn about socialist means of production. An agreement was signed with the Castro dictatorship for a student and faculty exchange between Havana University and Purdue. Of this, observed Professor Targ, "We have a real chance to change all levels of education."[776]

A secondary purpose of the trip was to protest the embargo the United States has placed on Cuba in the hopes of ending the Castro dictatorship's extensive violations of human rights. Naturally, Professor Targ had nothing to say about Castro's political prisons, but called the U.S. policy "draconian." As a member of the Committees of Correspondence for Democracy and Socialism, Professor Targ, a longtime Castro supporter, continues to hail the Cuban Revolution as "a radical and deeply egalitarian socialist experiment which has raised the bar to new heights on questions of race, gender and class equality and international solidarity."[777] Targ is also the co-founder of the local Lafayette Committee in Solidarity with the People of El Salvador, an organization created by Cuban intelligence to lend support to the Communist guerrilla movement in El Salvador during the 1980s.

See also: Professors Aptheker, Cloud, Davis, Marable

Research: Jacob Laksin

Professor Greg Thomas

Syracuse University

— Assistant professor of rhetoric, Syracuse University

— Teaches an accredited course on raunchy hip-hop icon Lil' Kim titled "Hip-Hop Eshu: Queen Bitch 101—The Life and Times of Lil' Kim."

— Advocates revolution in the United States

In the fall of 2004, through no intention of his own, Greg Thomas became a poster professor for academic degeneracy and decline. Contemptuous of the Great Books (University of Chicago) approach to literary study, the assistant professor of rhetoric at Syracuse University instead drew his texts from the Billboard charts for rap artists, introducing a new course devoted to the lyrics of Lil' Kim (real name: Kimberly Jones). The for-credit course, offered through the College of Arts and Sciences at Syracuse, was titled "Hip-Hop Eshu: Queen Bitch 101—The Life and Times of Lil' Kim."

Professor Thomas saw much to admire in Lil' Kim's foul-mouthed *repertoire*: "It's the art with the most profound sexual politics I've ever seen anywhere," he said.[778] "It's about her lyricism and the lyrical persona... new notions of sexual consciousness, sexual politics in her rhymes, how she deals with societies based on male domination in her rhymes and societies based on rigid gender categories and constructs."[779] Interviewed by ABC Radio, Professor Thomas stressed that "[h]er lyrical artistry is nothing short of revolutionary."[780]

Writing on the website allhiphop.com, Professor Thomas boasted that his course "overturns male domination, lyrically, and rigid, homophobic gender identity on record—way more effectively than any elite Women's or Gay & Lesbian Studies program in academia,"[781] and rhapsodized that Lil' Kim's "whole system of rhymes radically redistributes power, pleasure and privilege, always doing the unthinkable, embracing sexuality on her kind of terms."[782]

According to Professor Thomas, the course addressed another pressing dilemma: "How do we communicate the political absurdity of this brilliant Black female artist facing hard time [Lil Kim had been convicted of perjury] in the age of George 'Weapon of Mass Destruction' Bush, and all these corporate lies?"[783] The entire class, observed Professor Thomas, "developed out of my ongoing research on race and sex in the context of empire."[784]

Professor Thomas began the course by instructing his students to transcribe the lyrics of "Get Money," a song that Lil' Kim had recorded with her group Junior M*A*F*I*A. Among other colorful incantations, it featured the following lines:

> Niggas…betta grab a seatgrab on ya dick as this bitch gets deepDeeper than a pussy of a bitch 6 feetstiff dicks feel sweet in this little petite[785]

Professor Thomas described his classroom technique to a reporter this way: "After [the students] had basically been compelled to show respect to the song…then we did the video analysis," adding, "They got to see the way that that meaning was translated on video. They were blown away and we've been riding ever since."[786] To supplement the "analysis" of "Get Money," Professor Thomas had his students conduct comparative analyses with other rap music. The *Syracuse Post-Standard* reported a classroom exchange between Professor Thomas and his students:

> "Ya'll know that [rapper] Jay-Z joint? I got 99 problems?" [Thomas] asks his students. "How the chorus go?"

"If you having girl problems, I feel bad for you son," Thomas says along with the class. "I got 99 problems but a bitch ain't one."

"The chorus draws an equivalence between a girl and a bitch. Is the girl a positive or negative?" he asks. "Negative," they say in unison.

"(Jay-Z) says his problems are bigger than a bitch."

Then he plays a Lil' Kim joint. One where she uses Jay-Z's line about 99 problems except her meaning is different.

"It's a whole difference articulation of the same words," Thomas says.

"Jay-Z says they're beneath him. She says bitches are not her number one enemy. Men are. See how it's been flipped?"

Scribbling notes, several students nod.[787]

In November 2004, Professor Thomas turned his classroom into an unofficial rap venue when he invited Lil' Kim to speak before faculty and students. Though initially startled by the invitation—"I was shocked," the rapper confessed to one newspaper reporter—she enthusiastically accepted. And so, for ninety minutes, Lil Kim' proceeded to share her wisdom with the gathered students and faculty, before answering students' questions on topics such as "race, gender and sexuality." "At the same time you're learning from me, I'm learning from you," she gushed.[788]

Critics, largely outside the university, rebuked Professor Thomas for profaning a serious college curriculum. But he had no patience for their concerns. The intellectual appeal of Lil' Kim, he sniffed, was "beautifully clear to anyone who is not committed to illiteracy in the language and literature of Hip-Hop."[789] Professor Thomas's enthusiasm for Lil' Kim was unchastened by her conviction for perjury in a case involving a gunfight outside a radio station. In a sulfurous polemic, Professor Thomas condemned the court, whose action he termed

evidence of the persecution of "Black women who do not conform to white racist codes of sexual repression."[790] Said Professor Thomas: "This case was not about 'perjury' at all, no more
than the U.S. in Iraq is about 'liberation.' It's about whether or
not we cooperate with state power, however illegitimate, and
this includes its power to persecute us—as usual. It is about the
power of the government to criminalize and imprison us along
lines of race, class and Hip-Hop affiliation, over here, when they
don't send us to commit their own violence over there. And if
'lies' were actually 'immoral,' according to the U.S. state, its
prison-industrial complex might not be large enough to house
those who rule us."[791]

Such sentiments were signature Greg Thomas, whose radicalism had long preceded "Hip Hop Eshu: Queen Bitch 101."
Professor Thomas is a longtime devotee of the radical black
activist Elaine Brown, a former head of the Black Panther Party,
who views America as a racist, fascist state. Brown's autobiography, *A Taste of Power*, describes a criminal career and a criminal
mind,[792] but to Professor Thomas hers is a tale of "Bourgeois
Cancer vs. Revolutionary Love."[793]

In December 2002, Professor Thomas played an instrumental role in bringing Brown to the Syracuse campus to deliver a
well-paid speech. Brown more than lived up to her end of the
bargain by using her speech to call for the immediate overthrow
of the American government: "On behalf of black people and all
oppressed people, I am calling for unfettered action—I would
like a regime change in America by any means necessary," Brown
declared.[794] Brown followed up this call with a hagiographic
account of the Black Panther Party, which she hailed for its "ideological commitment to black people." Professor Thomas, who
regularly assigns Brown's book as mandatory reading, was particularly delighted by her presence at Syracuse. "When you go to

see Elaine Brown, you leave knowing what she's about, and you leave wanting to learn more," Professor Thomas enthused to the campus newspaper, *The Daily Orange.* "She's exciting, entertaining, knowledgeable—everything you could want."[795]

Professor Thomas is the founder and editor of *Proud Flesh.* In an editorial in its premiere issue, after praising the calumnies of convicted Black Panther felon George Jackson against "Urban Fascist Amerika," Professor Thomas explained the journal's agenda: "we seek revolutionary words and strive to make them flesh."[796] In the fall 2003 issue of *The New Centennial Review* Professor Thomas observed: "The entire history of our African presence in 'American' captivity is one that lays bare a raw sexual terror that defines the cult of 'white supremacy' here and elsewhere." Professor Thomas contended that the history of blacks in the United States could be explained as an uninterrupted procession of "direct and indirect colonization."

In a second article, Professor Thomas railed against the concept of "post-coloniality." Post-colonialism is a popular theme of left-wing academics, but according to Professor Thomas there is no post-colonial reality in a country in which black people are colonized. The article, not distinguished by its coherence, offered a final insight into Professor Thomas's bitter and conspiratorial mind:

Saying "Post-coloniality" is like saying President Bush your words cry "freedom" while your life is full of bombs, surveillance, police brutality, corporate looting, fire and brimstone, Black Death, comprador complicity, democratic fascism, unfreedom. When a CIA father invents a "dictator" chief, installs him against a people's will, then bombs these same people again and again; and when his unelected son continues, after said chief becomes disposable, after another chief "terrorist" and former employee cannot be found, all in the name of Liberty, in the name of white men's burdens; then it's time we remember that *Liberty* was a slave ship. That it *is* a slave ship.[797]

See also: Professors Baraka, Davis, Dyson
hooks, Marable, Richards

Research: Jacob Laksin

Professor Suzanne Toton
Villanova University

— Associate professor of theology, Villanova University
— Instructor in Villanova's Center for Peace and Justice Education
— Promotes liberation theology, a form of Marxism disguised as Christianity

Suzanne Toton is an associate professor of theology at Villanova University, and is a faculty member of the University's Center for Peace and Justice Education, an interdisciplinary program that offers students both a minor and a concentration in issues of "world peace and social justice."

Professor Toton teaches the course "Global Poverty: Liberation Theology & the Struggle for Justice." This class, which receives more attention than most others in the course description section of the center's website, is ostensibly dedicated to:

Examin[ing] from a Christian ethical perspective: a) the structural and systemic linkages that produced wealth for one region of the world and poverty for the other; b) the phenomenon of globalization and its potential to promote or set development back further; c) the responsibility of the affluent to reshape the global order into one that is more just, compassionate and peaceful; and d) what the Christian churches and the Roman Catholic church in particular are doing to address global poverty.[798]

"Liberation theology" is a form of Marxized Christianity.[799] Its objective is to show Christians how Marxist-Leninist ideology is really a secular form of the Christian gospels.

One book that Professor Toton requires her students to read is Dorothy Day's *Loaves and Fishes*. Day was a Marxist Catholic who in the 1930s helped found the Catholic Workers Movement, which was both socialist and pacifist. Today, the Catholic Worker's Movement still advances its agendas by promoting individuals like Noam Chomsky and organizations like the International Action Center founded by Ramsey Clark.[800]

Professor Toton's liberation theology pervades her teaching curriculum. In her course "Service and Education for Justice," for example, the writings of Latin American Liberation theologians provide her basic texts.[801]

Professor Toton is an advisor to Villanova's chapter of Bread for the World, a politicized "citizens" movement seeking "justice for the world's hungry people by lobbying our nation's decision makers." In the 2000 election year, Bread for the World graded every congressional representative, giving each a numerical score between 0 and 100, depending on the percentage of times he or she voted in a manner that was politically correct. Members of the radical Progressive Caucus consistently garnered scores of 100, the organization's highest rating, while Republicans commonly had scores of zero. Opposed to the war in Iraq, Bread for the World said, "The U.S. economy is mired in a significant slump. . . . But Congress and the president are preoccupied with war and security. They aren't paying attention to what's happening to poor people."[802] In 2004, Toton was one of thirty activists honored at Bread for the World's 30th Anniversary celebration.

Professor Toton is also Villanova University's contact for the Justice Union of Students Staff and Teachers. This is part of the Peace and Justice Consortium of Colleges and Universities in the Philadelphia Area, which is dedicated to sharing information "on events and resources with member schools for the purpose of involving faculty, staff and above all students in a process of educating, mentoring and modeling for social change."[803]

See also: Professors Berklowitz, Fellman,
Richards, Wolfe, Targ

Research: Thomas Ryan

Professor Haunani-Kay Trask
University of Hawaii, Manoa

— Professor of Hawaiian studies

— Advocate of Hawaii's independence from the U.S., and of the deportation of all non-ethnic Hawaiians

— "The enemy is the United States of America and everyone who supports it."

Haunani-Kay Trask is professor of Hawaiian studies at the University of Hawaii, Manoa. Professor Trask was born in San Francisco in 1949 and received her PhD from the University of Wisconsin in 1981. Her thesis was on "The Promise of Feminism." Although lacking any scholarly publications, she is a well-known "Hawaiian activist" and poet, the author of works like "Racist White Woman."

Racist White WomanI could kickYour face, punctureBoth eyes.You deserve this kindOf violence.No more vicious-Tongues, obsceneLies.Just a knifeSlitting your tightLittle heart.For all my peopleUnder your feetFor all those yearsLived smug and wealthyOff our landParasite arrogantA fistIn your paintedMouth, thickWith moneyAnd piety.[804]

Like other institutions of higher learning, the University of Hawaii instructs its teachers not to "let disparaging comments go unnoticed. Explain why a comment is insensitive or offensive. Let your students know that racist, sexist and other discriminatory remarks are unacceptable in class."[805] Apparently these precepts don't apply to professors of Hawaiian studies.

Professor Trask believes that the Hawaiian people have been subjugated by the "racist, colonialist United States of colonial

America."[806] In addition to being redundant, Professor Trask's assertion is inaccurate. Professor Trask insists that "disease-laden racists...took our government and imprisoned our queen," and continue forcibly to occupy Hawaii thorough military occupation and institutionalized racism.[807] This is an interesting claim when both of Hawaii's U.S. senators are of Asian descent, there are two democratically elected congressmen, and its citizens have full rights under the U.S. Constitution.

At a January 1993 protest rally commemorating the one-hundredth anniversary of Hawaii's monarchy, Trask explained: "Hawaii is presently a colony of the United States, not because we Hawaiians chose that status, but because the American government overthrew our Hawaiian government in 1883 [the actual date is 1893], and forcibly annexed our islands in 1898. With the overthrow, things Hawaiian were outlawed and things *haole* [derogatory word for 'white'] American were imposed." In the same speech she expressed her view that white people are irredeemable racists who share the "common characteristic" of "not understand[ing] racism at all." Invoking the standard radical re-definition of racism, she said: "Racism is a system of power in which one racially identified group dominates and exploits another racially identified group for the advantage of the dominating group.... That's what the so-called 'founding fathers' of the United States intended, and that's how American society operates today.... The hatred and fear people of color have of white people is based on that ugly history." Finally, she declared: "I am NOT an American. I will DIE before I am an American."[808]

Professor Trask is part of a movement of Hawaiian ethnic nationalists and racial separatists who seek a system of Hawaiian racial supremacy that would resemble the policy of South African apartheid. The ethnic nationalists and racial separatists Professor Trask represents "agree that Hawaiians are indigenous people of Hawaii and are therefore entitled to political and economic supremacy" over all non-indigenous Hawaiians.[809]

Professor Trask's view of the 9/11 attacks accords with Ward Churchill's. He received a warm welcome from Trask and her faculty colleagues when he visited their campus at the height of his controversy. Apropos the 9/11 attacks, Professor Trask said, "Chickens have come home to roost.... What it means is that those who have suffered under the imperialism and militarism of the United States have come back to haunt in the twenty-first century that same government.... Why should we support the United States, whose hands are soaked with blood?... We need to think very, very clearly about who the enemy is. The enemy is the United States of America and everyone who supports it."[810]

See also: Professors hooks, Jeffries, Mazrui, Navarro, Zinn
Research: Ryan O'Donnell[811]

Professor Michael Vocino
University of Rhode Island

— Professor of film and media studies and political science at the
  University of Rhode Island
— Sexually harassed his male students
— Intrudes his sexual obsessions into his classes

Michael Vocino is a long-term chief librarian on the University
of Rhode Island (URI). He is also a tenured, full professor of film
and media studies, library science, and political science at URI.
Professor Vocino does not have a doctorate in any of the fields
he is tasked with teaching—although he does have a "certificate"
in film and television studies from the University of Amsterdam
in the Netherlands.[812] Currently in his fifties, Vocino is still
merely a PhD candidate in his chosen field of "Cultural Studies."
An enthusiast of the off-color cable series *South Park*, Vocino has
made this cartoon show the subject of his uncompleted dissertation, which at this point is entitled "'They've Killed Kenny!'
Popular Culture, Public Ethics and the Televisual."[813]

Professor Vocino's scholarly work is most notable for its
absence. Aside from a short book on ethics for public administrators (1996), Professor Vocino has practically no original work
to his name. Most of his publications are simply descriptive bib-
liographies of journals and newspapers already available in
libraries—i.e., they are lists. His work in film studies consists of
a 1998 conference paper on the film *Titanic*. With his glaring
paucity of both graduate training and independent scholarly
achievement, Professor Vocino does not even qualify for the
position of an assistant professor, let alone associate professor
with tenure rank, let alone a full professor.

That has not prevented Professor Vocino from posturing as an expert in all the many fields he teaches, which run the astounding gamut from "Film Theory" and "Film History," to "Political Ideologies," to "Political Philosophy: Plato to Machiavelli," to "The American Presidency," to "Contemporary Italian Politics." Vocino teaches all these courses—although he is essentially a librarian with an MA. But what he lacks in scholarly and professional expertise, Vocino—a militant gay activist who describes himself as "firmly on the deep Left politically"[814]—compensates for with his aggressive personal biases. His course "Film Theory," for instance, is billed as "an introduction to the basics of film theory and film criticism."[815] Instead, the course indulges Professor Vocino's preferences for "Queer Theory," as well as "Gay and Lesbian Criticism." The course also includes a section called "Marxism and Film," for which students are required to watch the cinematic adaptation of the *Motorcycle Diaries of Che Guevara*.

Professor Vocino elaborated on his criteria for excellence in film in a June 2004 posting on URI's academic list serve. In it, he gushed over left-wing provocateur Michael Moore's *Fahrenheit 9/11*. Applauding the distinction bestowed on the film at the Cannes Film Festival, Professor Vocino wrote: "Now we all know that i [sic] am not the brightest apple on the tree, something i [sic] know myself, but if only through osmosis, i [sic] did pick up enough substance in many courses and seminars during that time in Amsterdam to firmly assert that Moore deserved to win the coveted Cannes best film award for this production."[816]

A student named Nathaniel Nelson who took Professor Vocino's political science class, "Political Philosophy: Plato to Machiavelli," was struck by the professor's aggressive disregard for professional standards of conduct. According to the student, Professor Vocino entered the classroom on the first day announcing, "My name is Michael Vocino and I like dick."[817]

Professor Vocino next asked the student, "Are you queer?" On another occasion, Professor Vocino, cognizant that the student was a Christian, demanded to know why Christians "hate fags."[818] Besides sexually harassing his male students—he informed one that he thought him "hot"—Professor Vocino urged them to try "making out" with other males and describe their experiences for the class.[819] Vocino has also been known to use the university email system to send to female URI faculty his gleeful announcements of his acquisition of new pornographic material for the university library.[820] According to Nelson, Professor Vocino devoted an entire class period of his political philosophy course to a discussion of masturbation; another class session centered on whether President Bush's decision to deploy troops in Iraq made him a "serial killer."[821] All this in a course listed as the history of ancient and medieval political philosophy.

That a person totally lacking the proper professional credentials or scholarly achievements should be a full professor at the University of Rhode Island is scandal enough; that his astoundingly harassing behavior in class, both ideologically and sexually, has gone unchecked by the university administration can only deepen one's concern for students at this institution.

See also: Professors Rubin, Sedgwick, Warner
Research: Jacob Laksin

Professor Michael Warner

Rutgers University

— Professor of English at Rutgers University

— Advocates anonymous, public homosexual encounters with strangers

— "The phenomenology of a sex club encounter is an experience of world making."

Michael Warner is a professor of English at Rutgers University. He received his BA from Oral Roberts University and his PhD from Johns Hopkins. Professor Warner's specialty is nineteenth-century American literature but he is best known for the books he has written and edited in the field of "Queer Studies," including *Fear of a Queer Planet* (Minnesota, 1993) and *The Trouble with Normal* (Harvard, 2000). Professor Warner teaches a graduate course in queer theory and is considered one of the most important academic theorists in that discipline. One of the leading radicals of the "Gay Rights" movement, Warner is the opponent of "not just the normal behavior of the social, but the idea of normal behavior."[822] The essence of queer theory rejects the view that sexuality is a universal human impulse; that sexual desire can exist apart from history and culture; and that any sexual inclination, including heterosexuality, is inherently natural or normal. "What identity," Professor Warner writes, "encompasses queer girls who fuck queer boys with strap-ons, or FTMs (female-to-male transsexuals) who think of themselves as queer, FTMs who think of themselves as straights, or FTMs for whom life is a project of transition and screw the categories anyway?" Warner wants to "overthrow" what he calls "hetero-normativity," the very idea of the normal, which he regards as a form of "oppression."[823]

Professor Warner does not view gay marriage or adoption rights as ideals for which homosexuals should fight. On the contrary, the professor has been an outspoken critic of such crusades, finding them to be demeaning attempts to "normalize" the gay experience. As such, he reasons, they can only serve to destroy the queer lifestyle, which for Professor Warner necessarily includes promiscuous, unprotected, and public sex acts—in bathhouses and elsewhere.

In 1997, during a resurgence of HIV/AIDS and other sexually transmitted diseases, particularly among gay men, Professor Warner and a number of likeminded activists founded "Sex Panic," an organization that aimed to counter measures taken by law enforcement and policy makers to shut down bathhouses and other institutions that catered to promiscuous, anonymous homosexual sex. At the National Sex Panic Conference—held in San Diego, November 13–15, 1997, activists gathered to "discuss the emerging culture war within the gay community."[824] A Sex Panic press release on the conference read: Sex Panic organizers are concerned about the "increased attack against marginalized sexualities including the harassment and closure of sex clubs, bathhouses and public sex spaces; racist selective enforcement and policing of lesbian/gay bars; anti-sex AIDS activism and education campaigns; increased policing of and attacks on sex workers; and the burgeoning demonizing of sex and party cultures appearing in current gay men's writings."[825]

"The phenomenology of a sex club encounter," Professor Warner writes, "is an experience of world making. It's an experience of being connected not just to this person but to potentially limitless numbers of people, and that is why it's important that it be with a stranger. Sex with a stranger is like a metonym."[826]

See also: Professors Aptheker, Rubin, Sedgwick
Research: Roberta Leguizamon

Professor Dessima Williams

Brandeis University

— Assistant professor of sociology and Caribbean studies, and a
member of the faculty of Peace, Conflict and Coexistence
Studies, Brandeis University

— Served as ambassador for the Marxist dictatorship of Grenada

Professor Dessima Williams teaches sociology and Caribbean
studies at Brandeis University, near Boston, Massachusetts, and is
on the faculty of Peace, Conflict and Coexistence Studies.[827]
Professor Williams has no scholarly publications and her only
text credit is co-editing a book of speeches and articles by the
deposed Marxist dictators of Grenada, which was published
twenty years ago (*In Nobody's Backyard:The Grenada Revoluton
In Its Own Words* [828]). The Caribbean-born Williams completed
her primary and secondary education in Grenada before traveling to the U.S., where she received her BA in International Relations from the University of Minnesota, and her PhD in
International Relations from American University in 1995. With
interests in international relations, global apartheid, feminism in
developing countries, and the peace movement, Williams was
hired as a professor of political science at Williams College in
Williamstown, Massachusetts, before taking a faculty position as
a visiting associate professor in the Sociology Department at
Brandeis in 1992. In the same year she was appointed "assistant
professor of sociology" at Brandeis, where she has remained ever
since. It is highly unusual for an assistant professor to remain so
for thirteen years. Normally, universities like Brandeis have a six-
year trial period before awarding or denying tenure. The fact
that Williams has produced no scholarship in this lengthy period

suggests that her retention is a political rather than an academic decision.

Prior to launching her university career, Professor Williams was an ambassador for the dictatorship of Grenada, which was established as the result of a coup d'etat carried out by the Marxist-Leninst New Jewel Movement led by Maruice Bishop. From 1979 to 1983, she was the Grenadan ambassador to the United Nations Educational, Scientific and Cultural Organization, and the Organization of American States. In 1982 the Reagan administration rejected her credentials to be the dictatorship's new ambassador to the United States as a gesture of its displeasure towards a regime that had suspended civil liberties and allied itself with Fidel Castro and the Communist bloc. Bishop had set Grenada on a collision course with the United States by allowing the Cubans to build a military airport that would accommodate Soviet nuclear bombers.

Professor Williams's career took a dramatic turn when Defense Minister Bernard Coard—himself a former Brandeis student and a New Jewel Movement Marxist—seized power for himself and murdered half of his fellow cabinet members, including Bishop and the pregnant minister of education, and put the entire population under house arrest. This precipitated an invasion by the United States Marines, which led to Grenada's return to a democratic regime. Sensing that her opportunities in liberated Grenada were limited by her role in the dictatorship, Professor Williams emigrated to the United States to begin her academic career. In 1984, carrying lapel buttons that said "The Spirit of Maurice Bishop Lives," she was arrested by INS agents, but subsequently released.

Professor Williams's courses at Brandeis reflect her continuing radicalism and pursuit of "social change activism." Professor Williams's "Global Apartheid, Global Social Movements"[829] is a for-credit introduction to Professor Williams's assorted radical interests. The course's stated mission is explicitly political—"expanding social justice." Course assignments and activities are specifically aimed at "developing an informed critique of injustices in the global system and a disposition toward social justice via social movement as intellectual and social action." Obviously this is not a course to conduct a scholarly examination of globalization. Among the assignments are what Professor Williams calls "re-empowerment" exercises. By way of example, Professor Williams urges students to adopt the proper social justice attitude by imagining that they are an "over-worked, under-paid, undocumented worker with very little English in a ritzy hotel on Martha's Vineyard." Still another assignment requires students to discuss approvingly "the social movement of feminism or environmentalism," while criticizing "the western over-consumer." Course readings include books like *Eyes of the Heart*, a Marxist tract written by the deposed Haitian ruler Jean-Bertrand Aristide. The texts reflect Professor Williams's ingrained Marxist prejudices.

Professor Williams is particularly critical of what she calls the "assumed dominance and assumed superiority of the analysis and experiences of the West."[830] This anti-Western mindset has guided Professor Williams's activist career in several organizations and agencies. One of these is Oxfam America, which she served as a board member and vice president. Oxfam[831] is a confederation of twelve organizations ostensibly dedicated "to find[ing] lasting solutions to poverty, suffering, and injustice." Oxfam's approach to these issues is notably one-sided. Oxfam routinely condemns Israeli policies, for example, while remaining silent about Palestinian-perpetrated human rights abuses, including suicide bombings and the use of children to carry out acts of terror. Oxfam America was a signatory to a November 1, 2001, document[832] characterizing the 9/11 attacks as a legal matter to be addressed by criminal-justice procedures rather than military means. Ascribing the hijackers' motives to alleged social injustices against which they were protesting, this document explained that "security and justice are mutually reinforcing goals that ultimately depend upon the promotion of all human rights for all people," and called on the United States "to promote fundamental rights around the world."

Professor Williams opposes America's war on terror for several reasons, but "one of the simplest . . . is that war hurts people." In 2001, Professor Williams received the Debs-Thomas-Bernstein Award, which is given by the Boston Democratic Socialists of America. At the presentation ceremony, "Williams delivered a moving and inspirational speech recount[ing] how a young graduate student in the U.S. came to find herself appointed UN Ambassador from Grenada's new revolutionary government," and lamenting "the bitterness and sorrow of seeing their promising movement collapse, leading to military coup and ultimately a U.S. invasion."[833] That such a person with no scholarly publications is teaching as "courses" what are essentially radical anti-Western rants at a prestigious academic institution reveals a great deal about the nature of American higher education today. One can only wonder what Justice Louis Brandeis—who was a promoter of the ideas and ideals of western civilization—would think if he knew that a former ambassador for a Communist dictatorship who continues to defend its principles and views was teaching at a university named after him.

> **See also:** Professors Aptheker, Davis, Feldman, Furr, Wolfe, Zinn
>
> **Research:** Thomas Ryan, Jacob Laksin

Professor George Wolfe
Ball State University

— Professor of music performance (saxophone)
— Director of the Center for Peace and Conflict Studies
— Recruits students to join an anti-war group he advises

George Wolfe is an accomplished saxophonist and professor of music performance at Ball State University in Muncie, Indiana. This is his field of competence, but it is the aggressively political notes that he routinely sounds in the one non-musical class he teaches, "Introduction to Peace Studies and Conflict Resolution," that have made Wolfe a controversial figure on campus.

Professor Wolfe teaches the course in conjunction with his role as director of the Center for Peace and Conflict Studies at Ball State. Despite his complete lack of scholarly qualifications in social science or any field related to international relations, Professor Wolfe was appointed to this position by the Ball State administration in April 2002. Pledging his support for the center's classes in "contemplative practice and meditation," Wolfe declared his interest in increasing "religious diversity," to which end he recommended holding a celebration of Mahatma Gandhi's birthday. A follower of Gandhi's teachings, Wolfe is convinced that "conflicts between people are really a projection of inner conflict."[834] Wolfe regularly gives talks on Gandhi at universities across the country; the topic of a speech he recently delivered at Anderson University, in Indiana was "Gandhian Philosophy: Slaying the Enemy Within."[835] Professor Wolfe is also on the board of the Toda Institute for Global Research and Peace, an offshoot of the Soka Gokkai Buddhist cult, whose members believe that if enough human beings across the globe simultaneously chant "Nam myoho, renge kyo," there will be world peace.

A fierce critic of Israel, Professor Wolfe raised funds through the center to sponsor what he called a "student research project in the Israeli occupied territory."[836] One of the anti-Israel speakers he invited to address his students in 2005 was Philip C. Wilcox Jr., president of the Foundation for Middle East Peace. Wilcox is a former American diplomat who blames Israel for Palestinian terrorism.[837]

The center's website explains that "It is the mission of the Center for Peace and Conflict Studies to promote nonviolent alternatives to conflict resolution."[838] This is a political vocation, not an academic pursuit. "The Center will continue to study, teach, and be an advocate for nonviolent philosophies and strategies that have been proven successful in various parts of the world."[839] Citing some groups it hopes to emulate, the website lists, among others, "nuclear disarmament" groups, and "the United Farm Workers movement," and "organized labor." The required textbook for Professor Wolfe's course is a widely used peace studies text, Barash and Webel's *Peace and Conflict Studies*, which instructs students that "revolutionary violence" is sometimes necessary and therefore justified.[840] Wolfe's fervent advocacy of Gandhian non-violence evidently goes only so far.

The Peace Studies and Conflict Resolution Minor offered at Ball State explores the "challenges of promoting peace and justice," and urges students to practice "mediation and other more equitable, cooperative, and nonviolent methods that can be used to transform unjust, violent, or oppressive situations."[841] Toward this end, Professor Wolfe's course, "Introduction to Peace Studies and Conflict Resolution," is also an introduction to "peace movements."

Brett Mock a Ball State student who took Professor Wolfe's introductory class in the spring of 2004, charged in a published article that the class was organized around "indoctrination rather than education," and noted that Professor Wolfe recruited students to activist groups.[842] Mock disclosed that Professor Wolfe had urged his students to join Peace Workers, a Ball State student activist group formed in January 2003 in opposition to the Iraq war. Professor Wolfe acts as faculty advisor to the organization, which regularly stages anti-war protests on campus, and receives its funds from the Center for Peace and Conflict Studies. Under Professor Wolfe's direction, the center has even devised awards for students who join Peace Workers opposed to U.S. military efforts. In April of 2003, for instance, the center presented a special "Social Activist Award" to Peace Workers for organizing a march and a sit-in expressing opposition to the Iraq war.

According to Brett Mock, Professor Wolfe showed "no tolerance whatsoever for any disagreement and said that he would never support the use of force as an instrument of peace,"[843] an ideological disposition reflected in the required readings for the course. Mock also claimed that Professor Wolfe regularly gave lower grades to students who did not share his ideological disposition. On the other hand, students who echoed Professor Wolfe's own positions that the U.S.-led war in Iraq was a "fiasco" that was "leading us down the wrong path," and traveled to Washington, D.C., to take part in anti-war demonstrations, were rewarded with extra credit.[844] So that there should be no doubt about the political opinions students were expected to hold, Professor Wolfe required his class to attend a screening of the anti-war film *Uncovered: The Whole Truth about the War in Iraq.*

In a letter to the national director of the organization Students for Academic Freedom, Ball State provost Beverley Pitts defended Professor Wolfe's classroom performance and academic credentials, citing his doctorate in education and his Toda Institute board membership.[845] With the administration behind him, Professor Wolfe dismissed the criticism of Mock and other students as the work of "propaganda artists." He claims that in finding fault with his politically motivated teaching methods, his detractors are "confusing liberal politics with liberal education."[846]

The pattern of academically untrained and unqualified faculty members allowed to vent personal prejudices and passions in the classroom (in this case at taxpayers' expense), while supported by a pliant or enthusiastic administration has been encountered multiple times throughout these profiles. It is an example of the degradation of professional standards, and in the case of a professor of the saxophone presuming to teach courses on international politics and the economic social causes of war and peace, hits an academic rock bottom.

> **See also:** Professors Barash, Berlowitz, Eck-
> stein, Fellman, Lembcke, Targ
> **Research:** Jacob Laksin

Professor Howard Zinn
Boston University

— Emeritus professor of political science at Boston University

— Author of *A People's History of the United States*, one of the most influential academic texts

— "The Founding Fathers ... created the most effective system of national control devised in modern times ..."

Howard Zinn is professor emeritus of political science at Boston University. He is best known for authoring the 1980 book *A People's History of the United States*, a Marxist tract, which claims to present American history through the eyes of workers, American Indians, slaves, women, blacks, and populists. *A People's History* has sold over a million copies, making it one of the bestselling history books of all time and, despite its lack of footnotes and other scholarly apparatus, is one of most influential texts in college classrooms on college campuses today. A review by Professor Eric Foner in the *New York Times* suggested that the book should be "required reading" for students and that "[h]istorians may well view it as a step toward a coherent new version of American history."[847] *A People's History* can be found on the class syllabus in such fields as economics, political science, literature, and women's studies, in addition to history. A course description at Evergreen State College noted: "This is an advanced class and all students should have read Howard Zinn's *A People's History of the United States* before the first day of class, to give us a common background to begin the class."[848]

Professor Zinn announces the overtly political agenda of *A People's History of the United States* in an explanatory coda to the 1995 edition. Zinn explains to the reader that he has no interest in striving for objectivity, and that his history is "a biased account." Professor Zinn explains: "I am not troubled by that. I wanted my writing of history and my teaching of history to be a part of social struggle. I wanted to be a part of history and not just a recorder and teacher of history. So that kind of attitude towards history, history itself as a political act, has always informed my writing and my teaching."[849]

Zinn begins his narrative not with the settling of North America, or the creation of the United States as one might expect, but with a long chapter on Columbus's "genocide" against the native inhabitants, an event—which even if it had happened as Zinn describes it—was an act committed by agents of the Spanish empire more than a century before the English settled North America and nearly three centuries before the creation of the United States, which is also geographically well-removed from the scene of the crime. It is Zinn's unintended way of announcing the tendentiousness of his entire project, which is really not a "history" of the American people, but an indictment of white people and the capitalist system.

The perspective that informs the nearly seven hundred pages of *A People's History* is a pedestrian Marxism encapsulated in the idea that nation states are merely a fiction, and only economic classes are "real" social actors: "Class interest has always been obscured behind an all-encompassing veil called 'the national interest.' My own war experience [in World War II], and the history of all those military interventions in which the United States was engaged, made me skeptical when I heard people in high political office invoke 'the national interest' or 'national security' to justify their policies. It was with such justifications that Truman initiated a 'police action' in Korea that killed several million people, that Johnson and Nixon carried out a war in Indochina in which perhaps three million died, that Reagan invaded Grenada, Bush attacked Panama and then Iraq, and Clinton bombed Iraq again and again."[850]

A Stalinist in his youth, Professor Zinn retains into his seventies the same ideological blinders he wore as a young man. America's defense of South Korea against a Communist invasion from the North was not initiated by the United States as the Communist propaganda machine maintained at the time and Professor Zinn still believes. It was a response to the Communist aggression, which was initiated by Stalin himself according to most recent historical accounts.[851] The war and subsequent American support for the South Koreans resulted in their liberation from both poverty and dictatorship. South Korea was, in 1950, one of the poorest Third World countries, with a per capita income of $250, on a level with Cuba and South Vietnam. Fifty years of American protection, trade, and investment has made South Korea a First World industrial nation with a reasonably stable democracy. By contrast, North Korea, which was the industrial heart of the Korean peninsula and which the American armies failed to liberate—thanks to Professor Zinn's political allies at the time—is an impoverished totalitarian state that has starved more than a million of its inhabitants in the last decade, while its Communist dictator hoards scarce funds to build an arsenal of nuclear intercontinental ballistic missiles. The rest of Professor Zinn's examples are equally tendentious.

In a twist of reality characteristic of this entire text, Professor Zinn describes the founding of the American Republic—the world's most successful democratic experiment—as an exercise in tyrannical control of the many by the few for greed and profit. "The American Revolution ... was a work of genius, and the Founding Fathers deserve the awed tribute they have received over the centuries. They created the most effective system of national control devised in modern times, and showed future generations of leaders the advantages of combining paternalism with command."[852] In Professor Zinn's reckoning, the Declaration of Independence was not so much a revolutionary statement of rights as a cynical means of manipulating popular groups into overthrowing the King to benefit the rich. The rights it appeared to guarantee were "limited to life, liberty and happiness for white males"—and actually for wealthy white males—because they excluded black slaves and "ignored the existing inequalities in property"[853] (in other words, they were not socialist rights). This is an ahistorical, not to say absurd view of the Declaration and of the history of the Republic to which it gave birth.

Of course, traducing the historical data is no problem for Professor Zinn. "Objectivity is impossible," the professor writes, "and it is also undesirable. That is, if it were possible it would be undesirable, because if you have any kind of a social aim, if you think history should serve society in some way; should serve the progress of the human race; should serve justice in some way, then it requires that you make your selection on the basis of what you think will advance causes of humanity."[854] Of course if you think socialism and Communism are systems that advance the cause of humanity and that America is a reactionary, terrorist state, as Professor Zinn does, then you get the kind of history on display in his book.

Through Professor Zinn's rose-colored glasses, Maoist China, site of history's bloodiest state-sponsored killings, is transformed into "the closest thing, in the long history of that ancient country, to a people's government, independent of outside control."[855] Castro's Cuba, Professor Zinn's readers learn, "had no bloody record of suppression."[856] The Marxist dictators of Nicaragua were "welcomed" by the people, while the opposition Contras, whose candidate triumphed when free elections were held as a result of U.S. pressure, were a "terrorist group" that "seemed to have no popular support inside Nicaragua."[857] In fact, the Contras were the largest peasant army in Latin America's modern history.

In *A People's History of the United States*, greed is the explanation for every major historical event. According to Professor Zinn, the separation from Great Britain, the Civil War, and World Wars I and II—to name some central examples—were all driven by base motives involving rich Americans seeking to enrich themselves even more at the expense of others: "Around 1776, certain important people in the English colonies made a discovery that would prove enormously useful for the next two hundred years. They found that by creating a nation, a symbol, a legal unity called the United States, they could take over land, profits, and political power from the favorites of the British Empire. In the process, they could hold back a number of potential rebellions and create a consensus of popular support for the rule of a new, privileged leadership."[858]

In Professor Zinn's account the answer is the same whatever the question. Thus Professor Zinn describes antebellum America as a uniquely cruel slaveholding society whose goal was subjugating man for profit. On the other hand, the war of the Union against the slaveholding system is portrayed in exactly the same terms: "It is money and profit, not the movement against slavery that was uppermost in the priorities of the men who ran the country."[859] The same explanation is given for America's entry into World War I (forget the sinking of the *Lusitania* or Germany's Zimmerman memorandum which promised Mexico the American Southwest for joining a war against the United States): "American capitalism needed international rivalry—and periodic war—to create an artificial community of interest between rich and poor."[860]

The explanation for World War II is also the same. Was America attacked? No, it was America and not Japan that was to blame for Pearl Harbor. The fight against fascism was a manipulated illusion to conceal America's real goals, which were empire and money. "Quietly, behind the headlines in battles and bombings, American diplomats and businessmen worked hard to make sure that when the war ended, American economic power would be second to none in the world. United States business would penetrate areas that up to this time had been dominated by England. The Open Door Policy of equal access would be extended from Asia to Europe, meaning that the United States intended to push England aside and move in."[861] Yet, despite defeating Japan and helping to vanquish Germany, afterwards America rebuilt the economies of both countries. Both are now among the chief economic rivals of the United States, hardly its colonies.

Not surprisingly, Professor Zinn's text abounds in factual inaccuracies. George Washington, for example, was not "the richest American" at the time of the revolution, nor did unemployment grow during the Reagan years. Even more impressive than his inaccuracies, on the other hand, are the events that are left out of his seven hundred–page text in order to concoct his Marxist fantasy. These include Washington's Farewell Address, Lincoln's Gettysburg Address, and Reagan's defiant speech at the Brandenburg Gate, "Tear down this wall!" Nowhere does a reader learn that Americans were first in flight, first to fly across the Atlantic, and first to walk on the moon. Alexander Graham Bell, Jonas Salk, and the Wright Brothers are absent. Instead, the reader is treated to the exploits of Speckled Snake, the anti-war folksinger Joan Baez, and the anti-war activist Berrigan brothers (Philip and Daniel.) While Zinn sees fit to mention that immigrants often went into professions like ditch-digging and prostitution, the fact that they also created Hollywood and the Federal Bank, among other prodigious achievements, or that America has an ongoing problem of too many people wanting to take advantage of its opportunities are missing. Valley Forge is mentioned but in a single fleeting reference, while the Normandy invasion, Gettysburg, and other historical turning points are omitted. In their place, the reader is given several pages on the My Lai massacre episode in the Vietnam War, and colorful descriptions of U.S. bombs falling on hotels, air-raid shelters, and markets during the Gulf War to stop Saddam's aggression in Kuwait. (Professor Zinn opposed the war.)

The historical progress Professor Zinn seeks to serve is evidently served by sympathizing with America's enemies and relentlessly denigrating the achievements of the American people. In a pamphlet-like tract published after 9/11 called *Terrorism and War*, Professor Zinn portrays America as the terrorist state, and—just as he did the Japanese during World War II—the terrorists as the people valiantly standing up to America's empire. Professor Zinn's book is part of what is now a dominant trend in the teaching of American history and the writing of American history texts: to see the American narrative through a Marx-tinted lens that puts its achievements in a negative light and its enemies in a sympathetic one.

Although Professor Zinn is retired, he remains an active presence on university campuses through a busy speaking schedule, a cohort of faculty disciples at universities across the country, and constant reprints of *A People's History*—not least because of its widespread use in academic courses.

> *See also:* Professors Chomsky, Kirstein
> *Research:* Dan Flynn[862]

CHAPTER 2

Why Administrators Fail to Maintain Academic Standards

Why have university administrators failed to enforce their own academic freedom guidelines or taken the violators of academic standards to task? Two recent episodes involving Harvard president Lawrence Summers provide elements of an answer.

In October 2001, Lawrence Summers was inaugurated as the twenty-seventh president of Harvard. Because of his unique credentials, he was probably the most powerful university president in the history of the modern research university. Summers had served as secretary of the treasury in the Clinton administration and came to Harvard with the aura and power of the Washington establishment. Before going to Washington he had been the youngest tenured professor in Harvard's modern history, respected as a scholar in his own right and a member of the academic elite. His liberal outlook fit comfortably with the prevailing social and political attitudes of Harvard. The combination of these factors seemed to assure that he would enjoy the confidence of the Harvard community; but three short years later, Summers became the first president in the history of the modern research university to be censured by a vote of his own faculty.

The change in Larry Summers's fortunes began at the very outset of his tenure during a celebrated meeting with African American studies professor Cornel West. West was one of only fourteen academics appointed to the post of "University Professor," a title of great distinction, which affords the bearer a higher salary than an ordinary full professor and requires him to report to the university president rather than to a departmental chair. This was the reason for the meeting between them. Cornel West was also known as an academic who prided himself on his social and political activism. In both roles, West's recent performance was a matter of concern to the new university president.

Cornel West was a paradoxical figure on the Harvard campus. An icon to faculty student "progressives," West had taught at Princeton, Yale, and the University of Paris, and was the recipient of twenty honorary university degrees. At the same, West was regarded far less positively outside the university environment, and had been characterized as an intellectual charlatan by his blunter detractors. A 1995 cover story on West in liberal *The New Republic* had drawn much attention at Harvard and elsewhere, in part because the editor-in-chief of *The New Republic*, Martin Peretz, was a longtime lecturer at Harvard himself. Written by literary editor Leon Wieseltier, the article was titled, "The Decline of the Black Intellectual," and was a review of West's work. Wieseltier's judgment on West's output was unambiguous: "Since there is no crisis in America more urgent than the crisis of race, and since there is no intellectual in America more celebrated for his consideration of race, I turned to West and read his books. They are almost completely worthless...monuments to the devastation of a mind by the squalls of theory."[1]

It was a judgment amply justified by the texts themselves. "I believe," wrote West in a passage typical of his writing, "that the major life-denying forces in our world are economic exploitation (resulting primarily from the social logic of capital accumulation), state repression (linked to the social logic of state augmentation), bureaucratic domination (owing to the social logic of administrative subordination), racial, sexual and hetero-sexual subjugation (due to the social logics of white, male and heterosexual supremacist practices) and ecological subjection (resulting, in part from modern values of scientific manipulation), I entertain a variety of social analyses and cultural critiques that yield not merely one grand synthetic social theory, but rather. . . ."[2] and so on. West was a perfect case of the Sokal phenomenon—someone who said all the politically correct things, the substance of which was vacuous.

Immensely popular among students and widely sought after as a campus speaker, West was politically ambitious as well and had spent a considerable amount of time on extra-curricular pursuits in the year prior to Summers's appointment. In 2000, which was a presidential election year, West served as an advisor to Senator Bill Bradley's primary run. When Bradley lost, West campaigned for Green Party candidate Ralph Nader. Finally, in August 2001 he announced that he had been tapped to head the presidential exploratory committee of racial demagogue Al Sharpton.[3] In addition to these political activities, West had also spent a significant part of the academic year composing a "rap" album on which he himself performed. In the *New Republic* article, Wieseltier had described West as "self-endeared." West's website said of his rap album that it "constituted a watershed in the history of music." The site also described him as "one of the pre-eminent minds of our time."

One of the problems Summers attempted to raise with Professor West was that he had not written an academic book since 1989. In that year he published *The Evasion of Philosophy*, a reworking of his PhD thesis. It consisted of summaries of the ideas of leading pragmatist philosophers along with a scolding by Professor West when they did not share his "progressive politics." This constituted the "evasion" of the title. Nor had West published shorter works of a scholarly nature. In fact, West had not published a scholarly article in a "peer-reviewed" journal since 1981. From that year—or to be charitable, since 1989—his output had been limited to political and religious tracts, and to editing collections of other people's writings.[4]

At their meeting, Summers expressed concern about West's distraction from academic pursuits and lack of a serious intellectual output. He asked the professor to spend the next year producing a proper scholarly book that would be reviewed in an academic journal, and not just in *Time* magazine or the *New York Review of Books*. Finally, he asked Professor West to refrain from giving so many of his students "A's," which contributed to "grade inflation" at Harvard.[5]

West took umbrage at these requests and—since this was the fulcrum of his entire affirmative-action-driven career—racial umbrage. He responded by insinuating publicly that Summers had disrespected him, and not only him personally, but the entire African American community at Harvard. Prominent African American radicals on the faculty, like law professor and slavery reparations advocate Charles Ogletree, were quick to respond to this appeal and both seconded and amplified the racial charge. Against the backdrop of this radical chorus, rumors began to surface that West and several other African Americans on the faculty were considering leaving Harvard because of their dissatisfaction with the way he had been treated.

It was a public relations nightmare for the president of America's premier liberal university. Summers beat a hasty retreat and apologized. But Cornel West was not about to be appeased by any self-abasing gesture by Harvard's president. Declaring the apology too little and too late, West threw in a little bigotry of his own, referring to Summers as the "Ariel Sharon of Harvard" (Summers is Jewish). He then announced his departure for

Princeton, where he had been offered a top-tier position by his friend and political soulmate, Princeton Provost Amy Gutmann.[6] The moral of the episode is that even the most powerful president at America's most prestigious university cannot hold a radical professor like Cornel West to account in regard to his academic responsibilities or to the institution's intellectual standards.

If the West episode was an instructive demonstration of the power of the faculty left, the issue that followed was even more so and led directly to Summers's censure. On January 15, 2005, Summers spoke to a small, closed faculty symposium on women in science, sponsored by the National Bureau of Economic Research. The symposium took place against the backdrop of a decline in the number of women faculty awarded tenure at Harvard during Summers's leadership. In his remarks, he attempted to defend his administration and to address the question of why there were not more women at the "high ends" of scientific fields in general and in tenured positions at Harvard in particular. He began with this comment:

> There are three broad hypotheses about the sources of the very substantial disparities that this conference's papers document and have been documented before with respect to the presence of women in high-end scientific professions. One is what I would call ... the high-powered job hypothesis. The second is what I would call different availability of aptitude at the high end, and the third is what I would call different socialization patterns of discrimination in a search. And in my own view, their importance probably ranks in exactly the order that I just described.[7]

Summers then elaborated his points, drawing on empirical data to sustain his hypotheses. In the midst of his remarks, however,

Nancy Hopkins, a professor of biology at M.I.T. who was sitting ten feet from the speaker, closed her computer, got up, and walked out. She then contacted a *Boston Globe* reporter and said that if she hadn't left, "I would've either blacked out or thrown up." Six other participants, including Denice D. Denton, chancellor designate of the University of California, Santa Cruz, said they were also "deeply offended" by Summers's suggestion that there might be a "different availability of aptitude at the high end" of scientific ability for men and women.[8] Even though Summers's remarks reflected the conclusions of a large body of neuro-scientific data and opinion,[9] and even though his remarks were unavailable to the general public, the protesters claimed that his views would injure the self-esteem of women at Harvard and cause them to feel "unwelcome," and were thus a form of sexual harassment.

Within days of the symposium, a group of faculty feminists had called on Summers to resign. The furor was so great that four days later, on January 19, Summers was forced to issue a formal letter of apology. "I was wrong to have spoken in a way that has resulted in an unintended signal of discouragement to talented girls and women,"[10] he said (even though the talented girls would only have learned of his remarks through Nancy Hopkins's tales to the press). Though he did confess to an unintentional thought crime, Summers tried to defend the integrity of his remarks: "Despite reports to the contrary, I did not say, and I do not believe, that girls are intellectually less able than boys, or that women lack the ability to succeed at the highest levels of science." This was factually accurate. Summers had merely suggested that there was a disparity at the high end of scientific intelligence (more men were capable of attaining those levels than women) and even observed that there were more men who had tested at the lower end of the scientific intelligence scale as well.

But his antagonists were not really interested in the intellectual issues involved, let alone fairness to Summers. What they were interested in was silencing one side of a scientific debate. That was the symbolic meaning of Professor Hopkins's peremptory departure. No discussion of such matters was tolerable, no matter what the facts might be. The only real concern of the faculty leftists was to punish Summers for voicing a politically incorrect idea. It is hard to imagine a more anti-intellectual position than the one taken by the feminists and other faculty radicals involved in this incident.

On March 14, members of the faculty convened a meeting to discuss Summers's offense. Stephan Thernstrom, one of Harvard's handful of conservatives, who years before had been driven from his classroom for expressing views that were politically incorrect,[11] made this trenchant observation at the meeting: "It is amazing to me that many of us here no longer seem to understand that the expression of controversial ideas and the freedom to debate them is at the heart of any greater institution of higher learning. The whole point of tenure, as I understand it, is to protect professors from the thought police. But now they are not just outside, on some congressional or state legislative committee. They are inside too in our midst."[12]

Professor Thernstrom had a pointed observation to make about Professor Hopkins's behavior: "If hearing ideas that she deeply disagrees with makes her physically ill, I suggest that Professor Hopkins's temperament is ill suited for academic life, the life-blood of which is free inquiry and unfettered debate." Thernstrom hoped that hers was not a majority view, but evidently it was. When the vote was taken, 218 members of the faculty voted that they "lacked confidence" in Summers's leadership, with 185 opposed and eighteen abstentions. On another vote, 253 expressed "regret" over Summers's "mid-January statements about women in science and the adverse consequences of those statements for individuals and for Harvard."[13] It was the first time in the history of American higher education that there had been a censure of a university president at a major research university, and the entire purpose of the censure was to suppress a politically objectionable (but scientifically grounded) idea.

Summers followed his defeat by conceding his antagonists' superior power in the institution he headed. In an attempt to appease his persecutors he offered them a $50 million tribute. The money would be used to set up "diversity programs" to recruit more women to Harvard's faculty and to promote them to higher positions—regardless of what the data revealed about the pool of intellectually qualified candidates. Summers's offer included the creation of a senior vice provost for diversity and faculty development who was to be "given priority in terms of office space," and three diversity deans to see that politically correct guidelines were enforced at three Harvard schools.[14]

Summers's defeat demonstrated the chilling power of a radical minority on the university's faculty. There were only 218 censure votes out of a Faculty of Arts and Sciences of 941, and an overall university faculty of more than 2,100.[15] As in the West case, the source of the radicals' power was their willingness to deploy the weapon of victimhood to stigmatize and silence their intellectual opposition. Unlike the incidents over Ward Churchill's appearance at Hamilton College, where an outraged public intervened to strengthen the president's hand, there was no public intervention over the arcane matters at issue in the conflict at Harvard. What the Summers affair revealed was that when the public was not a player, administrators challenged radical faculty at peril to themselves.

CHAPTER 3

The Representative
Nature of the Professors
Profiled in This Volume

The modern university is a decentralized unit, consisting of quasi-independent faculties that create their own intellectual standards. Thus the hard sciences have remained relatively free from ideological intrusions; the traditional humanities and social science fields—history, philosophy, literature—much less so; and the various inter-disciplinary "studies" departments generally not at all. The university is also by nature and structure a conformist institution regardless of who controls it. It is hierarchical in organization and the apprenticeship required for admission to its ascending levels of privilege is long in duration and closely observed. The committees that manage its hiring and promotion processes are collegial and secretive, and its ruling establishment is accountable only to itself. Because the performance on which advancement is based is ultimately the production of ideas, the pressure to share common assumptions and common attitudes is far greater in universities than in other social institutions, whether governmental or corporate. In these circumstances university and departmental elites create faculties in their own image. Consequently, far from being eccentric or peripheral figures the professors in this volume are integral to the intellectual life of the institutions they inhabit and to the course of higher education in America.

During the 1960s, complex procedures for hiring and promotion were developed in universities as reform measures to do away with the existing "old boys' network" in which candidates were hired and promoted on the basis of who they or their faculty mentors happened to know in positions of departmental power. The goal of these reforms was to maintain the highest professional standards in hiring, and to create a system in which the most qualified person judged by objective merit would be offered the position. Under the new system, positions are nationally advertised in the appropriate academic journals and the number of candidates for any one position can be well over a hundred.[1]

A "search committee" is chosen by the chair of the department, which normally consists of three faculty members who in the view of the department are known both for their diligence and good sense. The search committee sifts through and evaluates the applications, which include letters of recommendation and samples of written work, and chooses between 12–15 people to interview at the annual national convention of the profession. From these personal interviews, the search committee chooses three or four people to come to campus for several days. The high point of such campus visits is the presentation of a scholarly paper before the assembled department. Candidates may also be asked to teach a class in front of observers. They will meet for extensive interview sessions with the chair of the department, and often with the dean of the college as well. After the visits, the search committee writes a detailed report on the top candidates, and ranks them. The assembled department then votes on whether to accept the nominee of the search committee. If accepted by majority vote, the search committee report then goes up to the dean of the college, with an accompanying letter from the chair. This process is so painstaking and careful that it normally lasts nine months, from middle or late summer to the spring of the following year.

Obviously the departmental chair who selects the members of the search committee and the members themselves play a crucial role in determining both the "long short list" of 12–15 who are interviewed at the national convention and the "short short list" of 3–4 candidates who actually come for campus visits and on whom the department as a whole will eventually vote. It is easy to see how this system can be exploited by faculty members with activist agendas. The composition of the search committee chosen by the chair will go a long way in determining the orientation of the candidate likely to be hired. As one senior professor at a large research university observed, "If a departmental chair chooses a political radical to chair a search committee, it is more than likely that all three of the final candidates for the open faculty position will be people who are, more or less, sympathetic to such views. Among the faculty left, this is called 'Revolution by Search Committee.'"[2] This is Gramscian theory in practice.

Almost all of the professors profiled in this volume were not only hired by search committees and departmental votes, but were promoted at least once (to a tenured rank) and often twice (to a full professorship). A promotion committee also normally consists of three faculty who are chosen by the departmental chair, and the idea also is that they should be individuals with expertise in the field and noted for their diligence and fairness. In addition, at least four and often as many as eight nationally-prominent figures in the relevant field but outside the specific university itself are asked to write letters evaluating the work of the candidate for promotion. These "outside letters" are a crucial part of the process, because theoretically they offer an objective view of the work of the candidate, untainted by local faculty politics.

An academically untrained and intellectually inadequate political extremist like Ward Churchill had to pass the close scrutiny not only of his own department faculty but of more than a dozen members of his field at the national level, in addition to the dean of his college over a period of many years, to arrive at his full professorship (not to mention his chairmanship). Given what has come to light about Churchill's scholarship—that he simply invented historical incidents central to his academic work—not only are the scholarly *bona fides* of the Ethnic Studies Department at Colorado called into question by Churchill's repeated promotions, but the implication is that his entire field—ethnic studies—is intellectually corrupt. As this volume clearly demonstrates, such corruption is not confined to ethnic studies, but has spread throughout the liberal arts fields.

More than 90 percent of the professors profiled in this text have attained tenure rank, an indication that their academic work is approved by their peers both within their department and university, and nationally (through the requirement of outside letters approving the quality of their work). Their tenure also makes them eligible to vote for decades on who will be hired in the future to their departments and who will be promoted to tenure rank. Some of the professors profiled here hold especially prestigious and lucrative "endowed" chairs, which gives them added weight and prestige within their departments. At least fourteen of the professors profiled are (or have been) department chairs at one university and sometimes more. As chairs they are in a position to designate members of search committees and shape the composition of their departments. (An academic department can include as few as a half-dozen faculty and as many as seventy or more, depending on the size of the university.)

The professors in this volume are drawn from the broad spectrum of fields in the humanities and the social sciences. They are professors of African American studies, anthropology, criminology, communications, comparative literature, economics, education, English literature, ethnic studies history, international relations, Islamic studies, Jewish studies, journalism, law, Middle East studies, philosophy, peace studies, political science, psychology, religion, sociology, and women's studies. They teach at sixty-six representative institutions of higher learning, located in every geographical region: The Northeast (Boston University, Columbia, C.U.N.Y., M.I.T.); the Midwest (Ball State, Michigan, Northwestern); the South (Duke, Texas, Kentucky, North Carolina); and the West (Berkeley, Hawaii, Oregon, Stanford, U.C.L.A.). The list intentionally includes institutions large and small, and in many different categories: local public colleges (Metro State, Montclair State, San Francisco State); private liberal arts colleges and universities (Dayton, Emory, U.S.C.); major state universities (Colorado, Illinois, Penn State); and Ivy League giants (Penn, Princeton). The list includes Catholic institutions (De Paul, St. Xavier, Villanova), Jewish institutions (Brandeis), Protestant institutions (Baylor), and a Quaker institution (Earlham).

Thus the problems revealed in this text—the explicit introduction of political agendas into the classroom, the lack of professionalism in conduct, and the decline in professional standards—appear to be increasingly widespread throughout the academic profession and at virtually every type of institution of higher learning.

NOTES

Introduction
Trials of the Intellect in the Post-Modern Academy

1. Scott Smallwood, "Inside A Free Speech Firestorm: How a Professor's 3-year-old Essay Sparked a National Controversy," *Chronicle of Higher Education*, February 18, 2005.

2. Ward Churchill, "Some People Push Back: On the Justice of Roosting Chickens," *Pockets of Resistance #11*, September 2001 http://www.kersplebedeb.com/mystuff/s11/churchill.html.

3. The term was coined by Roger Kimball in a book of the same name.

4. When I was at Columbia College in the 1950s, there was a reluctance to look at events more recent than twenty-five years in the past because of the dangers of "present-mindedness" and the fear that events so fresh could not be examined with "scholarly disinterest."

5. These templates can be found in university catalogues. When I visited the president of Brandeis College, Yehuda Reinharz, he had throw pillows on his office sofa inscribed with the words, "Peace" and "Social Justice." Brandeis professors profiled in this volume include Gordon Fellman and Dessima Williams.

6. Bernardine Dohrn and Bill Ayers raised Kathy Boudin's child during the twenty years she was in prison. For an account of the Weather Underground, see Peter Collier and David Horowitz, *Destructive Generation*, 1996.

7. David Horowitz, "Prisoners of War," *FrontPageMag.com*, September 5, 2001.

8. James Taranto, "A Terrorist at Duke", *OpinionJournal*, January 16, 2003.

9. Jacob Laksin, "Terrorist Teacher," *FrontPageMag.com*, December 2, 2004.

10. Ibid.

11. Ibid.

12. Confidential faculty source.

13. Smallwood, "Inside a Free Speech Firestorm," op. cit.

14. Ibid.

15. At a speech at the University of Michigan, which I gave in the spring of 2002, university officials provided twelve armed guards and a German shepherd. In the previous spring during a controversy over my opposition to slave reparations paid to living Americans who had never been slaves, the University of California, Berkeley assigned thirty armed guards to maintain security at a speech I gave there. David Horowitz, *Uncivil Wars: The Controversy over Reparations for Slavery*, 2001.

16. Scott Jaschik, "Fallout at Hamilton," *Inside Higher Ed News*, July 5, 2005.

17. Interview with Colorado University regent Tom Lucero.

18. Profiled in this volume.

19. I, myself, filed an amicus brief in behalf of Jeffries, precisely because it was a free speech issue. I also wrote an op-ed column for the *Denver Rocky Mountain News* defending Ward Churchill's free speech rights, which were separate from the question of whether he had the qualifications to be a tenured professor.

20. "And the Verdict: He's Got to Go," *RockyMountainNews.com*, June 10, 2005; "Rocky Mountain News Earns Reader Respect," *Discarded Lies*, June 22, 2005; Berny Morson, "The Charge: Mischaracterization," *RockyMountainNews.com*, June 8, 2005.

21. Rafael Renteria, "Petition on Ward Churchill and Academic Free-dom," *University of Dayton*, February 2005 http://academic.udayton.edu/race/miscell/WardChurchill.htm; Jacob Laksin, "Churchill's Champions," *FrontPageMag.com*, February 28, 2005; Elizabeth Mattern Clark, "Ad Demands Halt to Review," *dailycamera.com buffzone*, February 26, 2005.

22. http://www.frontpagemag.com/Articles/ReadArticle.asp?ID=19081.

23. "Faculty Action in the Ward Churchill Case," *American Association of University Professors*, (Updated) March 2005 http://www.aaup.org/newsroom/Newsitems/Faculty&churchill.htm.

24. Dan Werner, "200 Teachers Sign Ad Asking that Churchill Inquiry Be Dropped," *9News.com*, February 26, 2005 (Updated March 3, 2005); Charlie Brennan, "Churchill Throws Down Gauntlet at Speech in Boulder," *RockyMountainNews.com*, February 9, 2005; Craig Gima, "Churchill Attacks Essay's Critics," *(Honolulu) Starbulletin.com*, February 23, 2005.

25. Lawrence Stone, "Prosopography" in F. Gilbert and S. Graubard, eds., *Historical Studies Today*, W. W. Norton & Co., New York, 1972.

26. One hundred and two, if one includes Ward Churchill and Cornel West.

27. This is a troubling indicator of the support of faculty abuses by university administrations on more than one count. Sensitivity towards and respect for the "Other" is the most cherished and enforced ethical value on university campuses today. The enforcement of "sensitivity" begins with orientation guidelines for freshmen, stipulating required and forbidden behavior (at the University of Connecticut at Storrs, this includes warnings against "inappropriate smiling"). It continues in the curriculum, with an ever-increasing smorgasbord of "diversity" courses to which faculty resources are devoted. There is also guidance at great length in faculty handbooks, which are issued to all new professors by administrations–about what to say, how to act, and to whom to report violations. Sensitivity, finally, is formally enshrined in official and written and often lengthy university rules, and there is usually a substantial enforcement bureaucracy to back it up (sometimes called "The Office of Human Relations"). "Embrace Diversity!" and "Be Sensitive to Others!" are slogans endlessly repeated on campuses across the country.

28. The incident is discussed in the conclusion to this volume.

29. Todd Gitlin, "Varieties of Patriotic Experience" in George Packer, ed. *The Fight Is For Democracy: Winning the War of Ideas in America and the World*, Perennial Books, 2003.

30. Collier and Horowitz, eds., *Surviving the PC University*, Center for the Study of Popular Culture, 1996.

31. An email from the panel chair, Professor Dvora Yanow of California State, Hayward, described the proposed session in these words: "The panel, which is co-sponsored by the Conference Group on Theory, Policy, & Society, the Latino Caucus, New Political Science, and the Women's Caucus, emerged from a question that [Professor] Kathy Ferguson started asking last winter-spring (at ISA and WPSA) to focus on both substantive aspects and strategic/tactical ones: Is there theoretical-definitional grounding to make a claim for the present US administration as fascist, and is it useful, critically, to use that language at this point in time? One of the original intentions was also to create a teaching tool out of this discussion—a handout that presents these questions and offers relevant information to students to think about it for themselves." The panel included professors from the Universities of Hawaii, California and Colorado, among other schools, and the suggestion that the "questions" should be handed to students—undigested—indicated an intention to disseminate their views of the Bush administrations to undergraduates, again for obvious political reasons. The email was relayed to the author by political scientist John Earl Haynes.

32. For a hundred more, see: http://www.discoverthenetwork.org/ IndividualDesc.asp?type=aca.

33. The profiles appear in alphabetical order.

34. Cf, Richard Rorty, *Achieving Our Country: Leftist Thought in Twentieth-Century America*, Harvard University Press, 1998.

35. Paul Campos, "Finding Responsive, Responsible Leadership at CU is Just a Dream," *Denver Rocky Mountain News*, January 29, 2005.

36. Stanley Fish, "Save the World on Your Own Time," *The Chronicle of Higher Education*, Jan. 23, 2003; Fish has written a book on the same subject, *Professional Correctness*, Oxford University Press, 1995.

37. See, for example, the profiles of professors Anton and Gordon in this volume.

38. Jim Downs and Jennifer Manion, eds., *Taking Back The Academy!: History of Activism, History as Activism*, Routledge Books, 2004.

39. Profiled in this volume.

40. Ibid. p. xi

41. Ibid. p. 188. [Emphasis in original]

42. Ibid.

43. Sokal was himself a leftist, disturbed over what he (correctly) saw as the corruption of "progressive" thought.

44. Profiled in this volume.

45. http://www.physics.nyu.edu/faculty/sokal/lingua_franca_v4/lingua_franca_v4.html

For a book on the controversy, see Alan Sokal and Jean Bricmont, *Fashionable Nonsense: Post-Modern Intellectuals' Abuse of Science*, Picador Books, 1998.

46. Cass Sunstein, "The Law of Group Polarization," *Social Science Research Network—University of Chicago Law School*, December 1999 http://papers.ssrn.com/sol3/papers.cfm?abstract_id=199668.

47. Daniel Klein and Charlotta Stern, "Surveys on Political Diversity in American Higher Education" http://www.studentsforacademicfreedom.org/reports/Surveys.html; Daniel Klein and Charlotta Stern, "How Politically Diverse Are The Social Sciences and Humanities?" http://www.ratio.se/pdf/wp/dk_ls_diverse.pdf.

48. Vincent Carroll, "Republican Professors? Sure, There's One," *Wall Street Journal*, May 11, 1998; Rob Natelson, "Academia Locks Out Conservative Professors," *The Billings Outpost*, February 17, 2005; David Horowitz and Eli Lehrer, "Political Bias in the Administrations and Faculties of 32 Elite Colleges and Universities," *FrontPageMag.com* http://www.frontpagemag.com/Content/read.asp?ID=55.

49. Daniel Klein and Charlotta Stern, "Surveys on Political Diversity in American Higher Education," http://www.ratio.se/pdf/wp/dk_aw_voter.pdf. They conducted a separate study of junior faculty at both schools reflecting this disparity.

50. Paul Krugman, "An Academic Question," *New York Times*, April 5, 2005.

51. http://www.studentsforacademicfreedom.org/archive/2005/November2005/LawJournalismStudyRevisedFinal112205.htm.

52. Klein and Western, op. cit.

53. Stanley Rothman, S. Robert Lichter, Neil Nevitte, "Politics and Professional Advancement Among College Faculty," *The Forum*, Vol. 3, Iss. 1, Art. 2, 2005 http://www.cmpa.com/documents/05.03.29.Forum.Survey.pdf.

54. Rothman, Lichter, Nevitte, op. cit.

55. On the importance of these committees see Chapter 4: The Representative Nature of the Professors Profiled in this Volume, below.

56. Herbert Marcuse, "Repressive Tolerance," 1965. http://grace.evergreen.edu/~arunc/texts/frankfurt/marcuse/tolerance.pdf

57. This and the following anecdote were related to the author personally.

58. "Politics in the Classroom," *The Skidmore News*, April 29, 2005.

59. Professor Shortell is profiled in this volume.

60. Daniel Klein and Andrew Western, "How Many Democrats per Republican at U.C. Berkeley and Stanford?," "Surveys on Political Diversity in American Higher Education" http://www.studentsforacademicfreedom.org/reports/Surveys.html.

61. Mike Adams, "Fear and loathing in faculty recruitment," *Townhall.com*, June 2, 2004.

62. The anthropology professor is Robert Moore and the question was asked by the author of this book on a visit to Rollins.

63. David French, "More on Viewpoint Discrimination," *Fire's The Torch*, April 6, 2005.

64. Cindy Yee, "DCU Sparks Various Reactions," *The Chronicle Online*, February 10, 2004.

65. Andrew Peyton Thomas, *The People v. Harvard Law*, 2005 http://www.law.harvard.edu/faculty/directory/; David Horowitz, *Campus Blacklist* (booklet), Students for Academic Freedom, Washington, D.C., 2003.

66. Thomas, op. cit. pp. 126-127.

67. Martin Trow, "Californians Redefine Academic Freedom," *Academic Questions*, Summer 2003 http://gspp.berkeley.edu/people/faculty/emeritus/calif_redefine_adademic_freedom.pdf; David Horowitz, "California's Betrayal of Academic Freedom," *FrontPageMag.com*, September 14, 2004; (Two incidents precipitated the change in U.C. policy on academic freedom. The first was the complaint of a student at U.C. Berkeley that her Middle Eastern studies lecturer had told students that the notorious Czarist forgery, *The Protocols of the Elders of Zion*, was true. The *Protocols* describes a Jewish plot to control the world and was a document used by the Nazis to justify the extermination of Jews. The student's complaint was dismissed by university authorities. An official of the U.C. academic senate defended the professor's preposterous and bigoted statement as coming under the protection of "academic freedom." The second incident involved a required freshman English writing class conducted by instructor Snehal Shingavi discussed below.

68. Roger Kimball, "The Intifada Curriculum," *OpinionJournal*, May 11, 2002; Marc J. Rauch, "America-Hating Professors," *FrontPageMag. com* October 14, 2002. Shingavi is the head of the International Socialist Organization, a group that describes itself as "Leninist" and calls for violent revolution. He is also head of Students for Justice in Palestine. Shingavi organized an anti-American demonstration on September 11, 2001, after the World Trade Center attacks and has been arrested for leading illegal and violent demonstrations on campus.

69. The author has personally interviewed students about such courses on scores of college campuses.

70. E.g., Penn State and Ohio State (and indeed, nine of eleven public colleges and universities in Ohio). http://www.studentsforacademicfreedom.org/archive/2005/April2005/OhioSummaryCurrentAF-Policies042705.htm.

71. See page 369.

72. National Center for Education Statistics 2003: http://nces.ed.gov/programs/digest/d03/lt3.asp#c3a_3.

Chapter 1
One Hundred and One Professors

1. "Northeastern University Prof Likens 9/11 Hijackers to American Founding Fathers," *Jihad Watch*, December 30, 2004.

2. M. Shahid Alam, "Testing Free Speech in America," *CounterPunch*, January 1/2, 2005.

3. Robert Spencer, "Northeastern U's Professor of Jihad," *Jihad Watch*, January 5, 2005.

4. Russell Schoch, "A Conversation with Hamid Algar," *California Monthly*, June 2003.

5. Message of Thaqalayn, Vol. 1, No. 4, 49–57, Published by *Ah al-beyt('a)World Assembly, Tehran, Islamic Republic of Iran*, October 1994.

6. Ibid.

7. Schoch, op. cit.

8. Ibid.

9. Ibid.

10. Ibid.

11. Joseph D'Hippolito, "Jihadism Is the Modern Equivalent of Nazism", *Mid-East Realities*, November 14, 2004.

12. Joseph D'Hippolito, "A Front for Jihad," *FrontPageMag.com*, September 22, 2004.

13. Jacob Gershman, "Columbia Lists Said Donors—UAE Contributes to Chair Named for Israel Critic," *Campus Watch*, March 29, 2004.

14. Amba Datta, "Officer of Said Chair to Khalidi Draws Fire," *Columbia Spectator*, November 14, 2002.

15. "A South African Conversation on Israel and Palestine," The Institute for African Studies, *Columbia University–Economics Department*, September 20/21, 2002.

16. Lisa Anderson, "President's Letter," *Campus Watch*, February 2003.

17. Hugh Fitzgerald, "Lisa Anderson: Apologist for Academic Radicalism," *FrontPageMag.com*, May 3, 2005.

18. http://www.columbia.edu/cu/ccls/academics/intro/crosslist/.

19. Interview with Gil Anidjar by Nermeen Shaikh, "Religion, Race and Ethnicity," *Asia Source*, 2003.

20. Ibid.

21. Ibid.

22. Hugh Fitzgerald, "Columbia Teaches 'Hate'," *History News Network*, June 6, 2005.

23. Ibid.

24. Interview with Gil Anidjar by Nermeen Shaikh, "The Problem of Universalism," *Asia Source*, 2003.

25. National Day of Action against Israeli Apartheid, *Columbia University*, November 13, 2002.

26. Gil Anidjar, "Columbia Strike Too", *Censoring Thought*, 2005.

27. Ibid.

28. Fitzgerald, op. cit.

29. Jennifer McNulty, "Faculty Panel Debates the Lecture as a Tool of Instruction," *U.C. Santa Cruz Currents Online*, February 18, 2002.

30. Barbara McKenna, "Landmark Women's Studies Program Turns 25 This Year," *U.C. Santa Cruz Currents Online*, March 27, 2000.

31. http://humwww.ucsc.edu/FMST/PDFs/courses2005_06.pdf.

32. http://humwww.ucsc.edu/humbooks/WLegacy.html.

33. Professor Davis is profiled in this volume.

34. Jennifer McNulty, "Hundreds Gather for Teach-in about the War," *U.C. Santa Cruz Currents Online*, April 7, 2003.

35. http://humwww.ucsc.edu/wst/wave_2003.pdf.

36. Leila Beckwith, "Bias Colors U.C. Santa Cruz Department," *The Jewish Journal*, February 4, 2005.

37. Cited in state of Michigan, Washtenaw County Circuit Court, Case 02-1150-CZ, *Richard Dorfman and Adi Neuman v. The University of Michigan*.

38. Steven Emerson, "*American Jihad: The Terrorists Living among Us*," Free Press, 2002, pp. 109 et seq.

39. Both men are profiled in this volume.

40. Robert Spencer, "Al-Arian: Terrorist Professor and His Campus Allies," *FrontPageMag.com*, February 26, 2003.

41. Eric Boehlert, "The Prime-time Searing of Sami Al-Arian," *Salon.com*, January 19, 2002.

42. Ken Timmerman, *Preachers of Hate*, p. 273; Ron Radosh, "The Case of Sami Al-Arian," *FrontPageMag.com*, February 8, 2002; Jonathan Schanzer, "Professors for Terrorist Al-Arian," *FrontPageMag.com*, February 24, 2003.

43. The AAUP's position is analyzed in Nathan Giller, "American Association of University Professors: Lobby for the Left," *FrontPageMag.com*, June 4, 2003.

44. *New York Sun*, December 7, 2005

45. David Horowitz, *Unholy Alliance: Radical Islam and the American Left*, Regnery Publishing, 2004.

46. Lee Kaplan, "The Foothills of Hatred," *FrontPageMag.com*, March 15, 2004 (Kaplan audited the course).

47. Ibid.

48. Ibid.

49. Ibid.

50. Kaplan audited Armitage's class.

51. The Sokal article is discussed in the introduction to this volume.

52. "The Loafing Class" in David Horowitz, *Hating Whitey and Other Progressive Causes*, Spence, 1999.

53. http://www.law.upenn.edu/cf/faculty/raustin/.

54. See Derrick Bell profile below.

55. http://www.law.upenn.edu/registrar/descriptions/descriptions.html#AdministrativeLaw.

56. Ibid.

57. Zazy Ivonne Lopez, Univ. of Penn. Law School http://www.law.upenn.edu/admissions/jd/profiles/lopez.html.

58. Heather MacDonald, "Law School Humbug," *City Journal*, Autumn 1995.

59. Ibid.

60. Interview with Professor Regina Austin conducted by Randy Lee, October, 21, 1999; http://www.law.upenn.edu/bll/oralhistory/biddle-rev-oral-history/interviews/transcripts/austin_transcript.html.

61. Ibid.

62. Ibid.

63. Ibid.

64. Ibid.

65. Ibid.

66. Jay Nordlinger, "The Perfect European, K-mart's Good Deed, a Personal Story, &c.," *National Review Online*, September 17, 2001.

67. Collier and Horowitz, *Destructive Generation*, Free Press, 1996 ed. p. 68

68. Ibid.

69. Thomas Ryan, "RNC Forecast: Severe 'Weather' Watch," *American-Daily*, September 2, 2004.

70. Ibid.

71. Paul Sperry, "Homeland Insecurity," *WorldNetDaily*, August 11, 2003.

72. Major Study Of American Muslims To Be Released, *The Institute For Social Policy And Understanding*, April 2, 2004.

73. Alison Bethel, "Metro Muslims Eschew Radicalism," *The Detroit News—detnews.com*, April 6, 2004.

74. Daniel Pipes, "The Moderation of American Muslims," *danielpipes.org*, April 8, 2004.

75. Ibid.

76. Daniel Pipes, "Reply to CAIR's Attack on Daniel Pipes," *danielpipes.org.*

77. Joel Mowbray, "CAIR's Message of Violence," *FrontPageMag.com*, March 18, 2004.

78. Free Muslims March against Terror, *The Dead Hand*, April 18, 2005.

79. http://www.wfu.edu/~caron/ssrs/watts.DOC.

80. Jerry Gafio Watts, "Amiri Baraka: The Politics and Art of a Black Intellectual," *New York University Press*, August 2001—reviewed by Justin Driver, *Powells.com*, April 25 2002.

81. Ibid.

82. Jeff Jacoby, "New Jersey's Bigot Laureate," *Boston Globe*, October 13, 2002.

83. Jerry Gafio Watts, "Amiri Baraka: The Politics and Art of a Black Intellectual," op. cit.

84. Sara Russo, "Bigoted Poem by SUNY Professor Emeritus Sparks Outrage," *Accuracy In Academia*, November 2002.

85. Compiled by James Lubinskas, "Expressions of Ethnic Animosity," *American Renaissance*.

86. Daniel Won-gu Kim, "In the Tradition: Amiri Baraka, black liberation, and Avant-garde Praxis in the U.S—Critical Essay," African American Review, Summer-Fall, 2003.

87. Richard Poe, "'What Kind of Skeeza Is A Condoleeza' And So On," *RichardPoe.com*, October 12, 2002.

88. Watts, op. cit.

89. Robert Hanley, "Black Poet Says Faculty 'Nazis' Blocked Tenure," *The New York Times*, March 15, 1990, p. B3.

90. Statement By Amiri Baraka, New Jersey Poet Laureate, "I Will Not 'Apologize', I Will Not 'Resign!,'" October 2, 2002.

91. John Perazzo, "Racist Yale Laureate," *FrontPageMag.com*, July 24, 2003.

92. http://faculty.washington.edu/dpbarash/.

93. Ibid.

94. David Barash and Charles Webel, *Peace and Conflict Studies*, op. cit., p. x.

95. Ibid., p. 498

96. Ibid., p. 499

97. Ibid., pp. 14-15, emphasis added.

98. GDP Per Capita: 1999 CIA World Factbook, *www.geographic.org* http://www.photius.com/wfb1999/rankings/gdp_per_capita_0.html.

99. Barash and Webel, op. cit., p. 211

100. Ibid., p. 80

101. Ibid.

102. Ibid., p. 81

103. Ibid.

104. David Horowitz, "One Man's Terrorist" in David Horowitz and Ben Johnson, *Campus Support For Terrorism* (pamphlet), Center for the Study of Popular Culture, Los Angeles, 2004.

105. Jonathan Calt Harris, "Hatem Bazian: Calls for an Intifada in the United States," *History News Network*, May 14, 2004.

106. Ibid.

107. Anonymous, "UCLA Sponsors of Terrorism," *FrontPageMag.com*, April 4, 2003.

108. Rory Miller, "UC Berkeley: A Safe Harbor For Hate," *FrontPageMag.com*, September 5, 2002.

109. Aleza, Goldsmith, "Swastika Stirs New Concerns at Washington High School," *Jewish Bulletin News*, June 2002.

110. Jonathan Calt Harris, "Hatem Bazian: His Record of Hatred for Jews and America," *History News Network*, April 15, 2004.

111. Jonathan Calt Harris, "A Berkeley Prof's 'Intifada' Against America," *FrontPageMag.com*, April 15, 2004.

112. Press Release and Statements, Report on May 31, 2003 Historian Against The War Meeting.

113. Ibid.

114. Marc Becker, "Columbus Day," October 12, 2003 http:// www.yachana.org/writings/columbus.html.

115. Ibid.

116. Alyssa A. Lappen, "Stanford's Islamist Threat," *FrontPageMag.com*, December 21, 2004,

117. Ibid.

118. Stanley Kurtz, "Get Real," *National Review Online*, December 7, 2002.

119. Ibid.

120. William E. Hudson, "We Must Always Remain Critical," *The Stanford Review*, Volume XXX, Issue 1, February 26, 2003.

121. Joe Fairbanks, "Beinin Watch," *The Stanford Review*, Volume XXX, Issue 3, March 13, 2003.

122. Lappen, op. cit.

123. University of Texas at Austin, Dr. Jim Scheurich, Introduction to Systems of Human Inquiry, Spring 2001, *The History of Critical Race Theory* Project http://www.edb.utexas.edu/faculty/scheurich/proj7/crthistory.htm.

124. Ibid., p. 21

125. Ibid., p. 35

126. Ibid., p. 34

127. Ibid., p. 35

128. See Regina Austin profile in this volume. In an essay called "The Black Community, Its Lawbreakers, and a Politics of Identification," published in 1992. Regina Austin compared "street women [who] accept the justifiability of engaging in illegal conduct to rectify past injustices and to earn a living" to political revolutionaries such as Malcolm X. She called for "a legal praxis ... [that] would find its reference points in the 'folk law' of those black people who, as a matter of survival, concretely assess what laws must be obeyed and what laws may be justifiably ignored." See Regina Austin, "The Black Community, Its Lawbreakers, and a Politics of Identification," 65 S. CAL. L. REV. 1769, 1771-72 (1992). According to Austin the politics of identification promotes an empathy with lawbreakers as rebels against oppression.

129. Thomas, op. cit., p. 41

130. Ibid., p. 42

131. http://www.education.uc.edu/programs/doctoral_degree_programs/educational_foundations_doctoral.htm.

132. Marvin Berlowitz, "The Chickens Will Come Home to Roost," *Cal. State—A Justice Site*, March 9, 2001.

133. Ibid.

134. http://www.education.uc.edu/faculty/biographies/ed_studies_faculty_bios.htm.

135. Marvin J. Berlowitz, "Racism and Conscription in the JROTC," *Peace Review 12*, September 2000—reprinted on *Liberal Slant*.

136. Jacob Laksin, "Midwest Marxists," *FrontPageMag.com*, April 15, 2005.

137. Ibid.

138. Dawn Fuller, "Conflict Management Course Open to Ohio Schoolteachers," *University of Cincinnati News*, March 26, 2001.

139. Laksin, op. cit.

140. Ibid.

141. Ibid.

142. http://www.uc.edu/sga/UFB_minutes.htm.

143. Books, Articles, Other Writings, *MaryFrancesBerry.com*.

144. Mary Frances Berry, "Judging Morality: Sexual Behavior and Legal Consequences in the Late Nineteenth-Century South," *The Journal of American History*, Vol. 78, No. 3, December 1991, 835–856.

145. Linda Chavez, "Bush Finally Fires Mary Frances Berry," *Human Events Online*, December 14, 2004.

146. Ibid.

147. John J. Miller, "'A Threat to Our Domestic Institutions' High Times for a Racial Ambulance Chaser," *National Review Online*, April 2, 2001.

148. Ibid.

149. News & Notes with Ed Gordon, "Roundtable: Courtroom Security, Cuba Criticized, Silicone Implants," *National Public Radio (NPR)*, April 15, 2005.

150. Joseph McLaughlin, "Still a Lot More to Do," *Penn Arts & Sciences*, Spring 2005. http://www.sas.upenn.edu/sasalum/newsltr/spring05/berry.pdf.

151. *Crime and the Black Community*, Albany: The Governor's Advisory Committee for Black Affairs, December 1987.

152. George E. Curry, "Mary Frances Berry: A Fearless Warrior for Civil Rights," *Chicago Standard Newspapers—Part of the BlackPressUSA Network*, December 16, 2004.

153. Ibid.

154. Michael Berube, "Should I Have Asked John to Cool It? Standards of Reason in the Classroom," *Chronicle of Higher Education*, December 5, 2003.

155. Michael Berube, "Peace Puzzle," *boston.com News—Boston Globe*, September 15, 2002.

156. Michael Berube, "Teaching Postmodern Fiction without Being Sure that the Genre Exists," *Chronicle of Higher Education*, May 19, 2000.

157. Ibid.

158. Michael Berube, "Days of Future Past," *Modern Language Association—Association of Departments of English*, Bulletin 131, Spring 2002, 20–26

159. http://www.michaelberube.com/essays/pdf/abuses_alh.pdf (Orig. publ. in *American Literary History*, 1998).

160. Jonathan Calt Harris, "The Middle East Studies Left," *FrontPageMag.com*, November 6, 2003.

161. Martin Kramer, "Profs Condemn Israel in Advance," *FrontPageMag.com*, December 27, 2002.

162. Martin Kramer, "Middle East 'Scholars' Unleash a New Brand of Bias," *FrontPageMag.com*, November 26, 2004.

163. Ibid.

164. "Time for a Change of Course," *CounterPunch*, October 12, 2004.

165. http://fp.arizona.edu/mesassoc/MESA04/2004pres.htm.

166. http://fp.arizona.edu/mesassoc/Bulletin/Pres%20Addresses/Brand.htm (One wonders about the extent of her outrage at Abu Zarqawi's fatwah announcing that Muslim civilians can be killed if they get in the way of Jihad, a religious pronouncement recently carried through in the deaths of 18 children in Bagdad on July 12, 2005).

167. http://www.sigmaxi.org/programs/lectureships/past.0102.shtml.

168. http://www.anatomy.usyd.edu.au/danny/anthropology/sci.anthropology.paleo/archive/march-1995/0012.html.

169. SUNY at Binghamton, *RATS—Radical Archaeology Theory Seminar*, October 17-18, 2003.

170. http://www.caut.ca/en/bulletin/issues/2004_dec/news_aaa.asp.

171. Russell MCulley, "Bad for Business?" *BizNewOrleans.com*, August 1, 2004.

172. http://www.aaanet.org/stmts/marriage.htm.

173. Ibid.

174. http://www.aaanet.org/president.htm.

175. David Gulliver, "Academic Teach-In, Not." *FrontPageMag.com*, November 4, 2002.

176. Ibid.

177. "Castellano Named Head of Criminal Justice," *Rochester Institute of Technology—News Events*, Volume 36, Number 6, November 6, 2003 http://www.rit.edu/~930www/Proj/News/viewstory.php3?id=1326.

178. Larissa MacFarquhar, "The Devil's Accountant," *New Yorker,* March 31, 2003.

179. Anders Lewis, "Chomsky's Stalinist Arguments," *History News Network,* April 9, 2004.

180. Noam Chomsky, *What Uncle Sam Really Wants,* Odonian Press, 2002, 59.

181. Keith Windschuttle, "A Disgraceful Career," *The New Criterion,* Vol. 23, No. 1, September 2004.

182. Robert Faurisson, "World Famous French Professor Says from All His Research Nazi Homicidal Gas Chambers Did Not Exist," *Rense.com,* July 18, 2004.

183. Noam Chomsky, "War In Afghanistan," *World Confrontation Now,* January/February 2002 (This article is an edited excerpt, with notes, from the Lakdawala Memorial Lecture "Peering Into the Abyss of the Future," presented by Noam Chomsky on November 3, 2001 in New Delhi, under the sponsorship of the Institue of Social Sciences, New Delhi, India).

184. Adapted from Peter Collier's Introduction to *The Anti-Chomsky Reader,* Collier and Horowitz, eds., Encounter Books, 2004, vii–xv.

185. David Horowitz, "Black Murder Inc." in *Hating Whitey and Other Progressive Causes,* 1999.

186. Weckea Lilly, "Kathleen Cleaver Speaks in Baltimore," *Independent Media Center,* May 11, 2005.

187. Kathleen Cleaver, "Black Panthers Today," interview from the PBS film by Aaron Matthews, "A Panther in Africa," *PBS POV,* September 21, 2004.

188. Hugh Pearson, *Shadow of The Panther,* Perseus Books, 1994.

189. Ibid.

190. http://ethics.emory.edu/news/archives/000312.html.

191. Ibid.

192. Ibid.

193. Aaron Shuman, "A Sit-down with Kathleen Cleaver," *Bad Subjects,* Issue #60, April 2002.

194. Ed Rampell, "3rd Degree—Kathleen Cleaver," *Los Angeles City Beat,* February 12, 2004.

195. Ibid.

196. http://www.law.emory.edu/faculty/publication/cleaverpub.pdf.

197. Dana Cloud, "UT Professor on Terrorism," *Progessive Activism in Austin, TX,* September 13, 2001.

198. Ibid.

199. Ibid.

200. Dateline Durban: Anti-Semitic Materials/Slogans Proliferate On Opening Day of UN Conference, *Anti-Defamation League*, August 31, 2001.

201. Herbert Keinon, "Festival of Hate," *Jerusalem Post*, September 7, 2001, cited in Timmerman, op. cit., 25.

202. Dana Cloud, "UT Professor on Terrorism," op. cit.

203. Ibid.

204. Jay Nordlinger, "The Luxury of a Movie Star, the Democrats' Odd Glee, Decapitating Margaret, &c.," *National Review Online*, July 8, 2002.

205. http://www.law.georgetown.edu/curriculum/tab_courses.cfm?Status=Course&Detail=1046.

206. David Cole, "Enemy Aliens and American Freedoms," *The Nation*, September 5, 2002.

207. "Statement of Conscience Against War and Repression," *Not In Our Name*, April 15, 2003.

208. Larry Neumeister (AP), "N.Y. Lawyer Convicted of Aiding Terrorists," *ABC News*, February 10, 2005.

209. David Cole, "The Lynne Stewart Trial," *The Nation*, February 17, 2005.

210. Ibid.

211. Chris O'Donnell, "Cole Condemns University Action Against Al-Arian," *Academic Free Speech*, March 29, 2002.

212. Ibid.

213. David Cole, "National Security State," *The Nation*, November 29, 2001.

214. David Cole, "Terrorizing Immigrants in the Name of Fighting Terrorism," *American Bar Association—Human Rights Magazine*, Winter 2002.

215. Juan Cole, "Kwiatkowski on the Neoconservative Coup at the Pentagon," *Informed Comment*, February 23, 2004.

216. Jonathan Calt Harris, "Juan Cole, Media—and MESA—Darling," *FrontPageMag.com*, December 7, 2004.

217. Juan Cole, "Wolfowitz Throws Tantrum at France, Germany, Russia and Canada: The Failure of Emotional Intelligence," *Informed Comment*, December 12, 2003.

218. Cole, op. cit.

219. Juan Cole, "Reply to Yglesias on Palestine," *Informed Comment*, February 3, 2004.

220. Juan Cole, "No WMD. Nada. Bupkes*," *Informed Comment*, January 9, 2004.

221. Juan Cole, "Arguing with Bush," *Informed Comment*, April 14, 2004.

222. Ibid.

223. Juan Cole, "The Passion of Christ in the World Religions," *Informed Comment*, February 26, 2004.

224. Juan Cole, "200,000 Israeli Fascists Demand Colonization of Gaza," *Informed Comment*, July 26, 2004.

225. Juan Cole, "The US 3rd Infantry Division Has Entered Southern Iraq Virtually without Opposition," *Informed Comment*, March 21, 2003.

226. Jonathan Calt Harris, "Juan Cole: The New Head of the Middle East Studies Association," *History News Network*, December 7, 2004.

227. Jonathan Calt Harris, "Juan Cole, Media—and MESA—Darling," *FrontPageMag.com*, December 7, 2004.

228. Miriam Cooke, "War, Its Machines and the Women Who Fight Them," *Duke University Forum: Faculty Viewpoints*, October 17, 2001 http://www.duke.edu/web/forums/cooke.html.

229. Ibid. This is the same hysterical and discredited accusation made by Noam Chomsky (see profile above).

230. Sally Hicks, "Miriam Cooke: Crusade! I Mean Democracy! You Know: Women!," *Duke University News*, April 3, 2003.

231. Cinnamon Stillwell, "Duke Feminist Gives Thumbs Up to Taliban," *Campus Watch*, September 27, 2004.

232. Hicks, op. cit.

233. Stillwell, op. cit.

234. Ibid.

235. Ibid.

236. Patrick G. Coy, "The Incarnational Spirituality of Dorothy Day," *Sprituality Today*, Vol. 39, Summer 1987, 114–125.

237. Patrick G. Coy, Gregory M. Maney and Lynne M. Woehrle, "Contesting Patriotism by the Post-9/11 Peace Movement in the United States," *Fellowship of Reconciliation*, (First published in *Peace Review: A Transnational Quarterly*, Volume 14, Number 4, 2003, 463–470).

238. Ibid.

239. Patrick G. Coy, "American Liberalism's Achilles Heel," *Common Dreams*, June 1, 2004.

240. Member New: Patrick Coy, *International Peace Research Association*, March 2005.

241. Interview with Hamid Dabashi conducted by Nermeen Shaikh, *Asia Source*, June 12, 2003.

242. Hamid Dabashi, "For a Fistful of Dust: A Passage to Palestine," *Al-Ahram*, September 23-29, 2004, Issue No. 709.

243. Ibid.

244. On the eagerness of the Columbia University administration to punish certain types of "insensitivity" though obviously not anti-Semitism, see Donald Alexander Downs, *Restoring Free Speech and Liberty on Campus*, Cambridge: Cambridge University Press, 2005, Chapter 3.

245. Douglas Feiden, "Climate of Hate Rocks Columbia University," *New York Daily News*, November 21, 2004.

246. Shaikh, op. cit.

247. Xan Nowakowski, "Students Organize Sit-In to Support Palestinians," *Columbia Spectator*, April 18, 2002.

248. Daniel Pipes and Jonathan Schnanzer, "Extremists on Campus," *History News Network*, July 1, 2002.

249. Hamid Dabashi, "The Hallowed Ground of Our Secular Institution," *Columbia Spectator*, May 3, 2002.

250. Hamid Dabashi, "Forget Reds Under the Bed, There's Arabs in the Attic," *University of Cork (Ireland) Palestine Solidarity Campaign*, October 18, 2003.

251. Margaret Hunt Gram, "Professors Condemn War in Iraq At Teach-in," *Columbia Spectator*, March 27, 2003.

252. Ibid.

253. Shaikh, op. cit.

254. Ibid.

255. Ibid.

256. Geneive Abdo, "In Shi'ite World, Anger Toward US Seen Growing," *The Muslim News*, April 12, 2003.

257. Shaikh, op. cit.

258. Hallinan was formerly an editor of the Communist Party newspaper, *The People's World*.

259. The interviewer was David Horowitz, who was doing background research for the portrait of Newton in *Destructive Generation*, 1989.

260. Angela Yvonne Davis biography, *marcuse.org*.

261. Lawrence Cott, "San Rafael Shootout: The Facts Behind the Angela Davis Case, " *Human Events*, June 17, 1972.

262. Gwyneth E. Hambley, "The Image of the Jury in Popular Culture," *Legal Reference Services Quarterly*, The University of Texas at Austin—Tarlton Law Library, Volume 12, Number 2/3, 1992 http://tarlton.law.utexas.edu/lpop/etext/hambley.htm.

263. Aleksandr Solzhenitsyn, *Warning to the West*, Farrar, Straus and Giroux, New York, 1976, 60–1.

264. Beth Potier, "Abolish Prisons, Says Angela Davis," *Harvard University Gazette*, March 13, 2003.

265. http://www4.ncsu.edu/~ga.dfll/223.html.

266. Gregory Dawes, "Objectives of Our Journal," *A Contracorriente—University of North Carolina*.

267. Gregory Dawes, "Against the Grain," *A Contracorriente*, Vol. 1, No. 1, Fall 2003.

268. Ibid.

269. Ibid.

270. Ibid.

271. Greg Dawes, "A Critique of the Post-Althusserian Conception of Ideology In Latin American Cultural Studies," *Postmodern Culture*, V. 1, N. 3, May 1991.

272. Ibid.

273. Greg Dawes, "Somewhere Beyond Vertigo and Amnesia: Updike's *Toward the End of Time* and Vonnegut's *Timequake*," (Book Review), *Cultural Logic*, Volume 1, Number 2, Spring 1998.

274. Greg Dawes, "Realism, Surrealism, Socialist Realism and Neruda's 'Guided Spontaneity'," *Cultural Logic*, Volume 6, 2003.

275. http://sasw.chass.ncsu.edu/fl/ma/cv/dawes.htm.

276. Ibid.

277. David Horowitz, "Moment of Truth for the Anti-American Left," *FrontPageMag.com*, March 31, 2003.

278. Gram, op. cit.

279. David A. Harris, "Letter from the Campus Front," *Buffalo Israel Link*, June 24, 2002,

280. David Horowitz, "Allies in War," *FrontPageMag.com*, September 17, 2001.

281. She did so to the *New York Times* reporter whose profile appeared in the *Times* on September 11, 2001. However, no one present to hear the remark at the Flint War Council (there were several written reports on her remarks) thought she was joking. Moreover, the formal statement of Weatherman's aims in calling for a global race war perfectly mirrors Manson's own homicidal fantasies of such a conflict.

282. Duane Dudek, "Weather Underground Took Couple on a Strange Journey," *Milwaukee Journal Sentinel*, January 22, 2003.

283. Collier and Horowitz, *Destructive Generation*, 1989.

284. The author has been interviewed by the police investigators.

285. See Ayers profile above.

286. Aacia Hussain, "What's Up with Today's Weather?" *Northern Illinois University, Northern Star Online*, April 4, 2003.

287. Shawn Macomber, "Graduation Gift for the Left," *Students For Academic Freedom*, July 2, 2004.

288. Collier and Horowitz, op. cit.

289. http://catalog.unco.edu/2002-2003/02_03Catalog/2002-2003-11-86.html.

290. Provided by Gloria Reynolds, spokesperson for the University of Northern Colorado.

291. Michael Eric Dyson biography, *Thomson Gale.*

292. Larry Elder, "The 'Today' Show Trashes Bill Cosby," *Human Events Online*, May 12, 2005.

293. Ibid.

294. Ibid.

295. Lee Hubbard, "Michael Eric Dyson on Terrorism and Tupac," *Africana Gateway to the Black World*, September 21, 2001.

296. Ibid.

297. http://www28.homepage.villanova.edu/rick.eckstein/imperialism.syl.pdf.

298. Ibid.

299. Ibid.

300. Katherine Amenta, "Nova's Political Climate, Hot Issues, Tepid Concern," *The Villanovan*, September 19, 2003, 2.

301. Ibid.

302. Paul Grobstein, "11 September 2001," *Bryn Mawr College Serendip*, September 18, 2001.

303. Paul Erlich, "Getting at the Roots of Terrorism," *Stanford University News Service*, November 15, 2002.

304. "Causes of 9/11: U.S. Troops in Saudia Arabia?" *Council on Foreign Relations*, 2004.

305. Ben Johnson, *57 Varieties of Radical Causes: Teresa Heinz Kerry's Tax Exempt Donations* (booklet), Center for the Study of Popular Culture, 2004.

306. Ernst Zundel, "Good Morning from the Zundelsite:," *The Zundelsite*, December 10, 2000.

307. Ernst Zundel, "Good Morning from the Zundelsite:," *The Zundelsite*, March 6, 2001.

308. Press Release, "Second Annual Palestinian Film Festival Dallas, Texas," *PRWeb*, September 14, 2004.

309. "Deir Yassin Remembered," Board of Advisors http://www.deiryassin.org/board.html,

310. Marc E. Ellis, "Speaking Truth to Power," *Al-Ahram Weekly Online*, Issue 649, July 31-August 6, 2003.

311. Steven Plaut, "Lying about Deir Yassin," *FrontPageMag.com*, April 11, 2005.

312. Steven Plaut, "Baylor University's Anti-Jewish Liberation 'Theologian'," *FrontPageMag.com*, May 5, 2005.

313. Mark Ensalaco, "Terrorism Course Added to Winter Semester Offerings," *University of Dayton*, September 21, 2001 http://www.udayton.edu/news/nr/092101b.html.

314. Mary Beth Marklein, "Everyone's Seeking Answers Right Now," *USA Today—Life*, October 7, 2001.

315. Marianne Wellendorf, "Dayton Council Of World Affairs," *The Guardian Online*, February 11, 2004.

316. Thomas Ryan, "Channeling Churchill at the University of Dayton," *FrontPageMag.com*, April 19, 2005.

317. John Esposito, "Political Islam: Beyond the Green Menace," *International Islamic University, Malaysia*, (Originally published in the journal *Current History*, January 1994).

318. More useful terms are Islamic revivalism and Islamic activism.

319. Campus Watch, "Esposito: Apologist for Militant Islam," *FrontPageMag.com*, September 3, 2002.

320. John L. Esposito, *The Islamic Threat: Myth or Reality?*, Oxford University Press, New York, 1992—Review by Daniel Pipes, *Wall Street Journal*, October 30, 1992.

321. Campus Watch, op. cit.

322. Andrea Levin, "Conflict of Interest Fits NPR Bias," *Committee for Accuracy in Middle East Reporting in America (CAMERA)*, October 2, 1995.

323. David W. Lesch, *1979: The Year that Shaped the Modern Middle East*, Westview Press, 2001—Review by Jonathan Schanzer, *The Middle East Quarterly*, Volume IX, Number 4, Fall 2002.

324. Campus Watch, op. cit.

325. Interview with John L. Esposito conducted by Nermeen Shaikh, *Asia Source*, May 13, 2002.

326. Ron Riggins, "Dean's Greeting," *Fairhaven College—Western Washington University*,
http://www.wwu.edu/depts/fairhaven/about/about.html.

327. http://www.wwu.edu/advising/MajorGuides/American%20Cultural%20Studies.pdf.

328. http://www.ac.wwu.edu/~wwuacs/.

329. http://www.ac.wwu.edu/~wwuacs/courses.html.

330. http://www.wwu.edu/depts/fairhaven/classes/2002summer descrip.html.

331. Isolde Raftery, "MV Schools Set Meeting to Discuss Diversity," *Skagit Valley Herald*, May 20, 2005.

332. Ralph de Unamuno, "The Facts Behinds the Myths: Fox News, the GOP, and MEChA," *AztecaNet*, 2004.

333. MEChA Constitution—Article II, Section 1, *American Patrol*, June 8, 2005.

334. Ibid.

335. Carol Denker, "Ethnic Studies Convention in Philadelphia," *Center City's Weekly Press*, April 7, 2004.

336. Ibid.

337. Scott Jaschik, "Showdown in Colorado," *Inside Higher Ed News*, February 3, 2005.

338. Ibid.

339. Ethnic Student Center—Western Washington University http:// www.ac.wwu.edu/~esc/about.html.

340. http://www.ac.wwu.edu/~esc/eventlist/0001.html.

341. http://www.ac.wwu.edu/~esc/eventlist/9899.html.

342. Shara Smith, "Lack of Cultural Studies Upsets Professors," *Western Front Online*, October 23, 2003.

343. Edmund Levin, "Reagan's Victory? How Did the Cold War End?" *Weekly Standard*, November 15, 2004.

344. Cornell Peace Studies Program http://www.einaudi.cornell.edu/ PeaceProgram/courses/listing.asp?detail=375

345. http://falcon.arts.cornell.edu/Govt/courses/S04/ courses.html#131.

346. Franklin Crawford, "Matthew Evangelista is Named Director of CU's Peace Studies Program," *Cornell Chronicle*, July 25, 2002

347. Kirshner, Strauss, Fanis and Evangelista, "Iraq and Beyond: The New U.S. National Security Strategy," *Cornell University—Peace Studies Program*, January 2003, p. 21 This despite the fact that the equipment of violence in Saddam's military and secret police came primarily from france, Germany and Russia (who receive no blame from Evangelista)—and none of it came from the United States.

348. Ibid., 22

349. Ibid., 26–27

350. Matthew Evangelista, "Living in a State of Perpetual War," *Cornell Daily Sun*, October 22, 2002.

351. Joseph Sabia, "Today's Lesson: Peace at Any Price," *FrontPageMag.com*, October 24, 2002.

352. http://www.geocities.com/cfjusticepeace/appeal.html.

353. Ibid.

354. Franklin Crawford, "Panelists Speak Out Against War on Iraq and on Civil Liberties," *Cornell Chronicle*, February 20, 2003.

355. Ibid.

356. Ibid.

357. "The Perils of Occupation," *Coalition for A Realistic Foreign Policy*, October 28, 2004.

358. Richard Bernstein, "No Sympathy for Terrorists, but Warnings about Overreaction," *Common Dreams*, October 6, 2001.

359. David Horowitz and John Perazzo, "The Unholy Alliance of American Radicals and Islamic Terrorists Against the Patriot Act," *FrontPageMag.com*, June 7, 2005.

360. Richard Falk, "Will the Empire be Fascist?" *The Transnational Foundation for Peace and Future Research*, March 24, 2003.

361. "Resisting the Global Domination Project: An Interview with Prof. Richard Falk," *Waging Peace—Nuclear Age Peace Foundation*, April 18, 2003.

362. Falk, "Will the Empire be Fascist?" op. cit.

363. Richard Falk and Andrew Strauss, "Globalization Needs a Dose of Democracy," *Earth Rainbow Network*, (From the *International Herald Tribune*, October 5, 1999, 8).

364. Richard Falk and David Krieger, "No War Against Iraq," *Counter-Punch*, August 24, 2002.

365. David Krieger, "Security in the Post 9/11 World," *Waging Peace— Nuclear Age Peace Foundation*, December 30, 2002.

366. "US Iran Policy," An Interview with Sasan Fayazmanesh by Foaad Khosmood, *Znet*, April 14, 2004.

367. Ibid.

368. Ibid.

369. Bruce S. Thornton, "The Absurdity of Campus 'Middle East Forums'," *FrontPageMag.com*, January 16, 2003.

370. Joe R. Feagin, *Racist America: Roots, Current Realities and Future Reparations*, Routledge, 2000, 16.

371. Ibid., 2.

372. Nijole V. Benokraitis and Joe R. Feagin, *Modern Sexism: Blatant, Subtle, and Covert Discrimination*, Prentice Hall, 1994, 184–210.

373. Joe Feagin, *Racist America*, op. cit., 5.

374. Rhiannon Meyers, "Prof Says Racism Still Present in Colleges," *Texas A&M—The Battalion*, October 21, 2004.

375. Adam Benson, "Feagin: Whites Need to Address All Racism Issues," *University of Utah—The Daily Utah Chronicle*, April 14, 2003.

376. Jake Maynard, "Professor Says Racism Is Subconscious, but Present," *Texas A&M—The Battalion*, October 29, 2004.

377. Joe Feagin & Hernan Vera, "Reparations for Catastrophic Human Waste," *Poverty & Race Research Action Council*, (From *Poverty & Race*, September/October 1994).

378. Ibid.

379. Benson, op. cit.

380. Feagin, *Racist America*, op. cit., 4

381. Ibid., 162

382. Jeannine Gage, "Racism Still Confronts Hispanics," *Deltona Diversidad*, July 12, 2004.

383. Meyers, op. cit.

384. Benson, op. cit.

385. http://www.brandeis.edu/departments/sociology/fellman.html.

386. Thomas Ryan, "Leftist War Studies at Brandeis," *FrontPageMag. com*, July 21, 2004.

387. Ibid.

388. Ibid.

389. Gordon Fellman, "The Starr Bangled Banner," *Brandeis University*, 1998 http://people.brandeis.edu/~fellman/starr.html.

390. Benjamin Freed, "Brandeis Divided over Impending War Against Iraq," *Brandeis University—the Justice*, March 18, 2003.

391. Ryan, op. cit.

392. Richard Baehr, "DePaul's Jihad Against Academic Freedom," *The American Thinker*, April 18, 2005.

393. "Interview with Controversial Prof. Norman Finkelstein In Die Welt, February 6, 2000," *Rense.com*, February 8, 2001.

394. Ibid.

395. Ibid.

396. Don Atapattu, "A Conversation with Professor Norman Finkelstein—How to Lose Friends and Alienate People," *Kaos2000, CounterPunch*, December 13, 2001.

397. Ibid.

398. Steven Plaut, "DeNial at DePaul—the Thomas Klocek Affair," *FrontPageMag.com*, April 18, 2005.

399. Eric Foner, "11 September," *London Review of Books*, Vol. 23, No. 19, October 4, 2001.

400. David Horowitz, "Moment of Truth (for the anti-American Left)," *Jewish World Review*, March 31, 2003.

401. Robert Spencer, "Exposing Leftists' Radical Islam Connection," *Human Events*, September 29, 2004.

402. Eric Foner, "Rethinking American History in a Post-9/11 World," *History News Network*, September 6, 2004.

403. John Patrick Diggins, "Fate and Freedom in History: The Two Worlds of Eric Foner," *The National Interest Magazine*, September 1, 2002.

404. http://hnn.us/articles/15810.html.

405. David Horowitz, *Unholy Alliance: Radical Islam and the American Left*, (Washington, DC: Regnery) 2005.

406. Interview with John Bellamy Foster, *Monthly Review*, Vol. 56, Number 6, November 2004.

407. John Bellamy Foster, "The End of Rational Capitalism," *Monthly Review*, Vol. 56, Number 10, March 2005.

408. Murray Feshback and Alfred Friendly, Jr., *Ecocide in the USSR: Health and Nature Under Siege*, NY, 1993.

409. Foster, op. cit.

410. Ibid.

411. Lowell Ponte, "The Art of Religious War," *FrontPageMag.com*, December 5, 2003.

412. Jim Martin, "America's Al-Qaeda: The SLA-Venceremos Connection," *Flatland Books.com*, 2003.

413. H. Bruce Franklin, "Discussion of Recent Controversy Over Soviet Document on U.S. Vietnam War POW's," *The Etext Archives*, appearance on CNN, April 13, 1993.

414. Rocco DiPippo, "A Scholar for Stalin," *FrontPageMag.com*, March 16, 2005.

415. http://www.chss.montclair.edu/english/furr/stalintalk.html.

416. http://www.h-net.org/~hoac/.

417. DiPippo, op. cit.

418. http://www.chss.montclair.edu/english/furr/rich3rd.html. Furr also vehemently denies that the Soviet government was the perpetrator of the Katyn Massacre of 15,000 Polish officers, claiming there is no "hard historical evidence" of this—even though as a result of an investigation under Gorbachev the Soviet government itself admitted to having perpetrated the massacre, and even apologized to Poland. Trained historians participating in the forum find Furr alternatively a figure of fun and an impossible irritation.

419. http://chss.montclair.edu/english/furr/gbi/gbi05.html.

420. http://www.chss.montclair.edu/english/furr/vnmont84.html.

421. http://www.chss.montclair.edu/english/furr/furrpope83.pdf.

422. http://www.chss.montclair.edu/~furrg/rcpage.html.

423. http://www.ratemyprofessors.com/index.jsp.

424. DiPippo, op. cit.

425. Ibid.

426. http://www.temple.edu/gus/faculty/gilbert.htm.

427. Ibid.

428. Melissa Gilbert and Michele Masucci, "Feminist Praxis in University-Community Partnerships: Reflections on Ethical Crises and Turning Points in Temple-North Philadelphia IT Partnerships," 2004, 147.

429. Ibid.

430. "Building Connections"—Philadelphia Higher Education Network for Neighborhood Development—Volume 1, Number 1, July 1998.

431. Gilbert and Masucci, op. cit., 151.

432. Ibid.

433. Ibid.

434. Melissa Gilbert, "'Race', Space and Power: The Survival Strategies of Working Poor Women," 1998, 595.

435. http://www.temple.edu/gus/faculty/gilbertdocs/R055Syllabus HTML.htm.

436. Ibid.

437. http://www.temple.edu/gus/faculty/gilbertdocs/GUSW120 HTML.htm.

438. Ibid.

439. http://www.temple.edu/gus/faculty/gilbertdocs/GUS410Syllabus HTML.htm.

440. http://www.temple.edu/gus/faculty/gilbertdocs/GUS445Syllabus HTML.htm.

441. Collier and Horowitz, op. cit.

442. David Horowitz, "9/11 and the 'Anti-War' Left," *FrontPageMag.com*, September 11, 2003.

443. Gitlin, op. cit., 133

444. Ibid., 134

445. Horowitz, *Unholy Alliance*.

446. http://www.temple.edu/philosophy/fac_gordon.html.

447. http://www.ocf.berkeley.edu/~marto/aip/purposes.htm.

448. http://www.ed.uiuc.edu/EPS/PES-Yearbook/1998/gordon.html.

449. Ibid.

450. David Horowitz, *Uncivil Wars: The Controversy Over Reparations For Slavery*, 2001.

451. http://www.temple.edu/temple_times/3-31-05/gordon.html.

452. Cf. the profiles of Derek Bell and Regina Austin in this volume.

453. www.temple.edu/temple_times/3-31-05/gordon.html.

454. http://www.temple.edu/ISRST/Events/BCSC/.

455. http://www.temple.edu/philosophy/New_Corses.html.

456. http://chronicle.com/colloquylive/2001/03/paper/.

457. http://www.columbia.edu/cu/news/04/11/ blacks_ivy_league.html.

458. Barry Loberfeld, "Social Justice: Code for Communism," *FrontPageMag.com*, February 27, 2004.

459. Alan Wall, "Who Is Jose Angel Gutierrez—And What Does He Want?" *Vdare.com*, June 2, 2004.

460. Ibid.

461. David Orland, "The Road to Aztlan," *Boundless Webzine*, September 22, 2003.

462. Platform of *Partido Nacional La Raza Unida* http://www.pnlru.org/platform.htm.

463. Wall, op. cit.

464. Ibid.

465. Hal Netkin, "Does Antonio Villaraigosa Have Two Faces?," *mayorno.com*, 2004.

466. Peter Ford, "Europe Cringes at Bush 'Crusade' Against Terrorists," *Christian Science Monitor*, September 19, 2001.

467. Jonathan Dowd-Gailey, "Yvonne Yazbeck Haddad: America's Islam 'Sensitivity' Trainer," *History News Network*, December 14, 2004.

468. Ibid.

469. Ibid.

470. J.R. O'Dwyer, "'Anti-Americanism' Is on the Rise in the Middle East," *O'Dwyer's PR Daily*, November 1, 2002.

471. Ibid.

472. Dowd-Gailey, op. cit.

473. Ibid.

474. Yvonne Yazbeck Haddad, "The Quest for 'Moderate' Islam," *American Perspectives on the Middle East*, March 2, 2004.

475. Dowd-Gailey, op. cit.

476. Ibid.

477. Associated Press, "Bin Laden Provides Fodder for Jokes," *FOX News*, October 15, 2001.

478. Chris Fusco, Mark Skertic, "Crushing Terrorism Will Require Careful Aim," *Chicago Sun Times*, September 16, 2001.

479. Paul Harris, "America Increase Pressure on Annan Over UN Scandals," *The Guardian*, December 5, 2004.

480. "Iraq: Decades of Suffering, Now Women Deserve Better," *Amnesty International*, February 22, 2005.

481. http://departments.oxy.edu/registrar/catalog/pols.html.

482. http://64.233.187.104/u/OccidentalCollege?q=cache:LU7Sx_IEmZAJ:0-departments.oxy.edu.oasys.lib.oxy.edu/library-reserve/course%2520archives/fall04/pol261/eres.htm + tom + hayden&hl=en&ie=UTF-8.

483. http://departments.oxy.edu/registrar/catalog/pols.html.

484. Chris Werner, "Activist Claims U.S. Trying to Create Empire," *Wisconsin Badger Herald*, October 4, 2002.

485. Tom Hayden, "It's Empire Versus Democracy," *AlterNet*, September 10, 2002.

486. Ibid.

487. Tom Hayden, "How to End the Iraq War," *AlterNet*, November 23, 2004.

488. Ibid.

489. http://www.earlham.edu/~pags/Empire_notes.pdf.

490. http://www.earlham.edu/~pags/syllabus/pags_374_ch/PAGS_374_1_CH.pdf.

491. Ibid.

492. Ibid.

493. http://www.earlham.edu/~pags/syllabus/pags_374_ch/PAGS_374_5_CH.pdf.

494. http://www.earlham.edu/~pags/syllabus/pags_374_ch/PAGS_374_2_CH.pdf.

495. Ibid.

496. http://www.earlham.edu/%7Epags/syllabus/pags_80_ch/pags_80_2_ch.pdf.

497. http://www.earlham.edu/~pags/syllabus/PAGS_370CF.pdf.

498. Ibid.

499. Ibid.

500. Ibid.

501. http://www.earlham.edu/%7Epags/syllabus/PAGS_346_sylCH.pdf.

502. Ibid.

503. http://www.english.buffalo.edu/faculty/holstun/.

504. Karen Welsh, "Buffalo's Bullying Professor," *FrontPageMage.com*, June 14, 2005.

505. Omer Bartov, "A Tale of Two Holocausts," *New York Times Book Review Desk*, August 6, 2000.

506. Welsh, op. cit.

507. Mitchell Bard, "Myths & Facts Online—The Palestinian Uprisings," *Jewish Virtual Library*, 2005.

508. Ibid.

509. Welsh, op. cit.

510. Ibid.

511. Mike Adams, "Cornel West and Friends," *FrontPageMag.com*, June 7, 2004.

512. bell hooks, "Rebel's Dilemma," *Shambhala Sun Online*, November 1998.

513. bell hooks, *A Killing Rage: Ending Racism*, Henry Holt Publ., 1995. Cf. the analysis of Hooks's essay in Horowitz, *Hating Whitey and Other Progressive Causes*, 1999.

514. David Ryan, "Author bell hooks Challenges Power Structure," *Oregon Daily Emerald*, May 14, 1999.

515. University of Washington Graduate Diversity Fellows Dinner, March 2, 2005. http://www.grad.washington.edu/gomap/fellowsdinner.htm.

516. bell hooks, *Teaching to Transgress: Education as the Practice of Freedom*, Routledge Books, 1994.

517. Ibid.

518. Ibid.

519. Marc Levin, "Majoring in Political Correctness: Commencements of 2002 Achieve New Degree of Wackiness," *Texas Education Review*, Spring/Summer 2002.

520. Jamie Glazov, "bell hooks and the Politics of Hate," *Front-Pagemag.com*, June 12, 2002.

521. Marc Levin, "Commencements of 2002 Achieve New Degree of Political Correctness, " *Political USA*, June 18, 2002.

522. Leslie Heineman, "Women Studies Winning Status," *Boulder (Col.) Community Network*, September 28, 1995.

523. Alison Jaggar, "On the Standpoint of Women," *Feminist Politics and Human Nature*, 1983.

524. Rosemarie Tong, *Feminist Thought: A More Comprehensive Introduction*, Westview Press, 2nd ed., 1998, 114–129.

525. Jaggar, op. cit.

526. Anne Maloney, "Say You Want a Revolution? Pro-Life Philosophy and Feminism," *Feminism & Nonviolence Studies*, Fall 1995.

527. Mark Shiel, "Why Call Them 'Cult Movies'? American Independent Filmmaking and the Counterculture in the 1960s," *University of Nottingham—Institute of Film Studies*, August 2, 2003.

528. http://www.aas.duke.edu/reg/synopsis/view.cgi?s=33&action=display&subj=WRITING&course=20&sem=0820.

529. Fredric Jameson, *Postmodernism: Or, the Cultural Logic of Late Capitalism*, Verso Books, 1990.

530. http://waww.dukedivest.org/petition.html.

531. Ibid.

532. Fredric Jameson, "Fredric Jameson on September 11," *InterActivist Info Exchange*, October 5, 2001.

533. Ibid.

534. Ibid.

535. Ibid.

536. Fredric Jameson, "The Dialectics of Disaster," *Duke News*, September 2002.

537. "The Future of Utopia: Is Innovation Still Possible in Politics, Culture, Theory?" *Humanities and Social Sciences Online*, Commencing April 24, 2003.

538. Lawrence Auster, "The Regents' Round Table," *National Review*, December 8, 1989.

539. "Anti-Semitism Among Black Student Groups," *Jewish Virtual Library*. (Originally published as *Schooled in Hate: Anti-Semitism on Campus*, Anti-Defamation League, 1997).

540. Leonard Jeffries, "Our Sacred Mission," *National Black United Front*, (*Text of a speech given to the Empire State Black Arts and Cultural Festival in Albany, New York, July 20, 1991*). "Anti-Semitism Among Black Student Groups," op. cit.

541. Jeffries, op. cit.

542. Ibid.

543. Ibid.

544. Ibid.

545. This information was revealed in an interview by Jacob Laksin with the president of Greek life at Lafayette.

546. Jeffries, op. cit.

547. Ibid.

548. Robert Jensen, "Real Hope Is Radical," *Thinking Peace*, 2005.

549. Robert Jensen, "A Defeat for an Empire," *Common Dreams*, December 9, 2004.

550. Joe Wilson, "A Texan Ward Churchill," *FrontPageMag.com*, March 21, 2005.

551. Ibid.

552. Steve Brown, "High Noon in Texas for Leftist Academics," *Cybercast News Service*, November 6, 2003.

553. Ibid.

554. *Los Angeles Times*, May 14, 1971.

555. Ann Coulter, "Kwanzaa: A Holiday from the FBI," *Jewish World Review*, December 26, 2002.

556. Brown, op. cit.

557. Maulana Karenga, "Statement on Peace, Justice and Resistance to War," *The Organization Us (United Slaves)*, February 28, 2003.

558. Sean Emery, "Faculty Enters War Conversation," *California State University, Long Beach—49er On-line*, Spring 2003.

559. Karenga, op. cit.

560. March 28, 1997 http://www.csulb.edu/~africana/mission.htm.

561. Maulana Karenga, *Introduction to Black Studies*, Kawaida Publications, 1982.

562. http://faculty.sxu.edu/~kirstein/.

563. http://www.sxu.edu/history/history_courses.asp.

564. http://faculty.sxu.edu/~kirstein/marx_old.html.

565. HNN Staff, "The Historian Who Denounced the Military for 'Baby-Killing' Tactics," *History News Network*, November 17, 2002.

566. Peter Kirstein, "Re: Not a Fair Comparison," *History News Network*, April 10, 2005.

567. Peter Kirstein, "Kirstein Denounces Potential Iraq War," *History News Network*, December 10, 2002.

568. Peter Kirstein, "Responding to Mr. Baker," *History News Network*, December 23, 2003.

569. Peter Kirstein, "My Turn Mr. Smith," *History News Network*, January 7, 2004.

570. Peter Kirstein, "How I Define Patriotism," *History News Network*, October 13, 2003.

571. http://faculty.sxu.edu/~kirstein/.

572. Jamie Glazov, "Symposium: Bush's Decision to Go to War. Was it Justified?," *FrontPageMag.com*, July 4, 2003.

573. Owen Jubandang, "Smoke Screen," *Arab News*, April 9, 2004.

574. Peter Kirstein, "Nations to Be Admired and Condemned for Being Part of the Coalition of the Vassals I," *Peter N. Kirstein Blog*, July 29, 2005.

575. Sara Russo, "Professor Disparages 'Baby Killing' Military; Calls Cadet a 'Disgrace'," *Accuracy in Academia*, December 2002.

576. David Horowitz, "Ideological Indoctrination at UCLA," *History News Network*, April 25, 2005.

577. David Horowitz, "Bias in the California University System," *History News Network*, September 14, 2004.

578. Vinay Lal, "Terrorism, Inc, or the Family of Fundamentalisms," *The little magazine*, Vol. II, Issue 5, September/October 2001.

579. Ibid.

580. Ibid.

581. "Holy Cross Experts Available for Special Commentary and Analysis of Hot Button Political Issues this Election Season," *College-News.org*, 2004.

582. Jack Shafer, "Drooling on the Vietnam Vets," *Slate*, May 2, 2000.

583. Derek Summerfield, "The Invention of Post-Traumatic Stress Disorder and the Social Usefulness of a Psychiatric Category," *British Medical Journal*, 2001.

584. Ibid.

585. Jerry Lembcke, "We Are What We Remember," *Holy Cross Magazine*, Volume 33, Number 2, April 1999.

586. Jerry Lembcke, "Why This Election Is All About Vietnam," *History News Network*, October 2004.

587. Ibid.

588. http://www.meaning.org/levinebio.html.

589. Mark LeVine, "Melting Away the Matrix: Modernity, Terrorism and Us," *TikkunOnline*, October 2001.

590. Mark LeVine, "The UN Arab Human Development Report: A Critique," *Middle East Report Online*, July 26, 2002.

591. Mark LeVine, "The Death of Rachel Corrie," *Tikkun*, March 24, 2003.

592. Tzvi Kahn, "The Marxist Strikes Back," *FrontPageMag.com*, April 7, 2005.

593. Ibid.

594. Thomas Ryan, "Teaching and Terror at DePaul," *FrontPageMag.com*, May 12, 2005.

595. Tzvi Kahn, "Academic Marxist Rock Star," *FrontPageMag.com*, March 31, 2005.

596. Robert McChesney, "The Media Crisis of Our Times," *Third World Traveler*, April 2003.

597. Ibid.

598. Ibid.

599. Robert McChesney & John Nichols, "The Making of a Movement," *The Nation*, December 20, 2001.

600. McChesney, op. cit.

601. Thomas Ryan, "The Fighting Islamists of Notre Dame," *FrontPageMag.com*, February 8, 2005.

602. Ryan, "Teaching and Terror at DePaul," op. cit.

603. Ibid.

604. Ibid.

605. Askia Muhammad, "Impact of a Nation on 20th Century America, " *The Final Call*, March 10, 2000.

606. Ryan, op. cit.

607. Ibid.

608. Manning Marable, "Living Black History: Resurrecting Intellectual Tradition," *WGBH Forum Network*, April 20, 2004.

609. http://www.columbia.edu/cu/ccbh/.

610. Loberfeld, "Social Justice: Code for Communism," op. cit.

611. Manning Marable, "Introduction," *Africana Criminal Justice Project*, 2003.

612. Ibid.

613. Ibid.

614. Manning Marable, "Imprisoning Black Minds: Neoliberalism and Education Apartheid," *The Free Press*, August 11, 2000.

615. Jonathan Calt Harris, "Tenured Extremism," *New York Sun*, May 4, 2004.

616. Ibid.

617. Ibid.

618. Ibid.

619. Ibid.

620. Ibid.

621. Mohammed el-Nawawy and Adel Iskandar, *Al-Jazeera: How the Free Arab News Network Scooped the World and Changed the Middle East*, Westview Press, 2002, (Book Review), *Middle East Forum*, Summer 2003.

622. See profile of Professor Hamid Dabashi in this volume.

623. Martin Kramer, "Saving Private Massad," *Campus Watch*, January 31, 2005.

624. Joseph Massad, "The Legacy of Jean-Paul Sartre," *Al-Ahram*, Issue No. 623, January 30-February 5, 2003.

625. Ibid.

626. Ibid.

627. Ibid.

628. Ibid.

629. Ibid.

630. Ibid.

631. Joseph Massad, "Semites and anti-Semites, That Is the Question," *Al-Ahram*, Issue No. 720, December 9-15, 2004.

632. Ibid.

633. Ibid.

634. Joseph Massad, "Palestinians and Jewish History: Recognition or Submission," *Arab Thought Forum*, Vol. 7, No. 31, March 2000.

635. Charlie Homans, "Palestinian Film Festival Draws Crowds," *Columbia Spectator*, January 27, 2003.

636. Joseph Massad, "Statement in Response to the Intimidation of Columbia University," *The Electronic Intifada*, November 2004.

637. *Ad Hoc Grievance Committee Report*, Ira Katznelson, Chair; Lisa Anderson; Farah Griffin; Jean E. Howard; and Mark Mazower, Columbia University, March 28, 2005.

638. Robin Finn, "Public Lives; At the Center of an Academic Storm, a Lesson in Calm," *New York Times*, April 8, 2005.

639. Michael Capel, "Free Speech, Individualism, Due Process under Assault on Campus," *Accuracy in Academia*, November 1998.

640. Mari J. Matsuda, Charles R. Lawrence III, Richard Delgado, Kimberlè Williams Crenshaw, *Words That Wound: Critical Race Theory, Assaultive Speech, and the First Amendment*, Westview Press, 1993, 35.

641. Ibid., 38

642. Georgetown University—Campus Spotlight, *Foundation For Individual Rights*, March 2005.

643. Carl Shier, "40th Annual Debs-Thomas-Harrington Dinner," *Chicago Democratic Socialists of America*, New Ground 59, July-August 1998.

644. http://www.law.georgetown.edu/curriculum/tab_courses.cfm? Status=Course&Detail=1289.

645. Ibid.

646. Ibid.

647. http://www.law.georgetown.edu/curriculum/tab_courses.cfm? Status=Course&Detail=1216%20.

648. Mari Matsuda, "A Dangerous Place," *Boston Review*, December 2002-January 2003.

649. Ibid.

650. http://www.law.georgetown.edu/curriculum/tab_courses.cfm? Status=Course&Detail=156%20.

651. Ibid.

652. Mari Matsuda, "Memo to Bush: We Will Not Be Used," April 1990 address to Asian Law Caucus, *modelminority*, February 1993.

653. Jerrold Nadler, "Nadler Criticizes American Muslim Council For Suggesting That Shuttle Disaster Was Act of G-D," *Congressional Press Release*, February 5, 2003.

654. Ali A. Mazrui and Tony Kleban Levine, eds., *The African: A Reader*, Praeger Publ., 1986.

655. Ali A. Mazrui, "Is Israel a Threat to American Democracy?" *SwahiliOnline.com*, April 17, 2002.

656. Ibid.

657. Ibid.

658. Ibid.

659. Ibid.

660. Lindsay Sandham, "Student Files Complaint Against Prof," *MetOnline—Metropolitan State College of Denver*, Volume 27, Issue 5, September 9, 2004; Sara Dogan, "Setting the Record Straight," *FrontPageMag.com*, December 8, 2004.

661. Cliopatria: A Group Blog, "Student Free Speech," *History News Network*, November 26, 2004.

662. Tom Elia, "Oneida Meranto's Racist Speech," *FrontPageMag.com*, February 27, 2004.

663. Sharyn Obsatz, "Insult Prompts a Lifetime of Activism," *UC Riverside—In The News*, November 20, 2003.

664. Armando Navarro, "El Mejor De Los Tiempos, El Peor De Los Tiempos," *La Voz de Aztlan*.

665. Ibid.

666. Armando Navarro, "Latino Summit Response to Proposition 187 at UC Riverside," *California Coalition for Immigration Reform*, January 15, 1995.

667. Hector Carreon, "Dr. Armando Navarro to Lead National Delegation on Zapatista March into Mexico City," *La Voz de Aztlan*, February 2, 2001.

668. Brock Meeks, "Minuteman Opposition Organizes Resistance," *MSNBC*, June 15, 2005.

669. Chris Richard, "Minuteman Border Project Challenged by Activists," *The Press-Enterprise*, March 19, 2005.

670. Roberto Hernandez, "Hispanics Protest Bush's Iraq Policy," *UC Riverside—In The News*, October 5, 2002.

671. "Mexican Political Party Will Meet in Riverside," *UC Riverside—In The News*, August 31, 2002.

672. Susan Stranahan, "Hot Air, All Around Us," *Columbia Journalism Review*, April 19, 2005.

673. Ibid.

674. Harvey Klehr, John Earl Haynes, Kyrill M. Anderson, *The Soviet World of American Communism,* Yale University Press, 1998

675. Victor Navasky, "On *The Nation* and the Historical Role of the Journal of Opinion," *The New School—Transregional Center for Democratic Studies,* December 5, 1996.

676. Ibid.

677. Priya Parmar, *Brooklyn College—Faculty Newsletter,* Volume 7, Number 1, Fall/Winter 2003, p. 8, http://www.brooklyn.cuny.edu/bc/pubs/fn/fall03/1103.pdf.

678. "Questions for Priya Parmar," *Brooklyn College Magazine,* Spring 2004, 10, http://www.brooklyn.cuny.edu/bc/pubs/bcmag/spr2004/bcmag.pdf.

679. Ibid.

680. Ibid.

681. Jacob Gershman, "'Disposition' Emerges as Issue at Brooklyn College," *New York Sun,* May 31, 2005.

682. Ibid.

683. Ibid.

684. Ibid.

685. Ibid.

686. Ibid.

687. http://www.colorado.edu/EthnicStudies/faculty/e_perez.html,

688. "Are Chicanos the Same as Mexicans?" *AztecaNet,* March 29, 2001.

689. Emma Perez, *The Decolonial Imaginary: Writing Chicanas into History,* Indiana Univ. Press, 1999, xiii.

690. Ibid., xiv.

691. Ibid.

692. Ibid., 126.

693. Ibid.

694. Ibid., 13.

695. Ibid., 81.

696. "On the Need to Truly Challenge Sexism Through National Liberation Focused Chicano Mexicano Struggle," *Unión del Barrio—La Verdad Publications,* June 14, 1993.

697. Jefferson Dodge, "Faculty Defend Free-speech Rights of UCB Prof Amid Public Outcry," *University of Colorado, Boulder—NewMedia,* February 3, 2005.

698. Emma Perez, "The Attacks on Ward Churchill," *CounterPunch,* February 28, 2005.

699. Ibid.

700. "Interview with Dr. Sam Richards—Co-Director," *Penn State— Race Relations Project*, 2004, http://www.racerelationsproject.psu.edu/ facil_richards.shtml.

701. Thomas Joscelyn, "Penn State's Ward Churchill Twin," *Front-PageMag.com*, March 28, 2005.

702. Ibid.

703. Navasky, "On *The Nation* and the Historical Role of the Journal of Opinion," op. cit.

704. Ibid.

705. Ibid.

706. Gerard Ungerman & Audrey Brohey, *The Oil Factor: Behind the War on Terror (DVD)*, 2004.

707. Joscelyn, op. cit.

708. Ibid.

709. David Halperin, "The Traffic in Women: Thirty Years Later," *Women's Studies Newsletter—University of Michigan*, Spring 2005.

710. Rabia Nafees Shah, "Gayle Rubin: 'The Traffic in Wom[a]n'—My Notes on Her Notes," *Bulletin Board—University of Florida*, September 10, 2003.

711. Ibid.

712. Micaela di Leonardo and Roger Lancaster, "Gender, Sexuality, Political Economy," *New Politics*, Vol. 6, No. 1, Whole No. 21, 1996.

713. Gayle Rubin, "'The Traffic in Women,'" *Society for Social Research*, 1975.

714. Rubin, 180.

715. Gay Shame Conference, March 27-29, 2003, *lesbian gay queer research initiative—University of Michigan*.

716. Bio of Gayle Rubin and description of *Cuir Underground, Ambrosio's BDSM Site*.

717. Gayle Rubin, "Old Guard, New Guard," (Excerpt of her speech given at the graduation ceremony for the Journeyman II Academy— October 4, 1997), *Cuir Underground*, Issue 4.2, Summer 1998.

718. Ibid.

719. "Out with the Outcasts; In with the Exiles," *Cuir Underground*, Issue 3.4, April/May 1997

720. Ibid.

721. Gayle Rubin, *Youth Liberation*, Leaping Lesbian, 1978, *NAMBLA*, 2003.

722. Elaine Audet, "Elisabeth Badinter Distorts Feminism the Better to Fight It," *Sisyphe*, October 1, 2003.

723. Daniel J. Flynn, "Academics Defend Pedophilia," *NewsMax.com*, September 23, 2004.

724. Ibid.

725. 12th Conference of Cuban and North American Philosophers and Social Scientists, 19-23 June 2000, Havana, Cuba (sponsored by the Radical Philosophy Association), *DitoMorales.com*, July 13, 2002.

726. Richard D. Lamm, "Too Controversial for the University of Denver," *EducatioNation*, April 15, 2005.

727. Ibid.

728. Richard Wolff and Steven Resnick, eds., *Rethinking Marxism*, Autonomedia, 2001,

729. "Interview with Orville Schell," *Whole Earth Review*, Winter 1988.

730. Ibid.

731. Dirk Olin, (Interview with) "Orville Schell," *Mother Jones*, September/October 1997.

732. Ibid.

733. Russell Schoch, "The Journalism Dean Searches for Intelligent Life in the Media," *California Monthly*, 1998.

734. Center for Study of Working Class Life—State University of New York at Stony Brook, http://www.as.ysu.edu/~cwcs/New%20 WCS%20Association.htm.

735. "New York City Labor Against the War," *Global Policy Forum*, September 27, 2001.

736. http://www.sunysb.edu/sociology/catalogue.htm.

737. David Horowitz, "Left-wing Traitors Debase the Left and the Silence of Patriotic Liberals Earns Contempt from Those Who Care," *FrontPageMag.com*, May 21, 2005.

738. Michael Schwartz, "The New US Strategy After the Battle of Najaf," *Global Policy Forum*, September 28, 2004.

739. Horowitz, op. cit.

740. Michael Schwartz, "Tomgram: Schwartz on Americans Rolling the Dice in Najaf," *TomDispatch.com—Nation Institute*, August 11, 2004.

741. Michael Schwartz, "Tomgram: Schwartz on Symbolic Sovereignty in Iraq," *TomDispatch.com—Nation Institute*, June 17, 2004.

742. Courtney McKay and Radeyah Hack, "Could You Be Drafted?" *People Against the Draft*, November 15, 2004.

743. Maria Russo, "Ivory Tower," *Salon.com*, September 27, 1999. Book Review of Eve Kosofsky Sedgwick, *A Dialogue on Love*, Beacon Press, 1999.

744. Eve Kosofsky Sedgwick, *Tendencies*, Duke University Press, 1993, 3.

745. http://web.gc.cuny.edu/English/courses_f01.html.

746. Ibid.

747. John J.P. Caporaso, "Culture or Else—'P.C.' Pompousassism," *Higheryet.com*, August 7, 2002.

748. Eve Kosofsky Sedgwick, *Between Men: English Literature and Male Homosocial Desire*, Columbia University Press, 1985, 172–173.

749. http://web.gc.cuny.edu/English/courses_f05.html.

750. Russo, "Ivory Tower," op. cit.

751. Eve Kosofsky Sedgwick, "The Beast in the Closet: Henry James and the Writing of Homosexual Panic," in Ruth Bernard Yeazell, ed., *Sex, Politics, and Science in the Nineteenth-Century Novel*, Johns Hopkins University Press, 1985.

752. Peter Monaghan, "With Sex and Sensibility, Scholars Redefine Jane Austen," *The Chronicle of Higher Education*, August 17, 2001.

753. http://web.gc.cuny.edu/English/courses_f99.html.

754. Ibid.

755. "Top Prof Sparks Outrage—Devout Are 'Moral Retards,' He Sez," *New York Daily News*, May 23, 2005.

756. Timothy Shortell, "Religion & Morality: A Contradiction Explained," in *Axis of Evil: Perforated Praeter Naturam*, Qualiatica Press, 2004, 106–116.

757. Ibid.

758. Shortell, op. cit.

759. Timothy Shortell, "Becoming the übermensch," *The Anti Naturals*, Issue 21, 2002.

760. Christopher Flickinger, "Social Marxist Moves Up University Ladder," *Human Events Online*, June 8, 2005.

761. Flickinger, op. cit.

762. Lisa Makson, "CUNY Promotes an Anti-Christian Hatemonger," *FrontPageMag.com*, June 1, 2005.

763. Timothy Shortell, "Brownshirts," *The Anti Naturals*, Issue 24, 2003.

764. Cliopatria: A Group Blog, "The Shame of Shortell," *History News Network*, May 21, 2005.

765. Harry Targ, "Building a Peace and Justice Movement in the New Age of Empire," *Committees of Correspondence for Democracy and Socialism*, April 10, 2003.

766. Ibid.

767. Ibid.

768. Marc Geller, "Professors Disagree on Dangers Posed by Iraq," *Lafayette (Ind.) Journal and Courier*, February 9, 2003.

769. Ibid.

770. David Horowitz and Thomas Ryan, "Indoctrination at Purdue," *FrontPageMag.com*, December 13, 2004.

771. Ibid.

772. http://www.cla.purdue.edu/academic/comm/html/grad/prospective_students_courses.htm.

773. Ibid.

774. Horowitz and Ryan, op. cit.

775. Harry Targ (Radical Philosophy Association), "Bush Bashing vs. Class Struggle: The Two Sides of Fahrenheit 9/11," *University of Tennessee—Listserv*, July 1, 2004.

776. Brent Forgues, "Lift the Travel Ban to Cuba," *Cuba Central*, June 21, 2004.

777. Harry Targ (Radical Philosophy Association), "50 Years After Moncada—A Statement of the Committees of Correspondence for Democracy and Socialism," *University of Tennessee—Listserv*, July 26, 2003.

778. Buck Wolf, "Queen B 101: College Lessons in Stardom," *ABC News*, November 9, 2004.

779. Katherine Ernst, "Lil' Kim 101," *City Journal*, April 25, 2005.

780. Wolf, op. cit.

781. Greg Thomas, "Lil' Kim: Dealing with the Trial for Real," *AllHipHop.com*, March 2005.

782. Ibid.

783. Ibid.

784. Jacob Laksin, "Syracuse's Hip-Hop Hate," *FrontPageMag.com*, May 26, 2005.

785. Junior M.A.F.I.A., "Get Money," from the *Conspiracy* album (1995), *Original Hip-Hop Lyrics Archive.*

786. Wolf, op. cit.

787. Laksin, op. cit.

788. "Lil' Kim Raps with Syracuse Students," *News & Events of Arts and Sciences—Syracuse University*, November 3, 2004.

789. Thomas, op. cit.

790. Ibid.

791. Ibid.

792. Horowitz, "Black Murder Inc." op. cit.

793. Greg Thomas Faculty page—Syracuse University. http://www-hl.syr.edu/depts/english/faculty/thomas.htm.

794. Laksin, op. cit.

795. Ibid.

796. Greg Thomas, "Proud Flesh: Editorial Statement," *Proud Flesh: A New Afrikan Journal of Culture, Politics & Consciousness*, 2002.

797. Laksin, op. cit.

798. http://www.peaceandjustice.villanova.edu/academics/spring%
202005_courses.htm.

799. Fr. Robert Sirico, "Catholics for Marx," *FrontPageMag.com*, June 3,
2004.

800. http://www.iacenter.org/.

801. http://64.233.161.104/search?q=cache:P61kw7eTx10J:
www.upenn.edu/ccp/PHENND/syllabi/THEO4350.html + toton + %
22Service + and + Education + for + Justice%22&hl=en.

802. David Anderson, "Religious Groups Mount Last-Ditch Anti-War
Effort," *Bread for the World*, October 10, 2002.

803. Justice Union of Students Staff and Teachers, "Minutes for Peace
and Justice Consortium," *Villanova University*, November 2, 2001.
http://www.peaceconsortium.villanova.edu/minutes/011102.htm.

804. Ryan O'Donnell, "Hate America Professor," *FrontPageMag.com*,
June 25, 2003.

805. Barbara Gross Davis, *Tools for Teaching*, Jossey-Bass Books, 1993.

806. O'Donnell, op. cit.

807. Ibid.

808. Ibid.

809. Ibid.

810. Ibid.

811. Ibid.

812. http://www.vocino.us/resume09june2004.html.

813. Ibid.

814. Michael Vocino, "Saw Moore's Fahrenheit 911," *University of
Rhode Island—The Forum*, June 26, 2004.

815. http://www.Professor Vocino.us/flm203syllabus05x.html.

816. Vocino, op. cit.

817. Nathaniel Nelson, "'My Name Is Michael Vocino and I Like
Dick," http://www.frontpagemag.com/Articles/ReadArticle.asp?ID=
18967.

818. Ibid.

819. Ibid.

820. Personal communication to the author from a member of the
faculty at Rhode Island University.

821. Ibid.

822. David Horowitz, "The Boys in the Bathhouses," *Salon.com*,
November 3, 1997.

823. Marjorie King, "Queering the Schools," *City Journal*, May 29,
2003.

824. http://www.managingdesire.org/sexpanic/sexpanicpressrelease.
html.

825. Ibid.

826. Michael Warner, *The Trouble With Normal: Sex, Politics, and the Ethics of Queer Life*, Free Press, 1999. Book Review by Peter Kurth, *Salon.com*, December 8, 1999.

827. http://www.brandeis.edu/facguide/one?unetid= 1101081091111115117113115.

828. http://www.amazon.com/gp/product/0912469161/102-2825913-7286504?v=glance&n=283155&s=books&v=glance.

829. www.brandeis.edu/departments/sociology/Syllabi/sociology107a Syllabus-Fall2004.doc.

830. www.brc21.org/newsletters/n13-02.html',1.

831. www.discoverthenetworks.org/groupProfile.asp?grpid=6579',1.

832. www.crlp.org_01_1101ngos.html',1.

833. www.dsaboston.org/2001DTB.htm,1.

834. Tony Barker, "New Peace Studies Director Named," *Ball State University—Newscenter*, April 23, 2002.

835. George Wolfe, Professor of Music Performance, *Ball State University Profile*. http://www.bsu.edu/common/profile/0,,4155—-search, 00.html.

836. George Wolfe, "Message from the Director," *Ball State University—Center for Peace and Conflict Studies*, April 15, 2005.

837. Philip Wilcox, "Israel and Palestine: Rescuing a Two-State Peace," *Sponsored by Ball State University, Office of the Provost—Center for Peace and Conflict Studies*, February 28, 2005 and March 1, 2005. http://www.bsu.edu/update/media/pdf/022505.pdf.

838. "History and Mission," *Ball State University—Center for Peace and Conflict Studies* http://www.bsu.edu/cpcs/article/0,,28186—,00.html.

839. Ibid.

840. See the profile of David Barash in this volume.

841. "Peace Studies and Conflict Resolution Minor," *Ball State University—Center for Peace and Conflict Studies*, http://www.bsu.edu/cpcs/article/0,,28182—,00.html.

842. Brett Mock, "Indoctrination in the Classroom," *FrontPageMag.com*, September 13, 2004.

843. Ibid.

844. Thomas Ryan, "Recruiting for Terror at Ball State," *FrontPageMag.com*, November 8, 2004.

845. "Response from Ball State University Provost Beverley Pitts," *Students for Academic Freedom*, September 23, 2004.

846. "Ball State Professors Respond to Complaints," *Muncie (Ind.) Star Press*, September 27, 2004; For Mock's response to Pitts see: "To Whom It May Concern" in *The "Peace Studies And Conflict Resolution" Program At Ball State University—Indocrination or Education* (booklet), Students for Academic Freedom, Washington, D.C., 2004, 29.

847. Roger Herbst, "Democracy, Plutocracy, or Hypocrisy," *Washington*   **4.**
Free Press, September/October 2002.   For

848. http://192.211.16.13/curricular/nchomsky/syllabus.htm.

849. Dan Flynn, "Master of Deceit," *FrontPageMag.com*, June 3, 2003.
Review of Howard Zinn's book. Zinn, *A People's History*, 646: "Objectivity is impossible, and it is also undesirable. That is, if it were possible
it would be undesirable, because if you have any kind of a social aim, if
you think history should serve society in some way; should serve the
progress of the human race; should serve justice in some way, then it
requires that you make your selection on the basis of what you think
will advance causes of humanity."

850. Zinn, op. cit., 658–9

851. "Scattered Soviet materials have shown that Soviet involvement
in preparing and planning an invasion after Stalin gave his reluctant
endorsement in January 1950 was higher than previous writers had
thought." Bruce Cumings, *Korea's Place in the Sun*, 1998, 263. As it
happens, Cumings is a left-wing historian.

852. Zinn, op. cit. 59

853. Zinn, 73

854. Flynn, op. cit.

855. Malcolm Kline, "From Abject to Zinn," *Campus Report Online*,
September 24, 2004.

856. Flynn, op. cit.

857. Ibid.

858. Ibid.

859. Ibid.

860. Ibid.

861. Ibid.

862. Ibid.

Chapter 2
Why Administrators Fail to Maintain Academic Standards

1. *The New Republic*, March 6, 1995. The author of the present text
has written his own critique of West and drawn a similar conclusion:
David Horowitz, "Cornel West: No Light in His Attic," *Salon.com*,
October 11, 1999.

2. Cited in Roger Kimball, "Dr. West and Mr. Summers: A Harvard
Tale—Cornel West vs. Larry Summers," *National Review Online*, January 28, 2002.

3. Richard Bradley, *Harvard Rules: The Struggle for the Soul of the
World's Most Powerful University*, Harper Collins, 2005, 97. This is an
account hostile to Summers.

Cornel West's bibliography, cf. http://www.pragmatism.org/library/
west/west_bibliography.htm.

5. Bradley, op. cit.

6. Gutmann has since been appointed the president of the University
of Pennsylvania.

7. Lawrence H. Summers, *Remarks at NBER Conference on Diversify-
ing the Science & Engineering Workforce*, January 14, 2005. http://
www.president.harvard.edu/speeches/2005/nber.html.

8. Marcella Bombardieri, "Summers' Remarks on Women Draw Fire,"
Boston Globe, January 17, 2005.

9. "The Science of Gender and Science," *The Edge Foundation—Pinker
vs. Spelke Debate*, May 16, 2005.

10. "Letter from President Summers on Women and Science," January
19, 2005. http://www.president.harvard.edu/speeches/2005/women-
sci.html.

11. *Lingua Franca*, April 1991.

12. Opinion Editorial, "At Stake Is Academic Freedom," *New York
Sun*, March 17, 2005.

13. Stephan Thernstrom, "Harvard's Crucible," *Wall Street Journal*,
April 11, 2005.

14. Heather Mac Donald, "Harvard's Diversity Grovel," *City Journal*,
Spring 2005.

15. http://vpf-web.harvard.edu/budget/factbook/current_facts/
Online_Harvard_Fact_Book_05.pdf.

Chapter 3
The Representative Nature of the
Professors Profiled in This Volume

1. The author is grateful to several professors, who wish to maintain
their anonymity, for the information that follows.

2. Personal communication to the author from a tenured full professor at the flagship campus of a major state university who has himself
chaired three tenure committees.

INDEX